Polynomials: Theory and Applications, 2nd Edition

Polynomials: Theory and Applications, 2nd Edition

Guest Editor

Cheon-Seoung Ryoo

MDPI

Basel • Beijing • Wuhan • Barcelona • Belgrade • Novi Sad • Cluj • Manchester

Guest Editor
Cheon-Seoung Ryoo
Department of Mathematics
Hannam University
Daejeon
Republic of Korea

Editorial Office
MDPI AG
Grosspeteranlage 5
4052 Basel, Switzerland

This is a reprint of the Special Issue, published open access by the journal *Mathematics* (ISSN 2227-7390), freely accessible at: https://www.mdpi.com/journal/mathematics/special_issues/60C7HKKPI2.

For citation purposes, cite each article independently as indicated on the article page online and as indicated below:

Lastname, A.A.; Lastname, B.B. Article Title. *Journal Name* **Year**, *Volume Number*, Page Range.

ISBN 978-3-7258-6722-6 (Hbk)
ISBN 978-3-7258-6723-3 (PDF)
https://doi.org/10.3390/books978-3-7258-6723-3

Contents

About the Editor

Cheon Seoung Ryoo

Cheon Seoung Ryoo received his Ph.D. from Kyushu University, Japan. He is the author of 20 books and more than 500 research papers published in reputable international journals. He currently serves as Editor-in-Chief of the *Journal of Applied Mathematics and Informatics* and the *Journal of Applied and Pure Mathematics*, and is a reviewer and Editorial Board Member of numerous international journals.

His research interests include numerical verification methods, scientific computing, functional analysis, analytic number theory, differential equations, dynamical systems, quantum calculus, and various classes of special functions.

Preface

Polynomials have long been fundamental objects in mathematics, providing essential tools for analysis, algebra, approximation theory, numerical methods, and mathematical modeling. Over the past few decades, the scope of polynomial research has expanded significantly, driven by new theoretical frameworks such as q-calculus, fractional calculus, and symbolic computation, as well as by increasing demands from applied sciences and engineering.

The articles collected in this Special Issue illustrate how classical polynomial theories are being extended and refined through modern approaches. Several contributions focus on generalized Appell-type and Sheffer-type polynomials, exploring their generating functions, structural properties, and operational methods. Other papers investigate orthogonal and exceptional polynomial systems, revealing new connections with differential equations, spectral theory, and special functions.

In addition to theoretical advances, this volume highlights practical applications of polynomial methods in physics, engineering, and applied mathematics. Topics such as quantum calculus-based models, fractional differential equations, asymptotic analysis, and symbolic computation demonstrate the versatility and continuing relevance of polynomials in contemporary scientific research.

As Guest Editor, I would like to express my sincere appreciation to all authors for their high-quality contributions, to the reviewers for their careful and constructive evaluations, and to the editorial staff of MDPI for their professional support in bringing this Special Issue to completion.

The Special Issue includes a diverse selection of published papers that collectively demonstrate the breadth and depth of current research on polynomials and special functions.

Several articles focus on generalized Appell and q-Appell polynomial families within the framework of quantum calculus, providing new convolution structures, generating functions, and operational techniques. These studies contribute to a deeper understanding of polynomial systems arising in discrete and quantum models.

Another group of papers investigates exceptional and orthogonal polynomial systems, including constructions based on Jacobi polynomials and pseudo-Wronskian techniques. These works reveal novel algebraic and analytical properties and establish connections with differential equations and spectral problems.

The volume also contains contributions on special functions and analytic number theory, such as studies on multiple zeta and zeta-star values, Sonin kernels expressed in terms of hypergeometric-type functions, and monotonicity properties of power series expansions. In addition, papers on Jacobsthal-type polynomials, polar Jacobi polynomials, and generating functions involving harmonic-like numbers further enrich the thematic scope of the Special Issue.

Together, these published works provide a coherent overview of recent developments in polynomial theory and its applications, highlighting both methodological innovations and emerging areas of interdisciplinary research.

Cheon-Seoung Ryoo
Guest Editor

mathematics

MDPI

Article

Finding the q-Appell Convolution of Certain Polynomials Within the Context of Quantum Calculus

Waseem Ahmad Khan [1,*], Khidir Shaib Mohamed [2,*], Francesco Aldo Costabile [3,*], Can Kızılateş [4] and Cheon Seoung Ryoo [5]

1 Department of Electrical Engineering, Prince Mohammad Bin Fahd University, P.O. Box 1664, Al Khobar 31952, Saudi Arabia
2 Department of Mathematics, College of Science, Qassim University, Buraydah 51452, Saudi Arabia
3 Department of Mathematics and Computer Science, University of Calabria, 87036 Rende, CS, Italy
4 Department of Mathematics, Faculty of Science, Zonguldak Bülent Ecevit University, 67100 Zonguldak, Turkey; cankizilates@gmail.com
5 Department of Mathematics, Hannam University, Daejeon 34430, Republic of Korea; ryoocs@hnu.kr
* Correspondence: wkhan1@pmu.edu.sa (W.A.K.); k.idris@qu.edu.sa (K.S.M.); francesco.costabile@unical.it (F.A.C.)

Abstract: This article introduces the theory of three-variable q-truncated exponential Gould–Hopper-based Appell polynomials by employing a generating function approach that incorporates q-calculus functions. This study further explores these polynomials by using a computational algebraic approach. The determinant form, recurrences, and differential equations are proven. Relationships with the monomiality principle are given. Finally, graphical representations are presented to illustrate the behavior and potential applications of the three-variable q-truncated exponential Gould–Hopper-based Appell polynomials.

Keywords: quantum calculus; q-truncated polynomials; q-truncated Gould–Hopper–Appell polynomials; quasi-monomiality; extension of monomiality principle; q-dilatation operator; partial differential equations; differential equations

MSC: 05A30; 11B83; 11B68

1. Introduction

Special polynomials are fundamental mathematical constructs that serve as versatile tools across various disciplines. Their significance lies in their capacity to simplify complex mathematical problems and provide elegant solutions to real-world challenges. These polynomials are particularly effective in approximating intricate functions, rendering them invaluable in numerical analysis and computational mathematics. Their orthogonality properties facilitate the efficient representation of functions in series expansions, which is crucial in areas such as signal processing and data compression. Furthermore, special polynomials frequently emerge as solutions to differential equations that model physical phenomena, thereby bridging the gap between abstract mathematics and practical applications in physics and engineering. The utility of special polynomials extends beyond their computational advantages. Their associated generating functions offer a compact means of representing infinite sequences, thereby aiding the study of combinatorial problems and probability distributions. The recurrence relations governing these polynomials not only allow for efficient computation but also reveal profound mathematical structures and patterns. Additionally, the symmetry properties exhibited by many special polynomials provide insights into the underlying mathematical and physical principles of the systems that they describe. This combination of theoretical elegance and practical utility renders special polynomials indispensable in fields ranging from quantum mechanics to financial modeling, cementing their status as essential tools in modern mathematics and its applications. Gould–Hopper polynomials are the subject of extensive research due to their distinctive characteristics and applicability in fields such as approximation theory, differential equations, and quantum mechanics. Gould–Hopper polynomials, which represent a generalization of Hermite polynomials, have been the focus of comprehensive investigations regarding their mathematical properties and practical applications.

Recent advancements in special polynomial, q-Appell, and truncated multivariate polynomial families have underscored their utility in operator theory, approximation, and discrete modeling [1–5]. These investigations have provided a comprehensive framework within which the proposed generalization can be contextualized. The 2-variable truncated exponential polynomials (2VTPs) denoted by $e_n^{(r)}(\tau,\phi)$ are specified by the generating relation [6–8]

$$\frac{e^{\tau t}}{1-\phi t^r}=\sum_{n=0}^{\infty} e_n^{(r)}(\tau,\phi)\frac{t^n}{n!}, \tag{1}$$

where

$$e_n^{(r)}(\tau,\phi)=n!\sum_{k=0}^{[\frac{n}{r}]}\frac{\phi^k\tau^{n-rk}}{(n-rk)!}. \tag{2}$$

Very recently, in [9], Özat et al. presented the general form of truncated exponential-based general-Appell polynomials, utilizing the framework of two-variable general-Appell polynomials as follows:

$$A(t)e^{\tau t}\psi(\phi,t)\frac{1}{1-\gamma t^m}=\sum_{s=0}^{\infty} {}_{e^{(m)}}T_s(\tau,\phi,\gamma)\frac{t^n}{n!}.$$

In addition, the authors successfully derived explicit and determinant representations, along with operators for lowering and raising, a recurrence relation, a differential equation, and various summation formulas pertinent to these polynomials.

The field of quantum calculus, alternatively known as q-calculus, represents an area of burgeoning research interest. For $q\to 1^-$, quantum calculus converges to classical calculus. In contemporary scientific discourse, quantum calculus has exhibited its utility across diverse disciplines, encompassing mathematical sciences, quantum physics, quantum mechanics, quantum algebra, approximation theory, and operator theory, among other domains. We now provide some basic properties of quantum analysis. For the following properties and more details, please see [1,10–13]. Assume that $0<q<1$. The q-shifted factorial $(\gamma;q)_v$ is defined as

$$(\vartheta;q)_u=\prod_{w=1}^{u-1}(1-q^w\vartheta),\ \ (u\in\mathbb{N}),\ \ (\vartheta;q)_0=1. \tag{3}$$

The q-analogue of a number γ is given by

$$[\vartheta]_q=\frac{1-q^\vartheta}{1-q},\ \ 0<q<1;\ \ \vartheta\in\mathbb{C}. \tag{4}$$

The q-factorial is given by

$$[\vartheta]_q! = \begin{cases} \prod_{w=1}^{\vartheta}[w]_q, & \vartheta \geq 1 \\ 1, & \gamma = 0 \end{cases}. \tag{5}$$

The following equality holds:

$$(\tau \pm \gamma)_q^v = \sum_{s=0}^{v} \binom{v}{s}_q q^{\binom{v-s}{2}} \tau^s (\pm\gamma)^{v-s}, \tag{6}$$

where

$$\binom{\vartheta}{w}_q = \frac{[\vartheta]_q!}{[\vartheta - w]_q! [w]_q!}.$$

The following equalities hold:

$$e_q(\tau) = \sum_{w=0}^{\infty} \frac{\tau^w}{[w]_q!}, \quad 0 < q < 1, \tag{7}$$

and

$$E_q(\tau) = \sum_{w=0}^{\infty} \frac{q^{\binom{w}{2}} \tau^w}{[j]_q!}, \quad 0 < q < 1. \tag{8}$$

The following equality holds:

$$e_q(\tau) E_q(\phi) = \sum_{n=0}^{\infty} \frac{(\tau + \phi)_q^n}{[n]_q!}. \tag{9}$$

Hence,

$$e_q(\tau) E_q(-\tau) = 1. \tag{10}$$

The following equality holds:

$$\widehat{D}_{q,\tau} h(\tau) = \frac{h(q\tau) - h(\tau)}{\tau(1-q)}, \quad 0 < q < 1, \quad \tau \neq 0. \tag{11}$$

In particular, we have

$$\widehat{D}_{q,\tau} \tau^w = [w]_q \tau^{w-1}, \tag{12}$$

$$\widehat{D}_{q,\tau} e_q(\alpha\tau) = \alpha e_q(\alpha\tau), \ \alpha \in \mathbb{C}, \tag{13}$$

and

$$\widehat{D}_{q,\tau}^{w} e_q(\alpha\tau) = \alpha^w e_q(\alpha\tau), \ w \in \mathbb{N}, \alpha \in \mathbb{C}, \tag{14}$$

where $\widehat{D}_{q,\tau}^{w}$ denotes the w^{th}-order q-derivative with respect to τ.

The q-derivative concerning the product of the functions $f(\tau)$ and $g(\tau)$ has been thoroughly examined in the existing literature.

$$\widehat{D}_{q,\tau}(h(\tau)k(\tau)) = h(\tau)\widehat{D}_{q,\tau}k(\tau) + k(q\tau)\widehat{D}_{q,\tau}h(\tau) \tag{15}$$

and

$$\widehat{D}_{q,\tau}\left(\frac{h(\tau)}{k(\tau)}\right) = \frac{k(q\tau)\widehat{D}_{q,\tau}h(\tau) - h(q\tau)\widehat{D}_{q,\tau}k(\tau)}{k(\tau)k(q\tau)}. \tag{16}$$

The q-integral of a function $h(\tau)$ is introduced as

$$\int_0^a h(\tau)d_q\tau = (1-q)a\sum_{w=0}^{\infty} q^w h(aq^w). \tag{17}$$

By virtue of (17), we get

$$\int_0^\tau \lambda^w d_q\lambda = (1-q)\tau\sum_{n=0}^{\infty} \tau^w q^{n(w+1)}$$

$$= \frac{\tau^{w+1}(1-q)}{1-q^{w+1}} = \frac{\tau^{w+1}}{[w+1]_q}, \quad w \in \mathbb{N} \sqcup \{0\}. \tag{18}$$

In particular, $\widehat{D}_{q,\tau}^{-1}\{1\} = \tau$, and then

$$\left(\widehat{D}_{q,\tau}^{-1}\right)^r\{1\} = \frac{\tau^r}{[r]_q!}, \qquad r \in \mathbb{N} \sqcup \{0\}. \tag{19}$$

The q-GHPs, symbolized as $H_{n,q}^{(m)}(\tau,\phi)$, are established through the use of the generating function [14]

$$e_q(\tau t)e_q(\phi t^m) = \sum_{n=0}^{\infty} H_{n,q}^{(m)}(\tau,\phi)\frac{t^n}{[n]_q!}, \tag{20}$$

and the series definition is

$$H_{n,q}^{(m)}(\tau,\phi) = [n]_q!\sum_{k=0}^{[\frac{n}{m}]} \frac{\phi^k\tau^{n-mk}}{[k]_q![n-mk]_q!}. \tag{21}$$

For $H_{n,q}^{(m)}(\tau,\phi)$, the following equality holds (see [15]):

$$H_{n,q}^{(m)}(\tau,\phi) = e_q\left(\phi D_{q,\tau}^m\right)\{\tau^n\}. \tag{22}$$

The q-dilatation operator T_z is characterized by its action on any function of the complex variable z as follows [2,16]:

$$T_z^k f(z) = f(q^k z), \quad k \in \mathbb{R}, \tag{23}$$

satisfying the property

$$T_z^{-1}T_z^1 f(z) = f(z). \tag{24}$$

The following equality holds [15]:

$$\widehat{D}_{q,t}e_q(\phi t^m) = \phi t^{m-1}T_{(\phi;m)}e_q(\phi t^m). \tag{25}$$

where

$$T_{(\phi;m)} = \frac{1-q^m T_\phi^m}{1-qT_\phi} = 1 + qT_\phi + \cdots + q^{m-1}T_\phi^{m-1}.$$

Al Salam provides a comprehensive explanation of the generating function for the q-Appell polynomials $\mathcal{A}_{n,q}(\tau)$, as articulated in the formula found in [17,18].

$$\mathcal{A}_q(t)\; e_q(\tau t) = \sum_{w=0}^{\infty} \mathcal{A}_{w,q}(\tau)\frac{t^w}{[w]_q!}, \tag{26}$$

$$\mathcal{A}_q(t) = \sum_{w=0}^{\infty} \mathcal{A}_{w,q}\frac{t^w}{[w]_q\;!}, \qquad \mathcal{A}_q(t) \neq 0, \qquad \mathcal{A}_{0,q} = 1. \tag{27}$$

The following represents a suitable option for specific individuals within the category of q-Appell polynomials (Table 1).

Table 1. Certain q-APF.

S. No.	q-APF	GF	$\mathcal{A}_q(t)$
I.	**The q-BP [3,19]**	$\dfrac{\delta}{e_q(\delta)-1}e_q(\tau\delta)=\sum_{v=0}^{\infty}\mathcal{B}_{v,q}(\tau)\frac{\delta^v}{[v]_q!}$	$\mathcal{A}_q(\delta)=\frac{\delta}{e_q(\delta)-1}$
II.	**The q-EP [3,19]**	$\dfrac{[2]_q}{e_q(\delta)+1}e_q(\tau\delta)=\sum_{v=0}^{\infty}\mathcal{E}_{v,q}(\tau)\frac{\delta^v}{[v]_q!}$	$\mathcal{A}_q(\delta)=\frac{[2]_q}{e_q(\delta)+1}$
III.	**The q-GP [3,19]**	$\dfrac{[2]_q\delta}{e_q(\delta)+1}e_q(\tau\delta)=\sum_{v=0}^{\infty}\mathcal{G}_{v,q}(\tau)\frac{\delta^v}{[v]_q!}$	$\mathcal{A}_q(\delta)=\frac{[2]_q\delta}{e_q(\delta)+1}$

Appell polynomials of the rth order, which are based on a two-variable q-truncated exponential function and are represented as ${}_{e^{(r)}}A_{n,q}(\tau,\phi)$, are characterized by the generating function provided in [6].

$$A_q(t)\frac{e_q(\tau t)}{1-\gamma t^r}=\sum_{n=0}^{\infty}{}_{e^{(r)}}A_{n,q}(\tau,\gamma)\frac{t^n}{[n]_q!}. \tag{28}$$

The higher-order q-truncated exponential Gould–Hopper polynomials in three variables, symbolized as ${}_{e^{(r)}}H_{n,q}^{(m)}(\tau,\phi,\gamma)$, are described by the following generating function:

$$\frac{e_q(\tau t)e_q(\phi t^m)}{1-\gamma t^r}=\sum_{n=0}^{\infty}{}_{e^{(r)}}H_{n,q}^{(m)}(\tau,\phi,\gamma)\frac{t^n}{[n]_q!}. \tag{29}$$

In [14], Raza et al. introduced the q-Gould–Hopper polynomials and examined various properties associated with them. Subsequently, in [20], the same authors defined the two-variable q-Gould–Hopper–Appell polynomials by convolving the q-Gould–Hopper polynomials with the q-Appell polynomials, utilizing an extended application of the monomial principle.

The classical Appell polynomial families and their q-analogs have garnered significant scholarly attention due to their applications in combinatorics, quantum theory, and operator analysis. Foundational studies, such as those conducted by Andrews, Askey, and Roy [1], Srivastava and Manocha [4], and Ernst [3], offer a comprehensive framework within which the current generalization can be contextualized.

In this paper, we define three-variable q-truncated exponential Gould–Hopper-based Appell polynomials, employing a generating function approach that incorporates q-calculus functions. The investigation extends to the analysis of these polynomials within the quasi-monomiality framework, facilitating the establishment of crucial operational identities. Subsequently, operational representations are derived, and both q-differential and partial differential equations are formulated for the aforementioned polynomials. To further elucidate their analytical properties, summation formulas are developed. The article concludes with graphical representations that demonstrate the behavior of the three-variable q-truncated exponential Gould–Hopper-based Appell polynomials and highlights their potential applications in various fields.

2. q-Appell Convolution

In this section, we introduce three-variable q-truncated exponential Gould–Hopper-based Appell polynomials or, shortly, 3VqTEGHbAPs denoted by ${}_{e^{(r)}}HA_{n,q}(\tau,\phi,\gamma)$, and we obtain their series definitions, partial derivatives, and explicit and implicit formulas. Therefore, we first define the 3VqTEGHbAPs.

Here, we define the three-variable q-truncated exponential Gould–Hopper-based Appell polynomials in the following form:

$$\frac{A_q(t)}{1-\gamma t^r}e_q(\tau t)e_q(\phi t^m) = \sum_{n=0}^{\infty} {}_{e^{(r)}}HA_{n,q}^{(m)}(\tau,\phi,\gamma)\frac{t^n}{[n]_q!}. \tag{30}$$

In other words, we note that

$$e_q\left(\phi\widehat{D}_{q,\tau}^m\right)\frac{A_q(t)}{1-\gamma t^r}e_q(\tau t) = \sum_{n=0}^{\infty} {}_{e^{(r)}}HA_{n,q}^{(m)}(\tau,\phi,\gamma)\frac{t^n}{[n]_q!}. \tag{31}$$

We observe that the generating function exhibits absolute convergence for $|t| < R$, where R is contingent upon the convergence radii of $A_q(t)$, $e_q(\tau t)$, and $e_q(\phi t^m)$. In this study, we assume $q \in (0,1)$ to ensure the validity of the q-calculus operations and convergence.

Theorem 1. *For the 3VqTEGHbAP, the following identity holds:*

$$ {}_{e^{(r)}}HA_{n,q}^{(m)}(\tau,\phi,\gamma) = \sum_{k=0}^{n}\binom{n}{k}_q A_{k,q}\,{}_{e^{(r)}}H_{n-k,q}^{(m)}(\tau,\phi,\gamma), \tag{32}$$

with $A_{k,q}$ given by Equation (27).

Proof. By virtue of Equations (29) and (30), we obtain

$$\sum_{n=0}^{\infty} {}_{e^{(r)}}HA_{n,q}^{(m)}(\tau,\phi,\gamma)\frac{t^n}{[n]_q!} = A_q(t)\sum_{n=0}^{\infty} {}_{e^{(r)}}H_{n,q}^{(m)}(\tau,\phi,\gamma)\frac{t^n}{[n]_q!}. \tag{33}$$

Utilizing the expansion (27) of $A_q(t)$ on the left-hand side of Equation (33), we simplify the expression and equate the coefficients of the corresponding powers of t on both sides of the equation, thereby establishing assertion (32). □

In a similar manner, we can derive the following equivalent forms of the series representations of ${}_{e^{(r)}}HA_{n,q}^{(m)}(\tau,\phi,\gamma)$.

Theorem 2. *The three-variable q-truncated exponential Gould–Hopper-based Appell polynomials are characterized by the following series:*

$$ {}_{e^{(r)}}HA_{n,q}^{(m)}(\tau,\phi,\gamma) = [n]_q!\sum_{k,m=0}^{k+sm\le n}\frac{A_{k,q}\phi^m\, E_{n-k-sm,q}^{(r)}(\tau,\gamma)}{[k]_q![m]_q![n-k-sm]_q!}, \tag{34}$$

$$ {}_{e^{(r)}}HA_{n,q}^{(m)}(\tau,\phi,\gamma) = [n]_q!\sum_{k,m=0}^{k+rm\le n}\frac{A_{k,q}\gamma^m H_{n-k-rm,q}^{(s)}(\tau,\phi)}{[k]_q![n-k-rm]_q!}, \tag{35}$$

$$ {}_{e^{(r)}}HA_{n,q}^{(m)}(\tau,\phi,\gamma) = [n]_q!\sum_{k,m=0}^{rm+sp\le n}\frac{\gamma^m\phi^p A_{n-rm-sp,q}^{(s)}(\tau)}{[n-rm-sp]_q!}. \tag{36}$$

Proof. In view of Equations (20) and (27)–(29), we can easily obtain (34)–(36). This completes the proof of the theorem. □

The determinant form plays a crucial role in deriving the exploration of q-special polynomials, offering a compact and refined representation that captures their core attributes. This formulation adeptly illustrates essential features, such as orthogonality, recurrence relations, and generating functions, establishing it as a valuable instrument for analysis and manipulation across diverse mathematical settings. Moreover, the determinant form serves as a link to other mathematical frameworks, enabling a deeper understanding of the foundational principles that govern q-special polynomials. Its importance extends beyond mere computational applications, contributing significantly to the theoretical progress in the field of special function theory.

Costabile and Longo [21], expanding on the techniques presented in [22], effectively derived the determinantal form of q-Appell polynomials.

Theorem 3. *The determinant form of the three-variable q-truncated exponential Gould–Hopper-based Appell polynomial with degree n is*

$$ {}_{e^{(r)}}HA^{(m)}_{0,q}(\tau,\phi,\gamma) = \frac{1}{\beta_{0,q}}, $$

$$ {}_{e^{(r)}}HA^{(m)}_{n,q}(\tau,\phi,\gamma) = \frac{(-1)^n}{(\beta_{0,q})^{n+1}} $$

$$ \times \begin{vmatrix} 1 & {}_{e^{(r)}}H^{(m)}_{1,q}(\tau,\phi,\gamma) & {}_{e^{(r)}}H^{(m)}_{2,q}(\tau,\phi,\gamma) & \cdots & {}_{e^{(r)}}H^{(m)}_{n-1,q}(\tau,\phi,\gamma) & {}_{e^{(r)}}H^{(m)}_{n,q}(\tau,\phi,\gamma) \\ \beta_{0,q} & \beta_{1,q} & \beta_{2,q} & \cdots & \beta_{n-1,q} & \beta_{n,q} \\ 0 & \beta_{0,q} & \binom{2}{1}_q\beta_{1,q} & \cdots & \binom{n-1}{1}_q\beta_{n-2,q} & \binom{n}{1}_q\beta_{n-1,q} \\ 0 & 0 & \beta_{0,q} & \cdots & \binom{n-1}{1}_q\beta_{n-3,q} & \binom{n}{2}_q\beta_{n-2,q} \\ \vdots & \vdots & \vdots & \cdots & \vdots & \\ 0 & 0 & 0 & \cdots & \beta_{0,q} & \binom{n}{n-1}_q\beta_{1,q} \end{vmatrix}, \tag{37} $$

$$ \beta_{n,q} = -\frac{1}{A_{0,q}}\left(\sum_{k=1}^{n}\binom{n}{k}_q A_{k,q}\beta_{n-k,q}\right), \quad n=0,1,2,\ldots, $$

where $\beta_{0,q} \neq 0$, $\beta_{0,q} = \frac{1}{A_{0,q}}$ and ${}_{e^{(r)}}H^{(m)}_{n,q}(\tau,\phi,\gamma)$, $n = 0,1,2,\ldots$, are the three-variable q-truncated exponential Gould–Hopper polynomials defined by Equation (29).

Proof. By integrating the series expressions of the newly generalized q-truncated exponential Gould–Hopper polynomials into the generating function of the three-variable q-truncated exponential Gould–Hopper-based Appell polynomials, we derive

$$ A_q(t)\sum_{n=0}^{\infty} {}_{e^{(r)}}H^{(m)}_{n,q}(\tau,\phi,\gamma)\frac{t^n}{[n]_q!} = \sum_{n=0}^{\infty} {}_{e^{(r)}}HA^{(m)}_{n,q}(\tau,\phi,\gamma)\frac{t^n}{[n]_q!}. \tag{38} $$

Multiplying both sides by

$$ \frac{1}{A_q(t)} = \sum_{\gamma=0}^{\infty}\beta_{\gamma,q}\frac{t^\gamma}{[\gamma]_q!}, \tag{39} $$

we get

$$ \sum_{n=0}^{\infty} {}_{e^{(r)}}H^{(m)}_{n,q}(\tau,\phi,\gamma)\frac{t^n}{[n]_q!} = \sum_{\gamma=0}^{\infty}\beta_{\gamma,q}\frac{\delta^\gamma}{[\gamma]_q!}\sum_{n=0}^{\infty} {}_{e^{(r)}}HA^{(m)}_{n,q}(\tau,\phi,\gamma)\frac{t^n}{[n]_q!}. \tag{40} $$

Applying the Cauchy product in (40) gives

$$ {}_{e^{(r)}}H^{(m)}_{n,q}(\tau,\phi,\gamma) = \sum_{\gamma=0}^{n}\binom{n}{\gamma}_q\beta_{\gamma,q}\, {}_{e^{(r)}}HA^{(m)}_{n-\gamma,q}(\tau,\phi,\gamma). \tag{41} $$

So, we obtain the system of equations as follows:

$$ {}_{e^{(r)}}H^{(m)}_{0,q}(\tau,\phi,\gamma) = \beta_{0,q}\, {}_{e^{(r)}}HA^{(m)}_{0,q}(\tau,\phi,\gamma), $$

$$
\begin{aligned}
{}_{e^{(r)}}H_{1,q}^{(m)}(\tau,\phi,\gamma) &= \beta_{0,q}\,{}_{e^{(r)}}HA_{1,q}^{(m)}(\tau,\phi,\gamma)+\beta_{1,q}\,{}_{e^{(r)}}HA_{0,q}^{(m)}(\tau,\phi,\gamma),\\
{}_{e^{(r)}}H_{2,q}^{(m)}(\tau,\phi,\gamma) &= \beta_{0,q}\,{}_{e^{(r)}}HA_{2,q}^{(m)}(\tau,\phi,\gamma)+\binom{2}{1}_q\beta_{1,q}\,{}_{e^{(r)}}HA_{1,q}^{(m)}(\tau,\phi,\gamma)+\beta_{2}\,{}_{e^{(r)}}HA_{0,q}^{(m)}(\tau,\phi,\gamma),\\
&\vdots\\
{}_{e^{(r)}}H_{n-1,q}^{(m)}(\tau,\phi,\gamma) &= \beta_{0,q}\,{}_{e^{(r)}}HA_{n-1,q}^{(m)}(\tau,\phi,\gamma)+\binom{n-1}{1}_q\beta_{1,q}\,{}_{e^{(r)}}HA_{n-2,q}^{(m)}(\tau,\phi,\gamma)+\cdots\\
&\quad+\beta_{n-1,q}\,{}_{e^{(r)}}HA_{0,q}^{(m)}(\tau,\phi,\gamma),\\
{}_{e^{(r)}}H_{n,q}^{(m)}(\tau,\phi,\gamma) &= \beta_{0,q}\,{}_{e^{(r)}}HA_{n,q}^{(m)}(\tau,\phi,\gamma)+\binom{n}{1}_q\beta_{1,q}\,{}_{e^{(r)}}HA_{n-1,q}^{(m)}(\tau,\phi,\gamma)+\cdots\\
&\quad+\beta_{n,q}\,{}_{e^{(r)}}HA_{0,q}^{(m)}(\tau,\phi,\gamma).
\end{aligned}
$$

Applying Cramers' rule, we get

$$
{}_{e^{(r)}}HA_{n,q}^{(m)}(\tau,\phi,\gamma)=\frac{\begin{vmatrix}
\beta_{0,q} & 0 & \cdots & 0 & {}_{e^{(r)}}H_{0,q}^{(m)}(\tau,\phi,\gamma)\\
\beta_{1,q} & \beta_{0,q} & \cdots & 0 & {}_{e^{(r)}}H_{1,q}^{(m)}(\tau,\phi,\gamma)\\
\beta_{2,q} & \binom{2}{1}_q\beta_{1,q} & \cdots & 0 & {}_{e^{(r)}}H_{2,q}^{(m)}(\tau,\phi,\gamma)\\
\beta_{3,q} & \binom{3}{2}_q\beta_{2,q} & \cdots & 0 & {}_{e^{(r)}}H_{3,q}^{(m)}(\tau,\phi,\gamma)\\
\vdots & \vdots & \vdots & \vdots & \vdots\\
\beta_{n-1,q} & \binom{n-1}{1}_q\beta_{n-2,q} & \cdots & \beta_{0,q} & {}_{e^{(r)}}H_{n-1,q}^{(m)}(\tau,\phi,\gamma)\\
\beta_{n,q} & \binom{n}{1}_q\beta_{n-1,q} & \cdots & \binom{n}{n-1}_q\beta_{1,q} & {}_{e^{(r)}}H_{n,q}^{(m)}(\tau,\phi,\gamma)
\end{vmatrix}}{\begin{vmatrix}
\beta_{0,q} & 0 & \cdots & 0 & 0\\
\beta_{1,q} & \beta_{0,q} & \cdots & 0 & 0\\
\beta_{2,q} & \binom{2}{1}_q\beta_{1,q} & \cdots & 0 & 0\\
\beta_{3,q} & \binom{3}{2}_q\beta_{2,q} & \cdots & 0 & 0\\
\vdots & \vdots & \vdots & \vdots & \vdots\\
\beta_{n-1,q} & \binom{n-1}{1}_q\beta_{n-2,q} & \cdots & \beta_{0,q} & 0\\
\beta_{n,q} & \binom{n}{1}_q\beta_{n-1,q} & \cdots & \binom{n}{n-1}_q\beta_{1,q} & \beta_{0,q}
\end{vmatrix}}.
$$

By taking the transpose in the last equation, we have

$$
{}_{e^{(r)}}HA_{n,q}^{(m)}(\tau,\phi,\gamma)=\frac{1}{(\beta_{0,q})^{n+1}}
$$

$$
\times\begin{vmatrix}
\beta_{0,q} & \beta_{1,q} & \cdots & \beta_{n-1,q} & \beta_{n,q}\\
0 & \beta_{0,q} & \cdots & \binom{n-1}{1}_q\beta_{n-2,q} & \binom{n}{1}_q\beta_{n-1,q}\\
0 & 0 & \cdots & \binom{n-1}{1}_q\beta_{n-3,q} & \binom{n}{2}_q\beta_{n-2,q}\\
\vdots & \vdots & \vdots & \vdots & \vdots\\
0 & 0 & \cdots & \beta_{0,q} & \binom{n}{n-1}_q\beta_{1,q}\\
{}_{e^{(r)}}H_{0,q}^{(m)}(\tau,\phi,\gamma) & {}_{e^{(r)}}H_{1,q}^{(m)}(\tau,\phi,\gamma) & \cdots & {}_{e^{(r)}}H_{n-1,q}^{(m)}(\tau,\phi,\gamma) & {}_{e^{(r)}}H_{n,q}^{(m)}(\tau,\phi,\gamma)
\end{vmatrix}.
$$

Thus, simple row operations are used to finish the proof. □

Theorem 4. *The following q-recurrence formula for the 3VqTEGHbAPs holds true:*

$$
{}_{e^{(r)}}HA^{(m)}_{n+1,q}(\tau,\phi,\gamma)=\tau\,{}_{e^{(r)}}HA^{(m)}_{n,q}(\tau,\phi,\gamma)+[n]_q!\phi\sum_{m=0}^{n-1}\frac{{}_{e^{(r)}}HA^{(m)}_{n-m+1,q}(\tau,\phi,\gamma)}{[n-m+1]_q!}T_{(\phi;m)}T_\tau
$$

$$
+\sum_{k=0}^{n}\binom{n}{k}_q {}_{e^{(r)}}HA^{(m)}_{n-k,q}(q\tau,q\phi,\gamma)A_{k+1,q}+[r]_q[n]_q!\sum_{k=0}^{[\frac{n-r+1}{r}]}\frac{q^{n-kr-r+1}\gamma^{k+1}{}_{e^{(r)}}HA^{(m)}_{n-kr-r+1,q}(\tau,\phi,\gamma)}{[n-kr-r+1]_q!}. \quad (42)
$$

Proof. By differentiating Equation (30) with respect to t using the q-partial derivative and by integrating Equation (15), we derive

$$
\sum_{n=0}^{\infty}{}_{e^{(r)}}HA^{(m)}_{n,q}(\tau,\phi,\gamma)\widehat{D}_{q,t}\frac{t^n}{[n]_q!}=\frac{A_q(t)}{1-\gamma t^r}\widehat{D}_{q,t}(e_q(\tau t)e_q(\phi t^m))+\frac{e_q(q\tau t)e_q(q\phi t^m)}{1-\gamma t^r}\widehat{D}_{q,t}A_q(t)
$$

$$
+A_q(qt)e_q(q\tau t)e_q(q\phi t^m)\widehat{D}_{q,t}\frac{1}{1-\gamma t^r}.
$$

Again, by using Equations (15), (16), (23), and (25) in the above equation, we obtain

$$
\sum_{n=0}^{\infty}{}_{e^{(r)}}HA^{(m)}_{n,q}(\tau,\phi,\gamma)\frac{t^{n-1}}{[n-1]_q!}=\tau\frac{A_q(t)}{1-\gamma t^r}e_q(\tau t)e_q(\phi t^m)+\phi t^{m-1}T_{(\phi;m)}\frac{A_q(t)}{1-\gamma t^r}e_q(q\tau t)e_q(\phi t^m)
$$

$$
+\frac{e_q(q\tau t)e_q(q\phi t^m)}{1-\gamma t^r}\widehat{D}_{q,t}A_q(t)+\left(\frac{[r]_q\gamma t^{r-1}}{1-\gamma t^r}\right)\left(\frac{A_q(qt)}{1-\gamma q^r t^r}e_q(q\tau t)e_q(q\phi t^m)\right). \quad (43)
$$

Using the series in the r.h.s of Equation (39), we get

$$
\widehat{D}_{q,t}A_q(t)=\sum_{n=0}^{\infty}A_{n+1,q}\frac{t^n}{[n]_q!}. \quad (44)
$$

Again, using Equations (30) and (44) in Equation (43), we achieve

$$
\sum_{n=0}^{\infty}{}_{e^{(r)}}HA^{(m)}_{n+1,q}(\tau,\phi,\gamma)\frac{t^n}{[n]_q!}
$$

$$
=\tau\sum_{n=0}^{\infty}{}_{e^{(r)}}HA^{(m)}_{n,q}(\tau,\phi,\gamma)\frac{t^n}{[n]_q!}+[n]_q!\phi\sum_{n=0}^{\infty}\sum_{m=0}^{n-1}\frac{{}_{e^{(r)}}HA^{(m)}_{n-m+1,q}(\tau,\phi,\gamma)}{[n-m+1]_q!}T_{(\phi;m)}T_\tau\frac{t^n}{[n]_q!}
$$

$$
+\sum_{n=0}^{\infty}\sum_{k=0}^{n}\binom{n}{k}_q{}_{e^{(r)}}HA^{(m)}_{n-k,q}(q\tau,q\phi,\gamma)A_{k+1,q}\frac{t^n}{[n]_q!}
$$

$$
+[r]_q\sum_{n=0}^{\infty}[n]_q!\sum_{k=0}^{[\frac{n-r+1}{r}]}\frac{q^{n-kr-r+1}\gamma^{k+1}{}_{e^{(r)}}HA^{(m)}_{n-kr-r+1,q}(\tau,\phi,\gamma)}{[n-kr-r+1]_q!}\frac{t^n}{[n]_q!}. \quad (45)
$$

By rearranging the series and equating the corresponding powers of t on both sides of the resulting equation, we derive assertion (42). □

Theorem 5. *The higher derivative formula for the 3VqTEGHbAPs holds true:*

$$
\widehat{D}^k_{q,t}{}_{e^{(r)}}HA^{(m)}_{n,q}(\tau,\phi,\gamma)=\frac{[n]_q!}{[n-k]_q!}{}_{e^{(r)}}HA^{(m)}_{n-k,q}(\tau,\phi,\gamma). \quad (46)
$$

Proof. By taking the kth-order q-partial derivative with respect to τ on both sides of the generating function (30) and subsequently applying Equation (13) to the left-hand side, it can be deduced that

$$\sum_{n=0}^{\infty} \widehat{D}^{k}_{q,t\,e^{(r)}} HA^{(m)}_{n,q}(\tau,\phi,\gamma)\frac{t^n}{[n]_q!} = t^k \frac{A_q(t)}{1-\gamma t^r} e_q(\tau t)e_q(\phi t^m) = \sum_{n=0}^{\infty} {}_{e^{(r)}}HA^{(m)}_{n,q}(\tau,\phi,\gamma)\frac{t^{n+k}}{[n]_q!}. \tag{47}$$

Upon reorganizing the given series and then equating the corresponding powers of t on both sides of the resulting equation, we confirm assertion (30). □

Theorem 6. *The 3VqTEGHbAPs satisfy the following addition formula:*

$$ {}_{e^{(r)}}HA^{(m)}_{n,q}(\tau+\delta,\phi,\gamma) = \sum_{k=0}^{w} \binom{w}{k}_q \delta^k \, {}_{e^{(r)}}HA^{(m)}_{w-k,q}(\tau,\phi,\gamma). \tag{48}$$

Proof. By changing τ by $\tau+\delta$ in (30) and then using Equation (7), we get

$$A_q(t)\frac{e_q(\tau t)e_q(\phi t^m)}{1-\gamma t^r} e_q(\delta t) = \sum_{w=0}^{\infty} {}_{e^{(r)}}HA^{(m)}_{w,q}(\tau+\delta,\phi,\gamma)\frac{t^w}{[w]_q!}. \tag{49}$$

Using Equations (7) and (30) in l.h.s. of the above equation, we have

$$\sum_{w=0}^{\infty}\sum_{k=0}^{\infty} \delta^k \, {}_{e^{(r)}}HA^{(m)}_{w,q}(\tau,\phi,\gamma)\frac{t^{w+k}}{[w]_q![k]_q!} = \sum_{w=0}^{\infty} {}_{e^{(r)}}HA^{(m)}_{w,q})(\tau+\delta,\phi,\gamma)\frac{t^w}{[w]_q!}.$$

Through the process of rearranging the series and equating the corresponding powers of t on each side, assertion (48) is substantiated. □

Theorem 7. *The summation formula for the ${}_{e^{(r)}}HA^{(m)}_{w,q}(\tau,\phi,\gamma)$ is explicitly defined as the product of $H^{(m)}_{w,q}(\tau,\phi)$ and $e^{(r)}_{w,q}(\tau,\phi)$, as demonstrated below:*

$$ {}_{e^{(r)}}HA^{(m)}_{w,q}(\tau,\phi,\gamma) = \sum_{s=0}^{w}\sum_{k=0}^{w-s} \binom{w}{s}_q \binom{w-s}{k}_q (-w)^s H^{(m)}_{w-k-s}(\tau,\gamma) e^{(r)}_{k,q}(w,\phi). \tag{50}$$

Proof. We examine the product formed by the generating function (20) of $H^{(m)}_{w,q}(\tau,\phi)$ and generating function (28) of ${}_{e^{(r)}}A_{w,q}(\tau,\phi)$ in the following form:

$$A_q(t)\frac{e_q(wt)}{1-\gamma t^r} e_q(\tau t)e_q(\phi t^r) = \sum_{w=0}^{\infty}\sum_{k=0}^{\infty} H^{(m)}_{w,q}(\tau,\gamma)\, {}_{e^{(r)}}A_{k,q}(\tau,\phi)\frac{t^{w+k}}{[w]_q![k]_q!}. \tag{51}$$

In the r.h.s. of Equation (51), using the identity

$$\sum_{w=0}^{\infty}\sum_{k=0}^{\infty} A(k,w) = \sum_{w=0}^{\infty}\sum_{k=0}^{w} A(k,w-k), \tag{52}$$

we get

$$A_q(t)\frac{e_q(wt)}{1-\gamma t^r} e_q(\tau t)e_q(\phi t^r) = \sum_{w=0}^{\infty}\sum_{k=0}^{w} H^{(m)}_{w-k,q}(\tau,\gamma)\, {}_{e^{(r)}}A_{k,q}(\tau,\phi)\frac{t^{w+k}}{[w-k]_q![k]_q!}, \tag{53}$$

which, on shifting the $e_q(wt)$ to the l.h.s. and using the series definition of the exponential, becomes

$$\frac{A_q(t)}{1-\gamma t^r} e_q(\tau t)e_q(\phi t^r) = \sum_{w=0}^{\infty}\sum_{s=0}^{\infty}\sum_{k=0}^{w} \binom{w}{k}_q (-w)^s H^{(m)}_{w-k,q}(\tau,\gamma) e^{(r)}_{k,q}(w,\phi)\frac{t^{w+s}}{[w]_q![s]_q!}. \tag{54}$$

Again, using Equation (28) in the r.h.s of Equation (54), we get

$$\frac{A_q(t)}{1-\gamma t^r}e_q(\tau t)e_q(\phi t^r) = \sum_{w=0}^{\infty}\sum_{s=0}^{w}\sum_{k=0}^{w-s}\binom{w-s}{k}_q(-w)^s H^{(m)}_{w-k-s,q}(\tau,\gamma)_{e^{(r)}}A_{k,q}(\tau,\phi)\frac{t^w}{[w-s]_q![s]_q!}. \quad (55)$$

Utilizing the equation generating function (30) on the left-hand side of Equation (55) and matching the coefficients of identical powers of t in the resulting equation, we establish assertion (50). □

3. Monomiality Characteristic and Operational Identities

This section presents the q-quasi-monomiality characteristic, operational identities, and q-differential equations pertinent to the 3VqTEGHbAPs, denoted as ${}_{e^{(r)}}HA^{(m)}_{n,q}(\tau,\phi,\gamma)$.

The notion of monomiality is a crucial tool for analyzing exceptional polynomials and their attributes. Initially introduced by J.F. Steffensen [23], this concept was later expanded into the realm of quasi-monomiality by Dattoli and his colleagues [24–26]. In the specific context of q-polynomials, Raza et al. [15] further extended the monomiality principle. This extension offers a robust methodology for examining the quasi-monomiality of certain q-special polynomials. Researchers have extensively utilized monomiality frameworks to construct and evaluate hybrid families of special polynomials [27]. The two q-operators, denoted as $\widehat{M}_q$ and $\widehat{P}_q$, are known as the q-multiplicative and q-derivative operators, respectively, for a q-polynomial set $p_{n,q}(\tau)(n \in \mathbb{N}, \tau \in \mathbb{C})$, as demonstrated by [2]

$$\widehat{M}_q\{p_{n,q}(\tau)\} = p_{n+1,q}(\tau), \quad (56)$$

and

$$\widehat{P}_q\{p_{n,q}(\tau)\} = [n]_q p_{n-1,q}(\tau). \quad (57)$$

The operators $\widehat{M}_q$ and $\widehat{P}_q$ adhere to the following commutation relation:

$$[\widehat{M}_q, \widehat{P}_q] = \widehat{P}_q\widehat{M}_q - \widehat{M}_q\widehat{P}_q. \quad (58)$$

The characteristics of the polynomials $p_{n,q}(\tau)$ can be inferred from the properties of the operators $\widehat{M}_q$ and $\widehat{P}_q$. If these operators, $\widehat{M}_q$ and $\widehat{P}_q$, have a differential realization, then the polynomials $p_{n,q}(\tau)$ are governed by the differential equation

$$\widehat{M}_q\widehat{P}_q\{p_{n,q}(\tau)\} = [n]_q p_{n,q}(\tau), \quad (59)$$

and

$$\widehat{P}_q\widehat{M}_q\{p_{n,q}(\tau)\} = [n+1]_q p_{n,q}(\tau). \quad (60)$$

In view of (56) and (57), we have

$$[\widehat{M}_q, \widehat{P}_q] = [n+1]_q - [n]_q. \quad (61)$$

From (56), we have

$$\widehat{M}_q^{\,r}\{p_{n,q}\} = p_{n+r,q}(\tau). \quad (62)$$

In particular, we have

$$p_{n,q}(\tau) = \widehat{M}_q^{\,n}\{p_{0,q}\} = \widehat{M}_q^{\,n}\{1\}, \quad (63)$$

where $p_{0,q}(\tau) = 1$ is the q-sequel of polynomial $p_{n,q}(\tau)$. Also, the generating function of $p_{n,q}(\tau)$ can be obtained as

$$e_q(\widehat{M}_q t)\{1\} = \sum_{n=0}^{\infty} p_{n,q}(\tau)\frac{t^n}{[n]_q!}. \quad (64)$$

Now, we establish the q-monomial characteristic of the three-variable q-truncated Gould–Hopper–Appell polynomials in the form of the following theorem.

Theorem 8. *The three-variable q-truncated exponential Gould–Hopper-based Appell polynomials exhibit quasi-monomial properties when subjected to the following q-multiplicative and q-derivative operators:*

$$\widehat{M}_{3VqTGAP} = \tau + \phi \widehat{D}_{q,\tau}^{m-1} T_{(\phi;m)} T_\tau + \frac{A_q'(\widehat{D}_{q,\tau})}{A_q(\widehat{D}_{q,\tau})} T_\tau T_\phi + \left(\frac{[r]_q \gamma \widehat{D}_{q,\tau}^{r-1}}{1 - q^r \gamma \widehat{D}_{q,\tau}^r}\right) \left(\frac{A_q(q\widehat{D}_{q,\tau})}{A_q(\widehat{D}_{q,\tau})}\right) T_\tau T_\phi, \tag{65}$$

or, alternatively,

$$\widehat{M}_{3VqTGAP} = \tau T_\phi + \phi \widehat{D}_{q,\tau}^{m-1} T_{(\phi;m)} + \frac{A_q'(\widehat{D}_{q,\tau})}{A_q(\widehat{D}_{q,\tau})} T_\tau T_\phi + \left(\frac{[r]_q \gamma \widehat{D}_{q,\tau}^{r-1}}{1 - q^r \gamma \widehat{D}_{q,\tau}^r}\right) \left(\frac{A_q(q\widehat{D}_{q,\tau})}{A_q(\widehat{D}_{q,\tau})}\right) T_\tau T_\phi, \tag{66}$$

and

$$\widehat{P}_{3VqTGAP} = \widehat{D}_{q,\tau}, \tag{67}$$

respectively, where T_τ and T_ϕ are the q-dilatation operators, as specified in Equation (23).

Proof. By taking the partial derivative of Equation (30) with respect to t and applying Equation (15), we derive

$$\sum_{n=1}^{\infty} {}_{e^{(r)}}HA_{n,q}^{(m)}(\tau,\phi,\gamma) \widehat{D}_{q,t} \frac{t^n}{[n]_q!}$$

$$= \frac{A_q(t)}{1-\gamma t^r} \widehat{D}_{q,t}(e_q(\tau t) e_q(\phi t^m)) + \frac{e_q(q\tau t) e_q(q\phi t^m)}{1-\gamma t^r} \widehat{D}_{q,t} A_q(t) + A_q(qt) e_q(q\tau t) e_q(q\phi t^m) \widehat{D}_{q,t} \frac{1}{1-\gamma t^r}. \tag{68}$$

By employing Equations (15) and (16) and setting $f_q(t) = e_q(\phi t)$ and $g_q(t) = e_q(\phi t^m)$, followed by simplifying the resulting equation using Equations (23) and (25) on the left-hand side, we obtain

$$\sum_{n=1}^{\infty} {}_{e^{(r)}}HA_{n,q}^{(m)}(\tau,\phi,\gamma) \frac{t^{n-1}}{[n-1]_q!}$$

$$= \left(\tau + \phi t^{m-1} T_{(\phi;m)} T_\tau + \frac{A_q'(t)}{A_q(t)} T_\tau T_\phi + \left(\frac{[r]_q \gamma t^{r-1}}{1 - q^r \gamma t^r}\right)\left(\frac{A_q(qt)}{A_q(t)}\right) T_\tau T_\phi\right) \frac{A_q(t)}{1-\gamma t^r} e_q(\tau t) e_q(\phi t^m). \tag{69}$$

Since

$$\widehat{D}_{q,\tau} \frac{A_q(t)}{1-\gamma t^r} e_q(\tau t) e_q(\phi t^m) = t \frac{A_q(t)}{1-\gamma t^r} e_q(\tau t) e_q(\phi t^m). \tag{70}$$

$A_q(t)$ is an invertible series of t, and $\frac{A_q'(t)}{A_q(t)}$ has q-power series expansion in t.

Therefore, using Equations (69) and (70), we get

$$\sum_{n=0}^{\infty} {}_{e^{(r)}}HA_{n+1,q}^{(m)}(\tau,\phi,\gamma) \frac{t^n}{[n]_q!}$$

$$= \left(\tau + \phi \widehat{D}_{q,\tau}^{m-1} T_{(\phi;m)} T_\tau + \frac{A_q'(\widehat{D}_{q,\tau})}{A_q(\widehat{D}_{q,\tau})} T_\tau T_\phi + \left(\frac{[r]_q \gamma \widehat{D}_{q,\tau}^{r-1}}{1 - q^r \gamma \widehat{D}_{q,\tau}^r}\right)\left(\frac{A_q(q\widehat{D}_{q,\tau})}{A_q(\widehat{D}_{q,\tau})}\right) T_\tau T_\phi\right)$$
$$\times \frac{A_q(t)}{1-\gamma t^r} e_q(\tau t) e_q(\phi t^m), \tag{71}$$

which, on using (30), gives

$$\sum_{n=0}^{\infty} {}_{e^{(r)}}HA_{n+1,q}^{(m)}(\tau,\phi,\gamma) \frac{t^n}{[n]_q!}$$

$$= \sum_{n=0}^{\infty}\left(\tau + \phi\widehat{D}_{q,\tau}^{m-1}T_{(\phi;m)}T_\tau + \frac{A_q'(\widehat{D}_{q,\tau})}{A_q(\widehat{D}_{q,\tau})}T_\tau T_\phi + \left(\frac{[r]_q\gamma\widehat{D}_{q,\tau}^{r-1}}{1-q^r\gamma\widehat{D}_{q,\tau}^r}\right)\left(\frac{A_q(q\widehat{D}_{q,\tau})}{A_q(\widehat{D}_{q,\tau})}\right)T_\tau T_\phi\right)$$
$$\times {}_{e^{(r)}}HA_{n,q}^{(m)}(\tau,\phi,\gamma)\frac{t^n}{[n]_q!}. \tag{72}$$

By equating the coefficients of t on both sides of Equation (72) and considering Equation (56), the resulting equation substantiates assertion (65).

By utilizing Equation (68) and defining $f_q(t) = e_q(\phi t^m)$ alongside $g_q(t) = e_q(\phi t)$ and by replicating the procedural steps detailed in the proof of Equation (65), we confirm assertion (66).

In view of (57), we note that Equation (46) (for $k = 1$) proves assertion (67). □

Theorem 9. *The following q-differential equations for ${}_{e^{(r)}}HA_{n,q}^{(m)}(\tau,\phi,\gamma)$ hold true:*

$$\left(\tau\widehat{D}_{q,\tau} + \phi\widehat{D}_{q,\tau}^{m}T_{(\phi;m)}T_\tau + \frac{A_q'(\widehat{D}_{q,\tau})}{A_q(\widehat{D}_{q,\tau})}\widehat{D}_{q,\tau}T_\tau T_\phi + \left(\frac{[r]_q\gamma\widehat{D}_{q,\tau}^{r}}{1-q^r\gamma\widehat{D}_{q,\tau}^r}\right)\left(\frac{A_q(q\widehat{D}_{q,\tau})}{A_q(\widehat{D}_{q,\tau})}\right)T_\tau T_\phi - [n]_q\right)$$
$$\times {}_{e^{(r)}}HA_{n,q}^{(m)}(\tau,\phi,\gamma) = 0, \tag{73}$$

and

$$\left(\tau\widehat{D}_{q,\tau}T_\phi + \phi\widehat{D}_{q,\tau}^{m}T_{(\phi;m)} + \frac{A_q'(\widehat{D}_{q,\tau})}{A_q(\widehat{D}_{q,\tau})}\widehat{D}_{q,\tau}T_\tau T_\phi + \left(\frac{[r]_q\gamma\widehat{D}_{q,\tau}^{r}}{1-q^r\gamma\widehat{D}_{q,\tau}^r}\right)\left(\frac{A_q(q\widehat{D}_{q,\tau})}{A_q(\widehat{D}_{q,\tau})}\right)T_\tau T_\phi - [n]_q\right)$$
$$\times {}_{e^{(r)}}HA_{n,q}^{(m)}(\tau,\phi,\gamma) = 0. \tag{74}$$

Proof. Using (65), (66), and (67) in (59), we get

$$\left(\tau\widehat{D}_{q,\tau} + \phi\widehat{D}_{q,\tau}^{m}T_{(\phi;m)}T_\tau + \frac{A_q'(\widehat{D}_{q,\tau})}{A_q(\widehat{D}_{q,\tau})}\widehat{D}_{q,\tau}T_\tau T_\phi + \left(\frac{[r]_q\gamma\widehat{D}_{q,\tau}^{r}}{1-q^r\gamma\widehat{D}_{q,\tau}^r}\right)\left(\frac{A_q(q\widehat{D}_{q,\tau})}{A_q(\widehat{D}_{q,\tau})}\right)T_\tau T_\phi\right)$$
$$\times {}_{e^{(r)}}HA_{n,q}^{(m)}(\tau,\phi,\gamma) = [n]_q\, {}_{e^{(r)}}HA_{n,q}^{(m)}(\tau,\phi,\gamma), \tag{75}$$

and

$$\left(\tau\widehat{D}_{q,\tau}T_\phi + \phi\widehat{D}_{q,\tau}^{m}T_{(\phi;m)} + \frac{A_q'(\widehat{D}_{q,\tau})}{A_q(\widehat{D}_{q,\tau})}\widehat{D}_{q,\tau}T_\tau T_\phi + \left(\frac{[r]_q\gamma\widehat{D}_{q,\tau}^{r}}{1-q^r\gamma\widehat{D}_{q,\tau}^r}\right)\left(\frac{A_q(q\widehat{D}_{q,\tau})}{A_q(\widehat{D}_{q,\tau})}\right)T_\tau T_\phi\right)$$
$$\times {}_{e^{(r)}}HA_{n,q}^{(m)}(\tau,\phi,\gamma) = [n]_q\, {}_{e^{(r)}}HA_{n,q}^{(m)}(\tau,\phi,\gamma), \tag{76}$$

Therefore, upon simplification, we get the assertions (73) and (74). □

The application of the monomiality principle in this context inherently results in the formulation of canonical q-differential operators, for which the polynomials serve as eigenfunctions. This structural characteristic implies that each polynomial family under consideration can be systematically linked to a q-difference equation, thereby reinforcing its analytical and spectral importance. We present the following theorem regarding the operational identities associated with the three-variable q-truncated Gould–Hopper polynomials.

Theorem 10. *The 3VqTEGHbAPs satisfy the following respective operational identities:*

$${}_{e^{(r)}}HA_{n,q}^{(m)}(\tau,\phi,\gamma) = e_q\left(\phi\widehat{D}_{q,\tau}^{m}\right)\left\{{}_{e^{(r)}}A_{n,q}(\tau,\gamma)\right\}, \tag{77}$$

or, equivalently,

$${}_{e^{(r)}}HA_{n,q}^{(m)}(\tau,\phi+l,\gamma) = e_q\left(l\widehat{D}_{q,\tau}^{m}\right)\left\{{}_{e^{(r)}}A_{n,q}(\tau,\gamma)\right\}, \tag{78}$$

and

$$E_q\left(-\phi\widehat{D}^m_{q,\tau}\right)_{e(r)}HA^{(m)}_{n,q}(\tau,\phi,\gamma) = {}_{e(r)}A_{n,q}(\tau,\gamma), \tag{79}$$

where $\widehat{D}^m_{q,\tau}$ is the mth q-derivative operator.

Proof. In view of Equation (7), we have

$$\widehat{D}^m_{q,\tau}\tau^w = \frac{[w]_q!}{[w-mr]_q!}\tau^{w-mr}. \tag{80}$$

Utilizing the preceding equation of Formula (30), we acquire

$${}_{e(r)}HA^{(m)}_{n,q}(\tau,\phi,\gamma) = \sum_{k=0}^{\infty}\frac{(\phi\widehat{D}^m_{q,\tau})^k}{[k]_q!}\,{}_{e(r)}A_{n,q}(\tau,\gamma). \tag{81}$$

Utilizing expression (5) on the r.h.s. of the preceding equation, we arrive at statement (77). Again, by using a similar method to (77) and (5), we get assertion (78). By operating $E_q\left(-\phi\widehat{D}^m_{q,\tau}\right)$ on both sides of Equation (77) and using Equation (10), we obtain (79). □

4. Reductions to Classical Families

This section presents specific cases of the polynomial previously discussed in Section 2, represented by Equation (30). Taking $A_q(t) = \frac{t}{e_q(t)-1}$ in (30), ${}_{e(r)}HA^{(m)}_{n,q}(\tau,\phi,\gamma)$ reduces to the q-truncated exponential Gould–Hopper-based Bernoulli polynomials (q-TEGHbBPs); ${}_{e(r)}HB^{(m)}_{n,q}(\tau,\phi,\gamma)$ are defined by the following generating function:

$$\frac{t}{e_q(t)-1}\frac{e_q(\tau t)e_q(\phi t^m)}{1-\gamma t^r} = \sum_{n=0}^{\infty}{}_{e(r)}HB^{(m)}_{n,q}(\tau,\phi,\gamma)\frac{t^n}{[n]_q!}. \tag{82}$$

In view of Equations (22) and (82), we have

$${}_{e(r)}HB^{(m)}_{n,q}(\tau,\phi,\gamma) = e_q\left(\phi\widehat{D}^m_{q,\tau}\right)\left\{{}_{e(r)}B_{n,q}(\tau,\gamma)\right\}. \tag{83}$$

Utilizing Equation (29), we proceed to expand the left-hand side of Equation (82), and we have

$${}_{e(r)}HB^{(m)}_{n,q}(\tau,\phi,\gamma) = \sum_{k=0}^{n}\binom{n}{k}_q B_{k,q}\,{}_{e(r)}H^{(m)}_{n-k,q}(\tau,\phi,\gamma). \tag{84}$$

Considering Equation (82), the following determinant form for ${}_{e(r)}HB^{(m)}_{n,q}(\tau,\phi,\gamma)$ is derived:

Theorem 11. *The determinant representation of q-truncated Gould–Hopper–Bernoulli polynomials of degree n is*

$${}_{e(r)}HB^{(m)}_{0,q}(\tau,\phi,\gamma) = 1,$$

$${}_{e(r)}HB^{(m)}_{n,q}(\tau,\phi,\gamma) = (-1)^n$$

$$\times\begin{vmatrix} 1 & {}_{e(r)}H^{(m)}_{1,q}(\tau,\phi,\gamma) & {}_{e(r)}H^{(m)}_{2,q}(\tau,\phi,\gamma) & \cdots & {}_{e(r)}H^{(m)}_{n-1,q}(\tau,\phi,\gamma) & {}_{e(r)}H^{(m)}_{n,q}(\tau,\phi,\gamma) \\ 1 & \frac{1}{[2]_q} & \frac{1}{[3]_q} & \cdots & \frac{1}{[n]_q} & \frac{1}{[n+1]_q} \\ 0 & 1 & \binom{2}{1}_q\frac{1}{[2]_q} & \cdots & \binom{n-1}{1}_q\frac{1}{[n-1]_q} & \binom{n}{1}_q\frac{1}{[n]_q} \\ 0 & 0 & 1 & \cdots & \binom{n-1}{1}_q\frac{1}{[n-2]_q} & \binom{n}{2}_q\frac{1}{[n-1]_q} \\ \vdots & \vdots & \vdots & \cdots & \vdots & \\ 0 & 0 & 0 & \cdots & 1 & \binom{n}{n-1}_q\frac{1}{[2]_q} \end{vmatrix}, \tag{85}$$

where ${}_{e^{(r)}}HB^{(m)}_{n,q}(\tau,\phi,\gamma)$ $(n = 1,2,\cdots)$ *and* ${}_{e^{(r)}}H^{(m)}_{n,q}(\tau,\phi,\gamma)$, $n = 0,1,2,\ldots$, *are the q-truncated Gould–Hopper polynomials defined by Equation (29).*

Furthermore, by taking $A_q(t) = \frac{2}{e_q(t)+1}$ in (30), ${}_{e^{(r)}}HA^{(m)}_{n,q}(\tau,\phi,\gamma)$ reduces to the q-truncated exponential Gould–Hopper-based Euler polynomials (q-TEGHbEPs); ${}_{e^{(r)}}HE^{(m)}_{n,q}(\tau,\phi,\gamma)$ are defined by the following generating function:

$$\frac{2}{e_q(t)+1}\frac{e_q(\tau t)e_q(\phi t^m)}{1-\gamma t^r} = \sum_{n=0}^{\infty} {}_{e^{(r)}}HE^{(m)}_{n,q}(\tau,\phi,\gamma)\frac{t^n}{[n]_q!}. \tag{86}$$

By virtue of (22) and (60), we have

$${}_{e^{(r)}}HE^{(m)}_{n,q}(\tau,\phi,\gamma) = e_q\left(\phi\widehat{D}^m_{q,\tau}\right)\left\{{}_{e^{(r)}}E_{n,q}(\tau,\gamma)\right\}. \tag{87}$$

Expanding the left-hand side of Equation (86) by using Equation (29), we have

$${}_{e^{(r)}}HE^{(m)}_{n,q}(\tau,\phi,\gamma) = \sum_{k=0}^{n}\binom{n}{k}_q E_{k,q}\,{}_{e^{(r)}}H^{(m)}_{n-k,q}(\tau,\phi,\gamma), \tag{88}$$

The following determinant form for ${}_{e^{(r)}}HE^{(m)}_{n,q}(\tau,\phi,\gamma)$ is obtained.

Theorem 12. *The determinant formulation of the q-truncated Gould–Hopper–Euler polynomials for a polynomial of degree n is*

$${}_{e^{(r)}}HE^{(m)}_{0,q}(\tau,\phi,\gamma) = 1,$$
$${}_{e^{(r)}}HE^{(m)}_{n,q}(\tau,\phi,\gamma) = (-1)^n$$

$$\times\begin{vmatrix} 1 & {}_{e^{(r)}}H^{(m)}_{1,q}(\tau,\phi,\gamma) & {}_{e^{(r)}}H^{(m)}_{2,q}(\tau,\phi,\gamma) & \cdots & {}_{e^{(r)}}H^{(m)}_{n-1,q}(\tau,\phi,\gamma) & {}_{e^{(r)}}H^{(m)}_{n,q}(\tau,\phi,\gamma) \\ 1 & \frac{1}{2} & \frac{1}{2} & \cdots & \frac{1}{2} & \frac{1}{2} \\ 0 & 1 & \binom{2}{1}_q\frac{1}{2} & \cdots & \binom{n-1}{1}_q\frac{1}{2} & \binom{n}{1}_q\frac{1}{2} \\ 0 & 0 & 1 & \cdots & \binom{n-1}{1}_q\frac{1}{2} & \binom{n}{2}_q\frac{1}{2} \\ \vdots & \vdots & \vdots & \cdots & \vdots & \\ 0 & 0 & 0 & \cdots & 1 & \binom{n}{n-1}_q\frac{1}{2} \end{vmatrix}, \tag{89}$$

where ${}_{e^{(r)}}HE^{(m)}_{n,q}(\tau,\phi,\gamma)$ $(n = 1,2,\cdots)$ *and* ${}_{e^{(r)}}H^{(m)}_{n,q}(\tau,\phi,\gamma)$, $n = 0,1,2,\ldots$, *are the q-truncated Gould–Hopper polynomials defined by Equation (29).*

By taking $A_q(t) = \frac{2t}{e_q(t)+1}$ in (30), ${}_{e^{(r)}}HA^{(m)}_{n,q}(\tau,\phi,\gamma)$ is reduced to the q-truncated exponential Gould–Hopper-based Genocchi polynomials (q-TEGHbGPs); ${}_{e^{(r)}}HG^{(m)}_{n,q}(\tau,\phi,\gamma)$ are defined by the following generating function:

$$\frac{2t}{e_q(t)+1}\frac{e_q(\tau t)e_q(\phi t^m)}{1-\gamma t^r} = \sum_{n=0}^{\infty} {}_{e^{(r)}}HG^{(m)}_{n,q}(\tau,\phi,\gamma)\frac{t^n}{[n]_q!}. \tag{90}$$

In view of Equations (22) and (64), we have

$${}_{e^{(r)}}HG^{(m)}_{n,q}(\tau,\phi,\gamma) = e_q\left(\phi\widehat{D}^m_{q,\tau}\right)\left\{{}_{e^{(r)}}G_{n,q}(\tau,\gamma)\right\}. \tag{91}$$

Expanding the left-hand side of Equation (65) by using Equation (29), we have

$${}_{e^{(r)}}HG^{(m)}_{n,q}(\tau,\phi,\gamma) = \sum_{k=0}^{n}\binom{n}{k}_q G_{k,q}\,{}_{e^{(r)}}H^{(m)}_{n-k,q}(\tau,\phi,\gamma), \tag{92}$$

Theorem 13. *The determinant representation of the q-truncated exponential Gould–Hopper-based Genocchi polynomials (q-TEGHbGPs)* ${}_{e^{(r)}}HG^{(m)}_{n,q}(\tau,\phi,\gamma)$ *of degree n is*

$$ {}_{e^{(r)}}HG^{(m)}_{0,q}(\tau,\phi,\gamma)=1, $$

$$ {}_{e^{(r)}}HG^{(m)}_{n,q}(\tau,\phi,\gamma)=(-1)^n $$

$$ \times\begin{vmatrix} 1 & {}_{e^{(r)}}H^{(m)}_{1,q}(\tau,\phi,\gamma) & {}_{e^{(r)}}H^{(m)}_{2,q}(\tau,\phi,\gamma) & \cdots & {}_{e^{(r)}}H^{(m)}_{n-1,q}(\tau,\phi,\gamma) & {}_{e^{(r)}}H^{(m)}_{n,q}(\tau,\phi,\gamma) \\ 1 & \frac{1}{2[2]_q} & \frac{1}{2[3]_q} & \cdots & \frac{1}{2[n]_q} & \frac{1}{2[n+1]_q} \\ 0 & 1 & \binom{2}{1}_q\frac{1}{2[2]_q} & \cdots & \binom{n-1}{1}_q\frac{1}{2[n-1]_q} & \binom{n}{1}_q\frac{1}{2[n]_q} \\ 0 & 0 & 1 & \cdots & \binom{n-1}{1}_q\frac{1}{2[n-2]_q} & \binom{n}{2}_q\frac{1}{2[n-1]_q} \\ \vdots & \vdots & \vdots & \cdots & \vdots & \\ 0 & 0 & 0 & \cdots & 1 & \binom{n}{n-1}_q\frac{1}{2[2]_q} \end{vmatrix}, \tag{93} $$

where ${}_{e^{(r)}}HG^{(m)}_{n,q}(\tau,\phi,\gamma)$ $(n=1,2,\cdots)$ *and* ${}_{e^{(r)}}H^{(m)}_{n,q}(\tau,\phi,\gamma)$, $n=0,1,2,\ldots$, *are the q-truncated exponential Gould–Hopper polynomials defined by Equation (29).*

Remark 1. *To further enhance clarity and confirm consistency with classical results, it is instructive to consider the limiting case as* $q\to 1$. *In this limit, the q-truncated exponential Gould–Hopper-based Appell polynomials reduce to their classical counterparts, including the Bernoulli, Euler, and Genocchi polynomials.*

For instance, taking the generating function of the q-truncated exponential Gould–Hopper-based Bernoulli polynomials with

$$ A_q(t)=\frac{t}{e_q(t)-1}, $$

and considering the classical limit $q\to 1$, *we obtain*

$$ \lim_{q\to 1}\left(\frac{t}{e_q(t)-1}e_q(\tau t)e_q(\phi t^m)\frac{1}{1-\gamma t^r}\right)=\frac{t}{e^t-1}e^{\tau t}e^{\phi t^m}\frac{1}{1-\gamma t^r}. $$

This expression corresponds to the generating function of the classical truncated exponential Gould–Hopper-based Bernoulli polynomials:

$$ \frac{t}{e^t-1}e^{\tau t}e^{\phi t^m}\frac{1}{1-\gamma t^r}=\sum_{n=0}^{\infty}{}_{e^{(r)}}HB^{(m)}_n(\tau,\phi,\gamma)\frac{t^n}{n!}. $$

Similar derivations can be performed for the Euler and Genocchi polynomials.

Remark 2 (On Time-Reversal Symmetry). *A critical yet frequently neglected aspect in the analysis of special polynomials is their behavior under the inversion of the dependent variable, specifically the transformation* $t\mapsto -t$. *This consideration of symmetry is of considerable importance in physical and engineering contexts, where it often corresponds to* time reversibility *or* irreversibility *in dynamical systems. For example, even functions* $p(t)=p(-t)$ *exhibit time-symmetric behavior, whereas odd or asymmetric functions indicate directional or irreversible processes.*

In the case of the three-variable q-truncated exponential Gould–Hopper-based Appell polynomials $e^{(r)}HA^{(m)}_{n,q}(\tau,\phi,\gamma)$, *a study of the generating function*

$$ \frac{A_q(t)}{1-\gamma t^r}\,e_q(\tau t)\,e_q(\phi t^m) $$

under the substitution $t\mapsto -t$ *could yield insights into the* parity structure *of the polynomials and their coefficients. Such an investigation could further distinguish between* even, odd, *or* asymmetrically structured *polynomial families, as well as elucidate deeper algebraic or physical symmetries embedded in the q-calculus framework.*

Remark 3 (On Canonical Differential Equations). *The introduction of the three-variable q-truncated exponential Gould–Hopper-based Appell polynomials in this study, along with the formulation of canonical q-differential equations, is both feasible and significant. By utilizing the generating function structure in conjunction with the monomiality principle and operational identities, one can systematically derive q-difference or q-differential equations for which these polynomials act as eigenfunctions. These equations not only elucidate the analytical structure of the polynomials but also facilitate applications in mathematical physics and integrable systems.*

5. Distribution of Zeros and Graphical Representation

In this section, we intend to present the graphical representations and zeros of the q-truncated exponential Gould–Hopper-based Bernoulli polynomials ${}_{e^{(r)}}HB^{(m)}_{n,q}(\tau,\phi,\gamma)$, as delineated in Section 3. For $m=3$, a few of ${}_{e^{(r)}}HB^{(3)}_{n,q}(\tau,\phi,\gamma)$ are as follows:

$$
\begin{aligned}
{}_{e^{(4)}}HB^{(3)}_{0,q}(\tau,\phi,\gamma) &= 1,\\
{}_{e^{(4)}}HB^{(3)}_{1,q}(\tau,\phi,\gamma) &= \tau - \frac{1}{[2]_q!},\\
{}_{e^{(4)}}HB^{(3)}_{2,q}(\tau,\phi,\gamma) &= -\tau + \tau^2 + \frac{1}{[2]_q!} - \frac{[2]_q!}{[3]_q!},\\
{}_{e^{(4)}}HB^{(3)}_{3,q}(\tau,\phi,\gamma) &= -\tau + \tau^3 + \frac{2}{[2]_q!} + \phi[3]_q! - \frac{[3]_q!}{[2]_q!^3} + \frac{\tau[3]_q!}{[2]_q^2} - \frac{\tau^2[3]_q!}{[2]_q!^2} - \frac{[3]_q!}{[4]_q!},\\
{}_{e^{(4)}}HB^{(3)}_{4,q}(\tau,\phi,\gamma) &= -\tau + \tau^4 + \frac{2}{[2]_q!} + \gamma[4]_q! + \tau\phi[4]_q! + \frac{[4]_q!}{[2]_q!^4} - \frac{\tau[4]_q!}{[2]_q!^3}\\
&\quad + \frac{\tau^2[4]_q!}{[2]_q!^3} - \frac{\phi[4]_q!}{[2]_q!} + \frac{[4]_q!}{[3]_q!^2} - \frac{3[4]_q!}{[2]_q!^2[3]_q!} + \frac{2\tau[4]_q!}{[2]_q![3]_q!}\\
&\quad - \frac{\tau^2[4]_q!}{[2]_q![3]_q!} - \frac{\tau^3[4]_q!}{[2]_q![3]_q!} - \frac{[4]_q!}{[5]_q!},
\end{aligned}
$$

$$
\begin{aligned}
{}_{e^{(4)}}HB^{(3)}_{5,q}(\tau,\phi,\gamma) &= -\tau + \tau^5 + \frac{2}{[2]_q!} + \gamma\tau[5]_q! - \frac{[5]_q!}{[2]_q!^5} + \frac{\tau[5]_q!}{[2]_q^4} - \frac{\tau^2[5]_q!}{[2]_q!^4}\\
&\quad + \frac{\phi[5]_q!}{[2]_q!^2} - \frac{\gamma[5]_q!}{[2]_q!} - \frac{\tau\phi[5]_q!}{[2]_q!} + \frac{\tau^2\phi[5]_q!}{[2]_q!} + \frac{\tau[5]_q!}{[3]_q!^2} - \frac{\tau^3[5]_q!}{[3]_q^2}\\
&\quad - \frac{3[5]_q!}{[2]_q![3]_q!^2} - \frac{\phi[5]_q!}{[3]_q!} + \frac{4[5]_q!}{[2]_q!^3[3]_q!} - \frac{3\tau[5]_q!}{[2]_q!^2[3]_q!}\\
&\quad + \frac{2\tau^2[5]_q!}{[2]_q!^2[3]_q!} + \frac{\tau^3[5]_q!}{[2]_q!^2[3]_q!} - \frac{3[5]_q!}{[2]_q!^2[4]_q!} + \frac{2\tau[5]_q!}{[2]_q![4]_q!}\\
&\quad - \frac{\tau^2[5]_q!}{[2]_q![4]_q!} - \frac{\tau^4[5]_q!}{[2]_q![4]_q!} + \frac{2[5]_q!}{[3]_q![4]_q!} - \frac{[5]_q!}{[6]_q!}.
\end{aligned}
$$

We conduct an investigation into the zeros of the q-truncated exponential Gould–Hopper-based Bernoulli polynomials, denoted as ${}_{e^{(r)}}HB^{(m)}_{n,q}(\tau,\phi,\gamma)=0$, utilizing computational methods. Specifically, we plot the zeros of the q-truncated Hopper–Bernoulli polynomials ${}_{e^{(r)}}HB^{(m)}_{n,q}(\tau,\phi,\gamma)=0$ for $n=30$ (see Figure 1).

In Figure 1 (top left), the parameters are set as follows: $m=3$, $r=4$, $\phi=2$, $\gamma=7$, and $q=\frac{3}{10}$. In Figure 1 (top right), the parameters are $m=3$, $r=4$, $\phi=2$, $\gamma=7$, and $q=\frac{5}{10}$. In Figure 1 (bottom left), the parameters are $m=3$, $r=4$, $\phi=2$, $\gamma=7$, and $q=\frac{7}{10}$. In Figure 1 (bottom right), the parameters are $m=3$, $r=4$, $\phi=2$, $\gamma=7$, and $q=\frac{9}{10}$.

Stacks of zeros of the q-truncated Hopper–Bernoulli polynomials ${}_{e^{(r)}}HB^{(m)}_{n,q}(\tau,\phi,\gamma)=0$ for $1\le n\le 30$, forming a 3D structure, are presented in Figure 2.

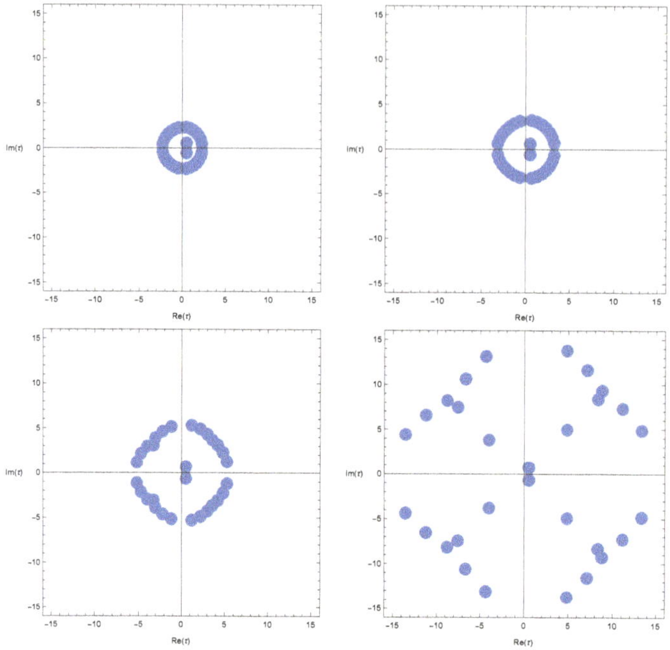

Figure 1. Zeros of ${}_{e^{(r)}}HB_{n,q}^{(m)}(\tau, \phi, \gamma) = 0$.

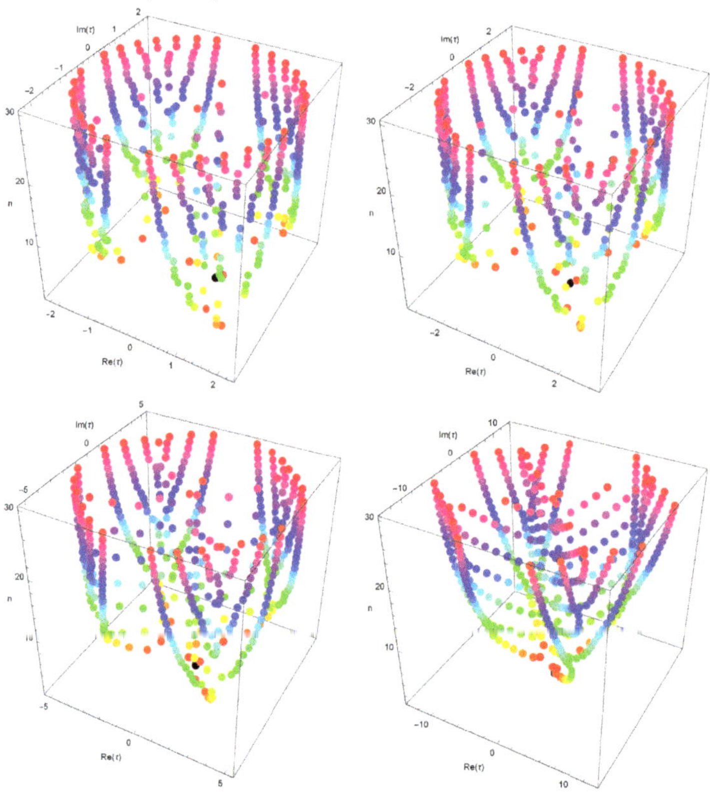

Figure 2. Zeros of ${}_{e^{(r)}}HB_{n,q}^{(m)}(\tau, \phi, \gamma) = 0$.

In Figure 2 (top left), the parameters are set as follows: $m = 3, r = 4, \phi = 2, \gamma = 7$, and $q = \frac{3}{10}$. In Figure 2 (top right), the parameters are $m = 3, r = 4, \phi = 2, \gamma = 7$, and $q = \frac{5}{10}$. In Figure 2 (bottom left), the parameters are $m = 3, r = 4, \phi = 2, \gamma = 7$, and $q = \frac{7}{10}$. In Figure 2 (bottom right), the parameters are $m = 3, r = 4, \phi = 2, \gamma = 7$, and $q = \frac{9}{10}$.

Plots of real zeros of q-truncated exponential Gould–Hopper-based Bernoulli polynomials ${}_{e^{(r)}}HB_{n,q}^{(m)}(\tau, \phi, \gamma) = 0$ for $1 \le n \le 30$ are presented in Figure 3.

In Figure 3 (top left), the parameters are set as follows: $m = 3$, $r = 4$, $\phi = 2$, $\gamma = 7$, and $q = \frac{3}{10}$. In Figure 3 (top right), the parameters are $m = 3$, $r = 4$, $\phi = 2$, $\gamma = 7$, and $q = \frac{5}{10}$. In Figure 3 (bottom left), the parameters are $m = 3$, $r = 4$, $\phi = 2$, $\gamma = 7$, and $q = \frac{7}{10}$. In Figure 3 (bottom right), the parameters are $m = 3$, $r = 4$, $\phi = 2$, $\gamma = 7$, and $q = \frac{9}{10}$.

Subsequently, we computed an approximate solution that satisfies the q-truncated exponential Gould–Hopper-based Bernoulli polynomials ${}_{e^{(r)}}HB_{n,q}^{(m)}(\tau, \phi, \gamma) = 0$ for the parameters $m = 3, r = 4, \phi = 2, \gamma = 7$, and $q = \frac{7}{10}$. The results are presented in Table 2.

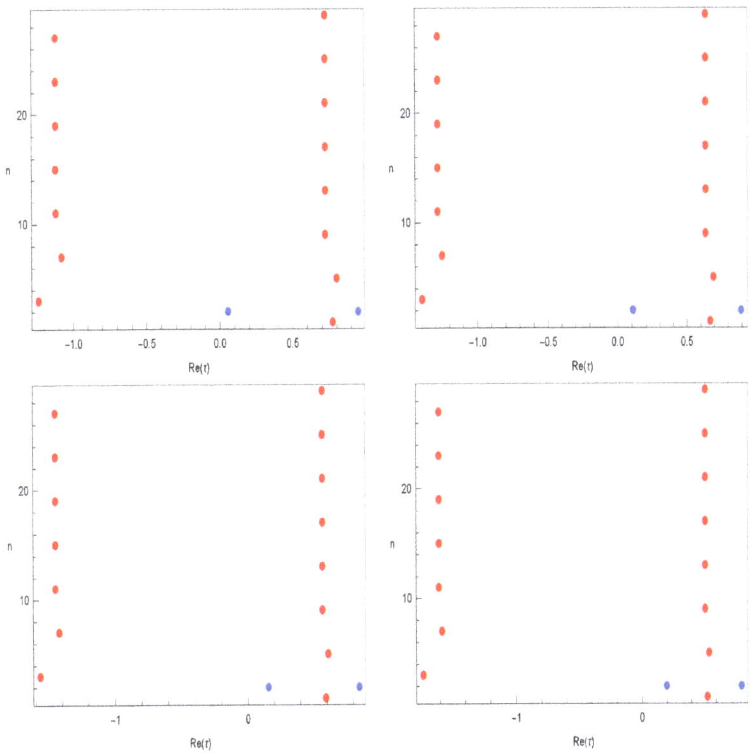

Figure 3. Real zeros of ${}_{e^{(r)}}HB_{n,q}^{(m)}(\tau, \phi, \gamma) = 0$.

Table 2. Approximate solutions of ${}_{e^{(r)}}HB_{n,q}^{(m)}(\tau, \phi, \gamma) = 0$.

Degree n	τ
1	0.58824
2	0.15593, 0.84407
3	-1.5676, $1.4279 - 1.6511i$, $1.4279 + 1.6511i$
4	$-1.6771 - 1.3048i$, $-1.6771 + 1.3048i$, $2.4221 - 2.5091i$, $2.4221 + 2.5091i$
5	$-2.3820 - 1.9547i$, $-2.3820 + 1.9547i$, 0.60620, $2.8945 - 3.1030i$, $2.8945 + 3.1030i$

Table 2. *Cont.*

Degree n	τ
6	$-2.8833-2.3341i, -2.8833+2.3341i, 0.54216-0.65641i, 0.54216+0.65641i, 3.2062-3.4847i, 3.2062+3.4847i$
7	$-3.1692-2.6645i, -3.1692+2.6645i, -1.4251, 1.3897-1.7140i, 1.3897+1.7140i, 3.3918-3.6791i, 3.3918+3.6791i$
8	$-3.3242-2.7625i, -3.3242+2.7625i, -1.6097-1.6085i, -1.6097+1.6085i, 2.5029-2.5017i, 2.5029+2.5017i, 3.3549-3.7042i, 3.3549+3.7042i$
9	$-3.4373-2.5476i, -3.4373+2.5476i, -2.2913-2.6109i, -2.2913+2.6109i, 0.56410, 2.8826-3.8504i, 2.8826+3.8504i, 3.5048-2.9482i, 3.5048+2.9482i$
10	$-3.8254-2.3390i, -3.8254+2.3390i, -2.4606-3.2866i, -2.4606+3.2866i, 0.50785-0.65764i, 0.50785+0.65764i, 2.7588-4.2451i, 2.7588+4.2451i, 3.9721-2.9318i, 3.9721+2.9318i$

For $m=3$, a few of ${}_{e^{(r)}}HE_{n,q}^{(3)}(\tau,\phi,\gamma)$ are as follows:

$$
\begin{aligned}
{}_{e^{(4)}}HE_{0,q}^{(3)}(\tau,\phi,\gamma) &= 1,\\
{}_{e^{(4)}}HE_{1,q}^{(3)}(\tau,\phi,\gamma) &= -\frac{1}{2}+\tau,\\
{}_{e^{(4)}}HE_{2,q}^{(3)}(\tau,\phi,\gamma) &= -\frac{1}{2}+\tau^2+\frac{1}{4}[2]_q!-\frac{1}{2}\tau[2]_q!,\\
{}_{e^{(4)}}HE_{3,q}^{(3)}(\tau,\phi,\gamma) &= -\frac{1}{2}+\tau^3-\frac{1}{8}[3]_q!+\frac{1}{4}\tau[3]_q!+\phi[3]_q!+\frac{[3]_q!}{2[2]_q!}-\frac{\tau[3]_q!}{2[2]_q!}-\frac{\tau^2[3]_q!}{2[2]_q!},\\
{}_{e^{(4)}}HE_{4,q}^{(3)}(\tau,\phi,\gamma) &= -\frac{1}{2}+\tau^4+\frac{1}{16}[4]_q!+\gamma[4]_q!-\frac{1}{8}\tau[4]_q!\\
&\quad -\frac{1}{2}\phi[4]_q!+\tau\phi[4]_q!+\frac{[4]_q!}{4[2]_q!^2}-\frac{\tau^2[4]_q!}{2[2]_q!^2}\\
&\quad -\frac{3[4]_q!}{8[2]_q!}+\frac{\tau[4]_q!}{2[2]_q!}+\frac{\tau^2[4]_q!}{4[2]_q!}+\frac{[4]_q!}{2[3]_q!}-\frac{\tau[4]_q!}{2[3]_q!}-\frac{\tau^3[4]_q!}{2[3]_q!},\\
{}_{e^{(4)}}HE_{5,q}^{(3)}(\tau,\phi,\gamma) &= -\frac{1}{2}+\tau^5-\frac{1}{32}[5]_q!-\frac{1}{2}\gamma[5]_q!+\frac{1}{16}\tau[5]_q!+\gamma\tau[5]_q!\\
&\quad +\frac{1}{4}\phi[5]_q!-\frac{1}{2}\tau\phi[5]_q!-\frac{3[5]_q!}{8[2]_q^2}+\frac{\tau[5]_q!}{4[2]_q^2}+\frac{\tau^2[5]}{2[2]_q!^2}+\frac{[5]_q!}{4[2]_q!}\\
&\quad -\frac{3\tau[5]_q!}{8[2]_q!}-\frac{\tau^2[5]_q!}{8[2]_q!}-\frac{\phi[5]_q!}{2[2]_q!}+\frac{\tau^2\phi[5]_q!}{[2]_q!}-\frac{3[5]_q!}{8[3]_q!}+\frac{\tau[5]_q!}{2[3]_q!}\\
&\quad +\frac{\tau^3[5]_q!}{4[3]_q!}+\frac{[5]_q!}{2[2]_q![3]_q!}-\frac{\tau^2[5]_q!}{2[2]_q![3]_q!}-\frac{\tau^3[5]_q!}{2[2]_q![3]_q!}+\frac{[5]_q!}{2[4]_q!}\\
&\quad -\frac{\tau[5]_q!}{2[4]_q!}-\frac{\tau^4[5]_q!}{2[4]_q!}.
\end{aligned}
$$

We investigate the beautiful zeros of the q-truncated exponential Gould–Hopper-based Euler polynomials ${}_{e^{(r)}}HE_{n,q}^{(m)}(\tau,\phi,\gamma)=0$ by using a computer. We plot the zeros of q-truncated Hopper–Euler polynomials ${}_{e^{(r)}}HE_{n,q}^{(m)}(\tau,\phi,\gamma)=0$ for $n=30$ (Figure 4).

In Figure 4 (top left), the parameters are set as follows: $m=3$, $r=4$, $\phi=5$, $\gamma=10$, and $q=\frac{3}{10}$. In Figure 4 (top right), the parameters are $m=3$, $r=4$, $\phi=5$, $\gamma=10$, and $q=\frac{5}{10}$. In Figure 4 (bottom left), the parameters are $m=3$, $r=4$, $\phi=5$, $\gamma=10$, and $q=\frac{7}{10}$. In Figure 4 (bottom right), the parameters are $m=3$, $r=4$, $\phi=5$, $\gamma=10$, and $q=\frac{9}{10}$.

Figure 5 illustrates the three-dimensional structure formed by the zeros of the q-truncated Hopper–Euler polynomials ${}_{e^{(r)}}HE_{n,q}^{(m)}(\tau,\phi,\gamma) = 0$ for $1 \leq n \leq 30$.

In Figure 5 (top left), the selected parameters are $m = 3$, $r = 4$, $\phi = 5$, $\gamma = 10$, and $q = \frac{3}{10}$. In Figure 5 (top right), the parameters remain as $m = 3$, $r = 4$, $\phi = 5$, and $\gamma = 10$, with q adjusted to $\frac{5}{10}$. In Figure 5 (bottom left), the parameters are consistent with $m = 3$, $r = 4$, $\phi = 5$, and $\gamma = 10$, and q is set to $\frac{7}{10}$. Finally, in Figure 5 (bottom right), the parameters are $m = 3$, $r = 4$, $\phi = 5$, and $\gamma = 10$, and q is increased to $\frac{9}{10}$.

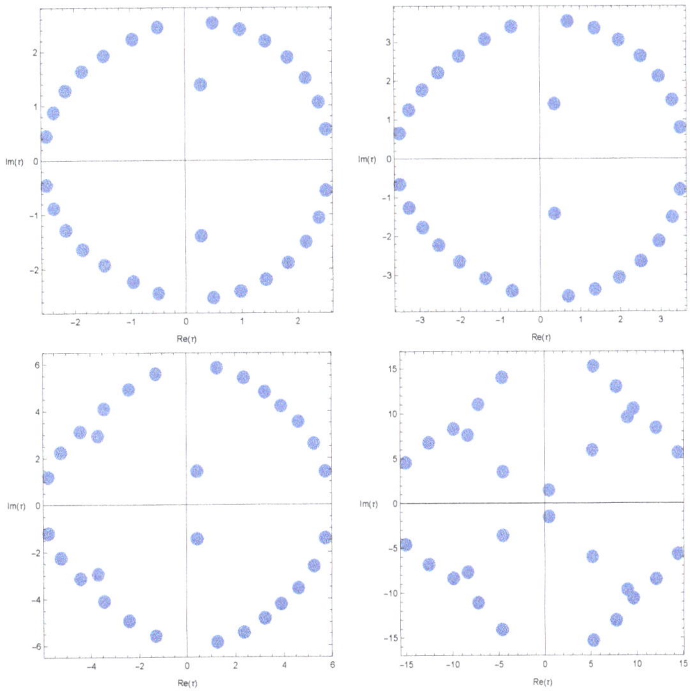

Figure 4. Zeros of ${}_{e^{(r)}}HE_{n,q}^{(m)}(\tau,\phi,\gamma) = 0$.

Plots of real zeros of q-truncated Hopper–Euler polynomials ${}_{e^{(r)}}HE_{n,q}^{(m)}(\tau,\phi,\gamma) = 0$ for $1 \leq n \leq 30$ are presented in Figure 6.

In Figure 6 (top left), the parameters are set as follows: $m = 3$, $r = 4$, $\phi = 5$, $\gamma = 10$, and $q = \frac{3}{10}$. In Figure 6 (top right), the parameters are $m = 3$, $r = 4$, $\phi = 5$, $\gamma = 10$, and $q = \frac{5}{10}$. In Figure 6 (bottom left), the parameters are $m = 3$, $r = 4$, $\phi = 5$, $\gamma = 10$, and $q = \frac{7}{10}$. In Figure 6 (bottom right), the parameters are $m = 3$, $r = 4$, $\phi = 5$, $\gamma = 10$, and $q = \frac{9}{10}$.

Subsequently, we computed an approximate solution that satisfies the q-truncated exponential Gould–Hopper-based Euler polynomials ${}_{e^{(r)}}HE_{n,q}^{(m)}(\tau,\phi,\gamma) = 0$, with the parameters set as $m = 3$, $r = 4$, $\phi = 5$, $\gamma = 10$, and $q = \frac{7}{10}$. The results are presented in Table 3.

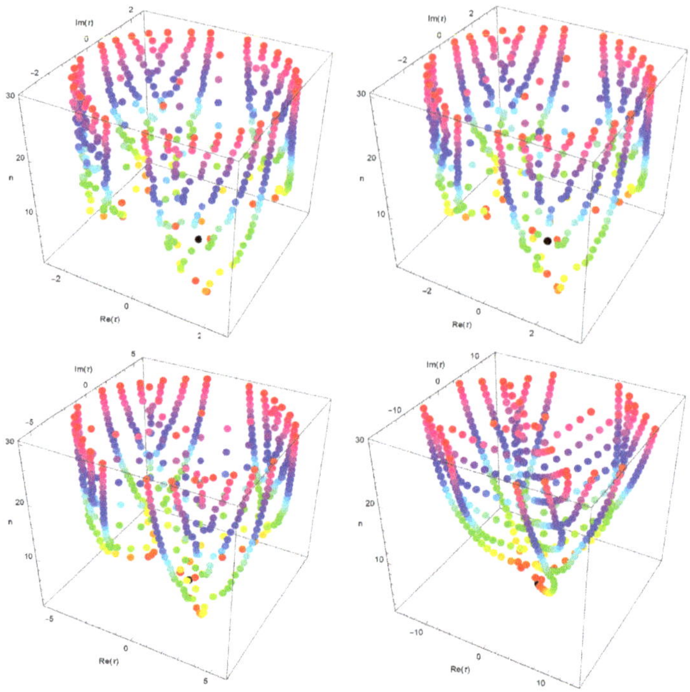

Figure 5. Zeros of ${}_{e^{(r)}}HE_{n,q}^{(m)}(\tau,\phi,\gamma)=0$.

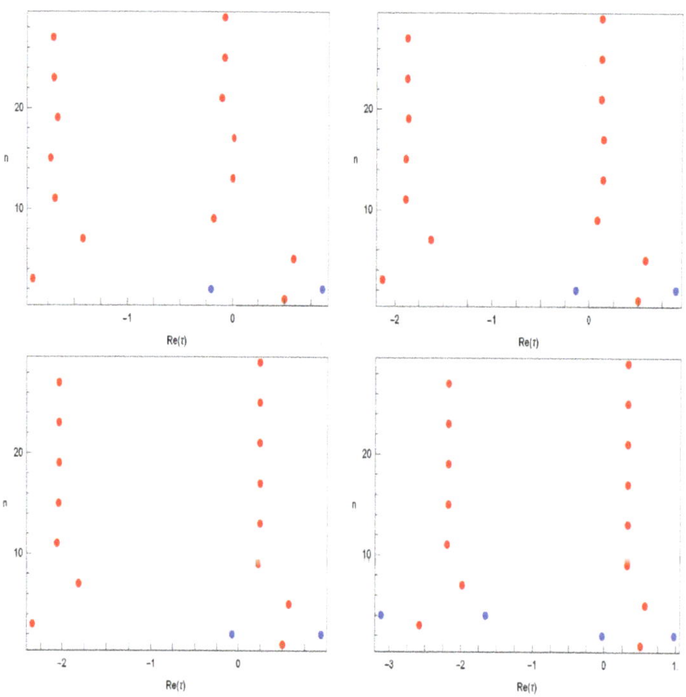

Figure 6. Real zeros of ${}_{e^{(r)}}HE_{n,q}^{(m)}(\tau,\phi,\gamma)=0$.

Table 3. Approximate solutions of ${}_{e^{(r)}}HE_{n,q}^{(m)}(\tau,\phi,\gamma)=0$.

Degree n	τ
1	0.50000
2	−0.080594, 0.93059
3	−2.3549, 1.7249 − 2.2326i, 1.7249 + 2.2326i
4	−2.0245 − 0.1768i, −2.0245 + 0.1768i, 2.6578 − 3.1756i, 2.6578 + 3.1756i
5	−2.7749 − 1.3907i, −2.7749 + 1.3907i, 0.56863, 3.1838 − 3.8462i, 3.1838 + 3.8462i
6	−3.4673 − 1.9184i, −3.4673 + 1.9184i, 0.6617 − 1.3704i, 0.6617 + 1.3704i, 3.5409 − 4.2425i, 3.5409 + 4.2425i
7	−3.7243 − 2.3058i, −3.7243 + 2.3058i, −1.8144, 1.6543 − 2.4440i, 1.6543 + 2.4440i, 3.7418 − 4.4043i, 3.7418 + 4.4043i
8	−3.9250 − 2.4629i, −3.9250 + 2.4629i, −1.6504 − 1.3176i, −1.6504 + 1.3176i, 2.6170 − 3.2519i, 2.6170 + 3.2519i, 3.7436 − 4.3541i, 3.7436 + 4.3541i
9	−4.1243 − 2.4363i, −4.1243 + 2.4363i, −2.1590 − 2.2507i, −2.1590 + 2.2507i, 0.22580, 3.0404 − 4.4562i, 3.0404 + 4.4562i, 3.9297 − 3.7151i, 3.9297 + 3.7151i
10	−4.4008 − 2.2964i, −4.4008 + 2.2964i, −2.6341 − 2.9269i, −2.6341 + 2.9269i, 0.4638 − 1.4799i, 0.4638 + 1.4799i, 2.9738 − 4.9105i, 2.9738 + 4.9105i, 4.4070 − 3.5880i, 4.4070 + 3.5880i

6. Conclusions

The concept of q-monomiality plays a pivotal role in the analysis of special polynomials, providing a framework for understanding their properties and relationships. This paper delves into a comprehensive examination of three-variable q-truncated exponential Gould–Hopper-based Appell polynomials within the context of q-monomiality. By systematically studying these polynomials, the authors uncover and elucidate various properties, contributing to a deeper understanding of their mathematical structure and behavior. The research extends beyond theoretical exploration, offering practical applications and insights. The authors present special cases of the newly established polynomials, accompanied by their determinantal forms. This approach not only demonstrates the versatility of the polynomials but also provides concrete examples for further study. Additionally, this paper includes an analysis of zeros and graphical representations for these special cases, offering visual and numerical insights into the polynomials' behavior. These findings serve as a valuable resource for researchers, enabling them to apply the q-monomiality principle to investigate the properties of various polynomials and potentially uncover new mathematical relationships.

Author Contributions: Conceptualization, W.A.K., K.S.M., F.A.C. and C.K.; methodology, W.A.K., K.S.M., F.A.C. and C.K.; software, C.S.R.; validation, W.A.K., K.S.M., F.A.C., C.K. and C.S.R.; formal analysis, W.A.K.; investigation, W.A.K.; resources, W.A.K.; data curation, C.S.R.; writing—original draft preparation, W.A.K., K.S.M., F.A.C., C.K. and C.S.R.; writing—review and editing, W.A.K.; visualization, W.A.K., K.S.M., F.A.C., C.K. and C.S.R.; supervision, W.A.K., K.S.M., F.A.C. and C.K.; project administration, W.A.K. and K.S.M.; funding acquisition, K.S.M. All authors have read and agreed to the published version of the manuscript.

Funding: The research received no external funding.

Data Availability Statement: No data were used to support this study.

Acknowledgments: The researchers would like to thank the Deanship of Graduate Studies and Scientific Research at Qassim University for financial support (QU-APC-2025).

Conflicts of Interest: The authors declare no conflicts of interest.

References

1. Andrews, G.E.; Askey, R.; Roy, R. *Special Functions;* Cambridge University Press: Cambridge, UK, 1999.
2. Cao, J.; Razab, N.; Fadel, M. Two-variable q-Laguerre polynomials from the context of quasi-monomiality. *J. Anal. Appl.* **2024**, *535*, 128126. [CrossRef]
3. Ernst, T. *A Comprehensive Treatment of q-Calculus, Birkhäuser;* Springer: Basel, Switzerland, 2012.
4. Srivastava, H.M.; Manocha, H.L. *A Treatise on Generating Functions;* Ellis Horwood Ltd.: Chichester, UK, 1984.
5. Choi, J. Recent Advances in Special Functions and Their Applications. *Symmetry* **2023**, *15*, 2159. [CrossRef]
6. Costabile, F.A.; Khan, S.; Ali, H. A Study of the q-Truncated Exponential-Appell Polynomials. *Mathematics* **2024**, *12*, 3862. [CrossRef]
7. Dattoli, G.; Migliorati, M.; Srivastava, H.M. A class of Bessel summation formulas and associated operational methods. *Frac. Calcu. Appl. Anal.* **2004**, *7*, 169–176.
8. Khan, S.; Yasmin, G.; Ahmad, N. A note on truncated exponential based Appell polynomials. *Bull. Malays. Math. Sci. Soc.* **2017**, *40*, 373–388. [CrossRef]
9. Özat, Z.; Çekim, B.; Özarslan, M.A.; Costabile, F.A. Truncated-Exponential-Based General-Appell Polynomials. *Mathematics* **2025**, *13*, 1266. [CrossRef]
10. Baxhaku, B.; Agrawal, P.N.; Shukla, R. Bivariate positive linear operators constructed by means of q-Lagrange polynomials. *J. Math. Anal. Appl.* **2020**, *491*, 124337. [CrossRef]
11. Kac, V.; Cheung, P. *Quantum Calculus;* Springer: New York, NY, USA, 2002.
12. Askey, R. Limits of some q-Laguerre polynomials. *J. Approx. Theory* **1986**, *46*, 213–216. [CrossRef]
13. Srivastava, H.M. Some characterization of Appell and q-Appell polynomials. *Ann. Mat. Pura Appl.* **1982**, *130*, 321–329. [CrossRef]
14. Raza, N.; Fadel, M.; Cesarano C. A note of q-truncated exponential polynomials. *Carpathian Math. Publ.* **2024**, *16*, 128–147. [CrossRef]
15. Raza, N.; Fadel, M.; Khan, S.; Cesarano, C. Monomiality principle for q-polynomials: Introduction and Applications. *Math. Mech. Complex Syst.* 2024, *in press.*
16. Florenini, R.; Vinet, L. Quantum algebras and q-special functions. *Ann. Phys.* **1993**, *221*, 53–70. [CrossRef]
17. Al-Salam, W.A. q-Bernoulli numbers and polynomials. *Math. Nachr.* **1958**, *17*, 239–260. [CrossRef]
18. Al-Salam, W.A. q-Appell polynomials. *Ann. Mat. Pura Appl.* **1967**, *77*, 31–45. [CrossRef]
19. Ernst, T. q-Bernoulli and q-Euler polynomials, an umbral calculus approach. *Int. J. Differ. Equ.* **2006**, *1*, 31–80.
20. Raza, N.; Fadel, M.; Cesarano, C. On monomiality property of q-Gould-Hopper-Appell polynomials. *Arab J. Basic Appl. Sci.* **2025**, *32*, 21–29. [CrossRef]
21. Costabile, F.A.; Longo, E. A Determinantal Approach to Appell Polynomials. *J. Comput. Appl. Math.* **2010**, *234*, 1528–1542. [CrossRef]
22. Costabile, F.A.; Gualtieri, M.T.; Napoli, A. General bivariate Appell polynomials via matrix calculus and related interpolation hints. *Mathematics* **2022**, *9*, 964. [CrossRef]
23. Steffensen, J.F. The poweroid, an extension of the mathematical notion of power. *Acta Math.* **1941**, *73*, 333–366. [CrossRef]
24. Dattoli, G. Hermite-Bessel and Laguerre-Bessel functions: A by-product of the monomiality principle. *Adv. Spec. Funct. Appl.* **2020**, *1*, 147–164.
25. Dattoli, G.; Lorenzutta, S.; Mancho, A.M.; Torre, A. Generalized polynomials and associated operational identities. *J. Comput. Appl. Math.* **1999**, *108*, 209–218. [CrossRef]
26. Dattoli, G.; Torre, A. Exponential operators, quasi-monomials and generalized polynomials. *Radiat. Phys. Chem.* **2000**, *57*, 21–26. [CrossRef]
27. Zayed, M.; Wani, S.A.; Ramirez, W.; Cesarano, C. Advancements in q-Hermite-Appell polynomials: A three-dimensional exploration. *AIMS Math.* **2024**, *9*, 26799–26824. [CrossRef]

mathematics

MDPI

Article

Exceptional Differential Polynomial Systems Formed by Simple Pseudo-Wronskians of Jacobi Polynomials and Their Infinite and Finite X-Orthogonal Reductions

Gregory Natanson

Independent Researcher, Silver Spring, MD 20904, USA; gregorynatanson@gmail.com

Abstract: The paper advances a new technique for constructing the exceptional differential polynomial systems (X-DPSs) and their infinite and finite orthogonal subsets. First, using Wronskians of Jacobi polynomials (JPWs) with a common pair of the indexes, we generate the Darboux–Crum nets of the rational canonical Sturm–Liouville equations (RCSLEs). It is shown that each RCSLE in question has four infinite sequences of quasi-rational solutions (q-RSs) such that their polynomial components from each sequence form a X-Jacobi DPS composed of simple pseudo-Wronskian polynomials (p-WPs). For each p-th order rational Darboux Crum transform of the Jacobi-reference (JRef) CSLE, used as the starting point, we formulate two rational Sturm–Liouville problems (RSLPs) by imposing the Dirichlet boundary conditions on the solutions of the so-called 'prime' SLE (p-SLE) at the ends of the intervals $(-1, +1)$ or $(+1, \infty)$. Finally, we demonstrate that the polynomial components of the q-RSs representing the eigenfunctions of these two problems have the form of simple p-WPs composed of p Romanovski–Jacobi (R-Jacobi) polynomials with the same pair of indexes and a single classical Jacobi polynomial, or, accordingly, p classical Jacobi polynomials with the same pair of positive indexes and a single R-Jacobi polynomial. The common, fundamentally important feature of all the simple p-WPs involved is that they do not vanish at the finite singular endpoints—the main reason why they were selected for the current analysis in the first place. The discussion is accompanied by a sketch of the one-dimensional quantum-mechanical problems exactly solvable by the aforementioned infinite and finite EOP sequences.

Keywords: rational Sturm-Liouville equation; pseudo-Wronskian polynomial; Darboux–Crum transformation; exceptional differential polynomial system; exceptional orthogonal polynomial system; exceptional orthogonal polynomials; Romanovski–Jacobi polynomials; Dirichlet problem

MSC: 34B24

1. Introduction

In the recently published paper [1] the author presented the systematic analysis of the Xm–Jacobi 'differential polynomial systems' (DPSs), with the term 'DPS' used in exactly the same sense as it was done by Everitt et al. [2,3] for the conventional polynomial sequences satisfying the (generally complex) second-order differential equations with polynomial coefficients (PDEs). The polynomial sequences are referred to as 'exceptional' [4,5], since each sequence either does not start from a constant or lacks the first-degree polynomial; the discovered polynomials are not covered by Bochner's classical proof [6]. As initially stressed by Kwon and Littlewood [7], Bochner himself did not mention the orthogonality of the polynomial systems that he found, and made no attempt to expand his argumentation to the real field—the problem initially analyzed in the 'ill-fated' [8] paper by Routh [9].

It has been proven by Kwon and Littlejohn [7] more recently that all the real field reductions of the complex DPSs constitute quasi-definite orthogonal polynomial sequences [10], and for this reason, the cited authors refer to the latter as 'OPSs'. However, this is not true for the X-DPSs, and we thus preserve the term 'X-OPS' solely for the sequences formed by positively definite orthogonal polynomials.

By further advancing the formalism put forward in [1], we then apply the sequential rational Rudjak–Zakhariev [11] transformations (RRZTs) to construct the new RCSLEs with quasi-rational solutions (q-RSs). For convenience, we sketch the main features of the generic Rudjak–Zakhariev transformations (RZTs) in Appendix A. We term a RZT rational if it uses a quasi-rational transformation function (q-RTF).

We then take advantage of Schulze-Halberg's formalism for the so-called 'foreign auxiliary equations' [12] to generalize the notion of the Darboux–Crum [13,14] transformations (DCTs) to the CSLEs. It is proven in Appendix B that sequential RZTs give rise to the DCT defined in the aforementioned way. Again, we refer to a DCT of the RCSLE as 'rational' (RDCT) if it uses quasi-rational seed functions. Below, these seed functions are represented by the four infinite sequences of the quasi-rational solutions (q-RSs) of the Jacobi-reference (JRef) CSLE, which is defined via (1)–(3) in Section 2.

In this paper, we focus solely on the RDCTs using quasi-rational seed functions with polynomial components formed by Jacobi polynomials with a common pair of the indexes λ_-, λ_+ [15]. The resultant net of the RCSLEs is introduced in Section 4. However, before switching the discussion to these RCSLEs, we found it useful to draw the reader's attention to one of most important element of our technique for generating infinite and finite sequences of exceptional orthogonal polynomials (EOPs), which has been already utilized in [1] for constructing rational Darboux transforms (RD$\mathscr{T}$s) of the Romanovski–Jacobi (R–Jacobi) polynomials [16–18].

Namely, to formulate the Sturm–Liouville problem (SLP), we introduce the so-called [19] 'prime' SLEs (p-SLEs) chosen in such a way that the two characteristic exponents (ChExps) for the poles at the endpoints differ only by sign. As a result, the energy spectrum of the given Sturm–Liouville problem can be obtained by solving the given p-SLE under the Dirichlet boundary conditions (DBCs). This, in turn, allows one to take advantage of the rigorous theorems proven in [20] for eigenfunctions of the generic SLE solved under the DBCs.

In Section 3, we introduce the prime forms of the JRef CSLE on the orthogonalization intervals $(-1, +1)$ and $(1, \infty)$ and then make use of the DBCs to select quasi-rational principal Frobenius solutions (q-RPFSs) near the singular endpoints in question. Our main interests lie in the q-RPFSs lying below the lowest eigenvalue of the JRef CSLEs. We have already used these solutions as the q-RTFs in [1] to construct infinite and finite subsets of X_m-Jacobi DPSs. In this paper, we extend this approach to the RDCTs, using the sequential RRZTs to generate sequences of q-RPFSs (see Appendix B for details).

In Section 5, we again take advantage of Schulze-Halberg's [12] technique to show that the RCSLEs constructed in Section 4 have four infinite sequences of the q-RSs with the polynomial components. While one of these sequences is formed by Jacobi polynomial Wronskians (JPWs), the polynomial components of the three others are represented by the so-called [1] 'simple' pseudo-Wronskian polynomials (p-WPs). Namely, we refer to a pseudo-Wronskian of Jacobi polynomials [21] as 'simple' if only a single polynomial in the given set of seed Jacobi polynomials has at least one Jacobi index with a different sign (compared with the sign of the common index of other Jacobi polynomials in the given set). As proven in Section 6, the simple p-WPs obey the Fuchsian differential equations with polynomial coefficients (FPDE), forming a X-Jacobi DPS. We have here a very specific example of Durán's fundamental theory of the X-Jacobi OPSs [22].

Section 7 constitutes the culminating point of our analysis. Namely, we prove that the rational Darboux-Crum transform (RDC$\mathcal{T}$) of eigenfunctions of the Jacobi p-SLEs on either finite or infinite interval in question represent the quasi-rational eigenfunctions of the corresponding Dirichlet problem formulated for the given RDC$\mathcal{T}$ of the JRef CSLE and therefore the polynomial components of these q-RSs form an orthogonal polynomial set satisfying (by the way it is constructed) to the FPDE.

While the RDC$\mathcal{T}$s of the classical Jacobi polynomials have been thoroughly covered in [22], the admissibility of the JPWs on the infinite interval $(1, \infty)$ represent the important new result. In Section 7.1, we thus verify our conclusions based on the more general theorems proven in [22] and then formulate the novel approach to the theory of the RDC$\mathcal{T}$s of the R-Jacobi polynomials.

Theorems proven in Section 7 are heavily based on the two cornerstones of the developed formalism thoroughly justified in Appendices C and D. Namely, Appendix C presents the proof that the RRZ$\mathcal{T}$ of the q-RPFS itself is the q-RPFs of the transformed RCSLE. In Appendix D we use this very broad result to prove that the latter RCSLE is exactly solvable and therefore the mentioned q-RPF lies below the lowest eigenvalue. This result in turn lays down the foundation for our crucial proof that the JPWs of our choice do not have zeros inside the given orthogonalization interval.

We illustrate this assertion in Appendix E, using the second-degree JPW as an example.

2. Four Distinguished Infinite Sequences of q-RSs

Let us start our analysis with the Jacobi-reference (JRef) CSLE

$$\left\{\frac{d^2}{d\eta^2} + I^o[\eta; \vec{\lambda}_o] + sgn(1-\eta^2)\varepsilon\rho[\eta]\right\}\Phi[\eta; \vec{\lambda}_o; \varepsilon] = 0, \tag{1}$$

with the single pole density function

$$\rho[\eta] := \frac{1}{|\eta^2 - 1|}, \tag{2}$$

and the reference polynomial fraction (RefPF) parameterized as follows:

$$I^o[\eta; \vec{\lambda}_o] \equiv \sum_{\aleph=\pm} \frac{1-\lambda^2_{o;\aleph}}{4(1-\aleph\eta)^2} + \frac{1-\lambda^2_{o;+}-\lambda^2_{o;-}}{4(1-\eta^2)}, \tag{3}$$

$$= \frac{1}{2(1-\eta^2)} \sum_{\aleph=\pm} \frac{1-\lambda^2_{o;\aleph}}{1-\aleph\eta} - \frac{1}{4(1-\eta^2)}, \tag{4}$$

where $\lambda_{o;\pm}$ are the ExpDiffs for the poles at ± 1 and the energy reference point is chosen by the requirement that the ExpDiff for the singular point at infinity vanishes at zero energy, i.e.,

$$\lim_{|\eta|\to\infty} \left(\eta^2 I^o[\eta; \vec{\lambda}_o]\right) = 1/4. \tag{5}$$

The energy sign is chosen in such a way

$$sgn(\varepsilon) = sgn(1-\eta^2) \tag{6}$$

that the sought-for eigenvalues are positive (negative) when the Sturm-Liouville problem in question is formulated on the finite interval $-1 < \eta < 1$ (or, respectively on the positive infinite interval $1 < \eta < \infty$). An analysis of solutions of the CSLE (1) on the negative infinite interval $-\infty < \eta < -1$ can be skipped without loss of generality due to the symmetry of the RefPF (2) under reflection of its argument, accompanied by the interchange of the exponents differences (ExpDiffs) $\lambda_{o;\pm}$ for the CSLE poles at ± 1.

Let us now consider the gauge transformation

$$\Phi\,[\eta;\vec{\lambda}_o;\,\varepsilon] = \phi_0[\eta;\vec{\lambda}_o]\,F\,[\eta;\vec{\lambda}_o;\,\varepsilon], \tag{7}$$

where

$$\phi_0[\eta;\vec{\lambda}] := (1+\eta)^{1/2(\lambda_-+1)}\,|1-\eta\,|^{1/2(\lambda_++1)}\;(-1<\eta\neq 1). \tag{8}$$

Keeping in mind that

$$ld\,\phi_0[\eta;\vec{\lambda}] := \dot{\phi}_0[\eta;\vec{\lambda}]/\phi_0[\eta;\vec{\lambda}] = \frac{\lambda_-+1}{2(\eta+1)} + \frac{\lambda_++1}{2(\eta-1)}, \tag{9}$$

coupled with (3), one finds

$$\ddot{\phi}_0[\eta;\vec{\lambda}]/\phi_0[\eta;\vec{\lambda}] = ld^2\phi_0[\eta;\vec{\lambda}] + l\dot{d}\phi_0[\eta;\vec{\lambda}] \tag{10}$$

$$= -I^o[\eta;\vec{\lambda}_o] - \frac{(\lambda_-+\lambda_++1)^2}{4(1-\eta^2)}, \tag{11}$$

with dot standing for the derivative with respect to η., i.e., the quasi-rational function (8) is the solution of the JRef CSLE at $|\varepsilon|$ equal to

$$\varepsilon_0(\vec{\lambda}) = 1/4(\lambda_-+\lambda_++1)^2. \tag{12}$$

It then directly follows from the identity

$$\begin{aligned}\ddot{\Phi}[\eta;\vec{\lambda};\varepsilon]/\phi_0[\eta;\vec{\lambda}] \equiv -\left\{I^o[\eta;\vec{\lambda}_o] + \tfrac{\varepsilon_0(\vec{\lambda})}{1-\eta^2}\right\}F[\eta;\vec{\lambda};\varepsilon] + \ddot{F}[\eta;\vec{\lambda};\varepsilon]\\ +2ld\phi_0[\eta;\vec{\lambda}]\times\dot{F}[\eta;\vec{\lambda};\varepsilon]\,,\end{aligned} \tag{13}$$

that the function (7) satisfies the FPDE

$$\left[(\eta^2-1)\frac{d^2}{d\eta^2} + 2P_1^{(\lambda_+,\lambda_-)}(\eta)\frac{d}{d\eta} + 1/4(\lambda_-+\lambda_++1)^2 - |\varepsilon|\right]\times F\,[\eta;\vec{\lambda};\,\varepsilon] = 0 \tag{14}$$

with the polynomial coefficients. It is essential that the resultant FPDE is well-defined for any real values of the variable η, including the border points $|\lambda_-| = 1$ or $|\lambda_+| = 1$ between the LP and LC regions (which require a special attention and were sidelined for this reason in our current discussion). The FPDE (14) turns into the conventional Jacobi equation

$$\begin{aligned}(\eta^2-1)\ddot{P}_m^{(\lambda_+,\lambda_-)}(\eta) + 2P_1^{(\lambda_+,\lambda_-)}(\eta)\dot{P}_m^{(\lambda_+,\lambda_-)}(\eta) +\\ m(\lambda_++\lambda_-+m+1)P_m^{(\lambda_+,\lambda_-)}(\eta) = 0\end{aligned} \tag{15}$$

at the energies

$$|\varepsilon| = \varepsilon_m(\vec{\lambda}) = 1/4(\lambda_++\lambda_-+2m+1)^2. \tag{16}$$

In following [2,3], we say that the polynomials in question form the Jacobi DPS.

Note that, in addition with the renowned polynomial solutions, the FPDE (14) has 3 other infinite sequences of the q-RSs listed in Table 1 in [22] (or Table 2 in [23]). It is worth pointing out to the difference in our terminology, compared with that in [22,23]. Namely, we restrict the term 'eigenfunction' only to a solution of a Sturm–Liouville problem (SLP), i.e., in our terms only the classical Jacobi polynomials constitute the eigenfunctions of the Sturm–Liouville differential expression (15), assuming that the corresponding polynomial SLP (PSLP] is formulated on the interval (−1, +1), using the boundary conditions (10) in [24].

Table 1. Correlation between labels t and signs of Jacobi indexes.

t	a	b	c	d
$\sigma_-\ \sigma_+$	+ −	− +	+ +	+ −

Table 2. Classification of JS solutions on the infinite interval (1, ∞) based on their asymptotic behavior near the endpoints.

$\underset{\sim}{t}_{\vec{\sigma},m}$	$\sigma_-\ \sigma_+\ \sigma_\infty$	m
$\underset{\sim}{a}$	+ + −	$0 \leq m < \infty$
$\underset{\sim}{a}'$	− + −	$m \geq n_{\underset{\sim}{c}} = j_{max} + 1$
$\underset{\sim}{b}$	− − +	$0 \leq m < 1/2(\lambda_{o;-} + \lambda_{o;+} - 1)$
$\underset{\sim}{b}'$	− + +	$0 \leq m < 1/2(\lambda_{o;+} - \lambda_{o;-} - 1)$
$\underset{\sim}{c}$	− + +	$0 \leq m \leq j_{max}$
$\underset{\sim}{d}$	+ − −	$1/2(\lambda_{o;+} - \lambda_{o;-} - 1) \leq m < \infty$
$\underset{\sim}{d}'$	− − −	$m > 1/2(\lambda_{o;-} + \lambda_{o;+} - 1)$

By choosing

$$\lambda_-,\ \lambda_+,\ \lambda_- + \lambda_+ + m \neq -k \text{ for any positive integer } k \leq m \tag{17}$$

(see §4.22(3) in [25]), we assure that the Jacobi polynomial in question has exactly m simple zeros $\eta_l(\vec{\lambda};m)$, i.e., using its monic form,

$$\hat{P}_m^{(\lambda_+,\lambda_-)}(\eta) = \Pi_m[\eta; \overline{\eta}(\vec{\lambda}; m)], \tag{18}$$

where by definition

$$\Pi_m[\eta; \overline{\eta}] := \prod_{l=1}^{m} [\eta - \eta_l]. \tag{19}$$

It is crucial that the Jacobi indexes do not depend on the polynomial degree, in contrast with the general case [26,27]. This remarkable feature of the CSLE under consideration is the direct consequence of the fact that the density function (2) has only simple poles in the finite plane [15] and as a result the ExpDiffs for the CSLE poles at ±1 become energy independent [28].

We conclude that the JRef CSLE with the density function (2) has four infinite sequences of the q-RSs

$$\phi_m[\eta; \vec{\lambda}] = |1+\eta|^{1/2(\lambda_-+1)} |1-\eta|^{1/2(\lambda_++1)} P_m^{(\lambda_+,\lambda_-)}(\eta) \quad (|\lambda_\pm| = \lambda_{o;\pm}) \tag{20}$$

at the energies (16), with the vector parameter $\vec{\lambda}$ restricted to the one of the four quadrants for each sequence.

Each infinite sequence starts from the q-RS (8) with $\vec{\lambda}$ restricted to the corresponding quadrant. Substituting (9) into the identity

$$\ddot{\phi}_0[\eta;\vec{\lambda}]/\phi_0[\eta;\vec{\lambda}] \equiv ld^2\phi_0[\eta;\vec{\lambda}] + \dot{ld}\phi_0[\eta;\vec{\lambda}], \tag{21}$$

where the symbolic expression ld f[η] denotes the logarithmic derivative of the function f[η], we find that the function (8) is the solution of the Riccati equation

$$\dot{ld}\ \phi_0[\eta;\vec{\lambda}] - ld^2\phi_0[\eta;\vec{\lambda}] + \mathrm{I^o}[\eta;\vec{\lambda}] + \frac{\varepsilon_0(\vec{\lambda})}{1-\eta^2} = 0. \tag{22}$$

3. Use of 'Prime' Forms of JRef CSLE to Select q-RPFSs

The gauge transformation

$$\Psi_{\mathscr{p}}[\eta;\vec{\lambda};\varepsilon] = \mathscr{p}^{-1/2}[\eta;\vec{\lambda}]\,\Phi[\eta;\vec{\lambda};\varepsilon], \tag{23}$$

with an arbitrarily chosen positive function $\mathscr{p}[\eta]$, converts the JRef CSLE (1) into the SLE of the generic form:

$$\{\frac{d}{d\eta}\mathscr{p}[\eta;\vec{\lambda}]\frac{d}{d\eta} - \mathscr{q}_{\mathscr{p}}[\eta;\vec{\lambda}] + sgn(1-\eta^2)\varepsilon w_{\mathscr{p}}[\eta;\vec{\lambda}]\}\ \Psi[\eta;\vec{\lambda};\varepsilon] = 0, \tag{24}$$

with the weight

$$w_{\mathscr{p}}[\eta;\vec{\lambda}] := \rho[\eta]/\mathscr{p}[\eta;\vec{\lambda}]. \tag{25}$$

The PF representing the zero-energy free term is given by the following generic formula [19]:

$$\mathscr{q}_{\mathscr{p}}[\eta;\vec{\lambda}] = \mathscr{p}[\eta;\vec{\lambda}]\,\mathrm{I^o}[\eta;\vec{\lambda}] + \mathscr{I}\{\mathscr{p}[\eta;\vec{\lambda}]\} \tag{26}$$

with

$$\tilde{\mathscr{I}}\{f[\eta]\} := {}^{1}/_{4}\dot{f}^2[\eta]/f[\eta] - {}^{1}/_{2}\ddot{f}[\eta] \tag{27}$$

and the sign of the sought-for spectral parameter ε is dictated by the constraint (6).

Let us choose the leading coefficient function in such a way:

$$\mathscr{p}[\eta] = \not{\mathscr{p}}[\eta] := \begin{cases} 1-\eta^2 \text{ for } -1<\eta<+1, \\ \eta-1 \text{ for } \eta>1 \end{cases} \tag{28}$$

that the SLP of our interest can be formulated as the Dirichlet problem:

$$\lim_{\eta\to\eta_\mp} \not{\psi}_j[\eta;\vec{\lambda}] = 0 \tag{29}$$

at the ends of the given interval of orthogonalization $\eta_\mp = \mp 1$ or $\eta_- = 1,\ \eta_+ = \infty$. It has been proven in [20] that the eigenfunctions of this Dirichlet problem must be square-integrable:

$$\int_{\eta_-}^{\eta_+} d\eta\, \not{\psi}_j^2[\eta;\vec{\lambda}]\not{w}[\eta] < \infty\,, \tag{30}$$

and mutually orthogonal:

$$\int_{\eta_-}^{\eta_+} d\eta \not{\psi}_j[\eta;\vec{\lambda}]\not{\psi}_{j'}[\eta;\vec{\lambda}]\not{w}[\eta] = 0\ (j \neq j'), \tag{31}$$

with the weight

$$\not{w}[\eta] := w_{\not{p}}[\eta] = \begin{cases} 1 & , \text{ for } -1 < \eta < +1, \\ (1+\eta)^{-1} < 1/2 & \text{for } \eta > 1. \end{cases} \quad (32)$$

Due to the very special choice of the leading coefficient function (28) for the *p*-SLE (24), the two ChExps for each singular endpoint differ by sign, while having exactly the same absolute value, which assures [19] that each DBC unambiguously selects PFS near the given end. In other words, the DBCs (28) unequivocally determine the PFSs nea both singular ends of the given interval of orthogonalization.

Substituting (28) into (27) gives [29]:

$$\mathcal{I}\{\not{p}[\eta]\} = \begin{cases} (1-\eta^2)^{-1} & \text{for } -1 < \eta < +1, \\ 1/4(\eta-1)^{-1} & \text{for } \eta > 1, \end{cases} \quad (33)$$

which shows the free-energy term of the *p*-SLE with the leading coefficient function (28) has simple poles in the finite plane.

As illuminated in Section 7, the concept of the *p*-SLEs allows one to select the sequences of the nodeless PFSs, which assures that the corresponding 'X-Bochner operators' (in terms of [30]) are regular inside the given orthogonalization interval. This is one of the most important achievements of this paper.

3.1. Dirichlet Problem on Interval (−1, +1)

The crucial advantage of representing the conventional Jacobi equation in the *p*-SLE form is that the q-RS

$$\psi_j[\eta; \vec{\lambda}] = (1+\eta)^{1/2\lambda_-}(1-\eta)^{1/2\lambda_+} P_j^{(\lambda_+,\lambda_-)}(\eta) \quad (34)$$

represents the PFS near the poles at ∓ 1 iff the corresponding Jacobi index $\lambda_\mp$ is positive. In particular, the q-RSs

$$\psi_j[\eta; \vec{\lambda}_o] = (1+\eta)^{1/2\lambda_{o;-}}(1-\eta)^{1/2\lambda_{o;+}} P_j^{(\lambda_{o;+},\lambda_{o;-})}(\eta)\ (-1 < \eta < 1) \quad (35)$$

formed by the classical Jacobi polynomials with positive indexes necessarily satisfy the DBCs at ∓ 1 and as a result constitute the eigenfunctions of the given Dirichlet problem. The orthogonality relations (30) thus turn into the conventional orthogonality relations for the classical Jacobi polynomials

$$\int_{-1}^{+1} d\eta P_j^{(\lambda_{o;+},\lambda_{o;-})}(\eta) P_{j'}^{(\lambda_{o;+},\lambda_{o;-})}(\eta) \mathscr{W}_m[\eta; \vec{\lambda}_o] = 0\ (j \neq j') \quad (36)$$

with the weight function

$$\mathscr{W}_m[\eta; \vec{\lambda}] := (1+\eta)^{\lambda_-}(1-\eta)^{\lambda_+} \text{ for } -1 < \eta < 1. \quad (37)$$

Since the (j + 1)-th solution has exactly j zeros between −1 and +1 and the positive eigenvalues converges to 0 as the polynomial degree tends to infinity, the Dirichlet problem in question may not have any other eigenfunctions.

One still needs to prove that the q-RSs (34) form the complete set of the eigenfunctions of the given Dirichlet problem. This can be performed, for example, by converting the JRef CSLE (1) to the hypergeometric equation on the interval (0, +1) and then follow the arguments presented by the author [26] for the exactly solvable JRef CSLE with the properly chosen density function.

On other hand, choosing

$$\mathscr{p}[\eta;\vec{\lambda}] := (1-\eta^2)W[\eta;\vec{\lambda}] = (1+\eta)^{\lambda_-+1}(1-\eta)^{\lambda_++1}, \tag{38}$$

we come to the Sturm–Liouville form [31] of the Jacobi equation:

$$\{\frac{d}{d\eta}\mathscr{p}[\eta;\vec{\lambda}]\frac{d}{d\eta} - \mathscr{q}_{\mathscr{p}}[\eta;\vec{\lambda}] + \varepsilon_j(\vec{\lambda})W[\eta;\vec{\lambda}]\}P_j^{(\lambda_+,\lambda_-)}(\eta) = 0. \tag{39}$$

It is crucial that the leading coefficient function (38) for $\lambda_\mp > -1$ vanishes at the ends of the interval $[-1, +1]$, which assures that the 'generalized' [32] Wronskian (g-W) of two classical Jacobi polynomials

$$\mathscr{W}_{\mathscr{p}}\{P_j^{(\lambda_+,\lambda_{o;-})}(\eta), P_{j'}^{(\lambda_+,\lambda_-)}(\eta)\} := \mathscr{p}[\eta;\vec{\lambda}]\,W\{P_j^{(\lambda_+,\lambda_{o;-})}(\eta), P_{j'}^{(\lambda_+,\lambda_-)}(\eta)\} \quad \text{for } 0 \le j' < j \le j_{max} \tag{40}$$

vanishes at ± 1.

Our next step is first to consider all the q-RSs of the given p-SLE, which vanish at one of the endpoints of the infinite interval $(-1, +1)$ and then select the subsets of the collected PFSs below the lowest eigenvalue.

Since our approach allows one to formulate the spectral problem only for positive values of the Jacobi indexes, this limitation restricts one's ability to construct the X-Jacobi OPSs formed by the RDC$\mathscr{T}$s of the classical Jacobi polynomials with negative indexes, as it has already become clear from our analysis [1] of the X_m-Jacobi OPSs. However, as demonstrated in [1], the certain advantage of our approach is that it allows one to treat in parallel the RSLPs for both intervals $(-1, +1)$ and $(1, \infty)$ and moreover to prove that the RDC$\mathscr{T}$s of the PFSs of the JRef CSLE are themselves the PFSs of the resultant RCSLEs. We refer the reader to Appendix C, where we present the proof of the latter assertion representing one of the pillars of our formalism.

In following our olden study [33] on the Darboux transforms (D$\mathscr{T}$s) of radial potentials, we use the letters $\mathtt{a}$ and $\mathtt{b}$ to specify the PFS near the singular endpoints ∓ 1 (cases I and II in Quesne's [34] commonly used classification scheme of q-RSs. According to their behavior near the endpoints). We use the letters $\mathtt{c}$ and $\mathtt{d}$ [33] to identify the $n_{\mathfrak{c}}$ eigenfunctions and, respectively all the q-RSs (34) not vanishing at both ends (case III in Quesne's classification scheme). For the given SLP there is the one-to-one correlation between the labels $\mathtt{t} = \mathtt{a}, \mathtt{b}, \mathtt{c}, \mathtt{d}$ and the sign $\sigma_\mp$ of the Jacobi indexes $\lambda_\mp$, as specified in Table 1.

Re-writing the dispersion Formula (16) for $\vec{\sigma} = \pm\mp$ as

$$\varepsilon_{\pm\mp,m}(\vec{\lambda}_o) = (\mp\lambda_{o;-} \pm \lambda_{o;+} - 2m - 1)^2, \tag{41}$$

we find that the PFSs of either type $\mathtt{a}$ or type $\mathtt{b}$ lie below the lowest eigenvalue

$$\varepsilon_{\mathtt{c},0}(\vec{\lambda}_o) = (\lambda_{\mathfrak{o};-} + \lambda_{\mathfrak{o};+} + 1)^2, \tag{42}$$

iff

$$m < -\lambda_+ = \lambda_{o;+} \; (\lambda_\mp = \pm\lambda_{o;\mp}), \tag{43}$$

or

$$m < -\lambda_- = \lambda_{o;-} \; (\lambda_\mp = \mp\lambda_{o;\mp}), \tag{44}$$

accordingly.

Using the Klein formulas [25], we have proved [28] that the m-degree Jacobi polynomial with the indexes λ_- and λ_+ does not have zeros between -1 and +1 iff

$$m \leq 1/2\,(|\lambda_-| - \lambda_- + |\lambda_+| - \lambda_+) \tag{45}$$

and

$$\begin{gathered}(-)^m\langle\lambda_- + 1\rangle_m\,\langle\lambda_+ + 1\rangle_m = \\ \langle-\lambda_- - m\rangle_m\langle\lambda_+ + 1\rangle_m = \langle\lambda_- + 1\rangle_m\langle-\lambda_+ - m\rangle_m > 0,\end{gathered} \tag{46}$$

where $\langle\nu\rangle_m$ is the rising factorial [35]. One can easily verify that the latter conditions do hold under both constraints (43) and (44).

3.2. Dirichlet Problem on Interval (1, ∞)

Examination of the q-RSs

$$\psi_j[[\eta; -\lambda_{o;-}, \lambda_{o;+}] = (1+\eta)^{1/2 - 1/2\lambda_{o;-}}\,(\eta-1)^{1/2\lambda_{o;+}}P_j^{(\lambda_{o;+}, -\lambda_{o;-})}(\eta) \tag{47}$$

reveals that they satisfy the DBCs at both ends of the interval $(1, \infty)$ for

$$0 \leq j < 1/2(\lambda_{o;-}, -\lambda_{o;+} - 1), \tag{48}$$

And, therefore, represent the eigenfunctions of the RSLP in question, which brings us to the orthogonality relations

$$\int_1^\infty d\eta\, P_j^{(\lambda_{o;+}, -\lambda_{o;-})}(\eta) P_{j'}^{(\lambda_{o;+}, -\lambda_{o;-})}(\eta)\mathscr{W}_m[\eta; \vec{\lambda}_o] = 0 \;\; (j \neq j'), \tag{49}$$

with the weight function

$$\mathscr{W}_m[\eta; \vec{\lambda}_o] := (1+\eta)^{-\lambda_{o;-}}\,(\eta-1)^{\lambda_{o;+}} \text{ for } \eta > 1. \tag{50}$$

One can easily verify that (49) is nothing but another form of the conventional orthogonality relations for the R-Jacobi polynomials

$$\int_0^\infty d\underset{\rightarrow}{z}\, J_j^{(\alpha,\beta)}(\underset{\rightarrow}{z}) J_{j'}^{(\alpha,\beta)}(\underset{\rightarrow}{z})\underset{\rightarrow}{\omega}_{\alpha,\beta}[\underset{\rightarrow}{z}] = 0 \;\; (j \neq j\prime), \tag{51}$$

with the weight function

$$\underset{\rightarrow}{\omega}_{\alpha,\beta}[\underset{\rightarrow}{z}] := \underset{\rightarrow}{z}^{\alpha}\,(\underset{\rightarrow}{z}+1)^{-|\beta|} \text{ for} \eta \in [1, \infty) \tag{52}$$

under constraint $\alpha > 0$, $\beta < 0$, where we adopted Askey's [36] definition of the R–Jacobi polynomials which, as proven by Chen and Srivastava [37], is equivalent to the elementary formula

$$J_n^{(\alpha,\beta)}(\underset{\rightarrow}{z}) := P_n^{(\alpha,\beta)}(2\underset{\rightarrow}{z}+1) \text{ for } \alpha > -1,\; \beta + 2n < 0, \tag{53}$$

with

$$\underset{\rightarrow}{z} := 1/2(\eta - 1). \tag{54}$$

Note that we [38] (see also [39]) changed the symbol R for J to avoid the confusion with R–Routh (Romanovski/pseudo-Jacobi [17,18]) polynomials denoted in the recent publications [40–43] by the same letter 'R'.

Our next step is to determine all the q-RSs vanishing at one of the endpoints of the infinite interval [+1, +∞] and then select the subsets of the collected PFSs which lie below the lowest eigenvalue. To explicitly reveal the behavior of the Jacobi-seed (JS) q-RSs (54) near the singular endpoints in question, we label them as indicated in Table 2 below, with σ_∞ specifying either the decay (+) or growth (−) of the given JS at infinity.

To indicate that the classification of the JS solutions is done on the infinite interval (1, ∞), we underline the symbol t by tilde. We then mark the given symbol by prime if the polynomial components of the given sequence of the q-RSs do not include a constant. (Note that the 'secondary' sequences of such a type do not exist for the potentials with infinitely many discrete energy levels which were the focal point of Quesne's analysis [34]).

By definition

$$\varepsilon_{\underset{\sim}{t}_{\vec{\sigma},m},m}(\vec{\lambda}_o) \equiv -\varepsilon_{\vec{\sigma},m}(\vec{\lambda}_o). \tag{55}$$

Note that the PFSs of the series $\underset{\sim}{b}'$ may exist only if the SLE does not have the discrete energy spectrum. We thus need to consider the three sequences of the quasi-rational PFSs: two 'primary' (starting from m = 0) sequences $\underset{\sim}{a}$ and $\underset{\sim}{b}$ as well as the infinite 'secondary' sequence $\underset{\sim}{a}'$ (starting from $m = n_{\underset{\sim}{c}}$).

The primary sequence $\underset{\sim}{a}$ is formed by classical Jacobi polynomials and consequently may not have zeros between 1 and ∞. As expected, all the PFSs of this type lie at the energies.

$$\varepsilon_{\underset{\sim}{a},m}(\vec{\lambda}_o) \equiv -\varepsilon_{++,m}(\vec{\lambda}_o) \tag{56}$$

below the lowest eigenvalue

$$\varepsilon_{\underset{\sim}{c},0}(\vec{\lambda}_o) \equiv -\varepsilon_{+-,0}(\vec{\lambda}_o). \tag{57}$$

The PFSs from the primary sequence $\underset{\sim}{b}$ at the energies

$$\varepsilon_{\underset{\sim}{b},m}(\vec{\lambda}_o) \equiv -\varepsilon_{--,m}(\vec{\lambda}_o) \tag{58}$$

for

$$0 \leq m < 1/2(\lambda_{o;-} + \lambda_{o;+} - 1) \tag{59}$$

do not have real zeros larger than 1 iff

$$\varepsilon_{\underset{\sim}{b},m}(\vec{\lambda}_o) - \varepsilon_{\underset{\sim}{c},0}(\vec{\lambda}_o) = -4(\lambda_{o;-} - m - 1)(\lambda_{o;+} - m) < 0, \tag{60}$$

i.e., iff

$$0 \leq m < \lambda_{o;+} < \lambda_{o;-} - 1. \tag{61}$$

Similarly, the PFSs from the secondary sequence $\underset{\sim}{a}'$ at the energies

$$\varepsilon_{\underset{\sim}{a}',m}(\vec{\lambda}_o) = -\varepsilon_{+-,m}(\vec{\lambda}_o) \text{ for } m \geq n_{\underset{\sim}{c}} \tag{62}$$

do not have real zeros larger than 1 iff

$$\varepsilon_{\underset{\sim}{a}',m}(\vec{\lambda}_o) - \varepsilon_{\underset{\sim}{c},0}(\vec{\lambda}_o) = -4m(\lambda_{o;+} - \lambda_{o;-} + m + 1) < 0 \tag{63}$$

or, in other words, iff

$$\mathtt{m} > \lambda_{o;-} - \lambda_{o;+} - 1. \tag{64}$$

4. RDCTs of JRef SLE Using Seed Jacobi Polynomials with Common Pair of Indexes

We call the DCT rational if it uses quasi-rational seed functions. In this section, we focus solely on the RDCTs using the seed functions (20) with the common Jacobi indexes $\vec{\lambda}$. Let us consider the RDCT using an arbitrary set of p seed functions,

$$\overline{M}_p := m_1, \ldots, m_p.$$

Denoting the Jacobi polynomial Wronskian (JPW) as

$$W^{(\lambda_+,\lambda_-)}_{\mathcal{N}(\overline{M}_p)}[\eta|\overline{M}_p] := W\{P^{(\lambda_+,\lambda_-)}_{m_{k=1,\ldots,p}}(\eta)\} \tag{65}$$

and substituting the Wronskian

$$W\{\phi_{m_{k=1,\ldots,p}}[\eta;\vec{\lambda}]\} = \phi_0^p[\eta;\vec{\lambda}]W^{(\lambda_+,\lambda_-)}_{\mathcal{N}(\overline{M}_p)}[\eta|\overline{M}_p] \tag{66}$$

into (A18), we come to the RCSLE

$$\left\{\frac{d^2}{d\eta^2} + I^o[\eta;\vec{\lambda}|\overline{M}_p] + sgn(1-\eta^2)\varepsilon\rho[\eta]\right\}\Phi[\eta;\vec{\lambda};\varepsilon|\overline{M}_p] = 0 \tag{67}$$

with the RefPF [12]

$$\begin{gathered} I^o[\eta;\vec{\lambda}|\overline{M}_p] = I^o[\eta;\vec{\lambda}_o] + 2p\sqrt{\rho[\eta]}\tfrac{d}{d\eta}\frac{ld\,\phi_0[\eta;\vec{\lambda}]}{\sqrt{\rho[\eta]}} - p(p-2)\mathcal{J}\{\rho[\eta]\} \\ +2\sqrt{\rho[\eta]}\tfrac{d}{d\eta}\frac{ld\,W^{(\lambda_+,\lambda_-)}_{\mathcal{N}(\overline{M}_p)}[\eta|\overline{M}_p]}{\sqrt{\rho[\eta]}}. \end{gathered} \tag{68}$$

Let us now show that the first three summands can be then re-arranged as

$$\begin{gathered} I^o[\eta;\vec{\lambda}+p\vec{1}] = I^o[\eta;\vec{\lambda}_o] + 2p\sqrt{\rho[\eta]}\tfrac{d}{d\eta}\frac{ld\,\phi_0[\eta;\vec{\lambda}]}{\sqrt{\rho[\eta]}} + \\ 2\sqrt{\rho[\eta]}\tfrac{d}{d\eta}\frac{ld\,W^{(\lambda_+,\lambda_-)}_{\mathcal{N}(\overline{M}_p)}[\eta|\overline{M}_p]}{\sqrt{\rho[\eta]}} - p(p-2)\mathcal{J}\{|1-\eta^2|\} \end{gathered} \tag{69}$$

and then prove that

$$I^o[\eta;\vec{\lambda}|\overline{M}_p] = I^o[\eta;\vec{\lambda}+p\vec{1}] + 2\,\dot{ld}\,W^{(\lambda_+,\lambda_-)}_{\mathcal{N}(\overline{M}_p)}[\eta|\overline{M}_p] - ld\,\rho[\eta]\,ld\,W^{(\lambda_+,\lambda_-)}_{\mathcal{N}(\overline{M}_p)}[\eta|\overline{M}_p] \tag{70}$$

which represents one of the most important results of this section. To prove (70), we first re-write the second summand in (69) as

$$2p\sqrt{\rho[\eta]}\frac{d}{d\eta}\frac{ld\,\phi_0[\eta;\vec{\lambda}]}{\sqrt{\rho[\eta]}} = 2p\,\dot{ld}\,\phi_0[\eta;\vec{\lambda}] - p\,ld\rho[\eta]ld\,\phi_0[\eta;\vec{\lambda}]. \tag{71}$$

Taking into account (9), coupled with

$$ld\rho[\eta] = -\frac{1}{\eta+1} - \frac{1}{\eta-1}, \tag{72}$$

gives

$$2p\sqrt{\rho[\eta]}\frac{d}{d\eta}\frac{ld\,\phi_0[\eta;\vec{\lambda}]}{\sqrt{\rho[\eta]}} = 2p\,\dot{ld}\phi_0[\eta;\vec{\lambda}] - p\,ld\rho[\eta]ld\,\phi_0[\eta;\vec{\lambda}] \tag{73}$$

$$= -\frac{p(\lambda_+ + 1)}{2(\eta-1)^2} - \frac{p(\lambda_- + 1)}{2(\eta+1)^2} + \frac{p(\lambda_- + \lambda_+ + 2)}{2(\eta^2-1)}. \tag{74}$$

Combining (74) with the definition (3) of the RefPF of the JRef CSLE (1), and also taking into account that [29]

$$\mathcal{I}\{|1-\eta^2|\} = \frac{1}{4(\eta-1)^2} + \frac{1}{4(\eta+1)^2} - \frac{1}{2(\eta^2-1)}, \tag{75}$$

one can directly confirm that the three distinguished singularities appearing in the right-hand side of (74) can be grouped as follows

$$\begin{aligned}2p\sqrt{\rho[\eta]}\tfrac{d}{d\eta}\tfrac{ld\,\phi_0[\eta;\vec{\lambda}]}{\sqrt{\rho[\eta]}} &= I^{o}[\eta;\vec{\lambda}+p\vec{1}] - I^{o}[\eta;\vec{\lambda}_o] + \\ &+ p(p-2)\mathcal{I}\{|1-\eta^2|\}.\end{aligned} \tag{76}$$

Before proceeding with the further analysis of the RefPF (70), let us first illuminate some remarkable features of the JPW (65). First, let us prove that the Wronskian of the Jacobi polynomials with the common positive integer does not vanish at the corresponding pole of the JRef CSLE (1), which simplifies the computation of the ExpDiffs for the pole of the RefPF (66) at this point.

Theorem 1. *The JPW (65) is finite at the singular point ∓ 1 if $\lambda_{\mp} > 0$.*

Proof. To verify this assertion, we take advantage of our generic observation that any DCT can be decomposed into the sequence of RZTs with the TFs given by the recurrence formulas (A19) in Appendix B. Making use of (66), one can easily verify that these TFs for the RDCTs under consideration have the following quasi-rational form

$$\phi_{m_{p+1}}[\eta;\vec{\lambda}|\overline{M}_p] = \frac{\phi_0[\eta;\vec{\lambda}]W^{(\lambda_+,\lambda_-)}_{\mathcal{N}(\overline{M}_{p+1})}[\eta|\overline{M}_{p+1}]}{\rho^{1/2p}[\eta]W^{(\lambda_+,\lambda_-)}_{\mathcal{N}(\overline{M}_p)}[\eta|\overline{M}_p]}, \tag{77}$$

i.e., taking into account (2) and (8),

$$\phi_{m_{p+1}}[\eta;\vec{\lambda}|\overline{M}_p] = \frac{\phi_0[\eta;\vec{\lambda}+p\vec{1}]W^{(\lambda_+,\lambda_-)}_{\mathcal{N}(\overline{M}_{p+1})}[\eta|\overline{M}_{p+1}]}{W^{(\lambda_+,\lambda_-)}_{\mathcal{N}(\overline{M}_p)}[\eta|\overline{M}_p]}. \tag{78}$$

Let us assume that the JPW in the denominator of the PF on the right remains finite at ∓ 1. Then examination of the RefPF (70), coupled with the definition of the Jref RefPF (3), reveals that the power exponent of $\eta \pm 1$ in the numerator of the PF (78) coincides with the positive ChExp for the pole of the RCSLE (67) at ∓ 1. Since the second ChExp, according to (3), is negative, the TF (78) necessarily represents the PFS near the pole in question if $\lambda_{\mp} > 0$, and therefore the numerator of the PF may not have the zero at ∓ 1. This completes the proof of Theorem 1 by mathematical induction, since the theorem necessarily holds for p = 1 due to the constraint (17) imposed on the seed Jacobi polynomial. □

In Appendix E, we explicitly confirm the theorem for the simplest second-degree JPW Wronskian formed by the Jacobi polynomials of degrees 1 and 2.

Corollary 1. *The Wronskian of the classical Jacobi polynomials with positive indexes may not have zeros at* ∓ 1.

As illuminated in Section 7.1, this corollary plays the crucial role in the theory of the RDC$\mathcal{T}$s of the R-Jacobi polynomials using the quasi-rational seed functions formed by the classical Jacobi polynomials with positive indexes.

We were unable to prove Theorem 1 for the case when the 2D vector $\vec{\lambda}$ lies in the third quarter so we make the following assumption specifically for this case:

Corollary 2. *The JPW does not generally have zeros at* ∓ 1, *regardless of the sign of* $\lambda_{\mp}$.

Proof. After representing the JPW as a polynomial in either $\eta - 1$ or $\eta + 1$ (instead of η), let us take advantage of the fact that the common leading coefficient is the polynomial in both λ_- and λ_+. According to Theorem 1, this coefficient remains finite at positive values of $\lambda_{\mp}$ and therefore does not vanish identically for any values of $\lambda_{\mp}$, which completes the proof. □

In [1], we implicitly used this assumption to construct the finitely many sequences of the RD$\mathcal{T}$s of the R-Jacobi polynomials using the TFs of type $\underset{\sim}{\mathfrak{b}}$ ($\lambda_{\mp} < 0$, without going into more details.

As explained below, we also have to disregard some specially designed exceptions [44], when the quasi-rational function (77) becomes regular at the two poles of the RCSLE (67), which leads us to the following assertion:

Preposition 1. *As a rule, the JPWs in the numerator and denominator of the fraction (77) do not have common zeros.*

Theorem 2. *The JPW in the numerator of the fraction (77) has only simple zeros as far as the Preposition 1 holds.*

Proof. Based on our prepositions, any zero of the JPW in the numerator of the fraction (77) is a regular point of the RCSLE (67) and therefore the polynomial in question may not have zeros of order higher than 1. (Otherwise, the solution (77) of the RCSLE (67) and its first derivative would vanish at the same point which is possible only for the trivial solution identically equal to zero). □

Let

$$\overline{\eta}(\vec{\lambda}\,|\overline{M}_p) := \eta_{l=1,\ldots,\mathcal{N}(\overline{M}_p)}(\vec{\lambda}\,|\overline{M}_p) \tag{79}$$

be the $\mathcal{N}(\overline{M}_p)$ zeros of the JPW (65), i.e.,

$$\hat{W}^{(\lambda_+,\lambda_-)}_{\mathcal{N}(\overline{M}_p)}[\eta|\overline{M}_p] = \Pi_{\mathcal{N}(\overline{M}_p)}[\eta;\overline{\eta}^{(\mathcal{N})}(\vec{\lambda}\,|\overline{M}_p)] := \prod_{\ell=1}^{\mathcal{N}(\overline{M}_p)} [\eta - \eta_\ell(\vec{\lambda}\,|\overline{M}_p)] \tag{80}$$

Re-writing (72) as

$$ld\rho[\eta] = -\frac{2\eta}{\eta^2 - 1} \tag{81}$$

and taking into account that

$$Q[\eta;\overline{\eta}] := l\dot{d}\Pi_m[\eta;\overline{\eta}] = -\sum_{l=1}^{m} \frac{1}{[\eta - \eta_l]^2}, \tag{82}$$

we can decompose the RefPF (70) as follows

$$\mathrm{I}^{\mathrm{o}}[\eta;\vec{\lambda}\,|\overline{\mathrm{M}}_{\mathrm{p}}] = \mathrm{I}^{\mathrm{o}}[\eta;\vec{\lambda}+\mathrm{p}\vec{1}] - \sum_{\ell=1}^{\mathcal{N}(\overline{\mathrm{M}}_{\mathrm{p}})} \frac{2}{[\eta-\eta_{l}(\vec{\lambda}\,|\overline{\mathrm{M}}_{\mathrm{p}})]^{2}} + \frac{2\eta}{\eta^{2}-1} \sum_{\ell=1}^{\mathcal{N}(\overline{\mathrm{M}}_{\mathrm{p}})} \frac{1}{\eta-\eta_{l}(\vec{\lambda}\,|\overline{\mathrm{M}}_{\mathrm{p}})}, \tag{83}$$

in agreement with (87) in [1] for p = 1.

The indicial equation for all the extraneous poles of the RCSLE (67) has exactly the same form:

$$\rho(\rho-1)-2=0. \tag{84}$$

The equation has two roots −1 and 2, which implies that the JPW in the numerator of the fraction (78) can formally have a zero of the third order [44]. However, as it becomes obvious from the analysis presented in [44], this is a relatively exotic case, when the solution becomes regular at two singular points, which will be simply disregarded here.

5. Four Infinite Sequences of q-RSs with Polynomial Components Represented by Simple p-WPs

In addition to (77), the RCSLE (67) has three infinite sequences of the q-RSs:

$$\phi_{\vec{\sigma},\mathrm{j}}[\eta;\vec{\lambda}\,|\overline{\mathrm{M}}_{\mathrm{p}}] = \frac{\mathrm{W}\{\phi_{\mathrm{m}_{\mathrm{k}=1,\ldots,\mathrm{p}}}[\eta;\vec{\lambda}],\phi_{\mathrm{j}}[\eta;\vec{\lambda}']\}}{\rho^{-1/2\mathrm{p}}[\eta]\mathrm{W}\{\phi_{\mathrm{m}_{\mathrm{k}=1,\ldots,\mathrm{p}}}[\eta;\vec{\lambda}]\}}\quad(\vec{\lambda}'\neq\vec{\lambda}), \tag{85}$$

where the indexes $\vec{\lambda}'$ may differ only by sign from the common indexes $\vec{\lambda}$ of the seed Jacobi polynomials:

$$\lambda'_{\mp} = \sigma_{\mp}\vec{\lambda}_{\mp} \tag{86}$$

and

$$|\lambda'_{\mp}| = |\lambda_{\mp}| = \lambda_{\mathrm{o};\mp}. \tag{87}$$

Here, we come to the most important result of this section: introducing the notion of the *simple p-WPs* which, by analogy with the JPWs, remain finite at ∓1.

Theorem 3. *The quasi-rational numerators of the fractions (85) can be expressed in terms of simple p-WPs defined via (92) below.*

Proof. In following [22], let us first introduce the eigenfunctions of the Jacobi operator:

$$\mathrm{f}[\eta;\vec{\lambda}\,|\vec{\sigma},\mathrm{j}] := \mathrm{f}[\eta;\vec{\lambda}\,|\vec{\sigma},0]\,\mathrm{P}_{\mathrm{j}}^{(\sigma_{+}\lambda_{+},\sigma_{-}\lambda_{-})}(\eta), \tag{88}$$

where

$$\mathrm{f}[\eta;\vec{\lambda}\,|\vec{\sigma},0] := \phi_{0}[\eta;\vec{\sigma}\times\vec{\lambda}]/\phi_{0}[\eta;\vec{\lambda}], \tag{89}$$

$$= \prod_{\aleph=\pm}|1-\aleph\eta|^{1/2(\sigma_{\aleph}1-1)\lambda_{\aleph}}, \tag{90}$$

(see Table 1 in [45] for details). We can then re-write the Wronskian in the numerator of the PF (85) as

$$\mathrm{W}\{\phi_{\mathrm{m}_{\mathrm{k}=1,\ldots,\mathrm{p}}}[\eta;\vec{\lambda}],\phi_{\mathrm{j}}[\eta;\vec{\lambda}']\} = \phi_{0}^{\mathrm{p}+1}[\eta;\vec{\lambda}]\times\mathrm{W}\{\mathrm{P}_{\mathrm{m}_{\mathrm{k}=1,\ldots,\mathrm{p}}}^{(\lambda_{+},\lambda_{-})}(\eta),\mathrm{f}[\eta;\vec{\lambda}\,|\vec{\sigma},\mathrm{j}]\}. \tag{91}$$

Though this paper is devoted solely to the EOP sequences associated with the particular case $\vec{\phi} = -+$ (as advocated in [45]), it seems enlightening to discuss in parallel all the three sequences of the simple p-WPs. First, it is worth noting that the net of X-Jacobi OPSs of our choice starts from the X_m-Jacobi OPSs of series J1, but not with the traditional X_m-Jacobi OPSs [24,46], referred to in our works [1,38] as being of series J2.

This is true [45] that the X_m-Jacobi OPSs in case $\vec{\phi} = --$ can be obtained by eliminating certain pairs of juxtaposed eigenfunctions [47,48]; however, the analysis of the RDC$\mathcal{T}$s of the JRef CSLE (1) obtained by sequential RRZTs is much easier as illustrated by the proofs presented in Appendices C and D. While the admissibility of the partitions composed of even-length segments for X-Jacobi OPSs has been proven by Durán in his renowned treatise [21], an extension of this assertion to the RDC$\mathcal{T}$s of the R–Jacobi polynomials constitutes a much more challenging problem (cf. the bulky arguments presented by us in [49] for the RDC$\mathcal{T}$s of the R-Routh polynomials).

Making use of Jacobi polynomial relations (92) in [21], we can tn represent the derivatives of functions (88) in in the explicitly quasi-rational form:

$$\frac{d^l}{d\eta^l} f[\eta; \vec{\lambda}|\vec{\phi}, j] = d^{(l)}_{\vec{\phi},j}(\vec{\lambda}') f[\eta; \vec{\lambda}|\vec{\phi}, 0] \Theta^{-l}_{\vec{\phi}}[\eta]\, P^{(\lambda'_+ + \phi_+ l, \lambda'_- + \phi_- l)}_{j-[\vec{\phi}]l/2}(\eta), \tag{92}$$

where

$$\Theta_{\vec{\phi}}[\eta] := \prod_{\aleph=\pm} (1 - \aleph\eta)^{1/2(1-\phi_\aleph 1)}, \tag{93}$$

$$[\vec{\phi}] := \phi_+ 1 + \phi_- 1, \tag{94}$$

and the indexes $\vec{\lambda}'$ appearing on the right are related to the indexes $\vec{\lambda}$ of the seed Jacobi polynomials via (86). The constant coefficient factors in (92) are determined by the elementary formulas [21]:

$$d^{(l)}_{\vec{\phi},j}(\vec{\lambda}') = \begin{cases} 2^{-l}\langle \lambda'_+ + \lambda'_- + j + 1\rangle_l & \text{if } \vec{\phi} = ++, \\ (-2)^l \langle j+1\rangle_l & \text{if } \vec{\phi} = --, \\ (-1)^l \langle j + \lambda'_+\rangle_l & \text{if } \vec{\phi} = -+, \\ \langle j + \lambda'_-\rangle_l & \text{if } \vec{\phi} = +-. \end{cases}, \tag{95}$$

The listed formulas can be directly verified by expressing the hypergeometric functions in terms of Jacobi polynomials in 2.1(20), 2.1(27), 2.1(24), and 2.1(22) in [50], with $a = -m$. While all four Jacobi polynomial relations (92) were obtained in [21] based on the translational shape-invariance of the trigonometric Pöschl–Teller (t-PT) potential, we prefer to refer the reader to the more general relations 2.1(7), 2.1(9), 2.1(8), and 2.1(22) for hypergeometric functions in [50], as the starting point for validating (92). The cited relations are valid within a broader range of the parameters, beyond the limits of the Liouville transformation implicitly used in [21].

Substituting the derivatives (92) into the Wronskian in the right-hand side of (86), we can represent the quasi-rational form

$$W\{P^{(\lambda_+,\lambda_-)}_{m_{k=1,\ldots,p}}(\eta), f[\eta; \lambda|\vec{\phi}, j]\} = f[\eta; \vec{\lambda}'|\vec{\phi}, 0]\Theta^{-p}_{\vec{\phi}}[\eta]\, \mathscr{P}_{\mathcal{N}(\overline{M}_p;\vec{\phi},j)}[\eta; \vec{\lambda}|\overline{M}_p; \vec{\phi}, j], \tag{96}$$

with the polynomial component represented by the simple p-WP ($\vec{\phi} \neq ++$):

$$\mathscr{P}_{\mathscr{N}(\overline{M}_p;\,\vec{\phi},j)}[\eta;\vec{\lambda}|\overline{M}_p;\,\vec{\phi},j] := \begin{vmatrix} P_{m_1}^{(\lambda_+,\lambda_-)}(\eta) & P_{m_2}^{(\lambda_+,\lambda_-)}(\eta) & \ldots & \Theta^p_{\vec{\phi}}[\eta]\,P_j^{(\lambda'_+,\lambda'_-)}(\eta) \\ \frac{d}{d\eta}P_{m_1}^{(\lambda_+,\lambda_-)}(\eta) & \frac{d}{d\eta}P_{m_2}^{(\lambda_+,\lambda_-)}(\eta) & \ldots & P^{(p,1)}_{n_{j;[\vec{\phi}]}(p-1)}[\eta;\vec{\lambda}'|\vec{\phi}] \\ & \ldots & & \\ \frac{d^p}{d^p\eta}P_{m_1}^{(\lambda_+,\lambda_-)}(\eta) & \frac{d^p}{d^p\eta}P_{m_2}^{(\lambda_+,\lambda_-)}(\eta) & \ldots & P^{(p,p)}_{n_{j;[\vec{\phi}]}(0)}[\eta;\vec{\lambda}'|\vec{\phi}] \end{vmatrix}, \tag{97}$$

where

$$P^{(p,l)}_{n_{j;[\vec{\phi}]}(p-l)}[\eta;\vec{\lambda}'\,|\,\vec{\phi}] := d^{(l)}_{\vec{\phi},j}(\vec{\lambda}')\,\Theta^{p-l}_{\vec{\phi}}[\eta]\;P^{(\lambda'_++\phi_+l,\,\lambda'_-+\phi_-l)}_{j-[\vec{\phi}]\frac{l}{2}}(\eta) \tag{98}$$

are the polynomials of the degree

$$n_{j;[\vec{\phi}]}(k) = j-1+(k+1)(1-1/2[\vec{\phi}]), \tag{99}$$

with the integer $[\vec{\phi}]$ defined via (94), which completes the proof. □

Here and below we use the symbol $\mathscr{P}$ for the polynomials forming a X-Jacobi DPS, with $\mathscr{N}$ standing for their degrees, while the nonnegative integer j counts the polynomials within the given X-DPS which is constructed using p seed Jacobi polynomials of degrees $m_1,\ldots,m_p$ with the common pair of the indexes $\vec{\lambda}$. The polynomial (97) thus represents the RDC$\mathscr{T}$ of the Jacobi polynomial of the degree j with the indexes $\vec{\lambda}'$ defined via (86) and (87).

Keeping in mind that

$$n_{j;[\vec{\phi}]}(0) = j-1/2[\vec{\phi}], \tag{100}$$

and using the cofactor expansion of the determinant (99) in terms of the ($p-l$, p + 1) minors (l = 0,. . .,p), we find that the first term in the sum has the degree

$$\mathscr{N}(\overline{M}_p;\,\vec{\phi},j) = \mathscr{N}(\overline{M}_p)+j-1/2[\vec{\phi}], \tag{101}$$

where [51]

$$\mathscr{N}(\overline{M}_p) = \sum_{k=1}^{p} m_k - 1/2p(p-1). \tag{102}$$

One can directly verify that

$$\mathscr{N}(\overline{M}_p;\,++,m_{p+1}) = \mathscr{N}(\overline{M}_p)+m_{p+1}-1 = \mathscr{N}(\overline{M}_{p+1}), \tag{103}$$

as expected. Taking into account that $[\mp\pm]=0$, we also find

$$n_{j;\mp\pm}(k) = j+k \tag{104}$$

and

$$\mathscr{N}(\overline{M}_p;\,\mp\pm,j) = \mathscr{N}(\overline{M}_p)+j. \tag{105}$$

Preposition 2. *In general, the degree of the simple p-WP (97) is equal to the positive integer specified by (101).*

Proof. One can easily verify that the degree of the $(p+1-l)$-th column element and degree of the corresponding cofactor polynomial minor increases and, respectively decreases by 1 as l grows, confirming that all the polynomial summands have the common degree (101). Based on Bonneux's [45] formula (2.10), we assert that the simple p-WP (97) has the degree (101) iff

$$\lambda_+ + \lambda_- + m_k \notin \{-1, -2, \ldots, -m_k\},\ \lambda'_+ + \lambda'_- + j \notin \{-1, -2, \ldots, -j\}. \tag{106}$$

The simplest way to avoid the degree reduction is to assume that the Jacobi indexes $\vec{\lambda}$ are non-integers. □

In [45], the positive integer (102) is termed 'length' $|\lambda|$ of the partition $\lambda := \lambda_1, \lambda_2, \ldots \lambda_p$ with $\lambda_k := m_k + p - k$ ($k = 1, \ldots, p$). Setting $\vec{\not{o}} = -+$, $\mu = j = |\mu|$, $r_1 = p$, $r_2 = 1$ confirms that the derived formula for the degree of the simple p-WP of the given type agrees with the more general formula $|\lambda| + |\mu|$ for the two partitions λ and μ [45].

To relate our analysis to Durán's theory [21], let us elaborate the case $\vec{\not{o}} = -+$ in more details, Keeping in mind that

$$\Theta_{-+}[\eta] = 1 + \eta \tag{107}$$

and choosing $\lambda_+ = \alpha$, $\lambda_- = -\beta$, so the function (89) takes form:

$$f[\eta; -\beta, \alpha| -+, 0] = (1+\eta)^{-\beta}, \tag{108}$$

we can re-write the Wronskian in the denominator of the fraction (85) as

$$W\{\phi_{m_{k=1,2,\ldots,p}}[\eta; -\beta, \alpha]\} = \phi_0^p[\eta; -\beta, \alpha]\Omega_{0/\mu}^{(\alpha,\beta)}, \tag{109}$$

where the polynomial

$$\Omega_{0/\mu}^{(\alpha,\beta)} = (1+\eta)^{p\beta}\, W\{f[\eta; -\beta, \alpha| -+, m_1], \ldots, f[\eta; -\beta, \alpha| -+, m_p]\} \tag{110}$$

is defined via (2.7) in [45] with $\mu := m_1 + p - 1, m_2 + p - 2, \ldots m_p$ and we also took into account that

$$\phi_0[\eta; \beta, \alpha](1+\eta)^{-\beta} = \phi_0[\eta; -\beta, \alpha]. \tag{111}$$

Comparing (109) with (66), we conclude that

$$\Omega_{0/\mu}^{(\alpha,\beta)} = W_{\mathcal{N}(\overline{M}_p)}^{(\alpha,-\beta)}[\eta|\overline{M}_p], \tag{112}$$

And, therefore, the requirement for the JPW in question not to have zeros in the closed interval [−1, +1] is the particular case of Lemma 5.1 and Theorem 6.3 in [22].

Similarly, we re-write the Wronskian in the numerator of the fraction (85) as

$$\begin{gathered} W\{\phi_{m_{k=1,\ldots,p}}[\eta; -\beta, \alpha], \phi_j[\eta; \beta, \alpha]\} = \phi_0^{p+1}[\eta; \beta, \alpha] \\ \times W\{f[\eta; \alpha, -\beta| -+, m_1], \ldots, f[\eta; \alpha, -\beta| -+, m_p], P_j^{(\alpha,\beta)}(\eta)\}, \end{gathered} \tag{113}$$

while setting $\vec{\not{o}} = -+$ and $\lambda_+ = \alpha$, $\lambda_- = -\beta$, in (91) and (96) gives

$$\begin{gathered} W\{\phi_{m_{k=1,\ldots,p}}[\eta; -\beta, \alpha], \phi_j[\eta; \beta, \alpha]\} = \phi_0^{p+1}[\eta; -\beta, \alpha] \\ \times (1+\eta)^{-\beta-p}\, P_{\mathcal{N}(\overline{M}_p)+j}[\eta; -\beta, \alpha|\overline{M}_p; -+, j]. \end{gathered} \tag{114}$$

Re-expressing (113) in terms of X-Jacobi polynomials (2.31) in [45]:

$$\begin{aligned} & \mathrm{P}_{0/\!\!\mu,\,p+j}^{(\alpha,\beta)} := (1+\eta)^{(\beta+1)p} \\ & \times \mathrm{W}\{f[\eta;\alpha,-\beta|-+,m_1],\ldots,f[\eta;\alpha,-\beta|-+,m_p],\mathrm{P}_j^{(\alpha,\beta)}(\eta)\}, \end{aligned} \tag{115}$$

making use of (111), and comparing the resultant expression

$$\mathrm{W}\{\phi_{m_{k=1,\ldots,p}}[\eta;-\beta,\alpha],\phi_j[\eta;\beta,\alpha]\} = \phi_0^{p+1}[\eta;-\beta,\alpha](1+\eta)^{-\beta-p}\mathrm{P}_{0/\!\!\mu,\,p+j}^{(\alpha,\beta)} \tag{116}$$

with (114) shows that

$$\mathrm{P}_{0/\!\!\mu,\,p+j}^{(\alpha,\beta)} \equiv \mathscr{P}_{\mathscr{N}(\overline{M}_p)+j}[\eta;-\beta,\alpha|\overline{M}_p;\,-+,j]. \tag{117}$$

Coming back to the q-RSs (85) for the simple p-WPs of the general type $\vec{\not{\sigma}} \neq ++$, note that the numerator of the fraction has the form:

$$\begin{aligned} \mathrm{W}\{\phi_{m_{k=1,\ldots,p}}[\eta;\vec{\lambda}],\phi_j[\eta;\vec{\lambda}']\} &= \phi_0^p[\eta;\vec{\lambda}]\Theta_{\vec{\not{\sigma}}}^{-p}[\eta]\phi_0[\eta;\vec{\lambda}'] \\ & \times \mathscr{P}_{\mathscr{N}(\overline{M}_p;\,\vec{\not{\sigma}},0)+j}[\eta;\vec{\lambda}|\overline{M}_p;\,\vec{\not{\sigma}},j] \end{aligned} \tag{118}$$

Making use of the identity

$$\Theta_{\vec{\not{\sigma}}}^{-p}[\eta]\phi_0[\eta;\vec{\lambda}'] = \phi_0[\eta;\vec{\lambda}' + p(\vec{\not{\sigma}} \times \vec{1} - \vec{1})], \tag{119}$$

we can then re-write (118) as

$$\begin{aligned} \mathrm{W}\{\phi_{m_{k=1,\ldots,p}}[\eta;\vec{\lambda}],\phi_j[\eta;\vec{\lambda}']\} &= \phi_0^p[\eta;\vec{\lambda}]\phi_0[\eta;\vec{\lambda}' + p(\vec{\not{\sigma}} \times \vec{1} - \vec{1})] \\ & \times \mathscr{P}_{\mathscr{N}(\overline{M}_p;\,\vec{\not{\sigma}},0)+j}[\eta;\vec{\lambda}|\overline{M}_p;\,\vec{\not{\sigma}},j], \end{aligned} \tag{120}$$

so the fraction takes the sought-for form:

$$\phi_{\vec{\not{\sigma}},j}[\eta;\vec{\lambda}|\overline{M}_p] = \phi_0[\eta;\vec{\not{\sigma}} \times (\vec{\lambda} + p\,\vec{1})]\frac{\mathscr{P}_{\mathscr{N}(\overline{M}_p;\,\vec{\not{\sigma}},0)+j}[\eta;\vec{\lambda}|\overline{M}_p;\,\vec{\not{\sigma}},j]}{\mathrm{W}_{\mathscr{N}(\overline{M}_p)}^{(\lambda_+,\lambda_-)}[\eta|\overline{M}_p]}. \tag{121}$$

Setting p = 1, $\overline{M}_1$ = m brings us to (124)–(125) in [1], as expected.

Let us now point to the very unique feature of the simple p-WP in the numerator of the PF in the right-hand side of (121):

Theorem 4. *The simple* p-WP *(97) does not have zeros at* ∓ 1, *assuming that both Jacobi indexes are non-integers.*

Proof. First, let us remind the reader that the ExpDiff for the pole of the RCSLE (67) at ∓ 1 and the corresponding ChExps are equal to $|\lambda_\pm + p|$ and, respectively $1/2 + |\lambda_\pm + p|$, $1/2 - |\lambda_\pm + p|$. On other hand, examination of the power function in front of the PF reveals that the power exponent of $\eta \pm 1$ coincides with one of these ChExps. For the p-WP in question to vanish at ∓ 1, the corresponding ExpDiff must be a positive integer, contradicts to the assumption that both Jacobi indexes are non-integers. □

As illuminated in the next Section, Theorem 4 assures that the p-WPs in question satisfy a FPDE and, therefore, form a X-DPS in our terminology.

6. X-Jacobi DPSs Composed of Simple p-WPs

Our next step is to prove that both JPW (65) and all three p-WPs in the numerator of the fraction in the right-hand side of (121) for $\vec{\phi} \neq ++$ constitute polynomial solutions of the second-order FPDEs. To construct the latter FPDEs, we make the four alternative gauge transformations

$$\Phi[\eta;\vec{\lambda}_o;\varepsilon|\overline{M}_p] = \phi_0[\eta;\vec{\lambda}|\overline{M}_p;\vec{\phi}] \times F[\eta;\vec{\lambda}_o;\varepsilon|\overline{M}_p;\vec{\phi}], \tag{122}$$

with the gauge functions

$$\phi_0[\eta;\vec{\lambda}|\overline{M}_p;\vec{\phi}] = \frac{\phi_0[\eta;\vec{\phi}\times(\vec{\lambda}+p\,\vec{1})]}{W^{(\lambda_+,\lambda_-)}_{\mathcal{N}(\overline{M}_p)}[\eta|\overline{M}_p]}, \tag{123}$$

satisfying the RCSLE

$$\ddot{\phi}_0[\eta;\vec{\lambda}|\overline{M}_p;\vec{\phi}] + \left\{ I^o_0[\eta;\vec{\lambda}|\overline{M}_p] - \frac{\varepsilon_0(\vec{\lambda}' + \vec{\phi}\times p\vec{1})}{\eta^2-1} \right\} \phi_0[\eta;\vec{\lambda}|\overline{M}_p;\vec{\phi}] = 0, \tag{124}$$

where

$$\begin{aligned} I^o_0[\eta;\vec{\lambda}|\overline{M}_p] &:= I^o[\eta;\vec{\lambda}+p\vec{1}] + 2\widehat{Q}[\eta;\overline{\eta}^{(\mathcal{N})}(\vec{\lambda}|\overline{M}_p)] \\ &+ 2\,ld\,\phi_0[\eta;\vec{\phi}\times(\vec{\lambda}+p\,\vec{1})]\,ld\,W^{(\lambda_+,\lambda_-)}_{\mathcal{N}(\overline{M}_p)}[\eta|\overline{M}_p], \end{aligned} \tag{125}$$

with [28]

$$\begin{aligned} \widehat{Q}[\eta;\overline{\eta}] &:= -1/2\,\Pi_m[\eta;\overline{\eta}]\frac{d^2}{d\eta^2}\Pi_m^{-1}[\eta;\overline{\eta}] \\ &= 1/2\frac{\ddot{\Pi}_m[\eta;\overline{\eta}]}{\Pi_m[\eta;\overline{\eta}]} - \frac{\dot{\Pi}^2_m[\eta;\overline{\eta}]}{\Pi^2_m[\eta;\overline{\eta}]}. \end{aligned} \tag{126}$$

The PF (126) is related to the Quesne PF [52–54]

$$Q[\eta;\overline{\eta}] := \frac{\ddot{\Pi}_m[\eta;\overline{\eta}]}{\Pi_m[\eta;\overline{\eta}]} - \frac{\dot{\Pi}^2_m[\eta;\overline{\eta}]}{\Pi^2_m[\eta;\overline{\eta}]} \tag{127}$$

in the elementary fashion:

$$\widehat{Q}[\eta;\overline{\eta}] = Q[\eta;\overline{\eta}] + \frac{\ddot{\Pi}_m[\eta;\overline{\eta}]}{2\Pi_m[\eta;\overline{\eta}]}, \tag{128}$$

$$= -\sum_{l=1}^{m}\frac{1}{[\eta-\eta_l]^2} + \frac{\ddot{\Pi}_m[\eta;\overline{\eta}]}{2\Pi_m[\eta;\overline{\eta}]}. \tag{129}$$

In our earlier works [28,55], we adopted the Quesne PF in the form (127) (see, i.g., (39) in [54], with $g^{(\alpha)}_{\mu}$ standing for $\Pi_m[\eta;\overline{\eta}]$ here), overlooking its alternative form (82), without any mixed simple poles at $\eta_{l=1,\ldots,m}$.

We are now ready to prove the assertion made by us at the beginning of the section:

Theorem 5. *The polynomials (97) satisfy the second-order FPDEs and, therefore, form four distinguished X-Jacobi DPSs.*

Proof. Substituting (122) into the RCSLE (67) and taking advantage of (125), coupled with (83), (124) and (129), we come to the second-order PDE:

$$\{D_\eta(\vec{\lambda}|\overline{M}_p;\vec{\phi}) + C_{\mathcal{N}(\overline{M}_p)}[\eta;\vec{\lambda};\varepsilon|\overline{M}_p;\vec{\phi}]\}F[\eta;\vec{\lambda}_o;\varepsilon|\overline{M}_p;\vec{\phi}] = 0, \tag{130}$$

where $D_\eta(\vec{\lambda}|\overline{M}_p;\vec{\phi})$ is an abbreviated notation for the second-order differential operator in η:

$$\begin{aligned} D_\eta(\vec{\lambda}|\overline{M}_p;\vec{\phi}) &= (1-\eta^2)W^{(\lambda_+,\lambda_-)}_{\mathcal{N}(\overline{M}_p)}[\eta|\overline{M}_p]\tfrac{d^2}{d\eta^2} \\ &+2B_{\mathcal{N}(\overline{M}_p)+1}[\eta;\vec{\lambda}|\overline{M}_p;\vec{\phi}]\tfrac{d}{d\eta} \end{aligned} \tag{131}$$

with the polynomial coefficient function of the first derivative

$$\begin{aligned} B_{\mathcal{N}(\overline{M}_p)+1}[\eta;\vec{\lambda}|\overline{M}_p;\vec{\phi}] &:= (1-\eta^2)\,W^{(\lambda_+,\lambda_-)}_{\mathcal{N}(\overline{M}_p)}[\eta|\overline{M}_p] \\ &\times\left(\sum_{\aleph=\pm}\frac{\phi_\aleph(\lambda_\aleph+p)+1}{2(\eta-\aleph 1)} - \sum_{l=1}^{\mathcal{N}(\overline{M}_p)}\frac{1}{\eta-\eta_l(\vec{\lambda};\overline{M}_p)}\right). \end{aligned} \tag{132}$$

The ε-dependent polynomial of degree m representing the free term of the PDE (130) is linear in the energy:

$$C_{\mathcal{N}(\overline{M}_p)}[\eta;\vec{\lambda};\varepsilon|\overline{M}_p;\vec{\phi}] = C_{\mathcal{N}(\overline{M}_p)}[\eta;\vec{\lambda}|\overline{M}_p;\vec{\phi}] - \varepsilon W^{(\lambda_+,\lambda_-)}_{\mathcal{N}(\overline{M}_p)}[\eta|\overline{M}_p], \tag{133}$$

with the energy-independent part represented by the following polynomial of degree $\mathcal{N}(\overline{M}_p)$:

$$\begin{aligned} &C_{\mathcal{N}(\overline{M}_p)}[\eta;\vec{\lambda}|\overline{M}_p;\vec{\phi}] + \varepsilon_0(\vec{\lambda}' + \vec{\phi}\times p\vec{1})W^{(\lambda_+,\lambda_-)}_{\mathcal{N}(\overline{M}_p)}[\eta|\overline{M}_p] \\ &= (1-\eta^2)W^{(\lambda_+,\lambda_-)}_{\mathcal{N}(\overline{M}_p)}[\eta|\overline{M}_p]\left\{I^o[\eta;\vec{\lambda}|\overline{M}_p] - I^o_0[\eta;\vec{\lambda}|\overline{M}_p]\right\} \\ &= 2P_1^{(\lambda'_++\phi_+p-1,\lambda'_-+\phi_-p-1)}(\eta)\dot{W}^{(\lambda_+,\lambda_-)}_{\mathcal{N}(\overline{M}_p)}[\eta|\overline{M}_p] \\ &\quad+(1-\eta^2)\ddot{W}^{(\lambda_+,\lambda_-)}_{\mathcal{N}(\overline{M}_p)}[\eta|\overline{M}_p]. \end{aligned} \tag{134}$$

The crucial point is that the polynomial coefficient of the second derivative in (131) has exactly $\mathcal{N}(\overline{M}_p)+2$ simple zeros while the degrees of the polynomials (132) and (134) are equal to $\mathcal{N}(\overline{M}_p)+1$ and $\mathcal{N}(\overline{M}_p)$ [25], which completes the proof. □

Setting $\vec{\phi} = -+$, $\lambda_- = -\beta$, $\lambda_+ = \alpha$ in (132) and (134), we come to the FPDE cited in Durán's Theorem 5.2 in [22] with $k_1 = 0$, $k_2 = p$:

$$\begin{aligned} h_1(\eta) &:= \frac{2B_{\mathcal{N}(\overline{M}_p)+1}[\eta;-\beta,\alpha|\overline{M}_p;-]}{W^{(\alpha,-\beta)}_{\mathcal{N}(\overline{M}_p)}[\eta|\overline{M}_p]} \\ &= \beta-\alpha-2p-(\alpha+\beta+2)\eta-(1-\eta^2)\dot{W}^{(\alpha,-\beta)}_{\mathcal{N}(\overline{M}_p)}[\eta|\overline{M}_p] \\ h_0(\eta) &:= C_{\mathcal{N}(\overline{M}_p)}[\eta;-\beta,\alpha|\overline{M}_p;-+] + \varepsilon_0(\beta-p,\alpha+p)W^{(\alpha,-\beta)}_{\mathcal{N}(\overline{M}_p)}[\eta|\overline{M}_p] \\ &= \alpha-\beta+2p+(\alpha+\beta)\eta\dot{W}^{(\alpha,-\beta)}_{\mathcal{N}(\overline{M}_p)}[\eta|\overline{M}_p] - (\eta^2-1)\ddot{W}^{(\lambda_+,\lambda_-)}_{\mathcal{N}(\overline{M}_p)}[\eta|\overline{M}_p] \end{aligned} \tag{135}$$

7. Prime Forms of RDC$\mathscr{T}$s of the J-Ref CSLE Solved Under DBCs on Intervals (−1, +1) and (1, ∞)

Starting from this point, we discuss only the admissible sets $\overline{M}_p = m_1, \ldots, m_p$ of JS solutions assuring that the corresponding JPWs do not have nodes within the given orthogonalization interval for the specified ranges of the parameters λ_-, λ_+.

Using the gauge transformations

$$\Psi[\eta; \vec{\lambda}; \varepsilon|\overline{M}_p] = (1-\eta^2)^{-1/2}\, \Phi[\eta; \vec{\lambda}; \varepsilon|\overline{M}_p] \tag{136}$$

and

$$\Psi[\eta; \vec{\lambda}; \underline{\varepsilon}|\overline{M}_p] = (\eta-1)^{-1/2}\, \Phi[\eta; \vec{\lambda}; \underline{\varepsilon}|\overline{M}_p], \tag{137}$$

we then convert the RCSLE (67) to its prime forms on the intervals $(-1,+1)$ and $(+1,\infty)$:

$$\left\{\tfrac{d}{d\eta}(1-\eta^2)\tfrac{d}{d\eta} - q[\eta; \vec{\lambda}|\overline{M}_p] + \varepsilon\right\} \Psi[\eta; \vec{\lambda}; \varepsilon|\overline{M}_p] = 0 \quad \text{for } \eta \in (-1,+1) \tag{138}$$

and

$$\left\{\tfrac{d}{d\eta}(\eta-1)\tfrac{d}{d\eta} - q[\eta; \vec{\lambda}|\overline{M}_p] + \tfrac{\underline{\varepsilon}}{\eta+1}\right\} \Psi[\eta; \vec{\lambda}; \underline{\varepsilon}|\overline{M}_p] = 0 \quad \text{for } \eta \in (1,\infty), \tag{139}$$

with the leading coefficient function and weight function defined via to (28) and (32), respectively. It is worth reminding the reader the main reasoning behind these particular transformations [19], namely, the leading coefficient functions in both cases were chosen in such a way that the ChExps at each of the singular endpoints have opposite signs and as a result the DBC imposed at the given end unambiguously determines the regular solution (or the PFS as we term it here).

In this paper we only discuss the seed solutions represented by the PFSs near the same endpoint under condition that they lie below the lowest eigenvalue. Since the RDCTs using the seed functions of types + − and − + are specified by same series of the Maya diagrams [21], any RCSLE using an arbitrary combination of these seed functions can be alternatively obtained by considering only infinitely many combinations $\overline{M}_p := \{m_1, m_2, \ldots, m_p\}$ of the PFSs of the same type + − or − + [21,56,57]. In particular, the Jacobi polynomial of order m with the indexes $\vec{\lambda}$ can be represented as the Wronskian of Jacobi polynomials of the sequential degrees $\tilde{m} = 1, \ldots, m$ with the indexes $-\vec{\lambda}$. The simplest case m = 2 is discussed in Appendix E.

Note that Gómez-Ullate et al. [24,45] derived the general expression for the X_m-Jacobi OPS, taking advantage of the Klein formulas [25] to select all the Jacobi polynomials without zeros between −1 and +1 under the constraint

$$\lambda_+ = -\alpha - 1 < 0, \;\; \lambda_- = \beta - 1 > -2,$$

whereas our approach allows us to identify only the bulk part of those polynomials with one of the first Jacobi indexes restricted solely to positive values. For the multi-indexed X-Jacobi OPSs the admissibility of the given set of seed Jacobi polynomials for the finite orthogonalization interval was thoroughly analyzed by Durán [22].

In this Section we consider the admissibility problem in parallel for both the finite and infinite orthogonalization intervals. While our study of the multi-indexed X-Jacobi OPSs constitutes the particular case of Durán's analysis, the results for the RDC$\mathscr{T}$s of the R-Jacobi polynomials constitute the state-of-the-art development. In particular, we prove that the Wronskians of the R-Jacobi polynomials with the common first and second Jacobi indexes, respectively positive and negative do not have zeros in the interval $[-1, +1]$ while the Wronskians of the classical Jacobi polynomials with common positive indexes may only have real zeros smaller than 1.

To determine the admissible sets $\overline{M}_p$ of seed Jacobi polynomials, we introduce the sequence of the q-RTFs

$$\psi_{++,m_{p+1}}[\eta;\vec{\lambda}\,|\overline{M}_p] = \psi_0[\eta;\lambda_- + p, \lambda_+ + p]\frac{\mathscr{P}_{\mathcal{N}(\overline{M}_{p+1})}[\eta;\vec{\lambda}\,|\overline{M}_p; ++, m_{p+1}]}{W^{(\lambda_+,\lambda_-)}_{\mathcal{N}(\overline{M}_p)}[\eta|\overline{M}_p]} \tag{140}$$

by setting $\vec{\phi} = +,+$ in (85) and also taking into account that the solutions of the p-SLEs (138) and (139) are related to the solutions of the RCSLE (67) via the gauge transformations (136) and (137), i.e.,

$$\psi_0[\eta;\beta,\alpha] = \begin{cases} (1+\eta)^{1/2\beta}(1-\eta)^{1/2\alpha} & \text{for } |\eta| < 1, \\ (1+\eta)^{1/2(\beta+1)}(\eta-1)^{1/2\alpha} & \text{for } \eta > 1. \end{cases} \tag{141}$$

While the sequences of the q-RSs (140) on the infinite interval are unlimited, we have to truncate the chain of the sequential RRZTs of the p-SLE (138) when the ExpDiff for the pole at -1 reaches its minimum value

$$0 < {*\lambda}^{(p_{max})}_{o;-} = \lambda_{o;-} - p_{max} < 1 \tag{142}$$

with

$$p_{max} = \lfloor \lambda_{o;-} \rfloor. \tag{143}$$

Below we always assume that p in (140) for $|\eta| < 1$ does not exceed (143), without explicitly mentioning this restriction.

Below we consider only the Wronskian net of the Jacobi polynomials with the indexes

$$\lambda_{\mp} = \mp\lambda_{o;\mp} \ \text{ for } |\eta| < 1 \text{ and } \vec{\lambda} = \vec{\lambda}_o \text{ for } \eta > 1, \tag{144}$$

while

$$\lambda'_{\mp} = \mp\lambda_{\mp} \ (\vec{\phi} = -+) \ \text{ in both cases.} \tag{145}$$

We refer to the X-Jacobi DPS constructed using p seed Jacobi polynomials of the degrees $m_1, m_2, \ldots, m_p$ as being of series J1(p). The selection (144), (145) for the p-WEOP sequences under consideration is consistent with (2.9) in [45], with $\alpha = \lambda_{o;+}, \beta = \lambda_{o;-}$.

Our next step is to prove that the q-RSs (140) constitute the PFSs near the singular endpoint +1 whether or not the polynomial denominator of the PF on the right has zeros inside the corresponding orthogonalization interval. Though the theorem stated below represents the very specific case of the general proposition proven in Appendix C, we feel useful to present an independent proof for the case of our current interest, which may be more appealing to the reader due to its simplicity.

Theorem 6. *The q-RSs (140) satisfy the DBC at the endpoint + 1.*

Proof. Based on Theorem 1, we first confirm that the JPW in the denominator of the PF in the right-hand side of (140) remains finite at η = +1, keeping in mind that $\lambda_+ = \lambda_{o;+} > 0$ in both cases. Examination of the q-RS (140) with $\alpha = \lambda_{o;+} + p$ then shows that it vanishes at η = +1, which completes the proof. □

It will be proven later that the q-RSs

$$\psi\!\!\!/_{-,j}[\eta; \vec{\lambda}\,|\overline{\mathtt{M}}_{\mathrm{p}}] = \psi\!\!\!/_{0}[\eta; -\lambda_{-} - \mathrm{p}, \lambda_{+} + \mathrm{p}]\frac{\mathscr{P}_{\mathcal{N}(\overline{\mathtt{M}}_{\mathrm{p}},-\,+,0)+\mathrm{j}}[\eta; \vec{\lambda}\,|\overline{\mathtt{M}}_{\mathrm{p}}; -\,,\mathrm{j}]}{W^{(\lambda_{+},\lambda_{-})}_{\mathcal{N}(\overline{\mathtt{M}}_{\mathrm{p}})}[\eta|\overline{\mathtt{M}}_{\mathrm{p}}]} \quad \text{for } 0 \leq \mathrm{j} \leq \mathrm{j}_{\max} \tag{146}$$

represent the eigenfunctions of the *p*-SLEs (138) or (139) if $\overline{\mathtt{M}}_{\mathrm{p}}$ is an admissible set, but before making the latter assumption, let us first show that

Theorem 7. *The q-RSs (146), with $\vec{\lambda}$ given by (144), satisfy the DBCs at the ends of the corresponding orthogonalization interval, l whether or not the JPW at the denominator of the PF in the right-hand side of (146) have zeros inside this interval.*

Proof. Setting $\alpha = \lambda_{o;+} + \mathrm{p}$, $\beta = \pm\lambda_{o;-} - \mathrm{p}$ in (146) confirms that the q-RSs in question vanishes at both ends of the interval $[-1, +1]$ as well as at the lower end of the interval $(1, \infty)$.

Furthermore, since the functions $\phi_0[\eta; -\lambda_{o,-}, \lambda_{o;+}]$ and $\phi_0[\eta; -\lambda_{o,-} - \mathrm{p}, \lambda_{o;+} + \mathrm{p}]$ have exactly the same asymptotics at infinity and the eigenfunction (47) of the *p*-SLE (24) on the interval $(+1, \infty)$ vanishes at the upper end by definition, we conclude that the q-RSs (146) also obey the DBC at infinity. □

Starting from this point, we assume that all the RCSLEs generated by the RDCTs with the seed solutions $\mathtt{m}_1, \overline{\mathtt{M}}_2, \ldots, \overline{\mathtt{M}}_{\mathrm{p}}$ have exactly the same energy spectrum and also that none of their poles lies inside the corresponding orthogonalization interval. We then need to prove that this also true for the set $\overline{\mathtt{M}}_{\mathrm{p}}, \mathtt{m}_{\mathrm{p}+1}$.

Corollary 3. *If $\overline{\mathtt{M}}_{\mathrm{p}}$ is an admissible set then the q-RSs (146) on the interval $(-1, +1)$ or $(1,\infty)$ represent the eigenfunctions of the p-SLE (138) or, respectively (139).*

Proof. The assertion directly follows from Theorem 6, since the RCSLE in question does not have singularities inside the orthogonalization interval. □

As pointed out in Section 3.1, the q-RS solutions of the JRef CSLE (1) with the polynomial components composed of the R-Jacobi polynomials (type $\mathfrak{b}$) represent PFSs of the *p*-SLE (24) near the pole at the upper end of the interval $(-1, +1)$ and lie below the lowest eigenvalue (42) of the corresponding SLP. We thus conclude that the PFSs (140) of the *p*-SLE (138) lie below the eigenvalue $\varepsilon_0(\vec{\lambda}')$.

Similarly, the q-RS solutions of the JRef CSLE (1) with the polynomial components composed of the classical Jacobi polynomials (type $\underset{\cdot}{\mathfrak{a}}$) represent PFSs of the *p*-SLE (24) near the pole at the lower end of the interval $(1, \infty)$ and lie below the lowest eigenvalue (56). We thus conclude that the PFSs (140) of the *p*-SLE (139) lie below the eigenvalue $\underset{\tilde{0}}{\varepsilon}(\vec{\lambda}') = -\varepsilon_0(\vec{\lambda}')$.

To confirm that the q-RPFs (140) do not have zeros inside the orthogonalization interval $(-1, +1)$ or $(1, \infty)$, we first need to prove that there is no eigenfunctions below the energies $\varepsilon_0(\vec{\lambda}')$ or accordingly $\underset{\tilde{0}}{\varepsilon}(\vec{\lambda}')$, i.e., that the latter are indeed the lowest eigenvalues of the *p*-SLE (138) or, respectively (139). To verify the latter assertion, we take advantage of the powerful theorem proven in Appendix D, which assures that the q-RPF (140), starting the sequence (j = 0), does not have zeros inside the given the orthogonalization interval.

The final preposition to prove that the PFSs lying below the eigenvalue in question do not have zeros inside this interval either.

Theorem 8. *A PFS near one of the endpoints ± 1 may not have zeros inside the given interval of orthogonalization if it lies below the lowest eigenvalue of the given Sturm-Liouville problem.*

Proof. For the Sturm–Liouville problem on the orthogonalization interval (−1, +1) the formulated assertion directly follows from the Sturm comparison theorem (see, i.g., Theorem 3.1 in Section XI of Hartman's monograph [58]), keeping in mind that the logarithmic derivatives for all the PFSs (including the eigenfunction in question) have the same asymptotics near the pole in question:

$$\lim_{\eta\to-1}\left[(1-\eta^2)\,ld\Psi[\eta;\lambda_{o;-},\lambda_+;\varepsilon|-+\vdots\overline{M}_p]\right]=-*\lambda_{o;-}^{(p)}, \tag{147}$$

and as a result the condition (3.4) in [58] turns into the identity. To apply the Sturm Theorem to the PFSs near the upper end +1, one simply needs to replace η for the reflected argument $-\eta$.

It is a more challenging problem to satisfy Sturm's constraint for the logarithmic derivatives in the limit $\eta\to\infty$ and we refer the reader to the proof of this assertion given in Appendix B in [1] for the PFSs of the *p*-SLE (24) solved under the DBCs at the ends of the interval (+1, ∞). The arguments presented in support of this proof are equally applied to the *p*-SLE (139) without any modification. □

Corollary 4. *The JPW (65) does not have zeros inside the corresponding orthogonalization interval assuming that the Jacobi indexes restricted by the conditions (144) and (145) and the order of the given RDCT on the interval (−1, +1) does not exceed the upper bound (143).*

It has been proven in [20] that the eigenfunctions of the generic SLE solved under the DBCs must be mutually orthogonal with the SLE weight function on the interval in question. Therefore,

$$\int_{\eta_-}^{\eta_+} d\eta\, \psi_{c,j}[\eta;\vec{\lambda}\,|\overline{M}_p]\psi_{c,j'}[\eta;\vec{\lambda}\,|\overline{M}_p]w[\eta]=0 \quad \text{for } 0\le j'<j\le j_{max},\ p\le p_{max}. \tag{148}$$

Consequently, the polynomial components of the quasi-rational eigenfunctions (146) must be mutually orthogonal with the weight function

$$W[\eta;\vec{\lambda}\,|\overline{M}_p;-+]:=\frac{\psi_0^2[\eta;-\lambda_--p,\lambda_++p]}{W^{(\lambda_+,\lambda_-)}_{\mathcal{N}(\overline{M}_p)}[\eta|\overline{M}_p]}w[\eta]\ \ (p\le p_{max}) \quad \text{for } |\eta|<1 \text{ or } \eta>1; \tag{149}$$

namely,

$$\int_{\eta_-}^{\eta_+} d\eta\, \mathscr{P}_{\mathcal{N}(\overline{M}_p)+j}[\eta;\vec{\lambda}\,|\overline{M}_p;-+,j]\,\mathscr{P}_{\mathcal{N}(\overline{M}_p)+j'}[\eta;\vec{\lambda}\,|\overline{M}_p;-+,j']\,W[\eta;\vec{\lambda}\,|\overline{M}_p;-+]=0 \quad \text{for } 0\le j'<j\le j_{max},\ p\le p_{max}. \tag{150}$$

In the following two subsections we discuss separately the X Jacobi OPSs on the interval (−1, +1) and the RDC$\mathscr{T}$s of the R–Jacobi polynomials forming finite EOP sequences on the infinite interval (1, ∞).

7.1. Finite Net of X-Jacobi OPSs Generated Using JPWs of R-Jacobi Polynomials with Positive First Index

As mentioned above, the purpose of this subsection is to discuss the finite net of the exactly solvable RCSLEs generated using the JPWs of R–Jacobi polynomials with the positive Jacobi index λ_{+}.

Let us set $\vec{\lambda} = -\lambda_{o;-}, \lambda_{o;+}, \vec{\lambda}' = \vec{\lambda}_o = \beta, \alpha, p_{max} = \lfloor \lambda_{o;-} \rfloor$, and $j_{max} = \infty$. This brings us to the net of the X-Jacobi OPSs composed of the p-WEOPs

$$\begin{gathered} P_{\mathcal{N}(\bar{M}_p)+j}[\eta; -\beta, \alpha|\bar{M}_p; -+, j] :=, \\ \begin{vmatrix} P_{m_1}^{(\alpha,-\beta)}(\eta) & P_{m_2}^{(\alpha,-\beta)}(\eta) & \dots & (1+\eta)^{\beta}\, P_j^{(\alpha,\beta)}(\eta) \\ \frac{d}{d\eta} P_{m_1}^{(\alpha,-\beta)}(\eta) & \frac{d}{d\eta} P_{m_2}^{(\alpha,-\beta)}(\eta) & \dots & P_{j+p-1}^{(1)}[\eta; \beta, \alpha| -+] \\ & \dots & & \\ \frac{d^p}{d^p\eta} P_{m_1}^{(\alpha,-\beta)}(\eta) & \frac{d^p}{d^p\eta} P_{m_2}^{(\alpha,-\beta)}(\eta) & \dots & P_j^{(p)}[\eta; \beta, \alpha| -+] \end{vmatrix}. \end{gathered} \tag{151}$$

Note that the first p elements of the first row are represented by the R–Jacobi polynomials, while the last element is the classical Jacobi polynomial multiplied by the *p*-th power of the first–first degree polynomial (93) with $\vec{\sigma} = -+$. The weight function (149) takes the form:

$$\begin{gathered} W\,[\eta; -\alpha, \beta|\bar{M}_p; -+] := \frac{\psi_0^2[\eta; \beta-p, \alpha+p]}{\left[W_{\mathcal{N}(\bar{M}_p)}^{(\alpha,-\beta)}[\eta\,|\,\bar{M}_p]\right]^2} \\ \text{for} -1 < \eta < 1 \;\; (p \le \lfloor \lambda_{o;-} \rfloor), \end{gathered} \tag{152}$$

where the polynomial Wronskian in the denominator is formed by the orthogonal R–Jacobi polynomials and, therefore is the subject of the general conjectures formulated in [51] for zeros of the Wronskians of orthogonal polynomials inside the normalization interval (real zeros larger than 1 in our case). Corollary 4 assures that this JPW remains finite inside the interval (−1, +1).

Substituting (141) into (152) and comparing the resultant expression

$$\begin{gathered} W\,[\eta; -\alpha, \beta|\bar{M}_p; -+] := \frac{(1+\eta)^{\alpha+p}\,(1-\eta)^{\beta-p}}{\left[W_{\mathcal{N}(\bar{M}_p)}^{(\alpha,-\beta)}[\eta\,|\,\bar{M}_p]\right]^2} \\ \text{for} -1 < \eta < 1 \;\; (p \le \lfloor \lambda_{o;-} \rfloor), \end{gathered} \tag{153}$$

with (2.36) in [22] once again confirms that our definition of the X-Jacobi OPSs apparently corresponds to the partition $\emptyset, \mu$ with $\mu_k := m_k + p - k$ (k = 1, …, p).

Our observation that the seed Jacob polynomials for the X-Jacobi OPSs composed of the simple p-WPs constitutes the finite orthogonal sequence of the R-Jacobi polynomials [1,38] may be useful for deriving some nontrivial properties of the JPWs in question. In particular, based on Theorem 2.1 in [51] (summarizing Karlin and Szego's results [59]), we assert that any Wronskian of an even number of the R–Jacobi polynomials of sequential degrees may have only negative real zeros smaller than −1.

7.2. Infinite Net of Finite EOPS Sequences Generated Using JPWs of Classical Jacobi Polynomials with Positive Indexes

Finally, we come to the discussion of the infinite net of the exactly solvable RCSLEs generated using the JPWs of classical Jacobi polynomials with the positive Jacobi indexes. Conjecture 4 assures that the JPW composed of the seed polynomials in question has no zeros larger than 1, which constitutes the question of fundamental significance for this study. Below we focus solely on the RDCTs using the infinitely many PFS of type a̤ as the seed functions, i.e., by definition $\vec{\lambda} = \vec{\lambda}_o$ and $p_{max} = \infty$. The corresponding eigenfunctions of the p-SLE (24) solved under the DBCs on the interval $(1, \infty)$ are formed by the R-Jacobi polynomials with the Jacobi indexes $\vec{\lambda}' = -\lambda_{o;-}, \lambda_{o;+}$, and their total number is equal to

$$n_{\varsigma} = j_{max} + 1 = \lceil \lambda_{o;-} \rceil. \tag{154}$$

This brings us to the finite net of the finite EOP sequences composed of the p-PWs

$$\mathscr{P}_{\mathcal{N}(\overline{M}_p)+j}[\eta; \lambda_{o;-}, \lambda_{o;+}|\overline{M}_p; -+, j] := \begin{vmatrix} P_{m_1}^{(\lambda_{o;+}, \lambda_{o;-})}(\eta) & P_{m_2}^{(\lambda_{o;+}, \lambda_{o;-})}(\eta) & \dots & \Theta_1^p[\eta]\, P_j^{(\lambda_{o;+}, -\lambda_{o;-})}(\eta) \\ \frac{d}{d\eta} P_{m_1}^{(\lambda_{o;+}, \lambda_{o;-})}(\eta) & \frac{d}{d\eta} P_{m_2}^{(\lambda_{o;+}, \lambda_{o;-})}(\eta) & \dots & P_{j+p-1}^{(1)}[\eta; -\lambda_{o;-}, \lambda_{o;+}| -+] \\ & \dots & & \\ \frac{d^p}{d^p\eta} P_{m_1}^{(\lambda_{o;+}, \lambda_{o;-})}(\eta) & \frac{d^p}{d^p\eta} P_{m_2}^{(\lambda_{o;+}, \lambda_{o;-})}(\eta) & \dots & P_j^{(p)}[\eta; -\lambda_{o;-}, \lambda_{o;+}| -+] \end{vmatrix}. \tag{155}$$

This time the first p elements of the first row are represented by the classical Jacobi polynomials with positive indexes while the last element is the R–Jacobi polynomial multiplied by a constant. The weight function (149) takes the form:

$$W[\eta; \lambda_{o;-}, \lambda_{o;+}| -+; \overline{M}_p] := \frac{\psi_0^2[\eta; -\lambda_{o;-} - p, \lambda_{o;+} + p]}{(\eta+1) W_{\mathcal{N}(\overline{M}_p)}^{(\lambda_{o;+}, \lambda_{o;-})}[\eta|\overline{M}_p]}, \tag{156}$$

where the Wronskian in the denominator is formed by the classical Jacobi polynomials with positive indexes.

Corollary 4 can be now reformulated as

Corollary 5. *The Wronskian of the classical Jacobi polynomials with positive indexes may not have real zeros larger than 1.*

In Appendix E, we explicitly confirm this corollary for the simplest second-degree JPW Wronskian formed by the Jacobi polynomials of degrees 1 and 2.

8. Discussion

Let us first point to the most essential element of our RSLP formalism—the advanced technique for selecting the sequences of the admissible RRZTs, using PFRs below the lowest eigenvalue as the q-RTFs. Each such sequence can then be re-interpreted as the admissible RDCT. To be more precise, we laid down the mathematical grounds for this innovation in Section 7 by converting the RCSLE (67) to its prime forms (138) and (139) on the intervals $(-1, +1)$ and $(1, \infty)$ accordingly and solving the resultant SLEs under the DBCs. The formulated SLPs allowed us to prove [19] that each RD$\mathcal{T}$ of the PFS itself constitutes the PFS of the transformed SLE at the same energy.

In summary, we have constructed three infinite nets of the X-Jacobi DPSs composed of the simple p-WPs. The current analysis was focused on the X-DPSs containing both the X-Jacobi OPSs formed by the RDC$\mathcal{T}$s of the classical Jacobi polynomials and finite EOP sequences formed by the RDC$\mathcal{T}$s of the R-Jacobi polynomials (using the seed R-Jacobi polynomials with the common pair of indexes and, respectively a set of the classical Jacobi polynomials with common pair of positive indexes). For $\vec{\phi} = -+$, $\lambda_- = -\beta$, $\lambda_+ = \alpha$ the constructed X-DPSs obey the second-order FPDEs cited in Theorem 5.2 in [22] with $k_1 = 0$, $k_2 = p$.

The fourth net of the X–Jacobi DPSs is composed of the Wronskians of the Jacobi polynomials with common pair of the indexes. Since the RDCTs generating these X-DPSs cannot be decomposed into the sequence of the admissible RRZTs, we skipped their analysis in this paper. However the infinite and finite orthogonal subsets of these X-DPSs form the eigenfunctions of the RCSLEs constructed from the JRef CSLE (1) using the 'juxtaposed' [60] pairs of its eigenfunctions, provided that the partition λ with $\lambda_k := m_k + p - k$ (k = 1, …, p) is composed of the even-length segments. For the X–Jacobi OPSs this assertion has been proven by Durán [22]. Comparing the weight

$$W\,[\eta;\alpha,\beta|\overline{M}_p;++] := \frac{(1+\eta)^{\alpha+p}\,(1-\eta)^{\beta+p}}{\left[W^{(\alpha,\beta)}_{\mathcal{N}(\overline{M}_p)}[\eta\,|\,\overline{M}_p]\right]^2}, \tag{157}$$

with (2.36) in [45] reveals that we deal with the partition $\lambda, 0'$ with $\lambda_k := m_k + p - k$ (k = 1, …, p).

The 'extension of the Adler theorem [61] to the Wronskians of the R-Jacobi polynomials can be done using the argumentation put forward by us in [49] for the Wronskians of the R-Routh polynomials.

The net of the trigonometric ($|\eta| < 1$) or radial ($\eta > 1$) quantum-mechanical potentials exactly solvable in terms of the constructed infinite or accordingly finite EOP sequences can be obtained in following the prescriptions outlined by us in [1] for p = 1.

The Liouville potentials quantized via the EOPs introduced in Sections 7.1 and 7.2 have the generic form:

$$\begin{aligned} V[\eta;-\lambda_{o;-},\lambda_{o;+}|\overline{M}_p] &= V_{t-PT}[\eta;\vec{\lambda}_o] \\ &+ (1-\eta^2)\left\{I^o[\eta;\vec{\lambda}_o] - I^o[\eta;-\lambda_{o;-},\lambda_{o;+}|\overline{M}_p]\right\} \text{ for } -1<\eta<1, \end{aligned} \tag{158}$$

and

$$\begin{aligned} V[\eta;\vec{\lambda}_o|\overline{M}_p] &= V_{h-PT}[\eta;\vec{\lambda}_o] \\ &+(\eta^2-1)\left\{I^o[\eta;\vec{\lambda}_o] - I^o[\eta;\vec{\lambda}_o|\overline{M}_p]\right\} \text{ for } \eta>1 \end{aligned} \tag{159}$$

after being expressed in terms of the variables:

$$\eta(x) = \mathit{cos}x\ (-\pi < x < 0) \tag{160}$$

and

$$\eta(r) = \mathit{cosh}r\ \ (0 < r < \infty), \tag{161}$$

respectively, where the t-PT potential on the finite interval and the radial h-PT potential are parametrized as follows:

$$V_{t-PT}[\eta(x);\lambda_{o;+},\lambda_{o;-}] = \frac{\lambda^2_{o;+} - 1/4}{4\mathit{sin}^2 x/2} + \lambda^2_{o;-} - 1/4/4\mathit{cos}^2\frac{x}{2}\ \ (-\pi < x < 0), \tag{162}$$

and

$$V_{h-PT}(r;\lambda_{o;+},\lambda_{o;-}) = \frac{\lambda^2_{o;+} - 1/4}{4\mathit{sinh}^2 r/2} + \lambda^2_{o;-} - 1/4/4\mathit{cosh}^2\frac{r}{2}\ \ (0 < r < \infty). \tag{163}$$

As mentioned in [1], the rigorous mathematical studies [30,47] on the X–Jacobi and X-Laguerre OPSs made a few misleading references to the quantum-mechanical applications of the EOPs. To a certain extent this misinformation is traceable to the fact that the cited applications do not properly distinguish between the terms 'X–Jacobi DPS', 'X–Jacobi OPS', and 'finite EOP' sequences' (formed by the RD$\mathcal{T}$s of the R-Jacobi polynomials), simply referring to the representatives of all the three manifolds as 'X–Jacobi polynomials'.

To be more precise, one has to distinguish between the X–Jacobi OPSs and the finite EOP sequences formed by the RDC$\mathcal{T}$s of the three families of the Romanovski polynomials [16]; namely, the finite EOP sequences composed of the Romanovski–Bessel (R–Bessel) and Romanovski–Routh (R–Routh) polynomials analyzed by us in [62] and [49], respectively, as well as the RDC$\mathcal{T}$s of the R–Jacobi polynomials discussed in this paper. The associated Liouville potentials all belong to group A in Odake and Sasaki's [48] classification scheme of the translationally shape-invariant potentials (TSIPs) and as a result their eigenfunctions are expressible via the finite EOP sequences.

In the general case of the rational density function, allowing the solution of the JRef CSLE in terms of hypergeometric functions [26], the energy-dependent PF in (1) has second-order poles in the finite plane and as a result the associated Liouville potentials are quantized by the Jacobi polynomials with degree-dependent indexes. If the numerator of the given rational density function has no zeros at regular points of the JRef CSLE (or similarly of its confluent counterpart), then the associated Liouville potential turns into a TSIP of group B, with eigenfunctions expressible via the Jacobi (or, respectively Laguerre) polynomials with at least one degree-dependent index, which have no direct relation to the theory of the EOPs.

To conclude, let us point to the crucial difference between the RDC$\mathcal{T}$s of the R-Jacobi polynomials and those of the R-Bessel and R-Routh polynomials analyzed by us in [62] and [49], respectively. The common feature of the latter RDCT nets is that each net is specified by a single series of Maya diagrams and, as a result, any finite EOP sequence allows the Wronskian representation [57]. On the other hand, the complete net of the RDCT$\mathcal{T}$s of the R–Jacobi polynomials is specified by the two series of Maya diagrams, similar to the RDC$\mathcal{T}$s in the classical Jacobi and classical Laguerre polynomials forming the X-Jacobi and X-Laguerre OPSs accordingly [21]. This implies that we managed to construct only a narrow manifold of the finite EOP sequences composed of the RDC$\mathcal{T}$s of the R–Jacobi polynomials.

For example, we can use different combinations of the PFSs $\underset{\sim}{\mathrm{a}}, \mathrm{k}$ and $\underset{\sim}{\mathrm{a}}', \mathrm{k}'$ below the lowest eigenvalue to construct the PFSs of the transformed RCSLEs. We refer the reader to [21] for the scrupulous analysis of the equivalence relations between the various p-WPs. It should be however stressed that grouping the equivalent p-WPs together represents only a part of the problem. The next step would be to select the preferable representation. For example, the RD$\mathcal{T}$ of the h-PT with the TF $\underset{\sim}{\mathrm{b}}, \mathrm{m}$ seems easier to deal with, compared with the RDC$\mathcal{T}$ of this potential with the m seed functions $\underset{\sim}{\mathrm{a}}, \mathrm{k} = 1, 2, \ldots, \mathrm{m}$, though the final results will be absolutely the same.

The additional complication comes from the fact that one has to analyze the order of p-WP zeros at ∓ 1 to construct the appropriate X-Jacobi DPSs. In this respect, Lemma 2.9 and Theorem 5.2 in [22] present the powerful alternative tool to generate the solved-by-polynomials FPDEs which, as proven in [22], do not have poles inside the interval $(-1, +1)$. However, to select finite EOP sequences from the constructed X-DPSs, one has to find the ranges of the parameters $\lambda_{\mp}$ such that the poles in question lie outside the infinite interval $(-1, \infty)$, which is the challenging problem of its own.

Funding: This research received no external funding.

Data Availability Statement: The original contributions presented in this study are included in the article.

Conflicts of Interest: The author declares no conflicts of interest.

Abbreviations

ChExp	characteristic exponent
CSLE	canonical Sturm-Liouville equation
DBC	Dirichlet boundary condition
DPS	differential polynomial system
DCT	Darboux-Crum transformation
DC$\mathscr{T}$	Darboux-Crum transform
DT	Darboux deformation
D$\mathscr{T}$	Darboux transform
EOP	exceptional orthogonal polynomial
ExpDiff	exponent difference
FPDE	Fuchsian differential equation with polynomial coefficients
GDT	generalized Darboux transformation
h-PT	hyperbolic Pöschl-Teller
JPW	Jacobi-polynomial Wronskian
JRef	Jacobi-reference
JS	Jacobi-seed
LC	limit circle
LDT	Liouville-Darboux transformation
LP	limit point
ODE	ordinary differential equation
OPS	orthogonal polynomial system
PD	polynomial determinant
PDE	polynomial differential equation
PF	polynomial fraction
PFS	principal Frobenius solution
p-SLE	prime Sturm-Liouville equation
p-WP	pseudo-Wronskian polynomial
p-WEOP	pseudo-Wronskian exceptional orthogonal polynomial
p-W$\mathscr{T}$	pseudo-Wronskian transform
q-RPFSs	quasi-rational principal Frobenius solution
q-RS	quasi-rational solution
q-RTF	quasi-rational transformation function
RCSLE	rational canonical Sturm-Liouville equation
RDC	rational Darboux-Crum
RDCT	rational Darboux-Crum transformation
RDC$\mathscr{T}$	rational Darboux-Crum transform
RDT	rational Darboux transformation
RD$\mathscr{T}$	rational Darboux transform
R-Jacobi	Romanovski-Jacobi
R-Routh	Romanovski-Routh
RRZ$\mathscr{T}$	rational Rudjak-Zakharov transform
TF	transformation function
W$\mathscr{T}$	Wronskian transform

Appendix A. RZT of Generic CSLE

Let $\phi_{\tau}[\eta; \vec{\lambda}_{o}]$ be a nodeless solution of a CSLE

$$\left\{ \frac{d^2}{d\eta^2} + I^{o}[\eta; \vec{\lambda}_{o}] + \varepsilon\, \rho[\eta] \right\} \Phi[\eta; \vec{\lambda}_{o}; \varepsilon] = 0 \tag{A1}$$

at the energy

$$\varepsilon = \varepsilon_{\tau}(\vec{\lambda}_{o}), \tag{A2}$$

i.e.,

$$\left\{ \frac{d^2}{d\eta^2} + I^{o}[\eta; \vec{\lambda}_{o}] + \varepsilon_{\tau}(\vec{\lambda}_{o})\, \rho[\eta] \right\} \phi_{\tau}[\eta; \vec{\lambda}_{o}] = 0. \tag{A3}$$

We define the RZT of the given CSLE via the requirement that the function

$$^{*}\phi_{\tau}[\eta; \vec{\lambda}_{o}] = \frac{\rho^{-1/2}[\eta]}{\phi_{\tau}[\eta; \vec{\lambda}_{o}]} \tag{A4}$$

is the solution of the transformed CSLE:

$$\left\{ \frac{d^2}{d\eta^2} + I^{o}[\eta; \vec{\lambda}_{o}|\tau] + \varepsilon\, \rho[\eta] \right\} \Phi[\eta; \vec{\lambda}_{o}; \varepsilon|\tau] = 0 \tag{A5}$$

at the same energy (A2), i.e.,

$$\left\{ \frac{d^2}{d\eta^2} + I^{o}[\eta; \vec{\lambda}_{o}|\tau] + \varepsilon_{\tau}(\vec{\lambda}_{o})\rho[\eta] \right\} {}^{*}\phi_{\tau}[\eta; \vec{\lambda}_{o}] = 0. \tag{A6}$$

Representing both CSLEs (A3) and (A6) in the Riccati form:

$$I^{o}[\eta; \vec{\lambda}_{o}] = -ld^{2}\phi_{\tau}[\eta; \vec{\lambda}_{o}] - \dot{ld}\, \phi_{\tau}[\eta; \vec{\lambda}_{o}] - \varepsilon_{\tau}(\vec{\lambda}_{o})\, \rho[\eta] \tag{A7}$$

and

$$I^{o}[\eta; \vec{\lambda}_{o}|\tau] := -ld^{2*}\phi_{\tau}[\eta; \vec{\lambda}_{o}] - \dot{ld}^{*}\phi_{\tau}[\eta; \vec{\lambda}_{o}] - \varepsilon_{\tau}(\vec{\lambda}_{o})\rho[\eta], \tag{A8}$$

subtracting one from another, and also taking into account that the logarithmic derivatives of the TF $\phi_{\tau}[\eta; \vec{\lambda}_{o}]$ and its reciprocal (A4) are related in the elementary fashion:

$$ld^{*}\phi_{\tau}[\eta; \vec{\lambda}_{o}] = -ld\, \phi_{\tau}[\eta; \vec{\lambda}_{o}] - 1/2 ld\rho\, [\eta] \tag{A9}$$

one finds [63]

$$I^{o}[\eta; \vec{\lambda}_{o}|\tau] = I^{o}[\eta; \vec{\lambda}_{o}] + 2\sqrt{\rho[\eta]} \frac{d}{d\eta} \frac{ld\, \phi_{\tau}[\eta; \vec{\lambda}_{o}]}{\sqrt{\rho[\eta]}} + \mathcal{J}\{\rho[\eta]\}, \tag{A10}$$

where the last summand represents the so-called [19] 'universal correction' defined via the generic formula

$$\mathcal{J}\{f[\eta]\} := 1/2\sqrt{f[\eta]} \frac{d}{d\eta} \frac{ld\, f[\eta]}{\sqrt{f[\eta]}}. \tag{A11}$$

Appendix B. DCT of the Generic CSLE as a Sequence of RZTs

Let $\phi_{\tau_2}[\eta; \vec{\lambda}_{o}]$ be another solution of a CSLE (A1) at the energy $\varepsilon_{\tau_2}(\vec{\lambda}_{o})$. Then the CSLE (A6) with $\tau \equiv \tau_1$ has the solution [63]

$$\phi_{\tau_2}[\eta; \vec{\lambda}_{o}|\tau_1] = \frac{W\{\phi_{\tau_{k=1,2}}[\eta; \vec{\lambda}_{o}]\}}{\rho^{1/2}[\eta]\, \phi_{1}[\eta; \vec{\lambda}_{o}]}. \tag{A12}$$

Using this solution as the TF for the next RZT, we come to the CSLE

$$\left\{\frac{d^2}{d\eta^2} + I^o[\eta;\vec{\lambda}_o|\tau] + \varepsilon\,\rho[\eta]\right\}\Phi[\eta;\vec{\lambda}_o;\varepsilon|\tau] = 0 \quad \text{(A13)}$$

with the zero-energy free term

$$\begin{gathered} I^o\,[\eta;\vec{\lambda}_o|\tau_{k=1,2}] = I^o[\eta;\vec{\lambda}_o|\tau_1] \\ +2\sqrt{\rho[\eta]}\frac{d}{d\eta}\frac{ld\,\phi_{\tau_2}[\eta;\vec{\lambda}_o|\tau_1]}{\sqrt{\rho[\eta]}} + \mathcal{J}\{\rho[\eta]\}. \end{gathered} \quad \text{(A14)}$$

Substituting (A12) into (A14), coupled with (A10) and (A11), then gives [63]

$$I^o\,[\eta;\vec{\lambda}_o|\tau_{k=1,2}] = I^o[\eta;\vec{\lambda}_o] + 2\sqrt{\rho[\eta]}\frac{d}{d\eta}\frac{ld\,W\{\phi_{\tau_{k=1,2}}[\eta;\vec{\lambda}_o]\}}{\sqrt{\rho[\eta]}}. \quad \text{(A15)}$$

Let us now assume that the function [12,64]

$$\phi_\tau[\eta;\vec{\lambda}_o|\tau_{k=1,\dots,p}] = \frac{W\{\phi_{\tau_{k=1,\dots,p}}[\eta;\vec{\lambda}_o],\phi_\tau[\eta;\vec{\lambda}_o]\}}{\rho^{\frac{p}{2}}\,[\eta]W\{\phi_{\tau_{k=1,\dots,p}}[\eta;\vec{\lambda}_o]\}} \quad \text{(A16)}$$

satisfies the CSLE

$$\left\{\frac{d^2}{d\eta^2} + I^o[\eta;\vec{\lambda}_o|\tau_{k=1,\dots,p}] + \varepsilon\,\rho[\eta]\right\}\Phi[\eta;\vec{\lambda}_o;\varepsilon|\tau_{k=1,\dots,p}] = 0 \quad \text{(A17)}$$

with the zero-energy free term [12]

$$\begin{gathered} I^o\,[\eta;\vec{\lambda}_o|\tau_{k=1,\dots,p}] = I^o[\eta;\vec{\lambda}_o] \\ +2\sqrt{\rho[\eta]}\frac{d}{d\eta}\frac{ld\,W\{\phi_{\tau_{k=1,\dots,p}}[\eta;\vec{\lambda}_o]\}}{\sqrt{\rho[\eta]}} - p(p-2)\,\mathcal{J}\{\rho[\eta]\}. \end{gathered} \quad \text{(A18)}$$

The RDT of the CSLE (A17) with the TF (A16) then results in the CSLE with the zero-energy free term defined by (A18) with p and $\tau_{k=1,\dots,p}$ replaced for p + 1 and $\tau_{k=1,\dots,p+1}$ accordingly.

Theorem A1. *The function (A16) is the solution of the CSLE (A17) at the energy* $\varepsilon_{\tau_p}(\vec{\lambda}_o)$.

Proof. Suppose that both functions $\phi_{\tau_p}[\eta;\vec{\lambda}_o|\tau_{k=1,\dots,p-1}]$ and $\phi_{\tau_{p+1}}[\eta;\vec{\lambda}_o|\tau_{k=1,\dots,p-1}]$ are solutions of the CSLE (A17) with p replaced by p − 1. It is also assumed that the energies are equal to $\varepsilon_{\tau_p}(\vec{\lambda}_o)$ and $\varepsilon_{\tau_{p+1}}(\vec{\lambda}_o)$ accordingly. Then, by definition of the CSLE (17), the function

$$\begin{gathered} \phi_{\tau_{p+1}}[\eta;\vec{\lambda}_o|\tau_{k=1,\dots,p}] \\ = \frac{W\{\phi_{\tau_p}[\eta;\vec{\lambda}_o|\tau_{k=1,\dots,p-1}],\phi_{\tau_{p+1}}[\eta;\vec{\lambda}_o|\tau_{k=1,\dots,p-1}]\}}{\rho^{1/2}\,[\eta]\,\phi_{\tau_p}[\eta;\vec{\lambda}_o|\tau_{k=1,\dots,p-1}]} \end{gathered} \quad \text{(A19)}$$

must be its solution at the energy $\varepsilon_{\tau_{p+1}}(\vec{\lambda}_o)$. Replacing p and $\tau_{k=1,\ldots,p}$ in the right-hand side of (A16) for $p-1$ and $\tau_{k=1,\ldots,p-1}$ accordingly and then setting $\tau=\tau_p,\tau_{p+1}$ we can re-write (A19) as

$$\phi_{\tau_{p+1}}[\eta;\vec{\lambda}_o|\tau_{k=1,\ldots,p}] = \frac{W\left\{W\{\phi_{\tau_{k=1,\ldots,p}}[\eta;\vec{\lambda}_o]\},W\{\phi_{\tau_p}[\eta;\vec{\lambda}_o|\tau_{k=1,\ldots,p-1}],\phi_{\tau_{p+1}}[\eta;\vec{\lambda}_o]\}\right\}}{\rho^{1/2p}[\eta]W\{\phi_{\tau_{k=1,\ldots,p-1}}[\eta;\vec{\lambda}_o]\}}. \tag{A20}$$

Choosing m = p − 1, n = p + 1, n − m = 2 in the general Wronskian decomposition formula in [65] then gives:

$$W\{\phi_{\tau_{k=1,\ldots,p+1}}[\eta;\vec{\lambda}_o]\} \frac{W\left\{W\{\phi_{\tau_{k=1,\ldots,p}}[\eta;\vec{\lambda}_o]\},W\{\phi_{\tau_p}[\eta;\vec{\lambda}_o|\tau_{k=1,\ldots,p-1}],\phi_{\tau_{p+1}}[\eta;\vec{\lambda}_o]\}\right\}}{W\{\phi_{\tau_{k=1,\ldots,p-1}}[\eta;\vec{\lambda}_o]} \tag{A21}$$

then brings us back to (A16) with $\tau=\tau_{p+1}$, which completes the proof. □

Here and in the other publications we refer to the CSLE (A17) with the zero-energy free term (A18) as 'Darboux-Crum transform' (DC$\mathcal{T}$) of the CSLE (1) with the seed functions $\tau_{k=1,\ldots,p}$.

Appendix C. RDC Sequences of PFSs Near a 2nd-Order Pole with an Energy-Independent ExpDiff

Let $\Phi_{\mp}[\eta;\vec{\lambda};\varepsilon\,|\overline{M}_p]$ be the PFS of the RCSLE (67) near the pole at ∓ 1. Then the functions

$$\Psi_{-}[\eta;\vec{\lambda};\varepsilon\,|\overline{M}_p] = (1-\eta^2)^{-1/2}\,\Phi_{-}[\eta;\vec{\lambda};\varepsilon\,|\overline{M}_p] \ \text{ for } |\eta|<1 \tag{A22}$$

and

$$\Psi_{+}[\eta;\vec{\lambda};\varepsilon\,|\overline{M}_p] = \begin{cases} (1-\eta^2)^{-1/2}\,\Phi_{+}[\eta;\vec{\lambda};\varepsilon\,|\overline{M}_p] & \text{for } |\eta|<1, \\ (\eta-1)^{-1/2}\,\Phi_{+}[\eta;\vec{\lambda};-\varepsilon\,|\overline{M}_p] & \text{for } \eta>1 \end{cases} \tag{A23}$$

are the solutions of the p-SLEs (138) and accordingly (1390), satisfying the DBCs at the corresponding singular endpoints:

$$\lim_{\eta\to\eta_{\mp}} \Psi_{\mp}[\eta;\vec{\lambda};\varepsilon\,|\overline{M}_p] = 0. \tag{A24}$$

Representing the RRZ$\mathcal{T}$s of the PFSs (A22) and (A23),

$$\Psi[\eta;\vec{\lambda};\varepsilon\,|\overline{M}_{p+1};\mp] = \frac{W\{\Psi[\eta;\vec{\lambda};\varepsilon_{m_{p+1}}(\vec{\lambda})\,|\overline{M}_p],\Psi_{\mp}[\eta;\vec{\lambda};\varepsilon\,|\overline{M}_p]\}}{\rho^{1/2}[\eta]\Psi[\eta;\vec{\lambda};\varepsilon_{m_{p+1}}(\vec{\lambda})\,|\overline{M}_p]}, \tag{A25}$$

as

$$\begin{aligned}\Psi[\eta;\vec{\lambda};\varepsilon\,|\overline{M}_{p+1};\mp] &= |1-\eta^2|^{1/2}\dot{\Psi}_{\mp}[\eta;\vec{\lambda};\varepsilon\,|\overline{M}_p] \\ &-|1-\eta^2|^{1/2}ld\,\Psi[\eta;\vec{\lambda};\varepsilon_{m_{p+1}}(\vec{\lambda})\,|M_p]\Psi_{\mp}[\eta;\vec{\lambda};\varepsilon\,|M_p]\end{aligned} \tag{A26}$$

shows that

$$\lim_{\eta\to\mp 1} \Psi[\eta;\vec{\lambda};\varepsilon\,|\overline{M}_{p+1};\mp] = 0 \tag{A27}$$

and therefore

$$\Psi[\eta;\vec{\lambda};\varepsilon\,|\overline{M}_{p+1};\mp] \equiv \Psi_{\mp}[\eta;\vec{\lambda};\varepsilon\,|\overline{M}_{p+1}] \tag{A28}$$

iff the ExpDiff for the corresponding pole of the RCSLE (67) lies within the LP range:

$$^{*}\lambda^{(p)}_{o;\mp} = |\lambda_{\mp} + p| > 1. \tag{A29}$$

Finally let us prove that the RRZ$\mathcal{T}$ of the PFS $\Psi_{\infty}[\eta; \vec{\lambda}; \underset{\sim}{\varepsilon}\, |\overline{M}_p]$ of the *p*-SLE (139) near the pole at infinity vanishes in the limit $\eta \to \infty$. Taking into account that differentiating of the function η^{α} decreases the power exponent, we find that both summands in

$$\begin{gathered}\Psi[\eta; \vec{\lambda}; \underset{\sim}{\varepsilon}\, |\overline{M}_{p+1}] = (\eta^2-1)^{1/2}\dot{\Psi}_{\infty}[\eta; \vec{\lambda}; \underset{\sim}{\varepsilon}\, |\overline{M}_p] \\ -(\eta^2-1)^{1/2} ld\,\Psi[\eta; \vec{\lambda}; -\varepsilon_{m_{p+1}}(\vec{\lambda})\, |\overline{M}_p]\Psi_{\infty}[\eta; \vec{\lambda}; \tilde{\varepsilon}\, |\overline{M}_p],\end{gathered} \tag{A30}$$

vanish at infinity which confirms that the q-RS (A30) is indeed the PFS of the transformed RCSLE near its pole at infinity.

Appendix D. Exact Solvability of the *p*-SLEs (138) and (139) Under the DBCs

The proof presented below constitutes the special of the general technique developed by the author [19] in support of the assertion that the RRZT of an exactly solvable RDC$\mathcal{T}$ of the JRef CSLE results in an exactly solvable RCSLE. In context of this paper we show that the q-RSs (146) represent the complete set of the eigenfunctions of the corresponding *p*-SLE (138) or (139). This proof assures that this set of the eigenfunctions starts from the nodeless solution, which in turns confirms that all the PFSs (146) under the conditions (144) and (145) lie below of the lowest eigenvalue of the *p*-SLE in question and therefore do not have zeros inside the orthogonalization interval under consideration.

Theorem A2. *All the Dirichlet problems for the p-SLEs (138) or alternatively (139) under the conditions (144) and (145) in both cases (coupled with the upper bound (143) for the degrees of the seed Jacobi polynomials in case of the former p-SLE), have exactly the same discrete energy spectrum as the precursor p-SLE (24) solved under the DBCs on the intervals (−1, +1) or (1, ∞) accordingly.*

Proof. For the *p*-SLE (139) with p = 1 this assertion has been proven in [1] and below reproduce similar arguments for the finite interval. We shall come back to these arguments, while proving the general case of p > 1. For now let us just assume that the cited statement is correct for both *p*-SLEs (138) and (139) with p = 1.

Re-writing (78) with p = 1 as

$$\begin{gathered}\psi_{\mp+,m_2}[\eta; \mp\lambda_{o;-}, \lambda_{o;+}|m_1] = \psi_0[\eta; \mp\lambda_{o;-}-1, \lambda_{o;+}+1]\times \\ \frac{W^{(\mp\lambda_{o;-},\lambda_{o;+})}_{m_1+m_2-1}[\eta|m_1,m_2]}{P^{(\mp\lambda_{o;-},\lambda_{o;+})}_{m_1}(\eta)},\end{gathered} \tag{A31}$$

we find that the power exponents of $\eta \pm 1$ coincide with halves of the corresponding ExpDiffs

$$^{*}\lambda^{(p)}_{o;\mp} = |\lambda_{\mp} + p| = \lambda_{o;\mp} \mp p > 0. \tag{A32}$$

Keeping in mind that the exponent power $(\lambda_{o;+}+1)/2$ is positive for the both intervals (−1, +1) and (1, ∞), we conclude that the listed solution vanishes in the limits $\eta \to 1\mp$ and therefore represents the PFS of the corresponding *p*-SLEs (138) or (139) near this singular endpoint. Since we assume that the formulated Dirichlet problems are exactly solvable for p = 1, this PFS lies below the lowest eigenvalue of the given *p*-SLE and therefore the JPW in the numerator of the PF in the right-hand side of (A31) may not have zeros inside the orthogonalization interval in question as far as the Jacobi indexes are restricted by the conditions (144).

Since the *p*-SLEs in question are exactly solvable for p = 1 and $\overline{M}_2$ is the admissible set of the polynomial seed solutions, we use the mathematical induction, assuming that the *p*-SLE (138) or (139) for the admissible set of the polynomial seed solutions, $\overline{M}_p = \overline{M}_{P-1}$, has exactly the same discrete energy spectrum as the *p*-SLE (24) with the leading coefficient function (28). Under the latter assumption one can then repeat the above arguments to prove that the JPW (65) with $\overline{M}_p = \overline{M}_P$ is nodeless inside the corresponding orthogonalization interval and therefore $\overline{M}_P$ is the admissible set of the polynomial seed solutions. Our final step is to prove that the given *p*-SLE with $\overline{M}_p = \overline{M}_P$ has exactly the same discrete energy spectrum as the *p*-SLE (24).

Suppose that the given *p*-SLE has another eigenfunction $\psi_{c,n}[\eta; \lambda' |\overline{M}_P]$ at an energy E_n with the absolute value $|E_n| \neq \varepsilon_j(\vec{\lambda}')$ for any $j \leq j_{max}$ and therefore, by definition, it must obey the DBCs

$$\lim_{\eta \to \eta_\mp} \psi_{c,n}[\eta; \vec{\lambda}' |\overline{M}_P] = 0. \tag{A33}$$

If $^*\lambda_{o;-}^{(P)} > 1$ (which assures ExpDiffs $*\lambda_{o;\mp}^{(P-1)}$ lie within the LP range) then we can take advantage of the arguments presented in Appendix C to show that the RRZT with the TF

$$*\phi_{m_P}[\eta; \vec{\lambda} |\overline{M}_{P-1}] = \frac{\rho^{-1/2}[\eta]}{\phi_{m_P}[\eta; \vec{\lambda} |\overline{M}_{P-1}]} \tag{A34}$$

converts the extraneous eigenfunction into the eigenfunction of the *p*-SLE (138) or (139) with $\overline{M}_p = \overline{M}_{P-1}$. However this conclusion contradicts the assumption that the *p*-SLE in question has exactly the same energy spectrum as the *p*-SLE (24). We thus assert that q-RSs (146) represent all possible eigenfunctions of the *p*-SLEs (138) and (139) accordingly.

Finally, one can easily verify that the presented arguments are fully applied to the starting instance *p* = 1, since we only need the presumption that the *p*-SLEs (24) with the leading coefficient functions (28) are exactly solvable under the DBCs imposed at the ends of the corresponding orthogonalization interval and that the TF of the given RRZT does not have zeros inside of this interval. □

The direct consequence of the proven theorem is that the p-WPs (97) with $\overline{M}_p = \overline{M}_P$ and $\vec{\sigma} = -+$ have exactly j real zeros larger than 1.

Appendix E. X_m-Jacobi DPS in the Second-Order Darboux-Crum Representation

It has been proven by the author in [66] that the JPW of degree 2 can be reduced to the second-degree Jacobi polynomial as follows

$$W_2^{(\lambda_+,\lambda_-)}[\eta|1,2] = 1/2(\lambda_+ + \lambda_- + 4)P_2^{(-\lambda_+-3,-\lambda_--3)}(\eta). \tag{A35}$$

At that time the author did not realized that it deals with the very special case of the equivalence theorem initially sketched in [47,48] and then scrutinized in great detail [21] (see [57] for additional comments).

In particular, this implies the Wronskian of two classical Jacobi polynomials with positive indexes can be written as

$$W_2^{(\lambda_{o;+},\lambda_{o;-})}(\eta|1,2) = 1/2(\lambda_{o;+} + \lambda_{o;-} + 4)P_2^{(-\lambda_{o;+}-3,-\lambda_{o;-}-3)}(\eta). \tag{A36}$$

Examination of the explicit formula for the second-degree Jacobi polynomial:

$$\begin{aligned}P_2^{(\lambda_+,\lambda_-)}(\eta) = \tfrac{1}{8}[&(\lambda_- + 2)(\lambda_- + 1)(1+\eta)^2 + (\lambda_+ + 2)(\lambda_+ + 1)(1-\eta)^2 \\ &-2(\lambda_0 + 2)(\lambda_1 + 2)(1-\eta^2)]\end{aligned} \tag{A37}$$

reveals that that the polynomial in the right-hand side of (A36) may not have a zero at $\eta = \mp 1$ since both Jacobi indexes are smaller than -3, in agreement with Theorem 1.

It can be shown that the discriminant of the polynomial (A37) is given by the simple formula:

$$\Delta(\vec{\lambda}) = \frac{1}{32}(\lambda_+ + \lambda_- + 3)(\lambda_- + 2)(\lambda_+ + 2) \tag{A38}$$

and therefore the second-degree Jacobi polynomial of our interest has the negative discriminant. Firstly, this observation confirms Theorem 2 stating all the zeros of the JPW with positive indexes may have only simple zeros. Secondly, we conclude that the second-degree polynomial (A36) has a pair of complex conjugated zeros and therefore remains finite on the interval $[1, \infty)$, in line with Corollary 5.

References

1. Natanson, G. On finite exceptional orthogonal polynomial sequences composed of rational Darboux transforms of Romanovski-Jacobi polynomials. *Axioms* **2025**, *14*, 218. [CrossRef]
2. Everitt, W.N.; Littlejohn, L.L. Orthogonal polynomials and spectral theory: A survey. In *Orthogonal Polynomials and Their Applications*; Brezinski, C., Gori, L., Ronveaux, A., Eds.; IMACS Annals on Computing and Applied Mathematics; J. C. Baltzer AG Publishers: Red Bank, NJ, USA, 1991; Volume 9, pp. 21–55.
3. Everitt, W.N.; Kwon, K.H.; Littlejohn, L.L.; Wellman, R. Orthogonal polynomial solutions of linear ordinary differential equations. *J. Comput. Appl. Math.* **2001**, *133*, 85–109.
4. Gómez-Ullate, D.; Kamran, N.; Milson, R. An extended class of orthogonal polynomials defined by a Sturm–Liouville problem. *J. Math. Anal. Appl.* **2009**, *359*, 352–367. [CrossRef]
5. Gómez-Ullate, D.; Kamran, N.; Milson, R. An extension of Bochner's problem: Exceptional invariant subspaces. *J. Approx. Theory* **2010**, *162*, 987–1006. [CrossRef]
6. Bochner, S. Über Sturm-Liouvillesche Polynomsysteme. *Math. Z.* **1929**, *29*, 730–736. [CrossRef]
7. Kwon, K.H.; Littlejohn, L.L. Classification of classical orthogonal polynomials. *J. Korean Math. Soc.* **1997**, *34*, 973–1008.
8. Natanson, G. Rediscovery of Routh polynomials after hundred years in obscurity. In *Recent Research in Polynomials*; Özger, F., Ed.; IntechOpen: London, UK, 2023; 27p.
9. Routh, E.J. On some properties of certain solutions of a differential equation of the second order. *Proc. Lond. Math. Soc.* **1884**, *16*, 245–262. [CrossRef]
10. Chihara, T.S. *An Introduction to Orthogonal Polynomials*; Gordon and Breach: New York, NY, USA, 1978.
11. Rudyak, B.V.; Zakhariev, B.N. New exactly solvable models for Schrödinger equation. *Inverse Probl.* **1987**, *3*, 125–133.
12. Schulze-Halberg, A. Higher-order Darboux transformations with foreign auxiliary equations and equivalence with generalized Darboux transformations. *Appl. Math. Lett.* **2012**, *25*, 1520–1527. [CrossRef]
13. Darboux, G. *Leçons sur la Théorie Générale des Surfaces et les Applications Géométriques du Calcul Infinitésimal*; Gauthier-Villars: Paris, France, 1915; Volume 2, pp. 210–215.
14. Crum, M.M. Associated Sturm-Liouville systems. *Q. J. Math.* **1955**, *6*, 121–127. [CrossRef]
15. Natanson, G. Use of Wronskians of Jacobi Polynomials with Common Complex Indexes for Constructing X-DPSs and Their Infinite and Finite Orthogonal Subsets. 2019. Available online: https://www.researchgate.net/publication/331638063 (accessed on 10 March 2019).
16. Romanovski, V.I. Sur quelques classes nouvelles de polynomes orthogonaux. *CR Acad. Sci.* **1929**, *188*, 1023–1025.
17. Lesky, P.A. Vervollstandigungderklassischen Orthogonalpolynomedurch Erganzungen zum Askey—Schema der hypergeometrischen orthogonalen Polynome. *Ost. Ak. Wiss* **1995**, *204*, 151–166.
18. Lesky, P.A. Endliche und unendliche Systeme von kontinuierlichen klassichen Othogonalpolynomen. *Z. Angew. Math. Mech.* **1996**, *76*, 181–184.
19. Natanson, G. Darboux-Crum Nets of Sturm-Liouville Problems Solvable by Quasi-Rational Functions I. General Theory. 2018. Available online: https://www.researchgate.net/publication/323831953 (accessed on 1 March 2018).
20. Gesztesy, F.; Simon, B.; Teschl, G. Zeros of the Wronskian and renormalized oscillation theory. *Am. J. Math.* **1996**, *118*, 571–594.

21. Gómez-Ullate, D.; Grandati, Y.; Milson, R. Shape invariance and equivalence relations for pseudo-Wronskians of Laguerre and Jacobi polynomials. *J. Phys. A Math. Theor.* **2018**, *51*, 345201.
22. Durán, A.J. Exceptional Hahn and Jacobi orthogonal polynomials. *J. Approx. Theory* **2017**, *214*, 9–48.
23. Garcia-Ferrero, M.; Gomez-Ullate, D.; Milson, R. Classification of Exceptional Jacobi Polynomials. *arXiv* **2024**, arXiv:2409.02656v1.
24. Gómez-Ullate, D.; Kamran, N.; Milson, R. On orthogonal polynomials spanning a non-standard flag. *Contemp. Math* **2012**, *563*, 51–71.
25. Szego, G. *Orthogonal Polynomials*; American Mathematical Society: New York, NY, USA, 1959.
26. Natanzon, G.A. Study of the one-dimensional Schrödinger equation generated from the hypergeometric equation. *Vestn. Len ingr. Univ.* **1971**, *10*, 22–28. (In Russian) [English translation is available online: https://doi.org/10.48550/arXiv.physics/9907032] [CrossRef]
27. Natanson, G. Survey of nodeless regular almost-everywhere holomorphic solutions for exactly solvable Gauss-reference Liouville potentials on the line I. Subsets of nodeless Jacobi-seed solutions co-existent with discrete energy spectrum. *arXiv* **2016**, arXiv:1606.08758.
28. Natanson, G. Gauss-seed nets of Sturm-Liouville problems with energy-independent characteristic exponents and related sequences of exceptional orthogonal polynomials I. Canonical Darboux transformations using almost-everywhere holomorphic factorization functions. *arXiv* **2013**, arXiv:1305.7453v1.
29. Natanson, G. Breakup of SUSY Quantum Mechanics in the Limit-Circle Region of the Darboux/Pöschl-Teller Potential. 2019. Available online: https://www.researchgate.net/publication/334960618 (accessed on 1 October 2019).
30. Garcia-Ferrero, M.; Gomez-Ullate, D.; Milson, R. A Bochner type characterization theorem for exceptional orthogonal polynomials. *J. Math. Anal. Appl.* **2019**, *472*, 584–626. [CrossRef]
31. Everitt, W.N. A Catalogue of Sturm-Liouville differential equations. In *Sturm-Liouville Theory, Past and Present*; Amrein, W.O., Hinz, A.M., Pearson, D.B., Eds.; Birkhäuser Verlag: Basel, Switzerland, 2005; pp. 271–331.
32. Weidmann, J. Spectral Theory of Sturm-Liouville Operators Approximation by Regular Problems. In *Sturm-Liouville Theory, Past and Present*; Amrein, W.O., Hinz, A.M., Pearson, D.B., Eds.; Birkhäuser Verlag: Basel, Switzerland, 2005; pp. 75–98.
33. Natanzon, G.A. Use of the Darboux theorem for constructing the general solution of the Schrödinger equation with the Pöschl-Teller potential. *Vestn. Leningr. Univ.* **1977**, 33–39. Available online: https://www.researchgate.net/publication/316150022 (accessed on 1 January 2010). (In Russian).
34. Quesne, C. Solvable rational potentials and exceptional orthogonal polynomials in supersymmetric quantum mechanics. *Symmetry Integr. Geom. Methods Appl.* **2009**, *5*, 84. [CrossRef]
35. Comtet, L. *Advanced Combinatorics: The Art of Finite and Infinite Expansions*; Reidel: Dordrecht, The Netherlands, 1974.
36. Askey, R. An integral of Ramanujan and orthogonal polynomials. *J. Indian Math. Soc.* **1987**, *51*, 27–36.
37. Chen, M.P.; Srivastava, H.M. Orthogonality relations and generating functions for Jacobi polynomials and related hypergeometric functions. *Appl. Math. Comput.* **1995**, *68*, 153–188. [CrossRef]
38. Natanson, G. Biorthogonal Differential Polynomial System Composed of X-Jacobi Polynomials from Different Sequences. 2018. Available online: https://www.researchgate.net/publication/322851312 (accessed on 22 January 2018).
39. Alhaidari, A.D.; AssiI, A. Finite-series approximation of the bound states for two novel potentials. *Physics* **2022**, *4*, 1067–1080. [CrossRef]
40. Raposo, A.P.; Weber, H.J.; Alvarez-Castillo, D.E.; Kirchbach, M. Romanovski polynomials in selected physics problems. *Open Phys.* **2007**, *5*, 253–284. [CrossRef]
41. Weber, H.J. Connections between Romanovski and other polynomials. *Cent. Eur. J. Math.* **2007**, *5*, 581–595. [CrossRef]
42. Avarez-Castillo, D.E.; Kirchbach, M. Exact spectrum and wave functions of the hyperbolic Scarf potential in terms of finite Romanovski polynomials. *Rev. Mex. Fŕsica E* **2007**, *53*, 143–154.
43. Martnez-Finkelshtein, A.; Silva Ribeiro, L.L.; Sri Ranga, A.; Tyaglov, M. Complementary Romanovski-Routh polynomials: From orthogonal polynomials on the unit circle to Coulomb wave functions. *Proc. Am. Math. Soc.* **2019**, *147*, 2625–2640. [CrossRef]
44. Ho, C.-L.; Sasaki, R.; Takemura, K. Confluence of apparent singularities in multi-indexed orthogonal polynomials: The Jacobi case. *J. Phys. A Math. Theor.* **2013**, *46*, 115205. [CrossRef]
45. Bonneux, N. Exceptional Jacobi polynomials. *J. Approx. Theory* **2019**, *239*, 72–112. [CrossRef]
46. Gómez-Ullate, D.; Marcellan, F.; Milson, R. Asymptotic and interlacing properties of zeros of exceptional Jacobi and Laguerre polynomials. *J. Math. Anal. Appl.* **2013**, *399*, 480–495. [CrossRef]
47. Gómez-Ullate, D.; Grandati, Y.; Milson, R. Extended Krein-Adler theorem for the translationally shape invariant poten-1220 tials. *J. Math. Phys.* **2014**, *55*, 043510. [CrossRef]
48. Odake, S.; Sasaki, R. Krein–Adler transformations for shape-invariant potentials and pseudo virtual states. *J. Phys. A Math. Theor.* **2013**, *46*, 245201. [CrossRef]
49. Natanson, G. Uniqueness of finite exceptional orthogonal polynomial sequences composed of Wronskian transforms of Romanovski-Routh polynomials. *Symmetry* **2024**, *16*, 282. [CrossRef]

50. Erdelyi, A.; Bateman, H. *Transcendental Functions*; McGraw Hill: New York, NY, USA, 1953; Volume 1.
51. Durán, A.J.; Pérez, M.; Varona, J.L. Some conjectures on Wronskian and Casorati determinants of orthogonal polynomials. *Exp. Math.* **2015**, *24*, 123–132. [CrossRef]
52. Quesne, C. Rationally-extended radial oscillators and Laguerre exceptional orthogonal polynomials in kth-order SUSYQM. *Int. J. Mod. Phys. A* **2011**, *26*, 5337–5347. [CrossRef]
53. Quesne, C. Higher-order SUSY, exactly solvable potentials, and exceptional orthogonal polynomials. *Mod. Phys. Lett. A* **2011**, *26*, 1843–1852. [CrossRef]
54. Quesne, C. Exceptional orthogonal polynomials and new exactly solvable potentials in quantum mechanics. *J. Phys. Conf. Ser.* **2012**, *380*, 012016. [CrossRef]
55. Natanson, G. Single-source nets of algebraically-quantized reflective Liouville potentials on the line I. Almost-everywhere holomorphic solutions of rational canonical Sturm-Liouville equations with second-order poles. *arXiv* **2015**, arXiv:1503.04798v2.
56. Odake, S. Equivalences of the multi-indexed orthogonal polynomials. *J. Math. Phys.* **2014**, *55*, 013502. [CrossRef]
57. Natanson, G. Equivalence Relations for Darboux-Crum Transforms of Translationally Form-Invariant Sturm-Liouville Equations. 2021. Available online: https://www.researchgate.net/publication/353131294 (accessed on 9 August 2021).
58. Hartman, P. *Ordinary Differential Equations*; John Wiley: New York, NY, USA, 1964.
59. Karlin, S.; Szegő, G. On Certain Determinants Whose Elements Are Orthogonal Polynomials. *J. d'Analyse Math.* **1960**, *8*, 1–157. [CrossRef]
60. Bagrov, V.G.; Samsonov, B.F. Darboux transformation and elementary exact solutions of the Schrödinger equation. *Pramana* **1997**, *49*, 563–580. [CrossRef]
61. Adler, V.E. A modification of Crum's method. *Theor. Math. Phys.* **1994**, *101*, 1381–1386. [CrossRef]
62. Natanson, G. Quantization of rationally deformed Morse potentials by Wronskian transforms of Romanovski-Bessel polynomials. *Acta Polytech.* **2022**, *62*, 100–117. [CrossRef]
63. Schnizer, W.A.; Leeb, H. Exactly solvable models for the Schrödinger equation from generalized Darboux transformations. *J. Phys. A Math. Gen.* **1993**, *26*, 5145–5156. [CrossRef]
64. Pozdeeva, E.; Schulze-Halberg, A. Propagators of generalized Schrödinger equations related by higher-order supersymmetry. *Int. J. Mod. Phys. A* **2011**, *26*, 191–207. [CrossRef]
65. Muir, T. *A Treatise on the Theory of Determinants*; Revised and enlarged by W. H. Metzler; Dover Publications: New York, NY, USA, 1960; p. 198.
66. Natanson, G. Quartet of Rationally-Deformed Non-PT-Symmetric Scarf II Potentials with Real Energy Spectra and Eigenfunctions Expressible in Terms of Complex X1 Differential Polynomial Systems. 2019. Available online: https://www.researchgate.net/publication/336839321 (accessed on 27 October 2019).

mathematics

MDPI

Article

Two-Variable q-General-Appell Polynomials Within the Context of the Monomiality Principle

Noor Alam [1], Waseem Ahmad Khan [2,*], Can Kızılateş [3] and Cheon Seoung Ryoo [4]

1 Department of Mathematics, College of Science, University of Ha'il, Ha'il 2440, Saudi Arabia; noor.alam@uoh.edu.sa
2 Department Electrical Engineering, Prince Mohammad Bin Fahd University, P.O. Box 1664, Al Khobar 31952, Saudi Arabia
3 Department of Mathematics, Faculty of Science, Zonguldak Bülent Ecevit University, Zonguldak 67100, Turkey; cankizilates@gmail.com
4 Department of Mathematics, Hannam University, Daejeon 34430, Republic of Korea; ryoocs@hnu.kr
* Correspondence: wkhan1@pmu.edu.sa or khan346@gmail.com

Abstract: In this study, we consider the two-variable q-general polynomials and derive some properties. By using these polynomials, we introduce and study the theory of two-variable q-general Appell polynomials (2VqgAP) using q-operators. The effective use of the q-multiplicative operator of the base polynomial produces the generating equation for 2VqgAP involving the q-exponential function. Furthermore, we establish the q-multiplicative and q-derivative operators and the corresponding differential equations. Then, we obtain the operational, explicit and determinant representations for these polynomials. Some examples are constructed in terms of the two-variable q-general Appell polynomials to illustrate the main results. Finally, graphical representations are provided to illustrate the behavior of some special cases of the two-variable q-general Appell polynomials and their potential applications.

Keywords: quantum calculus; two-variable q-general polynomials; two-variable q-general Appell polynomials; q-quasi monomiality principle; dilatation operators

MSC: 05A30; 11B83; 11B68

1. Introduction

Appell polynomials, a notable category of special functions, have found widespread utility in mathematical domains. Introduced by Paul Appell in 1880, these polynomials are characterized by distinctive properties that contribute to their significance across various mathematical and scientific fields.

The generating function for two-variable general polynomials (2VgP), represented as $p_n(\zeta,\eta)$, is established as follows in the literature [1,2]:

$$\exp(\zeta t)\phi(\eta,t) = \sum_{n=0}^{\infty} p_n(\zeta,\eta)\frac{t^n}{n!}, (p_0(\zeta,\eta) = 1), \tag{1}$$

where $\phi(\eta,t)$ has (at least the formal) series expansion

$$\phi(\eta,t) = \sum_{k=0}^{\infty} \phi_k(\eta)\frac{t^k}{k!}, (\phi_0(\eta) \neq 0). \tag{2}$$

In the 18th century, the foundation of q-calculus began, establishing a framework integral to the theory of special functions. Recently, q-calculus has garnered significant attention due to its applicability across fields like applied mathematics, mechanical engineering, and physics, bridging classical mathematics and quantum calculus. The development of q-analogues, inspired by classical calculus, has led to foundational results in combinatorics, number theory, and other mathematical disciplines. Key q-special polynomials, such as the q-binomial coefficient $\binom{n}{k}_q$ and the q-Pochhammer symbol $(\gamma; q)_v$, hold central roles in q-analog structures across combinatorics, representation theory, and statistical mechanics. The algebraic and analytic richness of these polynomials offers essential tools for exploring q-analogue phenomena. In this paper, we set $q \in \mathbb{C}$, with $|q| < 1$, and employ q-notations as per Andrews et al. [3]. In recent years, advancements have been made in the study of two-variable q-Hermite polynomials, notably by Zayed et al. [4] and Riyasat and Khan [5], highlighting their importance in extending classical Hermite polynomials into q-calculus frameworks. Additionally, q-special functions have been formulated and explored within the representations of quantum algebras [6–8] underscoring the role of q-calculus in quantum groups and quantum mechanics.

The q-shifted factorial $(\zeta; q)_\nu$ is defined as follows:

$$(\zeta; q)_\nu = \prod_{s=1}^{\nu-1}(1 - q^s\zeta), \quad \nu \in \mathbb{N}, \quad \zeta \in \mathbb{C}; \ 0 < q < 1. \tag{3}$$

In q-calculus, this notation assumes a fundamental significance, embodying the discrete characteristics of q-analogues and enabling a range of identities and transformations crucial to the theoretical framework.

For a complex number $\zeta \in \mathbb{C}$, the q-analogue of ζ is given by

$$[\zeta]_q = \frac{1 - q^\zeta}{1 - q}, \quad 0 < q < 1, \ \zeta \in \mathbb{C}. \tag{4}$$

The q-factorial is given by

$$[\zeta]_q! = \begin{cases} \prod_{s=1}^{\zeta}[s]_q, & 0 < q < 1, \ \zeta \neq 0 \in \mathbb{C} \\ 1, & \zeta = 0 \end{cases}. \tag{5}$$

The Gauss's q-binomial formula is given by [3]

$$(\zeta \pm \gamma)_q^v = \sum_{s=0}^{v} \binom{v}{s}_q q^{\binom{v-s}{2}} \zeta^s (\pm\gamma)^{v-s}, \tag{6}$$

where the Gauss q-binomial coefficient is

$$\binom{v}{s}_q = \frac{[v]_q!}{[s]_q![v-s]_q!}.$$

Two q-exponential functions are given by [9]

$$e_q(t) = \sum_{n=0}^{\infty} \frac{t^n}{[n]_q!}, \quad 0 < q < 1, \quad |\zeta| < \frac{1}{1-q} \tag{7}$$

and

$$E_q(t) = \sum_{n=0}^{\infty} \frac{q^{\binom{n}{2}} t^n}{[n]_q!}, \quad 0 < q < 1, \quad \zeta \in \mathbb{C}. \tag{8}$$

The product of both q-exponential functions is given by

$$e_q(\zeta)E_q(\eta) = \sum_{w=0}^{\infty} \frac{(\zeta+\eta)_q^w}{[w]_q!}. \tag{9}$$

Hence

$$e_q(\zeta)E_q(-\zeta) = 1, \quad |\zeta| < \frac{1}{1-q}. \tag{10}$$

The q-derivative of a function $f(\zeta)$ is defined as [10,11]

$$\widehat{D}_{q,\zeta} f(\zeta) = \frac{f(q\zeta) - f(\zeta)}{\zeta(q-1)}, \quad 0 < q < 1, \quad \zeta \neq 0. \tag{11}$$

In particular, we have

$$\widehat{D}_{q,\zeta} \zeta^w = [w]_q \zeta^{w-1}. \tag{12}$$

The q-derivative of the exponential function is given by

$$\widehat{D}_{q,\zeta} e_q(\alpha\zeta) = \alpha e_q(\alpha\zeta), \quad \alpha \in \mathbb{C} \tag{13}$$

and

$$\widehat{D}^k_{q,\zeta} e_q(\alpha\zeta) = \alpha^k e_q(\alpha\zeta), \quad k \in \mathbb{N},\ \alpha \in \mathbb{C}, \tag{14}$$

where $\widehat{D}^k_{q,\zeta}$ denotes the kth order q-derivative with respect to ζ.

The q-derivative of the product of functions $f(\zeta)$ and $g(\zeta)$ has been established in the literature [2,4,12]

$$\widehat{D}_{q,\zeta}(f(\zeta)g(\zeta)) = f(\zeta)\widehat{D}_{q,\zeta} g(\zeta) + g(q\zeta)\widehat{D}_{q,\zeta} f(\zeta). \tag{15}$$

The q-derivative of the division of functions $f(\zeta)$ and $g(\zeta)$ is given by

$$\widehat{D}_{q,\zeta}\left(\frac{f(\zeta)}{g(\zeta)}\right) = \frac{g(q\zeta)\widehat{D}_{q,\zeta} f(\zeta) - f(q\zeta)\widehat{D}_{q,\zeta} g(\zeta)}{g(\zeta)g(q\zeta)}, \quad g(\zeta) \neq 0, \quad g(q\zeta) \neq 0. \tag{16}$$

The q-integral of a function $f(\zeta)$ is defined as [3,4]

$$\int_0^a f(\zeta) d_q\zeta = (1-q)a \sum_{w=0}^{\infty} q^w f(aq^w). \tag{17}$$

By virtue of (17), we can conclude that

$$\int_0^\zeta \lambda^m d_q\lambda = (1-q)\zeta \sum_{w=0}^{\infty} \zeta^m q^{w(m+1)}$$

$$= \frac{\zeta^{m+1}(1-q)}{1-q^{m+1}} = \frac{\zeta^{m+1}}{[m+1]_q}, \quad m \in \mathbb{N} \sqcup \{0\}. \tag{18}$$

More specifically, $\widehat{D}^{-1}_{q,\zeta}\{1\} = \zeta$, and by using the method of mathematical induction, we have

$$\left(\widehat{D}^{-1}_{q,\zeta}\right)^r \{1\} = \frac{\zeta^r}{[r]_q!}, \quad r \in \mathbb{N} \sqcup \{0\}. \tag{19}$$

For some papers on q-generalizations of the special polynomials, we refer to [9,13–16]. The q-Gould–Hopper polynomials, denoted as $H^{(m)}_{w,q}(\zeta,\eta)$ ($qGHP$), can be defined following generating function

$$e_q(\zeta t)e_q(\eta t^m) = \sum_{w=0}^{\infty} H^{(m)}_{w,q}(\zeta,\eta)\frac{t^w}{[w]_q!} \tag{20}$$

and the series definition

$$H^{(m)}_{w,q}(\zeta,\eta) = [w]_q! \sum_{k=0}^{[\frac{w}{m}]} \frac{\eta^k \zeta^{w-mk}}{[k]_q![w-mk]_q!}. \tag{21}$$

For $m = 2$, (20) reduces to 2-variable q-Hermite polynomials defined by Raza et al. [11]. The operational identity of q-Gould–Hopper polynomials $H^{(m)}_{w,q}(\zeta,\eta)$ is as follows:

$$H^{(m)}_{w,q}(\zeta,\eta) = e_q\left(\eta D^m_{q,\zeta}\right)\{\zeta^w\}. \tag{22}$$

The q-dilatation operator T_ζ, which acts on any function of the complex variable ζ, in the following manner [8,10]

$$T^k_\zeta f(\zeta) = f(q^k\zeta), \quad k \in \mathbb{R}, \quad 0 < q < 1, \tag{23}$$

satisfies the property

$$T^{-1}_\zeta T^1_\zeta f(\zeta) = f(\zeta). \tag{24}$$

The q-derivative of the q-exponential function $e_q(\eta t^m)$ is given as [9]

$$\widehat{D}_{q,t} e_q(\eta t^m) = \eta t^{m-1} T_{(\eta;m)} e_q(\eta t^m). \tag{25}$$

where

$$T_{(\eta;m)} = \frac{1-q^m T^m_\eta}{1-qT_\eta} = 1 + qT_\eta + \cdots + q^{m-1}T^{m-1}_\eta.$$

The generating function of q-Appell polynomials $\mathcal{A}_{n,q}(\zeta)$ is elucidated by Al Salam, as delineated in the formula presented in [17,18].

$$\mathcal{A}_q(t)\, e_q(\zeta t) = \sum_{n=0}^{\infty} \mathcal{A}_{n,q}(\zeta)\frac{t^n}{[n]_q!}, \tag{26}$$

$$\mathcal{A}_q(t) = \sum_{n=0}^{\infty} \mathcal{A}_{n,q}\frac{t^n}{[n]_q!}, \qquad \mathcal{A}_q(t) \neq 0, \qquad \mathcal{A}_{0,q} = 1. \tag{27}$$

The following list (see Table 1) demonstrates an appropriate option for certain individuals within the class of q-Appell polynomials:

Table 1. Some q-Appell polynomial families.

S. No.	q-Appell Polynomials	Generating Function	$\mathcal{A}_q(t)$
I.	The q-Bernoulli Polynomials [16,19]	$\frac{t}{e_q(t)-1}e_q(\zeta t) = \sum_{n=0}^{\infty} \mathcal{B}_{n,q}(\zeta)\frac{t^n}{[n]_q!}$	$\mathcal{A}_q(t) = \frac{t}{e_q(t)-1}$
II.	The q-Euler Polynomials [16,19]	$\frac{[2]_q}{e_q(t)+1}e_q(\zeta t) = \sum_{n=0}^{\infty} \mathcal{E}_{n,q}(\zeta)\frac{t^n}{[n]_q!}$	$\mathcal{A}_q(t) = \frac{[2]_q}{e_q(t)+1}$
III.	The q-Genocchi Polynomials [16,19]	$\frac{[2]_q t}{e_q(t)+1}e_q(\zeta t) = \sum_{n=0}^{\infty} \mathcal{G}_{n,q}(\zeta)\frac{t^n}{[n]_q!}$	$\mathcal{A}_q(t) = \frac{[2]_q t}{e_q(t)+1}$

The elements of the q-Appell polynomials class $\mathcal{A}_{n,q}(\zeta)$ generate the corresponding q-numbers $\mathcal{A}_{n,q}$ when $\zeta = 0$. Table 2 illustrates the initial occurrences of three specific q-numbers: the q-Bernoulli numbers $\mathcal{B}_{n,q}$ [16,19], the q-Euler numbers $\mathcal{E}_{n,q}$ [16,19], and the q-Genocchi numbers $\mathcal{G}_{n,q}$ [16,19].

Table 2. The first five q-numbers of $\mathcal{B}_{n,q}$, $\mathcal{E}_{n,q}$ and $\mathcal{G}_{n,q}$.

n	0	1	2	3	4
$\mathcal{B}_{n,q}$ [16,19]	1	$-(1+q)^{-1}$	$q^2([3]_q!)^{-1}$	$(1-q)q^3([2]_q)^{-1}([4]_q)^{-1}$	$q^4(1-q^2-2q^3-q^4+q^6)([2]_q^2![3]_q[5]_q)^{-1}$
$\mathcal{E}_{n,q}$ [16,19]	1	$-\dfrac{1}{2}$	$\frac{1}{4}(-1+q)$	$\frac{1}{8}(-1+2q+q^2-q^3)$	$\frac{1}{16}(q-1)[3]_q!(q^2-4q+1)$
$\mathcal{G}_{n,q}$ [16,19]	0	$\dfrac{2-q}{1+q}$	$\frac{q(q-5)}{(1+q)^2}$	$-\frac{3q^2(q-5)}{(1+q)^3}-\frac{3q(2-q)}{(1+q)^2}-\frac{q}{(1+q)}$	$\frac{-3q}{1+q}\left(\frac{3q^3+10q^2-28q+7}{(1+q)^3}\right)$

The monomiality principle stands as a fundamental tool for investigating specific special polynomials and functions, as well as their properties. Originating from Steffensen's work in the early 19th century, this concept underwent significant refinement and expansion through Dattoli's contributions in 2000. Recent academic research has utilized the monomiality principle to explore innovative hybrid special polynomial sequences and families [14,15]. Notably, Cao et al. [10] extended the application of the monomiality principle to q-special polynomials, opening avenues for the creation of novel q-special polynomial families and shedding light on the quasi monomiality of certain existing q-special polynomials. Through the application of q-operation specific techniques, researchers can derive additional classes of q-generating functions and various generalizations of q-special functions. Among these techniques, the q-operational process demonstrates greater alignment with traditional mathematical approaches and implementations employed in the resolution of q-differential equations. In the context of a q-polynomial set $p_{n,q}(\zeta)(n \in \mathbb{N}, \zeta \in \mathbb{C})$, two q-operators are defined as $\widehat{M_q}$ and $\widehat{P_q}$. These operators, known as the q-multiplicative and q-derivative operators, respectively, are implemented as described in [10]

$$\widehat{M_q}\{p_{n,q}(\zeta)\} = p_{n+1,q}(\zeta) \tag{28}$$

and

$$\widehat{P_q}\{p_{n,q}(\zeta)\} = [n]_q p_{n-1,q}(\zeta). \tag{29}$$

The operators $\widehat{M_q}$ and $\widehat{P_q}$ satisfy the following commutation relation:

$$[\widehat{M_q}, \widehat{P_q}] = \widehat{P_q}\widehat{M_q} - \widehat{M_q}\widehat{P_q}. \tag{30}$$

An analysis of the $\widehat{M_q}$ and $\widehat{P_q}$ operators facilitates the determination of polynomial $p_{n,q}(\zeta)$ properties. When $\widehat{M_q}$ and $\widehat{P_q}$ demonstrate differential realization, the polynomials $p_{n,q}(\zeta)$ conform to a particular differential equation.

$$\widehat{M_q}\widehat{P_q}\{p_{n,q}(\zeta)\} = [n]_q p_{n,q}(\zeta) \tag{31}$$

and

$$\widehat{P_q}\widehat{M_q}\{p_{n,q}(\zeta)\} = [n+1]_q p_{n,q}(\zeta). \tag{32}$$

In view of (28) and (29), we have

$$[\widehat{M_q}, \widehat{P_q}] = [n+1]_q - [n]_q. \tag{33}$$

From (28), we have

$$\widehat{M_q}^r\{p_{n,q}\} = p_{n+r,q}(\zeta). \tag{34}$$

More specifically, we have

$$p_{n,q}(\zeta) = \widehat{M_q}^n\{p_{0,q}\} = \widehat{M_q}^n\{1\}, \tag{35}$$

where $p_{0,q}(\zeta) = 1$ is the q-sequel of polynomial $p_{n,q}(\zeta)$. Furthermore, the generating function of $p_{n,q}(\zeta)$ can be obtained as

$$e_q(\widehat{M_q}t)\{1\} = \sum_{n=0}^{\infty} p_{n,q}(\zeta)\frac{t^n}{[n]_q!}. \tag{36}$$

The subsequent q-multiplicative and q-derivative operators associated with the q-Appell polynomials $A_{n,q}$ are presented as follows [12]

$$\widehat{M}_{qA} = \eta + \frac{A_q'(\widehat{D}_{q,\eta})}{A_q(\widehat{D}_{q,\eta})}T_\eta, \tag{37}$$

or, alternatively,

$$\widehat{M}_{qA} = \eta\frac{A_q(q\widehat{D}_{q,\eta})}{A_q(\widehat{D}_{q,\eta})} + \frac{A_q'(\widehat{D}_{q,\eta})}{A_q(\widehat{D}_{q,\eta})}, \tag{38}$$

and

$$\widehat{P}_{qA} = \widehat{D}_{q,\eta}, \tag{39}$$

respectively.

Inspired by the above papers, in this paper, we examine the specific characteristics of two-variable q-general Appell polynomials through the implementation of the q-analog monomiality principle. Additionally, we present some applications of these newly established two-variable q-general Appell polynomials with graphical representations. Our findings suggest that these polynomials are promising for diverse applications across multiple disciplines.

2. Two-Variable q-General Appell Polynomials

In this section, we introduce the concept of two-variable q-general Appell polynomials, denoted as ${}_pA_{n,q}(\zeta,\eta)$. We elucidate their series definition, q-quasi-monomiality characteristics, operational identities, and associated q-differential equations. Our analysis begins with the formulation of two-variable q-general polynomials, referred to as 2VqgP $p_{n,q}(\zeta,\eta)$.

Here, we consider the two-variable q-general polynomials (2VqgP) $p_{n,q}(\zeta,\eta)$ defined by the following generating function:

$$e_q(\zeta t)\phi_q(\eta,t) = \sum_{n=0}^{\infty} p_{n,q}(\zeta,\eta)\frac{t^n}{[n]_q!}, \quad (p_{0,q}(\zeta,\eta) = 1), \tag{40}$$

where $\phi_q(\eta,t)$ has (at least the formal) series expansion

$$\phi_q(\eta,t) = \sum_{n=0}^{\infty} \phi_{n,q}(\eta)\frac{t^n}{[n]_q!}, \quad (\phi_{0,q}(\eta) \neq 0). \tag{41}$$

With the simplification of the left-hand side of Equation (40) through the application of Equations (7) and (41), the following series definitions of the two-variable q-general polynomials $p_{n,q}(\zeta,\eta)$ are obtained as follows:

$$p_{n,q}(\zeta,\eta) = \sum_{k=0}^{n} \binom{n}{k}_q \zeta^k \phi_{n-k,q}(\eta). \tag{42}$$

We hereby establish the following result concerning the q-quasi-monomial identities of the two-variable q-general polynomials $2VqgP$ $p_{n,q}(\zeta,\eta)$.

Theorem 1. *The two-variable q-general polynomials $2VqgP$ $p_{n,q}(\zeta,\eta)$ demonstrate quasi-monomial characteristics when subjected to the aforementioned q-multiplicative and q-derivative operators as follows:*

$$\widehat{M}_{2VqgP} = \zeta + \frac{\phi_q'(\eta,\widehat{D}_{q,\zeta})}{\phi_q(\eta,\widehat{D}_{q,\zeta})} T_{q,\zeta} \tag{43}$$

and

$$\widehat{P}_{2VqgP} = \widehat{D}_{q,\zeta}, \tag{44}$$

repectively, where $T_{q,\zeta}$ denote the q-dilation operator given by Equation (23).

Proof. Taking the q-derivative on both sides of Equation (40), partially with respect to t and by using Equation (15), we have

$$\sum_{n=1}^{\infty} p_{n,q}(\zeta,\eta)\widehat{D}_{q,t}\frac{t^n}{[n]_q!} = e_q(q\zeta t)\widehat{D}_{q,t}\phi_q(\eta,t) + \phi_q(\eta,t)\widehat{D}_{q,t}e_q(\zeta t), \tag{45}$$

which by using Equation (15) by taking $f_q(t) = \phi_q(\eta,t)$ and $g_q(t) = e_q(\zeta t)$, and then simplifying the resultant equation by using Equations (12), (26), and (28) on the right-hand side, we have

$$\left(\zeta + \frac{\phi_q'(\eta,t)}{\phi_q(\eta,t)} T_{q,\zeta}\right)\{e_q(\zeta t)\phi_q(\eta,t)\} = \sum_{n=0}^{\infty} p_{n+1,q}(\zeta,\eta)\frac{t^n}{[n]_q!}. \tag{46}$$

Since

$$\widehat{D}_{q,\zeta}\{e_q(\zeta t)\phi_q(\eta,t)\} = te_q(\zeta t)\phi_q(\eta,t), \tag{47}$$

and $\frac{\phi_q'(\eta,t)}{\phi_q(\eta,t)}$ has a q-power series expansion in t, as $\phi_q(\eta,t)$ is an invertible series of t.

Therefore, by (40) and (46), we have

$$\left(\zeta + \frac{\phi_q'(\eta,\widehat{D}_{q,\zeta})}{\phi_q(\eta,\widehat{D}_{q,\zeta})} T_{q,\zeta}\right)\left\{\sum_{n=0}^{\infty} p_{n,q}(\zeta,\eta)\frac{t^n}{[n]_q!}\right\} = \sum_{n=0}^{\infty} p_{n+1,q}(\zeta,\eta)\frac{t^n}{[n]_q!}. \tag{48}$$

Comparing the coefficients of like powers of t on both sides, gives

$$\left(\zeta + \frac{\phi_q'(\eta,\widehat{D}_{q,\zeta})}{\phi_q(\eta,\widehat{D}_{q,\zeta})} T_{q,\zeta}\right)\{p_{n,q}(\zeta,\eta)\} = p_{n+1,q}(\zeta,\eta). \tag{49}$$

In accordance with the monomiality principle Equation (28), the aforementioned equation substantiates assertion (43) of Theorem 1. Furthermore, with the application of identity (13) to Equation (40), we have

$$\widehat{D}_{q,\zeta}\left\{\sum_{n=0}^{\infty} p_{n,q}(\zeta,\eta)\frac{t^n}{[n]_q!}\right\} = \sum_{n=1}^{\infty} p_{n-1,q}(\zeta,\eta)\frac{t^n}{[n-1]_q!}. \tag{50}$$

Upon comparing the coefficients of equivalent powers of t on both sides of Equation (50), we derive

$$\widehat{D}_{q,\zeta}\{p_{n,q}(\zeta,\eta)\} = [n]_q p_{n-1,q}(\zeta,\eta), \quad (n \geqslant 1). \tag{51}$$

Upon examining the monomiality principle Equation (29), we can conclude that assertion (44) of Theorem 1 is validated. □

Theorem 2. *The following q-differential equation for two-variable q-general polynomials 2VqgP $p_{n,q}(\zeta,\eta)$ holds:*

$$\left(\zeta\widehat{D}_{q,\zeta}+\frac{\phi_q'(\eta,\widehat{D}_{q,\zeta})}{\phi_q(\eta,\widehat{D}_{q,\zeta})}T_{q,\zeta}\widehat{D}_{q,\zeta}-[n]_q\right)p_{n,q}(\zeta,\eta)=0. \tag{52}$$

Proof. In view of Equations (31), (43), and (44), we obtain the assertion (52) of Theorem 2. □

Remark 1. *Since $p_{0,q}(\zeta,\eta)=1$, in view of monomiality principle Equation (35), we have*

$$p_{n,q}(\zeta,\eta)=\left(\zeta+\frac{\phi_q'(\eta,\widehat{D}_{q,\zeta})}{\phi_q(\eta,\widehat{D}_{q,\zeta})}T_{q,\zeta}\right)^n\{1\}\quad(p_{0,q}(\zeta,\eta)=1). \tag{53}$$

Furthermore, in view of Equations (35), (40) and (43), we have

$$e_q\left(\widehat{M}_{2VqgP}\right)\{1\}=e_q(\zeta t)\phi_q(\eta,t)=\sum_{n=0}^{\infty}p_{n,q}(\zeta,\eta)\frac{t^n}{[n]_q!}. \tag{54}$$

Subsequently, we introduce the two-variable q-general-Appell polynomials ($2VqgAP$), in order to derive the generating functions for the two-variable q-general-Appell polynomials by means of exponentially generating the function of q-Appell polynomials. Thus, replacing ζ on the left-hand side of (43) by the q-multiplicative operator of $2VqgP$ $p_{n,q}(\zeta,\eta)$, given by (40) and denoting the resultant of two-variable q-general-Appell polynomials $2VqgAP$ ${}_pA_{n,q}(\zeta,\eta)$, we obtain

$$A_q(t)e_q\left(\widehat{M}_{2VqgP}\right)\{1\}=\sum_{n=0}^{\infty}{}_pA_{n,q}(\zeta,\eta)\frac{t^n}{[n]_q!}, \tag{55}$$

which, by using Equation (43), we obtain the following two equivalent forms of ${}_pA_{n,q}(\zeta,\eta)$:

$$A_q(t)e_q\left(\zeta+\frac{\phi_q'(\eta,\widehat{D}_{q,\zeta})}{\phi_q(\eta,\widehat{D}_{q,\zeta})}T_{q,\zeta}\right)\{1\}=\sum_{n=0}^{\infty}{}_pA_{n,q}(\zeta,\eta)\frac{t^n}{[n]_q!}. \tag{56}$$

The generating function for the two-variable q-general Appell polynomials ${}_pA_{n,q}(\zeta,\eta)$ can be formulated by applying the relation (54) to the left-hand side of Equation (55), resulting in the following representation:

$$A_q(t)e_q(\zeta t)\phi_q(\eta,t)=\sum_{n=0}^{\infty}{}_pA_{n,q}(\zeta,\eta)\frac{t^n}{[n]_q!}. \tag{57}$$

Theorem 3. *The two-variable q-general-Appell polynomials ${}_pA_{n,q}(\zeta,\eta)$ are defined by the following series:*

$${}_pA_{n,q}(\zeta,\eta)=\sum_{k=0}^{n}\binom{n}{k}_q A_{k,q}p_{n-k,q}(\zeta,\eta), \tag{58}$$

where $A_{k,q}$ is given by Equation (27).

Proof. In view of Equations (27) and (40), we can write

$$\sum_{n=0}^{\infty}{}_pA_{n,q}(\zeta,\eta)\frac{t^n}{[n]_q!}=A_q(t)\sum_{n=0}^{\infty}p_{n,q}(\zeta,\eta)\frac{t^n}{[n]_q!}. \tag{59}$$

By employing the expansion (27) of $A_q(t)$ on the left side of Equation (59), performing simplification, and subsequently comparing the coefficients of equivalent t powers on both sides of the resulting expression, we arrive at assertion (58). □

By using a similar approach given in [20,21], and in view of Equation (57), the following determinant form for ${}_pA_{n,q}(\zeta,\eta)$ is obtained.

Theorem 4. *The determinant representation of two-variable q-general Appell polynomials ${}_pA_{n,q}(\zeta,\eta)$ of degree n is*

$$ {}_pA_{0,q}(\zeta,\eta) = \frac{1}{\beta_{0,q}}, $$

$$ {}_pA_{n,q}(\zeta,\eta) = \frac{(-1)^n}{(\beta_{0,q})^{n+1}} \begin{vmatrix} 1 & p_{1,q}(\zeta,\eta) & p_{2,q}(\zeta,\eta) & \cdots & p_{n-1,q}(\zeta,\eta) & p_{n,q}(\zeta,\eta) \\ \beta_{0,q} & \beta_{1,q} & \beta_{2,q} & \cdots & \beta_{n-1,q} & \beta_{n,q} \\ 0 & \beta_{0,q} & \binom{2}{1}_q\beta_{1,q} & \cdots & \binom{n-1}{1}_q\beta_{n-2,q} & \binom{n}{1}_q\beta_{n-1,q} \\ 0 & 0 & \beta_{0,q} & \cdots & \binom{n-1}{1}_q\beta_{n-3,q} & \binom{n}{2}_q\beta_{n-2,q} \\ \vdots & \vdots & \vdots & \cdots & \vdots & \\ 0 & 0 & 0 & \cdots & \beta_{0,q} & \binom{n}{n-1}_q\beta_{1,q} \end{vmatrix}, \tag{60} $$

$$ \beta_{n,q} = -\frac{1}{A_{0,q}}\left(\sum_{k=1}^{n}\binom{n}{k}_q A_{k,q}\beta_{n-k,q}\right), \quad n = 0,1,2,\ldots, $$

where $\beta_{0,q} \neq 0$, $\beta_{0,q} = \frac{1}{A_{0,q}}$ and $p_{n,q}(\zeta,\eta)$, $n = 0,1,2,\ldots$ are the two-variable q-general polynomials defined by Equation (40).

Theorem 5. *The two-variable q-general Appell polynomials ${}_pA_{n,q}(\zeta,\eta)$ are quasi-monomials under the following q-multiplicative and q-derivative operators:*

$$ \widehat{M}_{2VqgAP} = \left(\zeta + \frac{\phi_q'(\eta,\widehat{D}_{q,\zeta})}{\phi_q(\eta,\widehat{D}_{q,\zeta})}T_{q,\zeta}\right)\frac{A_q(q\widehat{D}_{q,\zeta})}{A_q(\widehat{D}_{q,\zeta})} + \frac{A_q'(\widehat{D}_{q,\zeta})}{A_q(\widehat{D}_{q,\zeta})} \tag{61} $$

and

$$ \widehat{P}_{2VqgAP} = \widehat{D}_{q,\zeta}, \tag{62} $$

respectively, where $T_{q,\zeta}$ denote the q-dilatation operators given by Equation (23).

Proof. Taking the q-derivative on both sides of Equation (57) with respect to t by using Equation (15), we obtain

$$ \sum_{n=1}^{\infty} {}_pA_{n,q}(\zeta,\eta)\widehat{D}_{q,t}\frac{t^n}{[n]_q!} $$

$$ = A_q(qt)\widehat{D}_{q,t}(e_q(\zeta t)\phi_q(\eta,t)) + e_q(\zeta t)\phi_q(\eta,t)A_q'(t), \tag{63} $$

which by using Equation (15) by taking $f_q(t) = e_q(\eta t)\phi_q(\eta,t)$ and $g(t) = A_q(t)$, and then simplifying the resultant equation by using Equations (14), (23) and (28) on the left-hand side, we have

$$ \left(\left(\zeta + \frac{\phi_q'(\eta,t)}{\phi_q(\eta,t)}T_{q,\zeta}\right)\frac{A_q(qt)}{A_q(t)} + \frac{A_q'(t)}{A_q(t)}\right)A_q(t)e_q(\zeta t)\phi_q(\eta,t) $$

$$ = \sum_{n=1}^{\infty} {}_pA_{n,q}(\zeta,\eta)\frac{t^{n-1}}{[n-1]_q!}. \tag{64} $$

Let $A_q(t)$ and $\phi_q(\eta,t)$ be invertible series of t, $\frac{A_q'(t)}{A_q(t)}$ and $\frac{\phi_q'(\eta,t)}{\phi_q(\eta,t)}$ have a q-power series expansion in t. Since

$$\widehat{D}_{q,\eta}A_q(t)e_q(\zeta t)\phi_q(\eta,t)=tA_q(t)e_q(\zeta t)\phi_q(\eta,t), \tag{65}$$

Equation (64) becomes

$$\left(\left(\zeta+\frac{\phi_q'(\eta,\widehat{D}_{q,\zeta})}{\phi_q(\eta,\widehat{D}_{q,\zeta})}T_{q,\zeta}\right)\frac{A_q(q\widehat{D}_{q,\eta})}{A_q(\widehat{D}_{q,\eta})}+\frac{A_q'(\widehat{D}_{q,\eta})}{A_q(\widehat{D}_{q,\eta})}\right)A_q(t)e_q(\zeta t)\phi_q(\eta,t)$$
$$=\sum_{n=1}^{\infty}{}_pA_{n,q}(\zeta,\eta)\frac{t^{n-1}}{[n-1]_q!}, \tag{66}$$

which, by using (57), gives

$$\left(\left(\zeta+\frac{\phi_q'(\eta,\widehat{D}_{q,\zeta})}{\phi_q(\eta,\widehat{D}_{q,\zeta})}T_{q,\zeta}\right)\frac{A_q(q\widehat{D}_{q,\eta})}{A_q(\widehat{D}_{q,\eta})}+\frac{A_q'(\widehat{D}_{q,\eta})}{A_q(\widehat{D}_{q,\eta})}\right)\sum_{n=0}^{\infty}{}_pA_{n,q}(\zeta,\eta)\frac{t^n}{[n]_q!}$$
$$=\sum_{n=1}^{\infty}{}_pA_{n,q}(\zeta,\eta)\frac{t^{n-1}}{[n-1]_q!}. \tag{67}$$

An examination of the coefficients of t on both sides of Equation (67), in conjunction with a consideration of Equation (28), leads to the derivation of assertion (61). Furthermore, upon applying identity (13) to Equation (57), we have

$$\widehat{D}_{q,\zeta}\left\{\sum_{n=0}^{\infty}{}_pA_{n,q}(\zeta,\eta)\frac{t^n}{[n]_q!}\right\}=\sum_{n=1}^{\infty}{}_pA_{n-1,q}(\zeta,\eta)\frac{t^n}{[n-1]_q!}. \tag{68}$$

Upon comparing the coefficients of equivalent powers of t on both sides of Equation (68), we derive

$$\widehat{D}_{q,\zeta}\{{}_pA_{n,q}(\zeta,\eta)\}=[n]_q\,{}_pA_{n-1,q}(\zeta,\eta),\quad (n\geqslant 1). \tag{69}$$

Upon examining the monomiality principle Equation (29), we can conclude that assertion (62) of Theorem 5 is validated. □

Theorem 6. *The following q-differential equation for ${}_pA_{n,q}(\zeta,\eta)$ holds true:*

$$\left(\zeta\frac{A_q(q\widehat{D}_{q,\eta})}{A_q(\widehat{D}_{q,\eta})}\widehat{D}_{q,\zeta}+\frac{\phi_q'(\eta,\widehat{D}_{q,\zeta})}{\phi_q(\eta,\widehat{D}_{q,\zeta})}T_{q,\zeta}\frac{A_q(q\widehat{D}_{q,\eta})}{A_q(\widehat{D}_{q,\eta})}\widehat{D}_{q,\zeta}+\frac{A_q'(\widehat{D}_{q,\eta})}{A_q(\widehat{D}_{q,\eta})}\widehat{D}_{q,\eta}-[n]_q\right){}_pA_{n,q}(\zeta,\eta)=0. \tag{70}$$

Proof. Using (61) and (62) in (31), we obtain the assertion (70). □

3. Applications

Specifically, when considering the case where $\phi_q(\eta,t)=e_q(\eta t^m)$ in generating function (57), which results in the reduction of 2VqgAP ${}_pA_{n,q}(\zeta,\eta)$ to the q-Gould–Hopper-based Appell polynomials (q-GHbAP) ${}_HA_{n,q}^{(m)}(\zeta,\eta)$ can be characterized by a specific generating function as follows:

$$A_q(t)e_q(\zeta t)e_q(\eta t^m)=\sum_{n=0}^{\infty}{}_HA_{n,q}^{(m)}(\zeta,\eta)\frac{t^n}{[n]_q!}. \tag{71}$$

In other words, we have

$${}_HA_{n,q}^{(m)}(\zeta,\eta)=e_q(\eta\widehat{D}_{q,\eta}^{(m)})\{A_{n,q}(\zeta)\}. \tag{72}$$

Through the application of Equations (20) and (26), we can expand the left-hand side of Equation (71) as follows

$$ {}_HA_{n,q}^{(m)}(\zeta,\eta) = \sum_{k=0}^{n} \binom{n}{k}_q A_{k,q} H_{n-k,q}^{(m)}(\zeta,\eta). \tag{73} $$

By using a similar approach given in [20,21] and in view of Equation (71), the following determinant form for ${}_HA_{n,q}^{(m)}(\zeta,\eta)$ is obtained.

Theorem 7. *The determinant representation of q-Gould–Hopper-based Appell polynomials* ${}_HA_{n,q}^{(m)}(\zeta,\eta)$ *of degree n is*

$$ {}_HA_{0,q}^{(m)}(\zeta,\eta) = \frac{1}{\beta_{0,q}}, $$

$$ {}_HA_{n,q}^{(m)}(\zeta,\eta) = \frac{(-1)^n}{(\beta_{0,q})^{n+1}} \begin{vmatrix} 1 & H_{1,q}^{(m)}(\zeta,\eta) & H_{2,q}^{(m)}(\zeta,\eta) & \cdots & H_{n-1,q}^{(m)}(\zeta,\eta) & H_{n,q}^{(m)}(\zeta,\eta) \\ \beta_{0,q} & \beta_{1,q} & \beta_{2,q} & \cdots & \beta_{n-1,q} & \beta_{n,q} \\ 0 & \beta_{0,q} & \binom{2}{1}_q \beta_{1,q} & \cdots & \binom{n-1}{1}_q \beta_{n-2,q} & \binom{n}{1}_q \beta_{n-1,q} \\ 0 & 0 & \beta_{0,q} & \cdots & \binom{n-1}{1}_q \beta_{n-3,q} & \binom{n}{2}_q \beta_{n-2,q} \\ \vdots & \vdots & \vdots & \cdots & \vdots & \\ 0 & 0 & 0 & \cdots & \beta_{0,q} & \binom{n}{n-1}_q \beta_{1,q} \end{vmatrix}, \tag{74} $$

$$ \beta_{n,q} = -\frac{1}{A_{0,q}} \left(\sum_{k=1}^{n} \binom{n}{k}_q A_{k,q} \beta_{n-k,q} \right), \quad n = 0,1,2,\ldots, $$

where $\beta_{0,q} \neq 0$, $\beta_{0,q} = \frac{1}{A_{0,q}}$ *and* $H_{n,q}^{(m)}(\zeta,\eta)$, $n = 0,1,2,\ldots$ *are the q-Gould–Hopper polynomials defined by Equation (20).*

We shall now demonstrate the q-multiplicative and q-derivative operators of ${}_HA_{n,q}^{(m)}(\zeta,\eta)$. The following theorem is presented:

Theorem 8. *The q-Gould–Hopper-based Appell polynomials* ${}_HA_{n,q}^{(m)}(\zeta,\eta)$ *are quasi-monomial under the following q-multiplicative and q-derivative operators:*

$$ \widehat{M}_{2VqGHAP} = \left(\zeta T_\eta + \eta \widehat{D}_{q,\zeta}^{m-1} T_{(\eta;m)} \right) \frac{A_q(q\widehat{D}_{q,\eta})}{A_q(\widehat{D}_{q,\eta})} + \frac{A_q'(\widehat{D}_{q,\eta})}{A_q(\widehat{D}_{q,\eta})}, \tag{75} $$

or, equivalently,

$$ \widehat{M}_{2VqGHAP} = \left(\zeta + \eta \widehat{D}_{q,\zeta}^{m-1} T_{(\eta;m)} T_\zeta \right) \frac{A_q(q\widehat{D}_{q,\eta})}{A_q(\widehat{D}_{q,\eta})} + \frac{A_q'(\widehat{D}_{q,\eta})}{A_q(\widehat{D}_{q,\eta})} \tag{76} $$

and

$$ \widehat{P}_{2VqGHAP} = \widehat{D}_{q,\zeta}, \tag{77} $$

respectively, where T_ζ *and* T_η *denote the q-dilatation operators given by Equation (23), and* $D_{q,\zeta}^{-1}$ *is defined by Equation (19).*

Proof. By applying the q-derivative to both sides of Equation (71) with respect to t, utilizing Equation (15), we obtain

$$ \sum_{n=1}^{\infty} {}_HA_{n,q}^{(m)}(\zeta,\eta) \widehat{D}_{q,t} \frac{t^n}{[n]_q!} $$

$$= A_q(qt)e_q\widehat{D}_{q,t}(e_q(\zeta t)e_q(\eta t^m)) + e_q(\zeta t)e_q(\eta t^m)A_q'(t), \tag{78}$$

which, by using Equation (15) by taking $f(t) = e_q(\zeta t)e_q(\eta t^m)$ and $g(t) = A_q(t)$, and then simplifying the resultant equation by using Equations (14), (26), and (27) on the left-hand side, we have

$$\left(\left(\zeta T_\eta + \eta t^{m-1}T_{(\eta;m)}\right)\frac{A_q(qt)}{A_q(t)} + \frac{A_q'(t)}{A_q(t)}\right)A_q(t)e_q(\zeta t)e_q(\eta t^m)$$

$$= \sum_{n=1}^{\infty} {}_HA_{n,q}^{(m)}(\zeta,\eta)\frac{t^{n-1}}{[n-1]_q!}. \tag{79}$$

Since

$$\widehat{D}_{q,\zeta}A_q(t)e_q(\zeta t)e_q(\eta t^m) = tA_q(t)e_q(\zeta t)e_q(\eta t^m) \tag{80}$$

and $\frac{A_q'(t)}{A_q(t)}$ has a q-power series expansion in t, as $A_q(t)$ is an invertible series of t.

Therefore, by using Equation (71), we obtain

$$\left(\left(\eta T_\eta + \eta\widehat{D}_{q,\zeta}^{m-1}T_{(\eta;m)}\right)\frac{A_q(q\widehat{D}_{q,\eta})}{A_q(\widehat{D}_{q,\eta})} + \frac{A_q'(\widehat{D}_{q,\eta})}{A_q(\widehat{D}_{q,\eta})}\right)$$

$$\times \sum_{n=0}^{\infty} {}_HA_{n,q}^{(m)}(\zeta,\eta)\frac{t^n}{[n]_q!} = \sum_{n=1}^{\infty} {}_HA_{n,q}^{(m)}(\zeta,\eta)\frac{t^{n-1}}{[n-1]_q!}. \tag{81}$$

Comparing the coefficients of t on both sides of Equation (81), and then, in view of Equation (28), the resultant equation gives assertion (75).

Employing Equation (78) with $f_q(t) = e_q(\eta t^m)$ and $g_q(t) = e_q(\zeta t)$, and applying the methodology utilized in the proof of assertion (75), we obtain assertion (76).

Upon examining Equations (29) and (80), we establish assertion (77). □

Theorem 9. *The following q-differential equation for q-GAbP ${}_HA_{n,q}^{(m)}(\zeta,\eta)$ holds true:*

$$\left(\zeta\widehat{D}_{q,\zeta}\frac{A_q(q\widehat{D}_{q,\zeta})}{A_q(\widehat{D}_{q,\zeta})}T_\eta + \eta\widehat{D}_{q,\zeta}^{m}T_{(\eta;m)}\frac{A_q(q\widehat{D}_{q,\zeta})}{A_q(\widehat{D}_{q,\zeta})} + \frac{A_q'(\widehat{D}_{q,\eta})}{A_q(\widehat{D}_{q,\zeta})}\widehat{D}_{q,\zeta} - [n]_q\right){}_HA_{n,q}^{(m)}(\zeta,\eta) = 0, \tag{82}$$

or, equivalently

$$\left(\zeta\widehat{D}_{q,\zeta}\frac{A_q(q\widehat{D}_{q,\zeta})}{A_q(\widehat{D}_{q,\zeta})} + \eta\widehat{D}_{q,\zeta}^{m}T_{(\eta;m)}\frac{A_q(q\widehat{D}_{q,\zeta})}{A_q(\widehat{D}_{q,\zeta})}T_\zeta + \frac{A_q'(\widehat{D}_{q,\eta})}{A_q(\widehat{D}_{q,\zeta})}\widehat{D}_{q,\zeta} - [n]_q\right){}_HA_{n,q}^{(m)}(\zeta,\eta) = 0. \tag{83}$$

Proof. Using (75), (76), and (77) in (31), we obtain the assertions (82) and (83). □

4. Examples

In this section, we consider certain members of the family of two-variable q-Gould–Hopper-based Appell polynomials (71).

Through the appropriate selection of the function $A_q(t)$ in Table 1 in Equation (71), it is possible to establish the following generating functions for the q-Gould–Hopper-based Bernoulli ${}_H\mathbb{B}_{n,q}^{(m)}(\zeta,\eta)$, Euler ${}_H\mathbb{E}_{n,q}^{(m)}(\zeta,\eta)$, and Genocchi ${}_H\mathbb{G}_{n,q}^{(m)}(\zeta,\eta)$ polynomials:

$$\frac{t}{e_q(t)-1}e_q(\zeta t)e_q(\eta t^m) = \sum_{n=0}^{\infty} {}_H\mathbb{B}_{n,q}^{(m)}(\zeta,\eta)\frac{t^n}{[n]_q!}, \tag{84}$$

$$\frac{2}{e_q(t)+1}e_q(\zeta t)e_q(\eta t^m) = \sum_{n=0}^{\infty} {}_H\mathbb{E}_{n,q}^{(m)}(\zeta,\eta)\frac{t^n}{[n]_q!} \tag{85}$$

and

$$\frac{2t}{e_q(t)+1}e_q(\zeta t)e_q(\eta t^m)=\sum_{n=0}^{\infty}{}_H\mathbb{G}_{n,q}^{(m)}(\zeta,\eta)\frac{t^n}{[n]_q!}. \tag{86}$$

Furthermore, in view of expression (73), the polynomials ${}_H\mathbb{B}_{n,q}^{(m)}(\zeta,\eta)$, ${}_H\mathbb{E}_{n,q}^{(m)}(\zeta,\eta)$, and ${}_H\mathbb{G}_{n,q}^{(m)}(\zeta,\eta)$ satisfy the following explicit form:

$${}_H\mathbb{B}_{n,q}^{(m)}(\zeta,\eta)=\sum_{k=0}^{n}\binom{n}{k}_q \mathbb{B}_{k,q}\, H_{n-k,q}^{(m)}(\zeta,\eta), \tag{87}$$

$${}_H\mathbb{E}_{n,q}^{(m)}(\zeta,\eta)=\sum_{k=0}^{n}\binom{n}{k}_q \mathbb{E}_{k,q}\, H_{n-k,q}^{(m)}(\zeta,\eta) \tag{88}$$

and

$${}_H\mathbb{G}_{n,q}^{(m)}(\zeta,\eta)=\sum_{k=0}^{n}\binom{n}{k}_q \mathbb{G}_{k,q}\, H_{n-k,q}^{(m)}(\zeta,\eta). \tag{89}$$

Furthermore, in view of expressions (74), the polynomials ${}_H\mathbb{B}_{n,q}^{(m)}(\zeta,\eta)$, ${}_H\mathbb{E}_{n,q}^{(m)}(\zeta,\eta)$ and ${}_H\mathbb{G}_{n,q}^{(m)}(\zeta,\eta)$ satisfy the following determinant representations:

$${}_H\mathbb{B}_{0,q}^{(m)}(\zeta,\eta)=1,$$

$${}_H\mathbb{B}_{n,q}^{(m)}(\zeta,\eta)=(-1)^n\begin{vmatrix} 1 & H_{1,q}^{(m)}(\zeta,\eta) & H_{2,q}^{(m)}(\zeta,\eta) & \cdots & H_{n-1,q}^{(m)}(\zeta,\eta,) & H_{n,q}^{(m)}(\zeta,\eta) \\ 1 & \frac{1}{[2]_q} & \frac{1}{[3]_q} & \cdots & \frac{1}{[n]_q} & \frac{1}{[n+1]_q} \\ 0 & 1 & \binom{2}{1}_q\frac{1}{[2]_q} & \cdots & \binom{n-1}{1}_q\frac{1}{[n-1]_q} & \binom{n}{1}_q\frac{1}{[n]_q} \\ 0 & 0 & 1 & \cdots & \binom{n-1}{2}_q\frac{1}{[n-2]_q} & \binom{n}{2}_q\frac{1}{[n-1]_q} \\ . & . & . & \cdots & . & . \\ . & . & . & \cdots & . & . \\ 0 & 0 & 0 & \cdots & 1 & \binom{n}{n-1}_q\frac{1}{[2]_q} \end{vmatrix}, \tag{90}$$

$${}_H\mathbb{E}_{0,q}^{(m)}(\zeta,\eta)=1,$$

$${}_H\mathbb{E}_{n,q}^{(m)}(\zeta,\eta)=(-1)^n\begin{vmatrix} 1 & H_{1,q}^{(m)}(\zeta,\eta) & H_{2,q}^{(m)}(\zeta,\eta) & \cdots & H_{n-1,q}^{(m)}(\zeta,\eta) & H_{n,q}^{(m)}(\zeta,\eta) \\ 1 & \frac{1}{2} & \frac{1}{2} & \cdots & \frac{1}{2} & \frac{1}{2} \\ 0 & 1 & \binom{2}{1}_q\frac{1}{2} & \cdots & \binom{n-1}{1}_q\frac{1}{2} & \binom{n}{1}_q\frac{1}{2} \\ 0 & 0 & 1 & \cdots & \binom{n-1}{2}_q\frac{1}{2} & \binom{n}{2}_q\frac{1}{2} \\ . & . & . & \cdots & . & . \\ . & . & . & \cdots & . & . \\ 0 & 0 & 0 & \cdots & 1 & \binom{n}{n-1}_q\frac{1}{2} \end{vmatrix} \tag{91}$$

and

$${}_H\mathbb{G}_{0,q}^{(m)}(\zeta,\eta)=1,$$

$$
{}_{H}\mathbb{G}_{n,q}^{(m)}(\zeta,\eta)=(-1)^{n}\begin{vmatrix}
1 & H_{1,q}^{(m)}(\zeta,\eta) & H_{2,q}^{(m)}(\zeta,\eta) & \cdots & H_{n-1,q}^{(m)}(\zeta,\eta) & H_{n,q}^{(m)}(\zeta,\eta)\\
1 & \frac{1}{2[2]_q} & \frac{1}{2[3]_q} & \cdots & \frac{1}{2[n]_q} & \frac{1}{2[n+1]_q}\\
0 & 1 & \binom{2}{1}_q\frac{1}{2[2]_q} & \cdots & \binom{n-1}{1}_q\frac{1}{2[n-1]_q} & \binom{n}{1}_q\frac{1}{2[n]_q}\\
0 & 0 & 1 & \cdots & \binom{n-1}{2}_q\frac{1}{2[n-2]_q} & \binom{n}{2}_q\frac{1}{2[n-1]_q}\\
. & . & . & \cdots & . & .\\
. & . & . & \cdots & . & .\\
0 & 0 & 0 & \cdots & 1 & \binom{n}{n-1}_q\frac{1}{2[2]_q}
\end{vmatrix}, \tag{92}
$$

where $H_{n,q}^{(m)}(\zeta,\eta),\quad (n=0,1,2\cdots)$ are the q-Gould–Hopper polynomials of degree n.

5. Distribution of Zeros and Graphical Representation

In this section, we aim to provide the graphical representations and zeros for the q-Gould–Hopper-based Bernoulli ${}_{H}\mathbb{B}_{n,q}^{(m)}(\zeta,\eta)$ and q-Gould–Hopper-based Euler ${}_{H}\mathbb{E}_{n,q}^{(m)}(\zeta,\eta)$ polynomials. By appropriately choosing the function $A_q(t)$ from Table 1 in Equation (57), we can establish the following generating functions for the q-Gould–Hopper-based Bernoulli ${}_{H}\mathbb{B}_{n,q}^{(m)}(\zeta,\eta)$ polynomial:

$$
\frac{t}{e_q(t)-1}e_q(\zeta t)e_q(\eta t^m)=\sum_{n=0}^{\infty}{}_{H}\mathbb{B}_{n,q}^{(m)}(\zeta,\eta)\frac{t^n}{[n]_q!}. \tag{93}
$$

A few of them are

$$
\begin{aligned}
{}_{H}\mathbb{B}_{0,q}^{(3)}(\zeta,\eta))&=1,\\
{}_{H}\mathbb{B}_{1,q}^{(3)}(\zeta,\eta)&=\zeta-\frac{1}{[2]_q!},\\
{}_{H}\mathbb{B}_{2,q}^{(3)}(\zeta,\eta)&=-\zeta+\zeta^2+\frac{1}{[2]_q!}-\frac{[2]_q!}{[3]_q!},\\
{}_{H}\mathbb{B}_{3,q}^{(3)}(\zeta,\eta)&=-\zeta+\zeta^3+\frac{2}{[2]_q!}+\eta[3]_q!-\frac{[3]_q!}{[2]_q^3}+\frac{\zeta[3]_q!}{[2]_q!^2}-\frac{\zeta^2[3]_q!}{[2]_q!^2}-\frac{[3]_q!}{[4]_q!},\\
{}_{H}\mathbb{B}_{4,q}^{(3)}(\zeta,\eta)&=-\zeta+\zeta^4+\frac{2}{[2]_q!}+\zeta\eta[4]_q!+\frac{[4]_q!}{[2]_q!^4}-\frac{\zeta[4]_q!}{[2]_q!^3}+\frac{\zeta^2[4]_q!}{[2]_q!^3}\\
&\quad-\frac{\eta[4]_q!}{[2]_q!}+\frac{[4]_q!}{[3]_q!^2}-\frac{3[4]_q!}{[2]_q!^2[3]_q!}+\frac{2\zeta[4]_q!}{[2]_q![3]_q!}-\frac{\zeta^2[4]_q!}{[2]_q![3]_q!}-\frac{\zeta^3[4]_q!}{[2]_q![3]_q!}-\frac{[4]_q!}{[5]_q!},\\
{}_{H}\mathbb{B}_{5,q}^{(3)}(\zeta,\eta)&=-\zeta+\zeta^5+\frac{2}{[2]_q!}-\frac{[5]_q!}{[2]_q!^5}+\frac{\zeta[5]_q!}{[2]_q!^4}-\frac{\zeta^2[5]_q!}{[2]_q!^4}+\frac{\eta[5]_q!}{[2]_q!^2}-\frac{\zeta\eta[5]_q!}{[2]_q!}\\
&\quad+\frac{\zeta^2\eta[5]_q!}{[2]_q!}+\frac{\zeta[5]_q!}{[3]_q!^2}-\frac{\zeta^3[5]_q!}{[3]_q!^2}-\frac{3[5]_q!}{[2]_q![3]_q!^2}-\frac{\eta[5]_q!}{[3]_q!}+\frac{4[5]_q!}{[2]_q!^3[3]_q!}\\
&\quad-\frac{3\zeta[5]_q!}{[2]_q!^2[3]_q!}+\frac{2\zeta^2[5]_q!}{[2]_q!^2[3]_q!}+\frac{\zeta^3[5]_q!}{[2]_q!^2[3]_q!}-\frac{3[5]_q!}{[2]_q!^2[4,]_q!}+\frac{2\zeta[5]_q!}{[2]_q![4]_q!}\\
&\quad-\frac{\zeta^2[5]_!}{[2]_q![4]_q!}-\frac{\zeta^4[5]_q!}{[2]_q![4]_q!}+\frac{2[5]_q!}{[3]_q![4]_q!}-\frac{[5]_q!}{[6]_q!}.
\end{aligned}
$$

We investigate the beautiful zeros of the q-Gould–Hopper-based Bernoulli ${}_{H}\mathbb{B}_{n,q}^{(m)}(\zeta,\eta)=0$ by using a computer. We plot the zeros of q-Gould–Hopper-based Bernoulli ${}_{H}\mathbb{B}_{n,q}^{(m)}(\zeta,\eta)=0$ for $n=24$ (Figure 1).

In Figure 1 (top-left), we choose $m = 3, \eta = 6$, and $q = \frac{3}{10}$. In Figure 1 (top-right), we choose $m = 3, \eta = 6$, and $q = \frac{5}{10}$. In Figure 1 (bottom-left), we choose $m = 3, \eta = 6$, and $q = \frac{7}{10}$. In Figure 1 (bottom-right), we choose $m = 3, \eta = 6$, and $q = \frac{9}{10}$.

Stacks of zeros of the q-Gould–Hopper-based Bernoulli ${}_H\mathbb{B}_{n,q}^{(m)}(\zeta, \eta) = 0$ for $1 \leq n \leq 24$, forming a 3D structure, are presented (Figure 2).

In Figure 2 (top-left), we choose $m = 3, \eta = 6$, and $q = \frac{3}{10}$. In Figure 2 (top-right), we choose $m = 3, \eta = 6$, and $q = \frac{5}{10}$. In Figure 2 (bottom-left), we choose $m = 3, \eta = 6$, and $q = \frac{7}{10}$. In Figure 2 (bottom-right), we choose $m = 3, \eta = 6$, and $q = \frac{9}{10}$.

Plots of the real zeros of the q-Gould–Hopper-based Bernoulli ${}_H\mathbb{B}_{n,q}^{(m)}(\zeta, \eta) = 0$ for $1 \leq n \leq 24$ are presented (Figure 3).

In Figure 3 (top-left), we choose $m = 3, \eta = 6$, and $q = \frac{3}{10}$. In Figure 3 (top-right), we choose $m = 3, \eta = 6$, and $q = \frac{5}{10}$. In Figure 3 (bottom-left), we choose $m = 3, \eta = 6$, and $q = \frac{7}{10}$. In Figure 3 (bottom-right), we choose $m = 3, \eta = 6$, and $q = \frac{9}{10}$.

Next, we calculate an approximate solution satisfying the q-Gould–Hopper-based Bernoulli ${}_H\mathbb{B}_{n,q}^{(m)}(\zeta, \eta) = 0$ for $m = 3, \eta = 6$, and $q = \frac{9}{10}$. The results are given in Table 3.

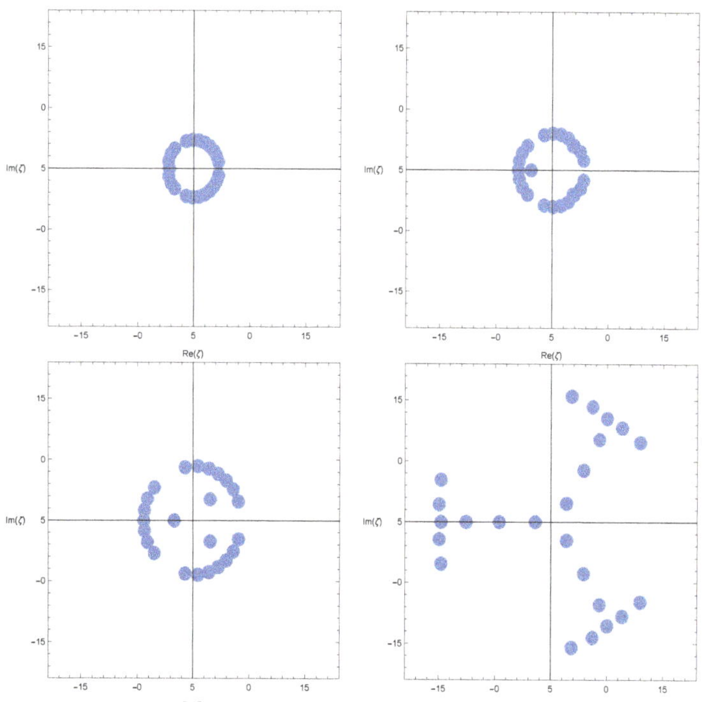

Figure 1. Zeros of ${}_H\mathbb{B}_{n,q}^{(m)}(\zeta, \eta) = 0$.

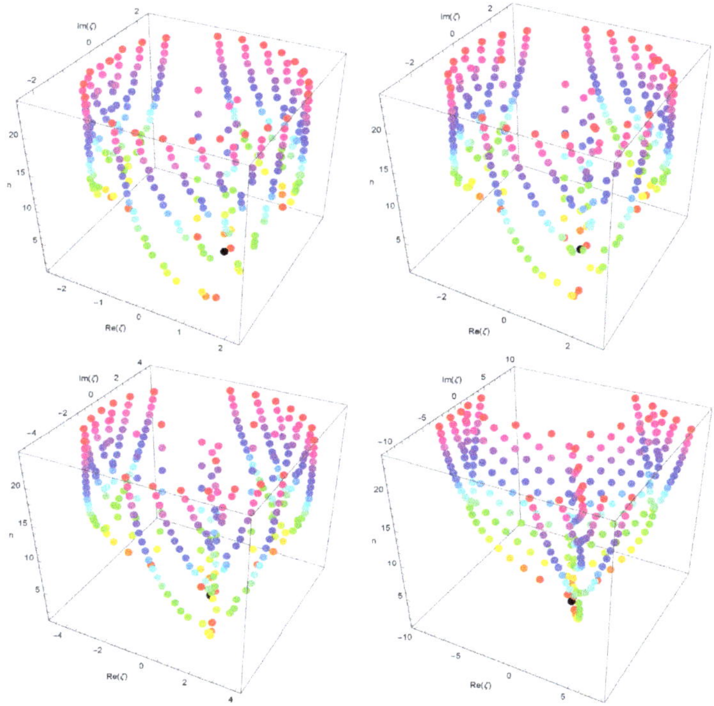

Figure 2. Zeros of ${}_H\mathbb{B}_{n,q}^{(m)}(\zeta,\eta) = 0$.

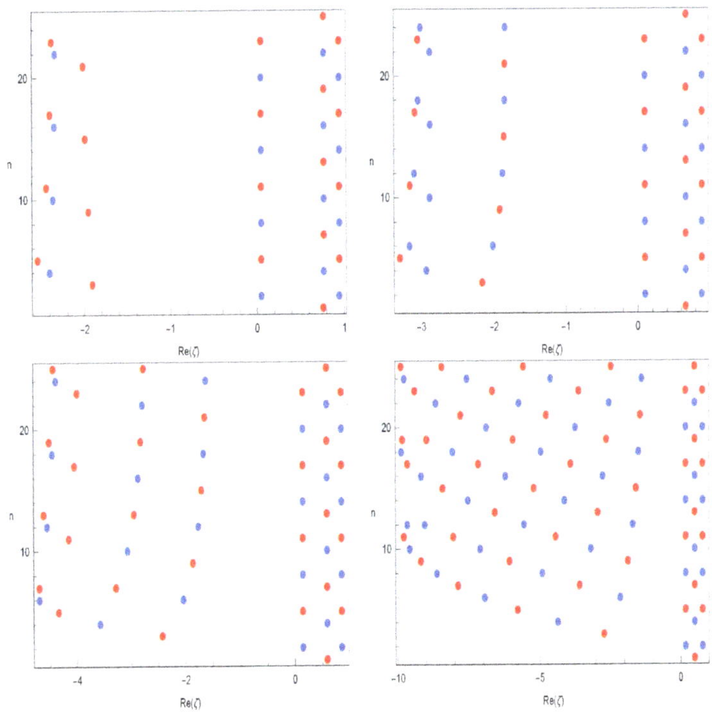

Figure 3. Real zeros of ${}_H\mathbb{B}_{n,q}^{(m)}(\zeta,\eta) = 0$.

Table 3. Approximate solutions of ${}_{H}\mathbb{B}_{n,q}^{(m)}(\zeta, \eta) = 0$.

Degree n	ζ
1	0.52632
2	0.19555, 0.80445
3	−2.6891, 2.0577 − 2.6942i, 2.0577 + 2.6942i
4	−4.3398, 0.52609, 2.8119 − 4.0737i, 2.8119 + 4.0737i
5	−5.7645, 0.19543, 0.80436, 3.4600 − 5.2700i, 3.4600 + 5.2700i
6	−6.9272, −2.1200, 1.7821 − 2.2002i, 1.7821 + 2.2002i, 3.9746 − 6.2386i, 3.9746 + 6.2386i
7	−7.8678, −3.5588, 0.52589, 2.4441 − 3.4039i, 2.4441 + 3.4039i, 4.3791 − 7.0171i, 4.3791 + 7.0171i
8	−8.6091, −4.8888, 0.19532, 0.80428, 3.0642 − 4.5295i, 3.0642 + 4.5295i, 4.6837 − 7.6242i, 4.6837 + 7.6242i
9	−9.1693, −6.0540, −1.8456, 1.6480 − 1.9596i, 1.6480 + 1.9596i, 3.6030 − 5.5115i, 3.6030 + 5.5115i, 4.8955 − 8.0749i, 4.8955 + 8.0749i
10	−9.5569, −7.0891, −3.1609, 0.52570, 2.2537 − 3.0594i, 2.2537 + 3.0594i, 4.0884 − 6.3858i, 4.0884 + 6.3858i, 5.0125 − 8.3748i, 5.0125 + 8.3748i

Similarly, by appropriately choosing the function $A_q(t)$ from Table 1 in Equation (57), we can obtain the following generating functions for the q-Gould–Hopper-based Euler ${}_{H}\mathbb{E}_{n,q}^{(m)}(\zeta, \eta)$ polynomial:

$$\frac{2}{e_q(t)+1}e_q(\zeta t)e_q(\eta t^m) = \sum_{n=0}^{\infty} {}_{H}\mathbb{E}_{n,q}^{(m)}(\zeta, \eta)\frac{t^n}{[n]_q!}. \tag{94}$$

A few of them are

$$\begin{aligned}
{}_{H}\mathbb{E}_{0,q}^{(2)}(\zeta,\eta)) &= 1,\\
{}_{H}\mathbb{E}_{1,q}^{(2)}(\zeta,\eta) &= -\frac{1}{2}+\zeta,\\
{}_{H}\mathbb{E}_{2,q}^{(2)}(\zeta,\eta) &= -\frac{1}{2}+\zeta^2+\frac{1}{4}[2]_q!-\frac{1}{2}\zeta[2]_q!+\eta[2]_q!,\\
{}_{H}\mathbb{E}_{3,q}^{(2)}(\zeta,\eta) &= -\frac{1}{2}+\zeta^3-\frac{1}{8}[3]_q!+\frac{1}{4}\zeta[3]_q!-\frac{1}{2}\eta[3]_q!+\zeta\eta[3]_q!\\
&\quad+\frac{[3]_q!}{2[2]_q!}-\frac{\zeta[3]_q!}{2[2]_q!}-\frac{\zeta^2[3]_q!}{2[2]_q!},\\
{}_{H}\mathbb{E}_{4,q}^{(2)}(\zeta,\eta) &= -\frac{1}{2}+\zeta^4+\frac{1}{16}[4]_q!-\frac{1}{8}\zeta[4]_q!+\frac{1}{4}\eta[4]_q!-\frac{1}{2}\zeta\eta[4]_q!+\frac{[4]_q!}{4[2]_q!^2}\\
&\quad-\frac{\zeta^2[4]_q!}{2[2]_q!^2}-\frac{3[4]_q!}{8[2]_q!}+\frac{\zeta[4]_q!}{2[2]_q!}+\frac{\zeta^2[4]_q!}{4[2]_q!}-\frac{\eta[4]_q!}{2[2]_q!}+\frac{\zeta^2\eta[4]_q!}{[2]_q!}\\
&\quad+\frac{\eta^2[4]_q!}{[2]_q!}+\frac{[4]_q!}{2[3]_q!}-\frac{\zeta[4]_q!}{2[3]_q!}-\frac{\zeta^3[4]_q!}{2[3]_q!},\\
{}_{H}\mathbb{E}_{5,q}^{(2)}(\zeta,\eta) &= -\frac{1}{2}+\zeta^5-\frac{1}{32}[5]_q!+\frac{1}{16}\zeta[5]_q!-\frac{1}{8}\eta[5]_q!+\frac{1}{4}\zeta\eta[5]_q!\\
&\quad-\frac{3[5]_q!}{8[2]_q!^2}+\frac{\zeta[5]_q!}{4[2]_q!^2}+\frac{\zeta^2[5]_q!}{2[2]_q!^2}+\frac{[5]_q!}{4[2]_q!}-\frac{3\zeta[5]_q!}{8[2]_q!}-\frac{\zeta^2[5]_q!}{8[2]_q!}\\
&\quad+\frac{\eta[5]_q!}{2[2]_q!}-\frac{\zeta\eta[5]_q!}{2[2]_q!}-\frac{\zeta^2\eta[5]_q!}{2[2]_q!}-\frac{\eta^2[5]_q!}{2[2]_q!}+\frac{\zeta\eta^2[5]_q!}{[2]_q!}\\
&\quad-\frac{3[5]_q!}{8[3]_q!}+\frac{\zeta[5]_q!}{2[3]_q!}+\frac{\zeta^3[5]_q!}{4[3]_q!}-\frac{\eta[5]_q!}{2[3]_q!}+\frac{\zeta^3\eta[5]_q!}{[3]_q!}+\frac{[5]_q!}{2[2]_q![3]_q!}\\
&\quad-\frac{\zeta^2[5]_q!}{2[2]_q![3]_q!}-\frac{\zeta^3[5]_q!}{2[2]_q![3]_q!}+\frac{[5]_q!}{2[4]_q!}-\frac{\zeta[5]_q!}{2[4]_q!}-\frac{\zeta^4[5]_q!}{2[4]_q!}.
\end{aligned}$$

We investigate the beautiful zeros of the q-Gould–Hopper-based Euler ${}_H\mathbb{E}_{n,q}^{(m)}(\zeta,\eta) = 0$ by using a computer. We plot the zeros of q-Gould–Hopper-based Euler ${}_H\mathbb{E}_{n,q}^{(m)}(\zeta,\eta) = 0$ for $n = 24$ (Figure 4).

In Figure 4 (top-left), we choose $m = 2, \eta = 6$, and $q = \frac{3}{10}$. In Figure 4 (top-right), we choose $m = 2, \eta = 6$, and $q = \frac{5}{10}$. In Figure 4 (bottom-left), we choose $m = 2, \eta = 6$, and $q = \frac{7}{10}$. In Figure 4 (bottom-right), we choose $m = 2, \eta = 6$, and $q = \frac{9}{10}$.

The stacks of zeros of the q-Gould–Hopper-based Euler ${}_H\mathbb{E}_{n,q}^{(m)}(\zeta,\eta) = 0$ for $1 \leq n \leq 24$, forming a 3D structure, are presented (Figure 5).

In Figure 5 (top-left), we choose $m = 2, \eta = 6$, and $q = \frac{3}{10}$. In Figure 5 (top-right), we choose $m = 2, \eta = 6$, and $q = \frac{5}{10}$. In Figure 5 (bottom-left), we choose $m = 2, \eta = 6$, and $q = \frac{7}{10}$. In Figure 5 (bottom-right), we choose $m = 2, \eta = 6$, and $q = \frac{9}{10}$.

Plots of the real zeros of the q-Gould–Hopper-based Euler ${}_H\mathbb{E}_{n,q}^{(m)}(\zeta,\eta) = 0$ for $1 \leq n \leq 24$ are presented (Figure 6).

In Figure 6 (top-left), we choose $m = 2, \eta = 6$, and $q = \frac{3}{10}$. In Figure 6 (top-right), we choose $m = 2, \eta = 6$, and $q = \frac{5}{10}$. In Figure 6 (bottom-left), we choose $m = 2, \eta = 6$, and $q = \frac{7}{10}$. In Figure 6 (bottom-right), we choose $m = 2, \eta = 6$, and $q = \frac{9}{10}$.

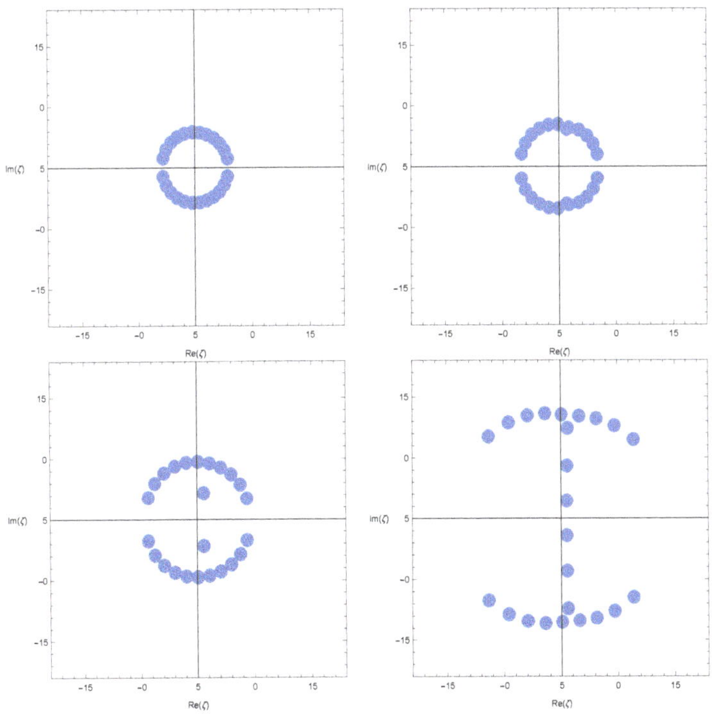

Figure 4. Zeros of ${}_H\mathbb{E}_{n,q}^{(m)}(\zeta,\eta) = 0$.

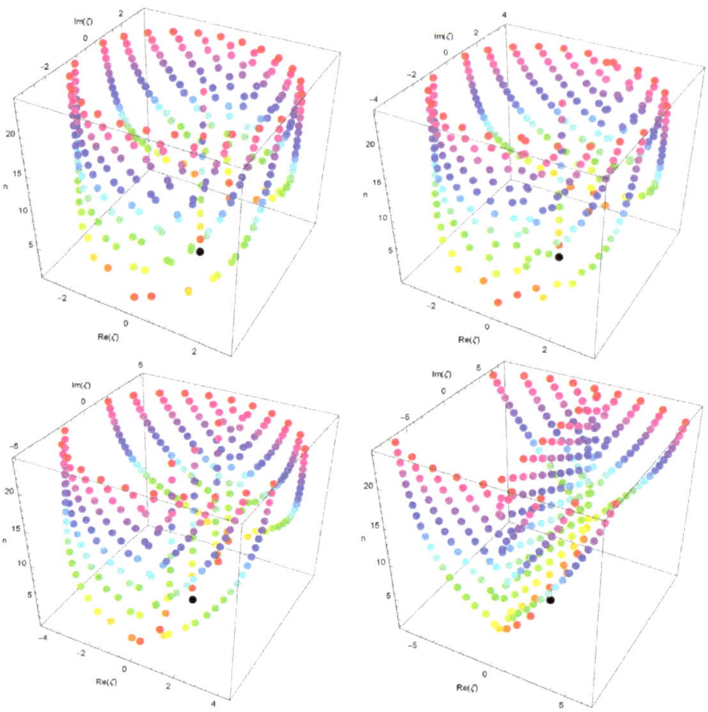

Figure 5. Zeros of ${}_H\mathbb{E}_{n,q}^{(m)}(\zeta,\eta) = 0$.

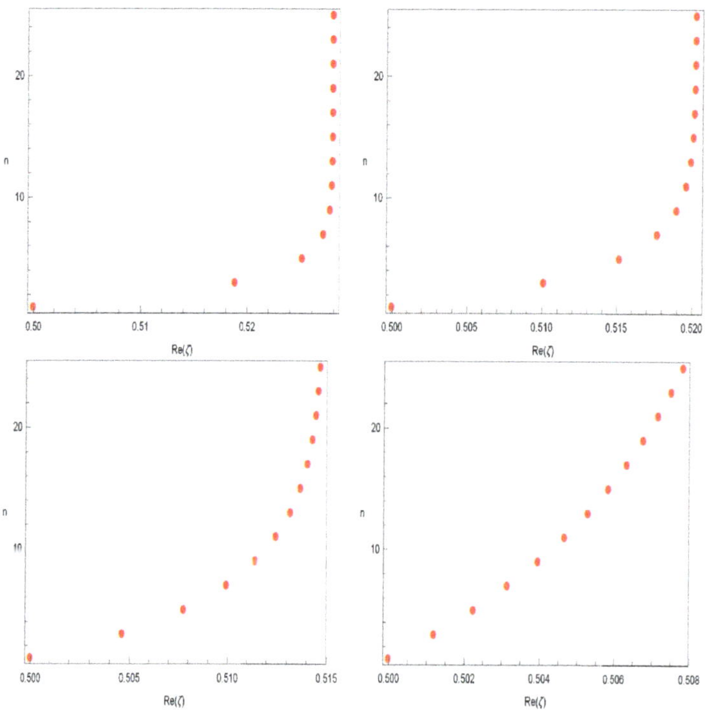

Figure 6. Real zeros of ${}_H\mathbb{E}_{n,q}^{(m)}(\zeta,\eta) = 0$.

Next, we calculated an approximate solution satisfying the q-Gould–Hopper-based Euler ${}_H\mathbb{E}_{n,q}^{(m)}(\zeta,\eta)=0$ for $m=2, \eta=6$, and $q=\frac{9}{10}$. The results are given in Table 4.

Table 4. Approximate solutions of ${}_H\mathbb{E}_{n,q}^{(m)}(\zeta,\eta)=0$.

Degree n	ζ
1	0.50000
2	$0.4750-3.3391i$, $0.4750+3.3391i$
3	$0.4269-5.4969i$, $0.4269+5.4969i$, 0.50120
4	$0.3686-6.9276i$, $0.3686+6.9276i$, $0.4912-2.5888i$, $0.4912+2.5888i$
5	$0.2992-7.8166i$, $0.2992+7.8166i$, $0.4734-4.6431i$, $0.4734+4.6431i$, 0.50224
6	$0.1944-8.2120i$, $0.1944+8.2120i$, $0.4795-6.3458i$, $0.4795+6.3458i$, $0.4975-2.2225i$, $0.4975+2.2225i$
7	$-0.3810-8.1652i$, $-0.3810+8.1652i$, $0.4901-4.1360i$, $0.4901+4.1360i$, 0.50316, $0.9436-7.7827i$, $0.9436+7.7827i$
8	$-0.9757-8.4614i$, $-0.9757+8.4614i$, $0.4911-5.8222i$, $0.4911+5.8222i$, $0.5012-1.9994i$, $0.5012+1.9994i$, $1.4072-8.2319i$, $1.4072+8.2319i$
9	$-1.4546-8.5648i$, $-1.4546+8.5648i$, $0.4537-7.3398i$, $0.4537+7.3398i$, $0.4993-3.7990i$, $0.4993+3.7990i$, 0.50396, $1.7811-8.2699i$, $1.7811+8.2699i$
10	$-1.9729-8.6021i$, $-1.9729+8.6021i$, $0.2771-8.2181i$, $0.2771+8.2181i$, $0.5036-1.8475i$, $0.5036+1.8475i$, $0.5055-5.4479i$, $0.5055+5.4479i$, $2.3151-8.2932i$, $2.3151+8.2932i$

6. Conclusions

In this paper, we have presented precise formulas and illuminated the fundamental characteristics of these polynomials, enhancing our comprehension of two-variable q-general-Appell polynomials and their relationships with established polynomial categories. Such advancements enrich the mathematical landscape and pave the way for novel research. The wide-ranging potential applications of these polynomials span quantum mechanics, mathematical physics, statistical mechanics, information theory, and computational science, warranting extensive investigation. Subsequent research may probe the structural properties and algebraic facets of these polynomials, potentially revealing profound insights and practical applications. Moreover, interdisciplinary collaboration can amplify the real-world impact of these polynomials across diverse fields. In summary, the introduction and examination of q-hybrid polynomials constitute a pivotal development in mathematics and science, catalyzing new research trajectories and applications across various disciplines.

Author Contributions: Conceptualization, W.A.K. and C.K.; Formal analysis, W.A.K. and C.K.; Funding acquisition, N.A. and W.A.K.; Investigation, W.A.K.; Methodology, W.A.K.; Project administration, N.A., W.A.K., C.K. and C.S.R.; Software, C.S.R.; Writing—original draft, W.A.K. and C.K.; Writing—review and editing, W.A.K., C.K. and C.S.R. All authors have read and agreed to the published version of the manuscript.

Funding: This research received no external funding.

Data Availability Statement: No data were used to support this study.

Conflicts of Interest: The authors declare no conflicts of interest.

References

1. Khan, S.; Raza, N. General Appell polynomials within the context of monomiality principle. *Int. J. Anal.* **2013**, *2013*, 328032. [CrossRef]
2. Riyasat, M.; Khan, S.; Haneef, M. Generalized 2D extension of q-Bessel polynomials. *Rep. Math. Phys.* **2024**, *90*, 63–80. [CrossRef]

3. Andrews, G.E.; Askey, R.; Roy, R. *Special Functions*; Cambridge University Press: Cambridge, UK, 1999.
4. Zayed, M.; Wani, S.A.; Ramírez, W.; Cesarano, C. Advancements in q-Hermite-Appell polynomials: A three-dimensional exploration. *AIMS Math.* **2024**, *9*, 26799–26824. [CrossRef]
5. Riyasat, M.; Khan, S. Some results on q-Hermite based hybrid polynomials. *Glas. Mat.* **2018**, *53*, 9–31. [CrossRef]
6. Florenini, R.; Vinet, L. Quantum algebras and q-special functions. *Ann. Phys.* **1993**, *221*, 53–70. [CrossRef]
7. Fadel, M.; Alatawi, M.S.; Khan, W.A. Two variable q-Hermite-based Appell polynomials and their applications. *Mathematics* **2024**, *12*, 1358. [CrossRef]
8. Wani, S.A.; Riyasat, M.; Khan, S.; Ramirez, W. Certain advancements in multidimensional q-Hermite polynomials. *Rep. Math. Phys.* **2024**, *94*, 117–141. [CrossRef]
9. Alatawi, M.S.; Khan, W.A.; Ryoo, C.S. Explicit properties of q-Cosine and q-Sine Array-type polynomials containing symmetric structures. *Symmetry* **2022**, *14*, 1675. [CrossRef]
10. Cao, J.; Raza, N.; Fadel, M. Two-variable q-Laguerre polynomials from the context of quasi-monomiality. *J. Anal. Appl.* **2024**, *535*, 128126. [CrossRef]
11. Raza, N.; Fadel, M.; Nisar, K.S.; Zakarya, M. On 2-variable q-Hermite polynomials. *AIMS Math.* **2021**, *6*, 8705–8727. [CrossRef]
12. Srivastava, H.M. Some characterization of Appell and q-Appell polynomials. *Ann. Mat. Pura Appl.* **1982**, *4*, 321–329. [CrossRef]
13. Askey, R. Limits of some q-Laguerre polynomials. *J. Approx. Theory* **1986**, *46*, 213–216. [CrossRef]
14. Dattoli, G. Hermite-Bessel and Laguerre-Bessel functions: A by-product of the monomiality principle. *Adv. Spec. Funct. Appl.* **2000**, *1*, 147–164
15. Dattoli, G.; Torre, A. Exponential operators, quasi-monomials and generalized polynomials. *Radiat. Phys. Chem.* **2000**, *57*, 21–26. [CrossRef]
16. Ernst, T. q-Bernoulli and q-Euler polynomials, an umbral calculus approach. *Int. J. Differ. Equ.* **2006**, *1*, 31–80.
17. Al-Salam, W.A. q-Bernoulli numbers and polynomials. *Math. Nachr.* **1958**, *17*, 239–260. [CrossRef]
18. Al-Salam, W.A. q-Appell polynomials. *Ann. Mat. Pura Appl.* **1967**, *77*, 31–45. [CrossRef]
19. Ernst, T. *A Comprehensive Treatment of q-Calculus;* Springer: Basel, Switzerland, 2012.
20. Costabile, F.A.; Gualtieri, M.T.; Napoli, A. General bivariate Appell polynomials via matrix calculus and related interpolation hints. *Mathematics* **2022**, *9*, 964. [CrossRef]
21. Costabile, F.A.; Gualtieri, M.T.; Napoli, A. Bivariate general Appell interpolation problem. *Numer. Algorithms* **2022**, *91*, 531–556. [CrossRef]

mathematics

MDPI

Article

New Results for Certain Jacobsthal-Type Polynomials

Waleed Mohamed Abd-Elhameed [1,2,*], Omar Mazen Alqubori [2] and Amr Kamel Amin [3,4]

[1] Department of Mathematics, Faculty of Science, Cairo University, Giza 12613, Egypt
[2] Department of Mathematics and Statistics, College of Science, University of Jeddah, Jeddah 23831, Saudi Arabia; ommohamad3@uj.edu.sa
[3] Department of Mathematics, Adham University College, Umm AL-Qura University, Makkah 28653, Saudi Arabia; akgadelrab@uqu.edu.sa
[4] Department of Mathematics and Computer Science, Faculty of Science, Beni-Suef University, Beni-Suef 62514, Egypt
* Correspondence: waleed@cu.edu.eg

Abstract: This paper investigates a class of Jacobsthal-type polynomials (JTPs) that involves one parameter. We present several new formulas for these polynomials, including expressions for their derivatives, moments, and linearization formulas. The key idea behind the derivation of these formulas is based on developing a new connection formula that expresses the shifted Chebyshev polynomials of the third kind in terms of the JTPs. This connection formula is used to deduce a new inversion formula of the JTPs. Therefore, by utilizing the power form representation of these polynomials and their corresponding inversion formula, we can derive additional expressions for them. Additionally, we compute some definite integrals based on some formulas of these polynomials.

Keywords: Jacobsthal polynomials; orthogonal polynomials; analytic and inversion formulas; linearization and connection coefficients; moment formulas; definite integrals

MSC: 33C45; 11B83; 33C20

1. Introduction

Special functions are fundamental in many fields of applied sciences. They help in addressing many problems in the applied sciences. Applications for some special functions can be found in [1,2]. The authors of [3] discussed the role of special functions in mathematical physics. Regarding some theoretical studies of special polynomials, the authors of [4] discussed probabilistic degenerate Fubini polynomials. In [5], the authors investigated probabilistic degenerate Stirling polynomials accompanied by some applications. The authors in [6] developed some results of Appell polynomials. Some generalized polynomials were discussed in [7], accompanied by some applications. Some new formulas concerned with the convolved Fibonacci polynomials were developed in [8]. A generalized class of polynomials associated with Hermite and Euler polynomials was introduced in [9]. A class of Poly-Genocchi polynomials was introduced in [10]. Some formulas and recurrence relations for general polynomial sequences were introduced in [11]. Some generalized Fibonacci and Lucas polynomials were investigated in [12]. Unified Chebyshev polynomials (CPs) were introduced and explored from a theoretical point of view in [13].

From a practical point of view, the different sequences of polynomials are crucial. For example, some applications of Hermite polynomials can be found in [14,15]. Many sequences of polynomials were utilized to solve various types of differential equations (DEs). For example, the Bernstein polynomial basis was employed in [16] to treat the

Korteweg–de Vries equation. The authors of [17] solved the Sobolev equation using mixed Fibonacci and Lucas polynomials. A certain Lucas polynomial sequence was used in [18] to solve the time-fractional generalized Kawahara equation. The shifted Vieta–Lucas polynomials were employed in [19] to treat the fractional advection-dispersion equation. In [20], Genocchi polynomials were used to treat a specific fractional model. The authors of [21] used Schröder polynomials to treat a particular fractional model. The authors of [22,23] used various types of CPs to solve some DEs. In [24], the authors followed a spectral method based on Genocchi polynomials to treat some singular fractional DEs. The authors of [25] used Changhee polynomials to treat high-dimensional chaotic Lorenz systems.

Generalized hypergeometric functions are a crucial family of special functions with extensive applications in engineering, mathematics, and physics. They serve to generalize a large class of special and elementary functions, enabling many essential functions to be expressed in terms of them. These functions significantly address important problems related to special functions, including connection and linearization formulas. Various approaches have been used to compute the connection coefficients between different polynomials. For more details, see, for example [26–31]. In addition, the expressions for the derivatives of different polynomials in terms of their original ones are crucial in numerical analysis. For example, the author in [32] has developed new derivative expressions for the sixth-kind CPs. Some terminating hypergeometric functions of the type ${}_4F_3(1)$ were involved in these equations.

Numerous studies have been conducted on some classes of the Lucas polynomial sequence. For example, the authors of [33] derived sums of Lucas and Pell polynomials. The authors of [34] studied some generalized polynomials. In [35], a study on generalized Fibonacci polynomials was presented. Some other contributions regarding these sequences can be found in [36–40]. However, there are fewer studies on Jacobsthal and Jacobsthal–Lucas polynomials compared to those on Fibonacci and Lucas polynomials. For example, Koshy in [41] has developed infinite sums involving Jacobsthal polynomials. The same author in [42,43] has derived some formulas related to Jacobsthal polynomials. Djordjevic in [44] has developed some results regarding the derivative sequences of generalized Jacobsthal and Jacobsthal–Lucas polynomials. Some results on third-order Jacobsthal polynomials were derived in [45]. In [46], some infinite sums involving Jacobsthal polynomials were developed. Other sums involving a class of Jacobsthal polynomial squares were developed in [47]. For some other studies regarding Jacobsthal polynomials and their related polynomials, one can refer to [48–50].

This paper introduces a class of JTPs. New formulas for these polynomials will be developed. We can summarize the main objectives of the current paper in the following items:

- Developing a new connection formula between the shifted CPs of the third kind and the JTPs.
- Deriving a new inversion formula of JTPs based on the above connection formula.
- Derivation of the moment and linearization formulas of the JTPs.
- Developing new derivative formulas for the JTPs using other polynomials. Additionally, we will also derive the inverse derivative formulas.
- Introducing some definite integrals using some of the introduced formulas.

The paper is structured as follows: Section 2 presents some properties of a certain generalized Lucas polynomial sequence. Some other polynomials are also accounted for. Two basic formulas of the JTPs are developed in Section 3. Moment and linearization formulas of the JTPs are presented in Section 4. New derivative expressions of the JTPs in terms of different polynomials are given in Section 5. Section 6 gives the inverse formulas to those provided in Section 5. Section 7 developed some definite integral formulas that are deduced as consequences of some of the developed formulas. Finally, Section 8 reports some findings.

2. Some Fundamentals and Basic Formulas

This section is devoted to presenting some characteristics of the Lucas polynomial sequence. In addition, some particular classes of this sequence are accounted for. This section also provides an account of certain other polynomials.

Horadam in [51] introduced two sequences of polynomials that can be generated, respectively, by the following two recursive formulas:

$$W_n(x) = p(x)\,W_{n-1}(x) + q(x)\,W_{n-2}(x), \quad W_0(x) = 0,\, W_1(x) = 1, \tag{1}$$
$$w_n(x) = \bar{p}(x)\,w_{n-1}(x) + \bar{q}(x)\,w_{n-2}(x), \quad w_0(x) = 2,\, w_1(x) = \bar{p}(x). \tag{2}$$

They can be written explicitly in the following forms:

$$W_n(x) = \frac{\left[p(x) + \sqrt{p^2(x) + 4\,q(x)}\right]^n - \left[p(x) - \sqrt{p^2(x) + 4\,q(x)}\right]^n}{2^n\sqrt{p^2(x) + 4\,q(x)}}, \tag{3}$$
$$w_n(x) = \frac{\left[\bar{p}(x) + \sqrt{\bar{p}^2(x) + 4\,\bar{q}(x)}\right]^n + \left[\bar{p}(x) - \sqrt{\bar{p}^2(x) + 4\,\bar{q}(x)}\right]^n}{2^n}. \tag{4}$$

Remark 1. *Many celebrated sequences are particular ones of the two polynomial sequences $W_n(x)$ and $w_n(x)$. Table 1 exhibits some of these polynomials.*

Table 1. Some special classes of the two sequences.

$p(x)$ $\bar{p}(x)$	$q(x)$ $\bar{q}(x)$	$W_n(x)$	$w_n(x)$
x	1	Fibonacci polynomial $F_n(x)$	Lucas polynomial $L_n(x)$
$2x$	1	Pell polynomial $P_n(x)$	Pell–Lucas polynomial $Q_n(x)$
1	$2x$	Jacobsthal polynomial $J_n(x)$	Jacobsthal–Lucas polynomial $j_n(x)$
$3x$	-2	Fermat polynomial $\mathcal{F}_n(x)$	Fermat–Lucas polynomial $f_n(x)$
$2x$	-1	CPs of the 2nd-kind $U_{n-1}(x)$	CPs of 1st-kind $2\,T_n(x)$

Many sequences generalize the two standard sequences of Fibonacci and Lucas sequences, which can also be extracted from the two sequences $W_n(x)$ and $w_n(x)$ as special cases. The two sequences $F_k^{a,b}(x)$ and $L_k^{c,d}(x)$, which are considered generalizations of Fibonacci and Lucas polynomials, can be generated from the following two recursive formulas:

$$F_k^{a,b}(x) = a\,x\,F_{k-1}^{a,b}(x) + b\,F_{k-2}^{a,b}(x), \quad F_0^{a,b}(x) = 1,\, F_1^{a,b}(x) = a\,x, \quad k \geq 2, \tag{5}$$
$$L_k^{c,d}(x) = c\,x\,L_{k-1}^{c,d}(x) + d\,L_{k-2}^{c,d}(x), \quad L_0^{c,d}(x) = 2,\, L_1^{c,d}(x) = c\,x, \quad k \geq 2. \tag{6}$$

Remark 2. *It is evident from Table 1 that the Jacobsthal polynomials can be constructed using the following recurrence relation:*

$$J_n(x) = J_{n-1}(x) + 2\,x\,J_{n-2}(x), \quad J_0(x) = 0,\, J_1(x) = 1. \tag{7}$$

These polynomials can be constructed using the following generating function [52]:

$$\sum_{n=0}^{\infty} t^n J_n(x) = \frac{t}{1-t-2\,x\,t^2}. \tag{8}$$

The series representation of the Jacobsthal polynomials is given by [53]

$$J_n(x) = \sum_{i=0}^{\lfloor \frac{n-1}{2} \rfloor} \binom{n-i-1}{i} x^i, \tag{9}$$

where $\lfloor z \rfloor$ denotes the well-known floor function.

Remark 3. *Many sequences generalize the sequence of Jacobsthal polynomials. Within these sequences is the sequence $\left\{ J_n^{a,b}(x) \right\}_{n\geq 0}$ that can be constructed with the aid of the following recurrence relation:*

$$J_n^{a,b}(x) = a\,J_{n-1}^{a,b}(x) + b\,x\,J_{n-2}^{a,b}(x), \quad J_0^{a,b}(x) = 0,\, J_1^{a,b}(x) = 1. \tag{10}$$

Based on the recurrence relation (10)*, it can be shown that the polynomials $\left\{ J_n^{a,b}(x) \right\}_{n\geq 0}$ can be generated using the following generating function:*

$$\sum_{n=0}^{\infty} t^n J_n^{a,b}(x) = \frac{t}{1-at-bxt^2}. \tag{11}$$

Remark 4. *From the representation in* (9)*, we can write the following representation for $J_{n+1}(x)$:*

$$\hat{J}_n(x) = J_{n+1}(x) = \sum_{i=0}^{\lfloor \frac{n}{2} \rfloor} \binom{i+n-\lfloor \frac{n}{2} \rfloor}{\lfloor \frac{n}{2} \rfloor - i} x^{\lfloor \frac{n}{2} \rfloor - i}. \tag{12}$$

In addition, the above representation can be split into the following two representations:

$$\hat{J}_{2n}(x) = \sum_{i=0}^{n} \binom{n+i}{n-i} x^{n-i},$$
$$\hat{J}_{2n+1}(x) = \sum_{i=0}^{n} \binom{n+i+1}{n-i} x^{n-i}.$$

Remark 5. *To the best of our knowledge, many formulas related to the Jacobsthal polynomials and their related polynomials are traceless in the literature, such as their derivative, moment, and linearization formulas. We also found no correlations between these formulas and orthogonal polynomials. This motivates us to investigate the JTPs further.*

This paper considers a kind of JTPs generated by the following recursive formula:

$$J_n^a(x) = a\,J_{n-1}^a(x) - \frac{a^2}{4} x\,J_{n-2}^a(x), \quad J_0(x) = 1,\, J_1(x) = a. \tag{13}$$

Remark 6. *In this paper, we restrict our study of the generalized Jacobsthal polynomials generated by* (10) *to the case corresponding to: $b = -\frac{a^2}{4}$, since in such a case, we will prove that the Chebyshev polynomials of the third kind can be written as a simple combination of them that does not involve any hypergeometric term. This pivotal formula in our study helped us develop further formulas related to these polynomials.*

An Overview of Some Polynomials

We will present an overview of a selection of orthogonal and non-orthogonal polynomials. Two families of polynomials, one symmetric and the other non-symmetric, are considered. We will refer to them as $\phi_m(x)$ and $\psi_m(x)$, and they have the following analytic representations:

$$\phi_m(x) = \sum_{\ell=0}^{\lfloor \frac{m}{2} \rfloor} H_{\ell,m}\, x^{m-2\ell}, \tag{14}$$

$$\psi_m(x) = \sum_{\ell=0}^{m} F_{\ell,m}\, x^{m-\ell}, \tag{15}$$

where $H_{r,s}$ and $F_{r,s}$ are known coefficients.

In addition, let us assume that the inversion formulas for (14) and (15) are as follows:

$$x^m = \sum_{\ell=0}^{\lfloor \frac{m}{2} \rfloor} \bar{H}_{\ell,m}\, \phi_{m-2\ell}(x), \tag{16}$$

$$x^m = \sum_{\ell=0}^{m} \bar{F}_{\ell,m}\, \psi_{m-\ell}(x), \tag{17}$$

where $\bar{H}_{\ell,m}$ and $\bar{F}_{\ell,m}$ are known coefficients.

We provide some famous polynomials that may be defined as in (14) and (15). The normalized shifted Jacobi polynomials are expressed as [8]:

$$\tilde{R}_m^{(\rho,\gamma)}(x) = \sum_{\ell=0}^{m} \frac{(-1)^\ell\, m!\, \Gamma(\rho+1)\, (\gamma+1)_m\, (\rho+\gamma+1)_{2m-\ell}}{\ell!\, (m-\ell)!\, \Gamma(m+\rho+1)\, (\rho+\gamma+1)_m\, (\gamma+1)_{m-\ell}}\, x^{m-\ell}. \tag{18}$$

$\tilde{R}_\ell^{(\rho,\gamma)}(x)$ are orthogonal on $[0,1]$ in the sense that

$$\int_0^1 (1-x)^\rho\, x^\gamma\, \tilde{R}_\ell^{(\rho,\gamma)}(x)\, \tilde{R}_k^{(\rho,\gamma)}(x)\, dx = \begin{cases} 0, & k \neq \ell, \\ \tilde{h}_\ell^{\rho,\gamma}, & k = \ell, \end{cases} \tag{19}$$

where

$$\tilde{h}_\ell^{\rho,\gamma} = \frac{k!\, \Gamma(\rho+1)^2\, \Gamma(k+\gamma+1)}{(2k+\rho+\gamma+1)\, \Gamma(k+\rho+1)\, \Gamma(k+\rho+\gamma+1)}. \tag{20}$$

Specifically, the ultraspherical polynomials are symmetric Jacobi polynomials. We have

$$C_m^{(\gamma)}(x) = \tilde{R}_m^{(\gamma-\frac{1}{2},\gamma-\frac{1}{2})}(x). \tag{21}$$

Moreover, we note that Jacobi polynomials involve four kinds of CPs. The following recurrence relation can generate all these kinds:

$$C_m(x) = 2\,x\, C_{m-1}(x) - C_{m-2}(x), \tag{22}$$

but with different initials.

In addition, the moment formula for $C_m(x)$ is given by

$$x^\ell\, C_m(x) = \frac{1}{2^\ell} \sum_{s=0}^{\ell} \binom{\ell}{s}\, C_{\ell+m-2s}(x). \tag{23}$$

Remark 7. *Examples of important non-symmetric polynomials are the shifted Jacobi polynomials* $\tilde{R}_m^{(\rho,\gamma)}(x)$ *that are expressed in* (18), *Schröder polynomials* $S_\ell(x)$, *and Bernoulli polynomials* $B_\ell(x)$. *Table 2 presents the power form and inversion coefficients for these non-symmetric polynomials.*

Remark 8. *Some examples of important symmetric polynomials are the ultraspherical polynomials that are given by* (21), *Hermite polynomials* $H_\ell(x)$, *and the two generalized classes of Fibonacci and Lucas polynomials that are generated, respectively, by* (5) *and* (6). *Table 3 represents the power form and inversion coefficients for these polynomials.*

Table 2. Power form and inversion coefficients for some non-symmetric polynomials.

Polynomial	$F_{\ell,m}$ in (15)	$\bar{F}_{\ell,m}$ in (17)
$\tilde{R}_\ell^{(\rho,\gamma)}(x)$	$\dfrac{(-1)^\ell\, m!\,\Gamma(1+\rho)\,(1+\gamma)_m\,(1+\rho+\gamma)_{2m-\ell}}{(m-\ell)!\,\ell!\,\Gamma(1+m+\rho)\,(1+\gamma)_{m-\ell}\,(1+\rho+\gamma)_m}$	$\dfrac{\binom{m}{\ell}\,(1+\rho)_{m-\ell}\,(1+m-\ell+\gamma)_\ell}{(2+2m-2\ell+\rho+\gamma)_L\,(1+m-\ell+\rho+\gamma)_{m-\ell}}$
$S_\ell(x)$	$\dfrac{\binom{m}{m-\ell}\binom{2m-\ell}{m-\ell}}{1+m-\ell}$	$\dfrac{i!(i+1)!((-1)^m(1+2i-2m))}{(2i-m+1)!m!}$
$B_\ell(x)$	$B_\ell\dbinom{m}{m-\ell}$	$\dfrac{\binom{m+1}{m-\ell}}{m+1}$

Table 3. Power form and inversion coefficients for some symmetric polynomials.

Polynomial	$H_{\ell,m}$ in (14)	$\bar{H}_{\ell,m}$ in (16)
$C_\ell^{(\lambda)}(x)$	$\dfrac{(-1)^\ell\,2^{-1+m-2\ell}\,m!\,\Gamma(m-\ell+\lambda)\,\Gamma(1+2\lambda)}{(m-2\ell)!\,\ell!\,\Gamma(1+\lambda)\,\Gamma(m+2\lambda)}$	$\dfrac{2^{-m+1}\,(m-2\ell+\lambda)\,m!\,\Gamma(\lambda+1)\,\Gamma(m-2\ell+2\lambda)}{(m-2\ell)!\,\ell!\,\Gamma(2\lambda+1)\,\Gamma(1+m-\ell+\lambda)}$
$H_\ell(x)$	$\dfrac{(-1)^\ell\,2^{-2\ell+m}\,m!}{\ell!\,(-2\ell+m)!}$	$\dfrac{2^{-m}\,m!}{\ell!\,(m-2\ell)!}$
$F_\ell^{A,B}(x)$	$\dfrac{A^{m-2\ell}\,B^\ell\,(m-2\ell+1)_\ell}{\ell!}$	$\dfrac{(-1)^\ell\,(m-2\ell+1)\,(m-\ell+2)_{\ell-1}\,B^\ell}{\ell!\,A^m}$
$L_\ell^{\bar{A},\bar{B}}(x)$	$\dfrac{\bar{A}^{m-2\ell}\,\bar{B}^\ell\,m\,(1-2\ell+m)_{\ell-1}}{\ell!}$	$\dfrac{c_{m-2\ell}\,(-1)^\ell\,\bar{A}^{-m}\,\bar{B}^\ell\,(1-\ell+m)_\ell}{\ell!}$

3. Two Basic Formulas of the Generalized Jacobsthal Polynomials

This section is devoted to developing two basic formulas of the JTPs: $J_i^a(x)$ generated by (7). The first is the series representation of $J_i^a(x)$, while the second formula exhibits the expression of x^m in terms of $J_i^a(x)$. These two formulas will be the backbone for many formulas in this paper.

Lemma 1. *For any non-negative integer m, one has*

$$J_m^a(x) = a^m \sum_{r=0}^{\lfloor \frac{m}{2} \rfloor} \left(-\frac{1}{4}\right)^r \binom{m-r}{r} x^r. \tag{24}$$

Proof. First, let

$$\xi_m^a(x) = a^m \sum_{r=0}^{\lfloor \frac{m}{2} \rfloor} \left(-\frac{1}{4}\right)^r \binom{m-r}{r} x^r.$$

It is easy to see that

$$\xi_0^a(x) = J_0^a(x) = 1, \quad \xi_1^a(x) = J_1^a(x) = a.$$

In addition, by performing some computations, we can show that the following relation holds:

$$\xi_m^a(x) - a\,\xi_{m-1}^a(x) + \frac{a^2}{4}x\,\xi_{m-2}^a(x) = 0. \tag{25}$$

This proves that

$$\xi_m^a(x) = J_m^a(x), \quad m \geq 0.$$

Lemma 1 is now proved. □

Remark 9. *Two representations may be obtained from the power form given in* (24):

$$J^a_{2m}(x) = a^{2m} \sum_{r=0}^{m} \frac{\left(-\frac{1}{4}\right)^{m-r} (m+r)!}{(2r)!(m-r)!} x^{m-r}, \tag{26}$$

$$J^a_{2m+1}(x) = a^{2m+1} \sum_{r=0}^{m} \frac{\left(-\frac{1}{4}\right)^{m-r} (m+r+1)!}{(2r+1)!(m-r)!} x^{m-r}. \tag{27}$$

Now, we are going to show that the shifted CPs of the third-kind $V^*_r(x)$, $r \geq 0$, can be written as a combination of the polynomials $J^a_i(x)$.

Theorem 1. *The formula that connects the third-kind CPs and the polynomials $J^a_i(x)$ is given by*

$$\begin{aligned} V^*_r(x) =& (-1)^r \sum_{s=0}^{r} \left(\frac{4}{a}\right)^{2r-2s} \binom{4r-2s+1}{2s} J^a_{2r-2s}(x) \\ &+ (-1)^{r+1} \sum_{s=0}^{r-1} \left(\frac{4}{a}\right)^{2r-2s-1} \binom{4r-2s}{2s+1} J^a_{2r-2s-1}(x), \quad r \geq 0. \end{aligned} \tag{28}$$

Proof. We will prove Formula (28) by induction on r. It is obvious that (28) holds for $r = 0$. Now, we are going to prove the following connection formula:

$$V^*_r(x) = \sum_{s=0}^{r} G_{s,r} \, J^a_{2r-2s}(x) + \sum_{s=0}^{r-1} \bar{G}_{s,r} \, J^a_{2r-2s-1}(x), \quad r \geq 1, \tag{29}$$

where

$$G_{s,r} = (-1)^r \left(\frac{4}{a}\right)^{2r-2s} \binom{4r-2s+1}{2s},$$

$$\bar{G}_{s,r} = (-1)^{r+1} \left(\frac{4}{a}\right)^{2r-2s-1} \binom{4r-2s}{2s+1}.$$

We proceed with the proof by induction. Assume that Formula (29) is valid for all $n < r$, i.e.,

$$V^*_n(x) = \sum_{s=0}^{n} G_{s,n} \, J^a_{2n-2s}(x) + \sum_{s=0}^{n-1} \bar{G}_{s,n} \, J^a_{2n-2s-1}(x), \tag{30}$$

and we must prove that (29) is itself valid.

Now, we start with the recurrence relation satisfied by $V^*_r(x)$:

$$V^*_r(x) = 2(2x-1) \, V^*_{r-1}(x) - V^*_{r-2}(x), \tag{31}$$

and apply the inductive assumption to write $V^*_{r-1}(x)$ and $V^*_{r-2}(x)$ to obtain

$$V^*_{r-1}(x) = \sum_{s=0}^{r-1} G_{s,r-1} J^a_{2r-2s-2}(x) + \sum_{s=0}^{r-2} \bar{G}_{s,r-1} \, J^a_{2r-2s-3}(x),$$

$$V^*_{r-2}(x) = \sum_{s=0}^{r-2} G_{s,r-2} J^a_{2r-2s-4}(x) + \sum_{s=0}^{r-3} \bar{G}_{s,r-2} \, J^a_{2r-2s-5}(x).$$

The last two expressions, along with (31), enable one to write $V_r^*(x)$ in the following form:

$$\begin{aligned} V_{r-1}^*(x) =& 2(2x-1)\left(\sum_{s=0}^{r-1} G_{s,r-1}\, J_{2j-2s-2}^a + \sum_{s=0}^{r-2} \bar{G}_{s,r-1}\, J_{2j-2s-3}^a\right) \\ & - \left(\sum_{s=0}^{r-2} G_{s,r-2}\, J_{2j-2s-4}^a + \sum_{s=0}^{r-2} \bar{G}_{s,r-2}\, J_{2j-2s-5}^a\right). \end{aligned} \tag{32}$$

Now, inserting the recurrence relation (13) in the form

$$x J_k^a(x) = -\frac{4}{a^2}\left(J_{k+2}^a(x) - a\, J_{k+1}^a(x)\right), \tag{33}$$

into (32) yields the following formula:

$$\begin{aligned} V_r^*(x) = &-\frac{16}{a^2}\left(\sum_{s=0}^{r-2} \bar{G}_{s,r-1}(-aJ^a_{-2+2j-2s}(x) + J^a_{-1+2j-2s}(x))\right. \\ &\left. + \sum_{s=0}^{r-1} G_{s,r-1}(-aJ^a_{-1+2j-2s}(x) + J^a_{2j-2s}(x))\right) \\ &- 2\left(\sum_{s=0}^{r-1} G_{s,r-1} J^a_{2j-2s-2}(x) + \sum_{s=0}^{r-2} \bar{G}_{s,r-1} J^a_{2j-2s-3}(x)\right) \\ &- \left(\sum_{s=0}^{r-2} G_{s,r-2} J^a_{2j-2s-4}(x) + \sum_{s=0}^{r-2} \bar{G}_{s,r-2} J^a_{2j-2s-5}(x)\right). \end{aligned}$$

Now, we can write

$$V_r^*(x) = \sum_1 + \sum_2, \tag{34}$$

where

$$\sum_1 = \frac{16}{a}\sum_{s=0}^{r-2} \bar{G}_{s,r-1} J^a_{-2+2j-2s}(x) - \frac{16}{a^2}\sum_{s=0}^{r-1} G_{s,r-1} J^a_{2j-2s}(x) \tag{35}$$

$$- 2\sum_{s=0}^{r-1} G_{s,r-1}\, J^a_{2j-2s-2}(x) - \sum_{s=0}^{r-2} G_{s,r-2} J^a_{2j-2s-4}(x), \tag{36}$$

$$\sum_2 = -\frac{16}{a^2}\sum_{s=0}^{r-2} \bar{G}_{s,r-1} J^a_{2j-2s-1}(x) + \frac{16}{a}\sum_{s=0}^{r-1} G_{s,r-1} J^a_{2j-2s-1}(x) \tag{37}$$

$$- 2\sum_{s=0}^{r-2} \bar{G}_{s,r-1} J^a_{2j-2s-3}(x) - \sum_{s=0}^{r-2} \bar{G}_{s,r-2} J^a_{2j-2s-5}(x). \tag{38}$$

Some algebraic manipulations transform $\sum_1$ and $\sum_2$ into the following forms:

$$\sum_1 = \sum_{s=0}^{r}\left(\frac{16}{a}\bar{G}_{s-1,r-1} - \frac{16}{a^2} G_{s,r-1} - 2G_{s-1,r-1} - G_{s-2,r-2}\right) J^a_{2j-2s}(x),$$

$$\sum_2 = \sum_{s=0}^{r-1}\left(-\frac{16}{a^2}\bar{G}_{s,r-1} + \frac{16}{a} G_{s,r-1} - 2\bar{G}_{s-1,r-1} - \bar{G}_{s-2,r-2}\right) J^a_{2j-2s-1}(x).$$

It is not difficult to show that the following two identities hold:

$$\frac{16}{a}\bar{G}_{s-1,r-1} - \frac{16}{a^2}G_{s,r-1} - 2G_{s-1,r-1} - G_{s-2,r-2} = G_{s,r}, \tag{39}$$

$$-\frac{16}{a^2}\bar{G}_{s,r-1} + \frac{16}{a}G_{s,r-1} - 2\bar{G}_{s-1,r-1} - \bar{G}_{s-2,r-2} = \bar{G}_{s,r}, \tag{40}$$

and this proves that

$$V_r^*(x) = \sum_{s=0}^{r} G_{s,r}\, J^a_{2r-2s}(x) + \sum_{s=0}^{r-1} \bar{G}_{s,r}\, J^a_{2r-2s-1}(x).$$

This finalizes the proof of Theorem 1. □

Theorem 2. *Let r be a non-negative integer. The following inversion formula for the JTPs holds:*

$$\begin{aligned} x^r =&(-1)^r\, 2^{2r} \sum_{s=0}^{r} \frac{a^{2s-2r}(1-2s+r)_{2s}}{(2s)!}\, J^a_{2r-2s}(x) \\ &+ (-1)^{r+1}\, 2^{2r} \sum_{s=0}^{r-1} \frac{a^{2s-2r+1}(-2s+r)_{1+2s}}{(2s+1)!}\, J^a_{2r-2s-1}(x). \end{aligned} \tag{41}$$

Proof. The inversion formula of $V_j^*(x)$ is given by [54]

$$x^r = 4^{-r}(2r+1)! \sum_{\ell=0}^{r} \frac{1}{\ell!(1-\ell+2r)!} V^*_{r-\ell}(x). \tag{42}$$

By virtue of the connection formula (28), one can write

$$\begin{aligned} x^r =& \sum_{i=0}^{r} \frac{(-1)^{i-r}4^{-r}(2r+1)!a^{2i-2r}}{i!(1-i+2r)!} \sum_{s=0}^{r-i} 4^{-2i-2s+2r} a^{2s} \binom{1-4i-2s+4r}{2s} J^a_{2r-2i-2s}(x) \\ &+ \sum_{i=0}^{r} \frac{(-1)^{i-r+1}4^{-r}(2r+1)!a^{2i-2r}}{i!(1-i+2r)!} \sum_{s=0}^{r-i-1} 2^{-2-4i-4s+4r} a^{2s+1} \binom{-4i-2s+4r}{1+2s} J^a_{2r-2i-2s-1}(x). \end{aligned} \tag{43}$$

Some calculations lead to the following formula:

$$\begin{aligned} x^r =& \sum_{s=0}^{r} 4^{-2s+r}(2r+1)!a^{2s-2r} \sum_{\ell=0}^{s} \frac{(-1)^{\ell+r}\binom{1-2\ell-2s+4r}{-2\ell+2s}}{\ell!(-\ell+2r+1)!} J^a_{2r-2s}(x) \\ &+ \sum_{s=0}^{r-1} 4^{-1-2s+r}(2r+1)!a^{2s-2r+1} \sum_{\ell=0}^{s} \frac{(-1)^{\ell+r+1}\binom{-2(\ell+s-2r)}{1-2\ell+2s}}{\ell!(-\ell+2r+1)!} J^a_{2r-2s-1}(x). \end{aligned} \tag{44}$$

To obtain a simplified formula for (44), let

$$W_{s,r} = \sum_{\ell=0}^{s} \frac{(-1)^{\ell+r}\binom{1-2\ell-2s+4r}{-2\ell+2s}}{\ell!(-\ell+2r+1)!}, \tag{45}$$

$$\bar{W}_{s,r} = \sum_{\ell=0}^{s} \frac{(-1)^{\ell+r+1}\binom{-2(\ell+s-2r)}{1-2\ell+2s}}{\ell!(-\ell+2r+1)!}. \tag{46}$$

We use Zeilberger's algorithm [55] to find a closed formula for the above two sums. They satisfy the following two recursive formulas:

$$(s+1)(2s+1)\,W_{s+1,r} - 8(r-2s-1)(r-2s)\,W_{s,r} = 0, \quad W_{0,r} = \frac{(-1)^r}{(2r+1)!}, \tag{47}$$

$$(s+1)(2s+3)\,\bar{W}_{s+1,r} - 8(r-2s-2)(r-2s-1)\,\bar{W}_{s,r} = 0, \quad \bar{W}_{0,r} = \frac{4\,r\,(-1)^{r+1}}{(2r+1)!}, \tag{48}$$

whose solutions are given as follows:

$$W_{s,r} = \frac{(-1)^r 4^{2s}\,(1-2s+r)_{2s}}{(2r+1)!(2s)!}, \tag{49}$$

$$\bar{W}_{s,r} = \frac{4^{2s+1}\,(-1)^{r+1}\,(-2s+r)_{2s+1}}{(2r+1)!(2s+1)!}, \tag{50}$$

and accordingly, Formula (44) reduces to Formula (41). This ends the proof. □

4. Moment and Linearization Formulas of the JTPs

This section is confined to presenting a new moment formula for $J_i^a(x)$. This formula will be the key to developing new linearization formulas for the polynomials $J_i^a(x)$.

4.1. Moment Formula of the JTPs

Now, we are going to state and prove a new moment formula for the polynomials $J_i^a(x)$.

Theorem 3. *Assume that s and i are two non-negative integers. We have*

$$x^s\,J_i^a(x) = 2^{2s}\sum_{r=0}^{s}(-1)^r\binom{s}{r}a^{-s-r}\,J^a_{i+s+r}(x). \tag{51}$$

Proof. We proceed by induction. For $s=0$, it is clear that the formula holds since each side in such a case is equal to $J_i^a(x)$. Now, assume that Formula (51) is valid, so to prove the inductive step, we have to prove that the following identity holds:

$$x^{s+1}\,J_i^a(x) = 2^{2s+2}\sum_{r=0}^{s+1}(-1)^r\binom{s+1}{r}a^{-s-r-1}J^a_{i+s+r+1}(x). \tag{52}$$

Now, using the recurrence relation (33) and multiplying both sides of (51) by x, we obtain

$$x^{s+1}\,J_i^a(x) = 2^{2s+2}\sum_{r=0}^{s}(-1)^{r+1}\binom{s}{r}a^{-s-r-2}\left(J^a_{i+s+r+2}(x) - a\,J^a_{i+s+r+1}(x)\right), \tag{53}$$

that can be written in the following form:

$$\begin{aligned} x^{s+1}\,J_i^a(x) = &-2^{2s+2}\sum_{r=0}^{s}(-1)^{r+1}\binom{s}{r}a^{-s-r-1}\,J^a_{i+s+r+1}(x) \\ &+ 2^{2s+2}\sum_{r=0}^{s+1}(-1)^r\binom{s}{r-1}a^{-s-r-1}\,J^a_{i+s+r+1}(x). \end{aligned}$$

If we note the following identity:

$$\binom{s+1}{r} = \binom{s}{r} + \binom{s}{r-1},$$

then, the following formula can be obtained after performing some simplifications:

$$x^{s+1}\,J_i^a(x) = 2^{2s+2}\sum_{r=0}^{s+1}(-1)^r\binom{s+1}{r}a^{-s-r-1}J_{i+s+r+1}^a(x). \tag{54}$$

This proves Formula (52). □

4.2. Linearization Formulas Involving the JTPs

This section is interested in developing new linearization formulas involving the JTPs. In this concern, the following linearization formulas will be introduced:

- The linearization formulas of $J_i^a(x)$.
- The product formulas of $J_i^a(x)$ and some celebrated polynomials.

Theorem 4. *For all non-negative integers r, s, one has the following linearization formulas:*

$$J_{2r}^a(x)\,J_s^a(x) = \sqrt{\pi}\,r!\left(\sum_{m=0}^{r}\frac{a^{2m}\,{}_3\tilde{F}_2\left(\begin{matrix}-m,\frac{1}{2}-m,r+1\\ \frac{1}{2},r+1-2m\end{matrix};1\right)}{(2m)!}J_{s+2r-2m}^a(x)\right.$$
$$\left.-\sum_{m=0}^{r-1}\frac{a^{2m+1}\,{}_3\tilde{F}_2\left(\begin{matrix}-m,-m-\frac{1}{2},r+1\\ \frac{1}{2},r-2m\end{matrix};1\right)}{(2m+1)!}J_{s+2r-2m-1}^a(x)\right), \tag{55}$$

$$J_{2r+1}^a(x)\,J_s^a(x) = \frac{1}{2}\sqrt{\pi}(r+1)!\left(\sum_{m=0}^{r}\frac{a^{2m+1}\,{}_3\tilde{F}_2\left(\begin{matrix}-m,\frac{1}{2}-m,r+2\\ \frac{3}{2},r+1-2m\end{matrix};1\right)}{(2m)!}J_{s+2r-2m}^a(x)\right.$$
$$\left.-\sum_{m=0}^{r-1}\frac{a^{2m+2}\,{}_3\tilde{F}_2\left(\begin{matrix}-m,-m-\frac{1}{2},r+2\\ \frac{3}{2},r-2m\end{matrix};1\right)}{(2m+1)!}J_{s+2r-2m-1}^a(x)\right), \tag{56}$$

where ${}_3\tilde{F}_2(z)$ is the regularized hypergeometric function [56].

Proof. We will prove (55). The proof of (56) is similar. The analytic formula of $J_{2r}^a(x)$ enables one to write

$$J_{2r}^a(x)\,J_s^a(x) = a^{2r}\sum_{\ell=0}^{r}(-4)^{\ell-r}\binom{r+\ell}{r-\ell}x^{r-\ell}J_s^a(x). \tag{57}$$

The application of the moment formula (51) yields

$$J_{2r}^a(x)\,J_s^a(x) = a^{2r}\sum_{\ell=0}^{r}(-1)^{r-\ell}\binom{r+\ell}{r-\ell}\sum_{m=0}^{r-\ell}(-1)^m a^{\ell-m-r}\binom{r-\ell}{m}J_{s+m+r-\ell}^a(x), \tag{58}$$

which may be written alternatively after some manipulations in the form

$$\begin{aligned}J_{2r}^{a}(x)\,J_{s}^{a}(x)=&\sum_{m=0}^{r}a^{2m}\sum_{\ell=0}^{m}\binom{r-\ell}{\ell-2m+r}\binom{\ell+r}{r-\ell}\,J^{s+2r-2m}(x)\\&-\sum_{m=0}^{r-1}a^{2m+1}\sum_{\ell=0}^{m}\binom{r-\ell}{-1+\ell-2m+r}\binom{\ell+r}{r-\ell}J_{s+2r-2m-1}^{a}(x),\end{aligned}\tag{59}$$

which leads to (55). □

Theorem 5. *Let r and s be two non-negative integers. Let also $C_s(x)$ be any of the four kinds of CPs. One has the following linearization formulas:*

$$\begin{aligned}J_{2r+1}^{a}(x)\,C_s(x)=&\left(-\frac{1}{8}\right)^{r}a^{2r+1}(r+1)\times\\&\sum_{m=0}^{r}\binom{r}{m}\,{}_4F_3\left(\left.\begin{matrix}-m,\frac{r}{2}+\frac{3}{2},m-r,\frac{r}{2}+1\\\frac{1}{2},\frac{3}{4},\frac{5}{4}\end{matrix}\right|1\right)C_{r+s-2m}(x)\\&+\frac{1}{3}(-1)^{r+1}2^{2-3r}a^{2r+1}(r+2)!\sum_{m=0}^{r-1}\frac{1}{m!(r-m-1)!}\times\\&{}_4F_3\left(\left.\begin{matrix}-m,\frac{r}{2}+2,m-r+1,\frac{r}{2}+\frac{3}{2}\\\frac{5}{4},\frac{3}{2},\frac{7}{4}\end{matrix}\right|1\right)C_{r+s-2m-1}(x),\end{aligned}\tag{60}$$

$$\begin{aligned}J_{2r}^{a}(x)C_s(x)=&\left(-\frac{1}{8}\right)^{r}a^{2r}\sum_{m=0}^{r}\binom{r}{m}\,{}_4F_3\left(\left.\begin{matrix}-m,\frac{r}{2}+1,m-r,\frac{r}{2}+\frac{1}{2}\\\frac{1}{4},\frac{1}{2},\frac{3}{4}\end{matrix}\right|1\right)C_{r+s-2m}(x)\\&+(-1)^{r+1}2^{2-3r}a^{2r}(r+1)!\sum_{m=0}^{r-1}\frac{1}{m!(r-m-1)!}\times\\&{}_4F_3\left(\left.\begin{matrix}-m,\frac{r}{2}+\frac{3}{2},m-r+1,\frac{r}{2}+1\\\frac{3}{4},\frac{5}{4},\frac{3}{2}\end{matrix}\right|1\right)C_{r+s-2m-1}(x).\end{aligned}\tag{61}$$

Proof. Based on the analytic Formula (27), one can write

$$J_{2r+1}^{a}(x)\,C_s(x)=a^{2r+1}\sum_{\ell=0}^{r}\frac{(-4)^{\ell-r}(1+\ell+r)!}{(2\ell+1)!(r-\ell)!}x^{r-\ell}\,C_s(x).\tag{62}$$

Based on the moment formula of $C_s(x)$ in (23), Formula (62) can be written as

$$J_{2r+1}^{a}(x)\,C_s(x)=a^{2r+1}\sum_{\ell=0}^{r}\frac{(-8)^{\ell-r}(1+\ell+r)!}{(2\ell+1)!(r-\ell)!}\sum_{m=0}^{r-\ell}\binom{r-\ell}{m}C_{r+s-\ell-2m},\tag{63}$$

which may be written again as

$$\begin{aligned}J_{2r+1}^{a}(x)\,C_s(x)=&a^{2r+1}\sum_{m=0}^{\lfloor\frac{r+s}{2}\rfloor}\sum_{\ell=0}^{m}\frac{(-8)^{2\ell-r}\binom{-2\ell+r}{-\ell+m}(2\ell+r+1)!}{(-2\ell+r)!(4\ell+1)!}C_{r+s-2m}(x)\\&+a^{2r+1}\sum_{m=0}^{\lfloor\frac{1}{2}(r+s-1)\rfloor}\sum_{\ell=0}^{m}\frac{(-8)^{2\ell-r+1}\binom{-1-2\ell+r}{-\ell+m}(2\ell+r+2)!}{(4\ell+3)!(-1-2\ell+r)!}C_{r+s-2m-1}(x)\end{aligned}\tag{64}$$

The last formula can be written as in (60). Formula (61) can be similarly proved. □

Theorem 6. *For non-negative integers r and s. The linearization formulas for $J_r^a(x)$ and generalized Fibonacci polynomials are given by*

$$\begin{aligned}
J_{2r}^a(x)\, F_s^{A,B}(x) =& a^{2r} A^{-r} \sum_{m=0}^{r} \left(-\frac{1}{4}\right)^r (-B)^m \binom{r}{m} \times \\
& {}_4F_3\left(\begin{matrix} -m, 1+\frac{r}{2}, \frac{1}{2}+\frac{r}{2}, -r+m \\ \frac{1}{4}, \frac{1}{2}, \frac{3}{4} \end{matrix} \middle| -\frac{A^2}{4B} \right) F_{r+s-2m}^{A,B}(x) \\
& + (-1)^{r+1} 2^{1-2r} a^{2r} A^{1-r} (r+1)! \sum_{m=0}^{r-1} \frac{1}{m!(r-m-1)!} (-B)^m \times \\
& {}_4F_3\left(\begin{matrix} -m, \frac{3}{2}+\frac{r}{2}, 1+\frac{r}{2}, 1-r+m \\ \frac{3}{4}, \frac{5}{4}, \frac{3}{2} \end{matrix} \middle| -\frac{A^2}{4B} \right) F_{r+s-2m-1}^{A,B}(x),
\end{aligned} \tag{65}$$

$$\begin{aligned}
J_{2r+1}^a(x)\, F_s^{A,B}(x) =& \left(-\frac{1}{4}\right)^r a^{1+2r} A^{-r} (r+1) \sum_{m=0}^{r} (-B)^m \binom{r}{m} \times \\
& {}_4F_3\left(\begin{matrix} -m, \frac{3}{2}+\frac{r}{2}, 1+\frac{r}{2}, -r+m \\ \frac{1}{2}, \frac{3}{4}, \frac{5}{4} \end{matrix} \middle| -\frac{A^2}{4B} \right) F_{r+s-2m}^{A,B}(x) \\
& + \frac{1}{3} (-1)^{r+1} 2^{1-2r} a^{1+2r} A^{1-r} (r+2)! \sum_{m=0}^{r-1} \frac{1}{m!(r-m-1)!} (-B)^m \times \\
& {}_4F_3\left(\begin{matrix} -m, 2+\frac{r}{2}, \frac{3}{2}+\frac{r}{2}, 1-r+m \\ \frac{5}{4}, \frac{3}{2}, \frac{7}{4} \end{matrix} \middle| -\frac{A^2}{4B} \right) F_{r+s-2m-1}^{A,B}(x).
\end{aligned} \tag{66}$$

Proof. The proof is similar to the proof of Theorem 5. □

5. New Derivative Expressions of the JTPs in Terms of Different Polynomials

This section focuses on developing new expressions for the derivatives of $J_k^a(x)$. We begin by providing derivative expressions for these polynomials as combinations of their original forms. Additionally, we present alternative expressions for the derivatives in terms of both symmetric and non-symmetric polynomials.

5.1. Derivatives in Terms of Their Original Ones

Theorem 7. *Consider the two non-negative integers k and p with $k \geq p$. The derivatives of $J_k^a(x)$ can be expressed as*

$$\begin{aligned}
D^p J_{2k}^a(x) = 4^{-p} a^{2p} \sqrt{\pi} (-1)^p k! \Bigg(& \sum_{\ell=0}^{k-p} \frac{a^{2\ell}\, {}_3\tilde{F}_2\left(\begin{matrix} -\ell, \frac{1}{2}-\ell, 1+k \\ \frac{1}{2}, 1+k-2\ell-p \end{matrix} \middle| 1 \right)}{(2\ell)!} J_{2k-2p-2\ell}^a(x) \\
& - \sum_{\ell=0}^{k-p-1} \frac{a^{2\ell+1}\, {}_3\tilde{F}_2\left(\begin{matrix} -\ell, -\frac{1}{2}-\ell, 1+k \\ \frac{1}{2}, k-2\ell-p \end{matrix} \middle| 1 \right)}{(2\ell+1)!} J_{2k-2p-2\ell-1}^a(x) \Bigg),
\end{aligned} \tag{67}$$

$$D^p J^a_{2k+1}(x) = (-1)^p 2^{-1-2p} \sqrt{\pi}\,(k+1)! \left(\sum_{\ell=0}^{k-p} \frac{a^{1+2\ell+2p}\, {}_3\tilde{F}_2\left(\begin{array}{c} -\ell, \frac{1}{2}-\ell, 2+k \\ \frac{3}{2}, 1+k-2\ell-p \end{array} \middle| 1 \right)}{(2\ell)!} J^a_{2k-2p-2\ell}(x) \right.$$
$$\left. - \sum_{\ell=0}^{k-p-1} \frac{a^{2(1+\ell+p)}\, {}_3\tilde{F}_2\left(\begin{array}{c} -\ell, -\frac{1}{2}-\ell, 2+k \\ \frac{3}{2}, k-2\ell-p \end{array} \middle| 1 \right)}{(2\ell+1)!} J^a_{2k-2p-2\ell-1}(x) \right). \tag{68}$$

Proof. We prove (67). The analytic form (26) enables one to write

$$D^p J^a_{2k}(x) = a^{2k} \sum_{r=0}^{k-p} \frac{(-4)^{r-k}(k+r)!}{(k-p-r)!(2r)!} x^{k-r-p}, \tag{69}$$

which may be written in terms of $J^a_i(x)$ using the inversion formula (41) as

$$\begin{aligned} D^p J^a_{2k}(x) = a^{2k} \sum_{r=0}^{k-p} & \frac{(-1)^{k-p-r}(-4)^{r-k}(k+r)!\left(\frac{2}{a}\right)^{2(k-p-r)}}{(k-p-r)!(2r)!} \\ & \times \left(\sum_{\ell=0}^{k-r-p} \frac{a^{2\ell}(1+k-2\ell-p-r)_{2\ell}}{(2\ell)!} J^a_{2k-2r-2p-2\ell}(x) \right. \\ & \left. - \sum_{\ell=0}^{k-r-p-1} \frac{a^{2\ell+1}(k-2\ell-p-r)_{2\ell+1}}{(2\ell+1)!} J^a_{2k-2r-2p-2\ell-1}(x) \right). \end{aligned} \tag{70}$$

The last formula can be rearranged to be written as

$$\begin{aligned} D^p J^a_{2k}(x) =& 4^{-p} a^{2p} (-1)^p \left(\sum_{\ell=0}^{k-p} a^{2\ell} \sum_{m=0}^{\ell} \frac{(k+m)!}{(2m)!(2\ell-2m)!(k-2\ell+m-p)!} J^a_{2k-2p-2\ell}(x) \right. \\ & \left. - \sum_{\ell=0}^{k-p-1} a^{2\ell+1} \sum_{m=0}^{\ell} \frac{(k+m)!}{(2m)!(2\ell-2m+1)!(k-2\ell+m-p-1)!} J^a_{2k-2p-2\ell-1}(x) \right), \end{aligned} \tag{71}$$

which may be written alternatively as in (67). Formula (68) can be similarly proved. □

5.2. Derivatives of Jacobsthal Polynomials in Terms of Non-Symmetric Polynomials

In this part, we will find a general expression for the derivatives of $J^a_k(x)$ in terms of any non-symmetric polynomial. In addition, some specific derivative expressions are given.

Theorem 8. *If we consider any non-symmetric polynomial $\psi_i(x)$ expressed as in (15), then for all non-negative integers p and k with $k \geq p$, we have the following two derivative expressions:*

$$D^p J^a_{2k}(x) = \sum_{m=0}^{k-p} R_{m,k}\, \psi_{k-p-m}(x), \tag{72}$$

$$D^p J^a_{2k+1}(x) = \sum_{m=0}^{k-p} \bar{R}_{m,k}\, \psi_{k-p-m}(x), \tag{73}$$

where

$$R_{m,k} = a^{2k}\sum_{r=0}^{m}(-4)^{r-k}\binom{k+r}{k-r}(1+k-p-r)_p\,\bar{F}_{m-r,k-r-p}, \tag{74}$$

$$\bar{R}_{m,k} = a^{2k+1}\sum_{r=0}^{m}(-4)^{r-k}\binom{k+r+1}{k-r}(1+k-p-r)_p\bar{F}_{m-r,k-r-p}, \tag{75}$$

and $\bar{F}_{\ell,m}$ *are the inversion coefficients appear in* (17).

Proof. We start from Formula (69), and after that, apply the inversion formula in (17) to obtain the following formula:

$$D^p J^a_{2k}(x) = a^{2k}\sum_{r=0}^{k-p}(-4)^{r-k}\binom{k+r}{k-r}(1+k-p-r)_p\sum_{t=0}^{k-r-p}\bar{F}_{t,k-r-p}\,\psi_{k-r-p-t}(x), \tag{76}$$

which can be arranged to give the following formula:

$$D^p J^a_{2k}(x) = a^{2k}\sum_{m=0}^{k-p}\sum_{r=0}^{m}(-4)^{r-k}\binom{k+r}{k-r}(1+k-p-r)_p\,\bar{F}_{m-r,k-r-p}\,\psi_{k-p-m}(x). \tag{77}$$

This proves (72). Formula (73) can be similarly proved. □

As a result of Theorem 8, we will present some derivative formulas for the JTPs as combinations of specific non-symmetric polynomials. The following corollaries display these results.

Corollary 1. *Consider the two non-negative integers k and p with* $k \geq p$. *In terms of the shifted Jacobi polynomials* $\tilde{R}^{(\rho,\gamma)}_\ell(x)$, *the derivatives* $D^p J^a_k(x)$ *have the following expressions:*

$$\begin{aligned} D^p J^a_{2k}(x) = & \frac{\left(-\frac{1}{4}\right)^k a^{2k}\Gamma(1+k-p+\gamma)k!}{\Gamma(1+\rho)}\times \\ & \sum_{m=0}^{k-p}\frac{(1+2k-2m-2p+\rho+\gamma)\Gamma(1+k-m-p+\rho)\Gamma(1+k-m-p+\rho+\gamma)}{m!(k-m-p)!\Gamma(1+k-m-p+\gamma)\Gamma(2+2k-m-2p+\rho+\gamma)}\times \\ & {}_3F_2\left(\left.\begin{matrix}-m,1+k,-1-2k+m+2p-\rho-\gamma\\ \frac{1}{2},-k+p-\gamma\end{matrix}\right|1\right)\tilde{R}^{(\rho,\gamma)}_{k-p-m}(x), \end{aligned} \tag{78}$$

$$\begin{aligned} D^p J^a_{2k+1}(x) = & \frac{\left(-\frac{1}{4}\right)^k a^{2k+1}\Gamma(1+k-p+\gamma)(k+1)!}{\Gamma(1+\rho)}\times \\ & \sum_{m=0}^{k-p}\frac{(1+2k-2m-2p+\rho+\gamma)\Gamma(1+k-m-p+\rho)\Gamma(1+k-m-p+\rho+\gamma)}{m!(k-m-p)!\Gamma(1+k-m-p+\gamma)\Gamma(2+2k-m-2p+\rho+\gamma)}\times \\ & {}_3F_2\left(\left.\begin{matrix}-m,2+k,-1-2k+m+2p-\rho-\gamma\\ \frac{3}{2},-k+p-\gamma\end{matrix}\right|1\right)\tilde{R}^{(\rho,\gamma)}_{k-p-m}(x). \end{aligned} \tag{79}$$

Proof. Based on Theorem 8 along with the inversion coefficients of $\tilde{R}^{(\rho,\gamma)}_\ell(x)$ in the first row and last column of Table 2. □

Corollary 2. *Consider the two non-negative integers k and p with $k \geq p$. In terms of Schröder polynomials, $D^p J^a_{2k}(x)$ have the following expressions:*

$$D^p J^a_{2k}(x) = 4^{-k} a^{2k} (1+k-p)!k! \sum_{m=0}^{k-p} \frac{(-1)^{k+m}(1+2k-2m-2p)}{m!(1+2k-m-2p)!} \times \\ {}_3F_2\left(\begin{matrix} -m, 1+k, -1-2k+m+2p \\ \frac{1}{2}, -1-k+p \end{matrix} \middle| -1\right) S_{k-p-m}(x), \tag{80}$$

$$D^p J^a_{2k+1}(x) = 4^{-k} a^{1+2k} (k+1)!(1+k-p)! \sum_{m=0}^{k-p} \frac{(-1)^{k+m}(1+2k-2m-2p)}{m!(1+2k-m-2p)!} \times \\ {}_3F_2\left(\begin{matrix} -m, 2+k, -1-2k+m+2p \\ \frac{3}{2}, -1-k+p \end{matrix} \middle| -1\right) S_{k-p-m}(x). \tag{81}$$

Proof. Based on Theorem 8 along with the inversion coefficients of $S_\ell(x)$ in the second row and last column of Table 2. □

Corollary 3. *Consider the two non-negative integers k and p with $k \geq p$. In terms of Bernoulli polynomials, $D^p J^a_{2k}(x)$ have the following expressions:*

$$D^p J^a_{2k}(x) = \frac{\left(-\frac{1}{4}\right)^k a^{2k} \sqrt{\pi}}{\Gamma\left(-\frac{1}{2}-k\right)} \sum_{m=0}^{k-p} \frac{k!\,\Gamma\left(\frac{1}{2}-k+m\right) + (-1)^m \Gamma\left(-\frac{1}{2}-k\right)(1+k+m)!}{\Gamma\left(\frac{3}{2}+m\right)(m+1)!(k-m-p)!} B_{k-p-m}(x), \tag{82}$$

$$D^p J^a_{2k+1}(x) = \frac{a^{2k+1}}{\sqrt{\pi}} \sum_{m=0}^{k-p} \frac{4^{-2k+m}\left(-(2k+2)!\,\Gamma\left(\frac{1}{2}-k+m\right) + (-1)^{m+k} 4^{1+k} \sqrt{\pi}(2+k+m)!\right)}{(2m+3)!(k-m-p)!} B_{k-p-m}(x). \tag{83}$$

Proof. By applying Theorem 8 using the inversion coefficients of $B_m(x)$ in the third row and last column of Table 2. □

5.3. Derivatives of Jacobsthal Polynomials in Terms of Symmetric Polynomials

In this part, we will find a general expression for the derivatives of $J^a_k(x)$ in terms of any symmetric polynomial. In addition, some specific derivatives of the JTPs in terms of symmetric polynomials are given.

Theorem 9. *If we consider any symmetric polynomial $\phi_i(x)$ expressed as in (14), then for any non-negative integers p and k with $k \geq p$, then we have the following two derivative expressions:*

$$D^p J^a_{2k}(x) = \sum_{m=0}^{\left\lfloor \frac{k-p}{2} \right\rfloor} M_{m,k,p}\, \phi_{k-p-2m}(x) + \sum_{m=0}^{\left\lfloor \frac{1}{2}(k-p-1) \right\rfloor} \sum_{r=0}^{m} \bar{M}_{m,k,p}\, \phi_{k-p-2m-1}(x), \tag{84}$$

$$D^p J^a_{2k+1}(x) = \sum_{m=0}^{\left\lfloor \frac{k-p}{2} \right\rfloor} W_{m,k,p}\, \phi_{k-p-2m}(x) + \sum_{m=0}^{\left\lfloor \frac{1}{2}(k-p-1) \right\rfloor} \sum_{r=0}^{m} \bar{W}_{m,k,p}\, \phi_{k-p-2m-1}(x), \tag{85}$$

where

$$M_{m,k,p} = a^{2k} \sum_{r=0}^{m} \frac{\left(-\frac{1}{4}\right)^{k-2r} (k+2r)!}{(k-p-2r)!(4r)!} \bar{H}_{m-r,k-2r-p}, \tag{86}$$

$$\bar{M}_{m,k,p} = a^{2k} \sum_{r=0}^{m} \frac{\left(-\frac{1}{4}\right)^{k-2r-1} (k+2r+1)!}{(k-p-2r-1)!(4r+2)!} \bar{H}_{m-r,k-2r-p-1}, \tag{87}$$

$$W_{m,k,p} = a^{2k+1} \sum_{r=0}^{m} \frac{\left(-\frac{1}{4}\right)^{k-2r} (1+k+2r)!(1+k-p-2r)_p}{(k-2r)!(1+4r)!} \bar{H}_{m-r,k-2r-p}, \tag{88}$$

$$\bar{W}_{m,k,p} = a^{2k+1} \sum_{r=0}^{m} \frac{\left(-\frac{1}{4}\right)^{k-2r-1} (2+k+2r)!(k-p-2r)_p}{(k-2r-1)!(3+4r)!} \bar{H}_{m-r,k-2r-p-1}. \tag{89}$$

and $\bar{H}_{\ell,m}$ are the inversion coefficients of $\phi_i(x)$ appear in (16).

Proof. The proofs of (84) and (85) are similar. We prove (85). Starting from Formula (69), and making use of the inversion formula of $\phi_k(x)$ in (16), we get

$$D^p J^a_{2k+1}(x) = a^{2k+1} \sum_{r=0}^{k-p} \frac{\left(-\frac{1}{4}\right)^{k-r} (1+k+r)!(1+k-p-r)_p}{(k-r)!(2r+1)!} \sum_{t=0}^{\lfloor \frac{1}{2}(k-r-p) \rfloor} \bar{H}_{t,k-r-p}\, \phi_{k-r-p-2t}(x). \tag{90}$$

The following formula is the result of some manipulations:

$$\begin{aligned} D^p J^a_{2k+1}(x) =& a^{2k+1} \sum_{m=0}^{\lfloor \frac{k-p}{2} \rfloor} \sum_{r=0}^{m} \frac{\left(-\frac{1}{4}\right)^{k-2r} (k+1+2r)!(k+1-p-2r)_p}{(k-2r)!(4r+1)!} \bar{H}_{m-r,k-2r-p}\, \phi_{k-p-2m}(x) \\ &+ a^{2k+1} \sum_{m=0}^{\lfloor \frac{k-p-1}{2} \rfloor} \sum_{r=0}^{m} \frac{\left(-\frac{1}{4}\right)^{k-2r-1} (k+2+2r)!(k-p-2r)_p}{(k-2r-1)!(4r+3)!} \bar{H}_{m-r,k-2r-p-1}\, \phi_{k-p-2m-1}(x). \end{aligned} \tag{91}$$

Similarly, we can show that

$$\begin{aligned} D^p J^a_{2k}(x) =& a^{2k} \sum_{m=0}^{\lfloor \frac{k-p}{2} \rfloor} \sum_{r=0}^{m} \frac{\left(-\frac{1}{4}\right)^{k-2r} (k+2r)!}{(k-p-2r)!(4r)!} \bar{H}_{m-r,k-2r-p}\, \phi_{k-p-2m}(x) \\ &+ a^{2k} \sum_{m=0}^{\lfloor \frac{1}{2}(k-p-1) \rfloor} \sum_{r=0}^{m} \frac{\left(-\frac{1}{4}\right)^{k-2r-1} (k+2r+1)!}{(k-p-2r-1)!(4r+2)!} \bar{H}_{m-r,k-2r-p-1}\, \phi_{k-p-2m-1}(x). \end{aligned} \tag{92}$$

The two formulas (91), and (92) can be written as:

$$D^p J^a_{2k}(x) = \sum_{m=0}^{\lfloor \frac{k-p}{2} \rfloor} M_{m,k,p}\, \phi_{k-p-2m}(x) + \sum_{m=0}^{\lfloor \frac{1}{2}(k-p-1) \rfloor} \bar{M}_{m,k,p}\, \phi_{k-p-2m-1}(x), \tag{93}$$

$$D^p J^a_{2k+1}(x) = \sum_{m=0}^{\lfloor \frac{k-p}{2} \rfloor} W_{m,k,p}\, \phi_{k-p-2m}(x) + \sum_{m=0}^{\lfloor \frac{1}{2}(k-p-1) \rfloor} \bar{W}_{m,k,p}\, \phi_{k-p-2m-1}(x), \tag{94}$$

where the coefficients $M_{m,k,p}$, $\bar{M}_{m,k,p}$, $W_{m,k,p}$, $\bar{W}_{m,k,p}$ are given, respectively, as in (86)–(89). This proves Theorem 9. □

In the following, we give two expressions for the derivatives of the JTPs in terms of the ultraspherical and Hermite polynomials as applications of Theorem 9.

Corollary 4. *Consider the two non-negative integers k and p with $k \geq p$. In terms of the ultraspherical polynomials $C_i^{(\gamma)}(x)$, the derivatives $D^p J_k^a(x)$ have the following expressions:*

$$
\begin{aligned}
D^p J_{2k}^a(x) = {} & \frac{(-1)^k 2^{1-3k+p-2\gamma} a^{2k} \sqrt{\pi} k!}{\Gamma\left(\frac{1}{2}+\gamma\right)} \sum_{m=0}^{\left\lfloor \frac{k-p}{2} \right\rfloor} \frac{(k-2m-p+\gamma)\Gamma(k-2m-p+2\gamma)}{m!(k-2m-p)!\Gamma(1+k-m-p+\gamma)} \times \\
& {}_4F_3\left(\begin{matrix} -m, \frac{1}{2}+\frac{k}{2}, 1+\frac{k}{2}, -k+m+p-\gamma \\ \frac{1}{4}, \frac{1}{2}, \frac{3}{4} \end{matrix} \middle| 1\right) C_{k-p-2m}^{(\gamma)}(x) \\
& + \frac{(-1)^{1+k} 2^{3-3k+p-2\gamma} a^{2k} \sqrt{\pi}(1+k)!}{\Gamma\left(\frac{1}{2}+\gamma\right)} \times \\
& \sum_{m=0}^{\left\lfloor \frac{1}{2}(k-p-1) \right\rfloor} \frac{(-1+k-2m-p+\gamma)\Gamma(-1+k-2m-p+2\gamma)}{m!(-1+k-2m-p)!\Gamma(k-m-p+\gamma)} \times \\
& {}_4F_3\left(\begin{matrix} -m, 1+\frac{k}{2}, \frac{3}{2}+\frac{k}{2}, 1-k+m+p-\gamma \\ \frac{3}{4}, \frac{5}{4}, \frac{3}{2} \end{matrix} \middle| 1\right) C_{k-p-2m-1}^{(\gamma)}(x),
\end{aligned} \tag{95}
$$

$$
\begin{aligned}
D^p J_{2k+1}^a(x) = {} & \frac{(-1)^k 2^{1-3k+p-2\gamma} a^{1+2k} \sqrt{\pi}(1+k)!}{\Gamma\left(\frac{1}{2}+\gamma\right)} \sum_{m=0}^{\left\lfloor \frac{k-p}{2} \right\rfloor} \frac{(k-2m-p+\gamma)\Gamma(k-2m-p+2\gamma)}{m!(k-2m-p)!\Gamma(1+k-m-p+\gamma)} \times \\
& {}_4F_3\left(\begin{matrix} -m, 1+\frac{k}{2}, \frac{3}{2}+\frac{k}{2}, -k+m+p-\gamma \\ \frac{1}{2}, \frac{3}{4}, \frac{5}{4} \end{matrix} \middle| 1\right) C_{k-p-2m}^{(\gamma)}(x) \\
& + \frac{(-1)^{k+1} 2^{3-3k+p-2\gamma} a^{1+2k} \sqrt{\pi}(2+k)!}{3\Gamma\left(\frac{1}{2}+\gamma\right)} \times \\
& \sum_{m=0}^{\left\lfloor \frac{1}{2}(k-p-1) \right\rfloor} \frac{(-1+k-2m-p+\gamma)\Gamma(-1+k-2m-p+2\gamma)}{m!(-1+k-2m-p)!\Gamma(k-m-p+\gamma)} \times \\
& {}_4F_3\left(\begin{matrix} -m, \frac{3}{2}+\frac{k}{2}, 2+\frac{k}{2}, 1-k+m+p-\gamma \\ \frac{5}{4}, \frac{3}{2}, \frac{7}{4} \end{matrix} \middle| 1\right) C_{k-p-2m-1}^{(\gamma)}(x).
\end{aligned} \tag{96}
$$

Proof. By applying Theorem 9 using the inversion coefficients of $C_\ell^{(\gamma)}(x)$ in the first row, last column of Table 3. □

Corollary 5. *Consider the two non-negative integers k and p with $k \geq p$. In terms of Hermite polynomials $H_\ell(x)$, the derivatives $D^p J_k^a(x)$ have the following expressions:*

$$
\begin{aligned}
D^p J_{2k}^a(x) = {} & (-1)^k 2^{-3k+p} a^{2k} k! \sum_{m=0}^{\left\lfloor \frac{k-p}{2} \right\rfloor} \frac{1}{m!(k-2m-p)!} \times \\
& {}_3F_3\left(\begin{matrix} -m, \frac{1}{2}+\frac{k}{2}, 1+\frac{k}{2} \\ \frac{1}{4}, \frac{1}{2}, \frac{3}{4} \end{matrix} \middle| -1\right) H_{k-p-2m}(x) \\
& + (-1)^{1+k} 2^{2-3k+p} a^{2k} (k+1)! \sum_{m=0}^{\left\lfloor \frac{1}{2}(k-p-1) \right\rfloor} \frac{1}{m!(k-2m-p-1)!} \times \\
& {}_3F_3\left(\begin{matrix} -m, 1+\frac{k}{2}, \frac{3}{2}+\frac{k}{2} \\ \frac{3}{4}, \frac{5}{4}, \frac{3}{2} \end{matrix} \middle| -1\right) H_{k-p-2m-1}(x),
\end{aligned} \tag{97}
$$

$$
\begin{aligned}
D^p J^a_{2k+1}(x) = {} & (-1)^k 2^{-3k+p} a^{1+2k}(k+1)! \sum_{m=0}^{\left\lfloor \frac{k-p}{2} \right\rfloor} \frac{1}{m!(k-2m-p)!} \times \\
& {}_3F_3\left(\begin{matrix} -m, 1+\frac{k}{2}, \frac{3}{2}+\frac{k}{2} \\ \frac{1}{2}, \frac{3}{4}, \frac{5}{4} \end{matrix} \middle| -1 \right) H_{k-p-2m}(x) \\
& + \frac{1}{3}(-1)^{k+1} 2^{2-3k+p} a^{1+2k}(k+2)! \sum_{m=0}^{\left\lfloor \frac{1}{2}(k-p-1) \right\rfloor} \frac{1}{m!(k-2m-p-1)!} \times \\
& {}_3F_3\left(\begin{matrix} -m, \frac{3}{2}+\frac{k}{2}, 2+\frac{k}{2} \\ \frac{5}{4}, \frac{3}{2}, \frac{7}{4} \end{matrix} \middle| -1 \right) H_{k-p-2m-1}(x).
\end{aligned} \tag{98}
$$

Proof. By applying Theorem 9 using the inversion coefficients of $H_\ell(x)$ in the second row, last column of Table 3. □

6. Derivatives of Different Polynomials in Terms of the JTPs

This section is confined to presenting new derivative expressions for various polynomials as combinations of the JTPs.

6.1. Derivatives of Non-Symmetric Polynomials in Terms of Jacobsthal Polynomials

We give a general theorem in which we express the derivatives of any non-symmetric polynomial represented as (15) in terms of the JTPs.

Theorem 10. *Consider any symmetric polynomial $\psi_k(x)$. In addition, consider the two non-negative integers k and p with $k \geq p$. We have*

$$
\begin{aligned}
D^p \psi_k(x) = {} & \sum_{t=0}^{k-p} a^{2(-k+t+p)} \times \\
& \left(\sum_{m=0}^{t} \frac{F_{m,k}\,(1+k-m-p)_p (-1)^{k-m-p} 2^{2(k-m-p)} (1+k+m-2t-p)_{-2m+2t}}{(2t-2m)!} \right) J^a_{2k-2p-2t}(x) \\
& + \sum_{t=0}^{k-p-1} a^{1-2k+2t+2p} \left(\sum_{m=0}^{t} \frac{F_{m,k}\,(1+k-m-p)_p (-1)^{1+k-m-p} 2^{2(k-m-p)} (k+m-2t-p)_{1-2m+2t}}{(2t-2m+1)!} \right) J^a_{2k-2p-2t-1}(x),
\end{aligned} \tag{99}
$$

where $F_{m,k}$ are the power form coefficients given in the second column of Table 2.

Proof. If we consider the power form representation in (15), then we can write

$$
D^p \psi_k(x) = \sum_{r=0}^{k-p} F_{r,k}\,(k-r-p+1)_p\, x^{k-r-p}.
$$

If the inversion formula (41) is applied, then the last formula transforms into the following form:

$$
\begin{aligned}
D^p \psi_k(x) = {} & \sum_{r=0}^{k-p} F_{r,k}\,(1+k-p-r)_p \times \\
& \left(\sum_{t=0}^{k-r-p} \frac{(-1)^{k-p-r} 2^{2(k-p-r)} a^{2(-k+t+p+r)} (1+k-2t-p-r)_{2t}}{(2t)!} J^a_{2k-2r-2p-2t}(x) \right. \\
& \left. + \sum_{t=0}^{k-r-p-1} \frac{(-1)^{1+k-p-r} 2^{2(k-p-r)} a^{1-2k+2t+2p+2r} (k-2t-p-r)_{1+2t}}{(2t+1)!} J^a_{2k-2r-2p-2t-1}(x) \right).
\end{aligned} \tag{100}
$$

Some tedious manipulations on the right-hand side of the last formula enable one to write (100) in the following form

$$D^p\psi_k(x) = \sum_{t=0}^{k-p} a^{2(-k+t+p)} \times \\ \left(\sum_{m=0}^{t} \frac{F_{m,k}\,(1+k-m-p)_p(-1)^{k-m-p}2^{2(k-m-p)}(1+k+m-2t-p)_{-2m+2t}}{(2t-2m)!}\right) J^a_{2k-2p-2t}(x) \\ + \sum_{t=0}^{k-p-1} a^{1-2k+2t+2p}\left(\sum_{m=0}^{t} \frac{F_{m,k}\,(1+k-m-p)_p(-1)^{1+k-m-p}2^{2(k-m-p)}(k+m-2t-p)_{1-2m+2t}}{(2t-2m+1)!}\right) J^a_{2k-2p-2t-1}(x). \tag{101}$$

This completes the proof. □

The following corollary gives an application to Theorem 10. The formula expressing the Jacobi polynomials' derivatives in terms of the JTPs is given.

Corollary 6. *Consider the two non-negative integers k and p with $k \geq p$. The following expression holds:*

$$D^p \tilde{R}_k^{(\gamma,\rho)}(x) = \sum_{t=0}^{k-p} V_{t,k,p}\, J^a_{2k-2p-2t}(x) + \sum_{t=0}^{k-p-1} \bar{V}_{t,k,b}\, J^a_{2k-2p-2t-1}(x), \tag{102}$$

where

$$V_{t,k,p} = \frac{(-1)^{k-p}2^{2(k-p)}a^{2(-k+p+t)}\, k!\,\Gamma(1+\gamma)\,\Gamma(1+2k+\gamma+\rho)}{(k-p-1-2t)!\,(2t)!\,k!\,\Gamma(1+k+\gamma+\rho)} \times \\ {}_3F_2\left(\begin{matrix} -t, \frac{1}{2}-t, -k-\rho \\ 1+k-p-2t, -2k-\gamma-\rho \end{matrix}\,\middle|\, 1\right), \tag{103}$$

$$\bar{V}_{t,k,p} = \frac{(-1)^{1+k-p}2^{2(k-p)}a^{1-2k+2p+2t}\,\Gamma(1+k)\,\Gamma(1+\gamma)\,\Gamma(1+2k+\gamma+\rho)}{\Gamma(k-p-2t)\,\Gamma(2(1+t))\,\Gamma(1+k+\gamma)\,\Gamma(1+k+\gamma+\rho)} \times \\ {}_3F_2\left(\begin{matrix} -t, -\frac{1}{2}-t, -k-\rho \\ k-p-2t, -2k-\gamma-\rho \end{matrix}\,\middle|\, 1\right). \tag{104}$$

Proof. Direct application of Theorem 10 considering the power form coefficients of $\tilde{R}_k^{(\gamma,\rho)}(x)$ in the first row, second column of Table 2. □

6.2. Derivatives of Symmetric Polynomials in Terms of the JTPs

Theorem 11. *Consider any symmetric polynomial $\phi_k(x)$. For all non-negative integers k, p with $k \geq p$, the following derivative expression for $\phi_k(x)$ is valid:*

$$
\begin{aligned}
D^p\phi_k(x) =&(-1)^{k-p}\sum_{t=0}^{\left\lfloor\frac{k-p}{2}\right\rfloor} a^{-2k+2p+4t}\left(\sum_{m=0}^{t}\frac{\left(2^{2(k-2m-p)}(k-2m)!\right)H_{m,k}}{(4t-4m)!(k+2m-p-4t)!}\right)J^a_{2k-2p-4t}(x)\\
&+(-1)^{1+k-p}\sum_{t=0}^{\left\lfloor\frac{k-p}{2}\right\rfloor} a^{1-2k+2p+4t}\left(\sum_{m=0}^{t}\frac{\left(2^{2(k-2m-p)}(k-2m)!\right)H_{m,k}}{(4t-4m+1)!(k+2m-p-4t-1)!}\right)J^a_{2k-2p-4t-1}(x)\\
&+(-1)^{k-p}\sum_{t=0}^{\left\lfloor\frac{k-p}{2}\right\rfloor-1} a^{2-2k+2p+4t}\left(\sum_{m=0}^{t}\frac{\left(2^{2(k-2m-p)}(k-2m)!\right)H_{m,k}}{(4t-4m+2)!(k+2m-p-4t-2)!}\right)J^a_{2k-2p-4t-2}(x)\\
&+(-1)^{1+k-p}\sum_{t=0}^{\left\lfloor\frac{k-p}{2}\right\rfloor-1} a^{3-2k+2p+4t}\left(\sum_{m=0}^{t}\frac{\left(2^{2(k-2m-p)}(k-2m)!\right)H_{m,k}}{(4t-4m+3)!(k+2m-p-4t-3)!}\right)J^a_{2k-2p-4t-3}(x),
\end{aligned}
\tag{105}
$$

where $H_{m,k}$ are the power form coefficients given in the second column of Table 3.

Proof. The analytic form of a symmetric polynomial given in (14) allows one to write

$$
D^p\phi_k(x) = \sum_{r=0}^{\left\lfloor\frac{k-p}{2}\right\rfloor} H_{r,k}(1+k-p-2r)_p\, x^{k-2r-p}. \tag{106}
$$

The inversion formula of the JTPs allows one to convert the last formula into the following one:

$$
\begin{aligned}
D^p\phi_k(x) =& \sum_{r=0}^{\left\lfloor\frac{k-p}{2}\right\rfloor} H_{r,k}(-1)^{k-p}2^{2(k-p-2r)}(1+k-p-2r)_p\times\\
&\left(\sum_{t=0}^{k-2r-p}\frac{a^{2(-k+p+2r+t)}(1+k-p-2r-2t)_{2t}}{(2t)!}J^a_{2k-4r-2p-2t}(x)\right.\\
&\left.-\sum_{t=0}^{k-2r-p-1}\frac{a^{1-2k+2p+4r+2t}(k-p-2(r+t))_{1+2t}}{(2t+1)!}J^a_{2k-4r-2p-2t-1}(x)\right).
\end{aligned}
\tag{107}
$$

Some tedious computations lead to the formula in (105). □

As an application to Theorem 11, the derivatives of the ultraspherical polynomials can be expressed in terms of the JTPs as in the following corollary.

Corollary 7. *Consider the two non-negative integers k and p with $k \geq p$. The derivatives of the ultraspherical polynomials can be expressed in terms of $J^a_k(x)$ as follows:*

$$
\begin{aligned}
D^pC^{(\gamma)}_k(x) =& \sum_{t=0}^{\left\lfloor\frac{k-p}{2}\right\rfloor} Q_{1,t,k,p}J^a_{2k-2p-4t}(x) + \sum_{t=0}^{\left\lfloor\frac{k-p}{2}\right\rfloor} Q_{2,t,k,p}J^a_{2k-2p-4t-1}(x)\\
&+\sum_{t=0}^{\left\lfloor\frac{k-p}{2}\right\rfloor-1} Q_{3,t,k,p}J^a_{2k-2p-4t-2}(x) + \sum_{t=0}^{\left\lfloor\frac{k-p}{2}\right\rfloor-1} Q_{4,t,k,p}J^a_{2k-2p-4t-3}(x),
\end{aligned}
\tag{108}
$$

where

$$
\begin{aligned}
Q_{1,t,k,p} =& \frac{(-1)^{k-p}\, 2^{-1+3k-2p+2\gamma}\, a^{-2k+2p+4t}\, k!\,\Gamma\left(\frac{1}{2}+\gamma\right)\Gamma(k+\gamma)}{\sqrt{\pi}\,(k-p-4t)!\,(4t)!\,\Gamma(k+2\gamma)} \times \\
& {}_4F_3\left(\begin{matrix} -t, \frac{1}{4}-t, \frac{1}{2}-t, \frac{3}{4}-t \\ \frac{1}{2}+\frac{k}{2}-\frac{p}{2}-2t, 1+\frac{k}{2}-\frac{p}{2}-2t, 1-k-\gamma \end{matrix}\middle| 1\right) \\
Q_{2,t,k,p} =& \frac{(-1)^{1+k-p}\, 2^{-1+3k-2p+2\gamma}\, a^{1-2k+2p+4t}\, k!\,\Gamma\left(\frac{1}{2}+\gamma\right)\Gamma(k+\gamma)}{\sqrt{\pi}\,(k-p-4t-1)!\,(4t+1)!\,\Gamma(k+2\gamma)} \times \\
& {}_4F_3\left(\begin{matrix} -t, -\frac{1}{4}-t, \frac{1}{4}-t, \frac{1}{2}-t \\ \frac{k}{2}-\frac{p}{2}-2t, \frac{1}{2}+\frac{k}{2}-\frac{p}{2}-2t, 1-k-\gamma \end{matrix}\middle| 1\right) \\
Q_{3,t,k,p} =& \frac{(-1)^{k-p}\, 2^{-1+3k-2p+2\gamma}\, a^{2-2k+2p+4t}\, k!\,\Gamma\left(\frac{1}{2}+\gamma\right)\Gamma(k+\gamma)}{\sqrt{\pi}\,(k-p-4t-2)!\,(4t+2)!\,\Gamma(k+2\gamma)} \times \\
& {}_4F_3\left(\begin{matrix} -t, -\frac{1}{2}-t, -\frac{1}{4}-t, \frac{1}{4}-t \\ -\frac{1}{2}+\frac{k}{2}-\frac{p}{2}-2t, \frac{k}{2}-\frac{p}{2}-2t, 1-k-\gamma \end{matrix}\middle| 1\right) \\
Q_{4,t,k,p} =& \frac{(-1)^{1+k-p}\, 2^{-1+3k-2p+2\gamma}\, a^{3-2k+2p+4t}\, k!\,\Gamma\left(\frac{1}{2}+\gamma\right)\Gamma(k+\gamma)}{\sqrt{\pi}\,(k-p-4t-3)!\,(4t+3))!\,\Gamma(k+2\gamma)} \times \\
& {}_4F_3\left(\begin{matrix} -t, -\frac{3}{4}-t, -\frac{1}{2}-t, -\frac{1}{4}-t \\ -1+\frac{k}{2}-\frac{p}{2}-2t, -\frac{1}{2}+\frac{k}{2}-\frac{p}{2}-2t, 1-k-\gamma \end{matrix}\middle| 1\right)
\end{aligned}
$$

Proof. Direct application of Theorem 11 considering the power form coefficients $C_k^{(\gamma)}(x)$ in the first row and second column of Table 3. □

7. Some Definite Integrals

This section is confined to deducing closed formulas for some definite integrals of the Jacobsthal polynomials, their moments, and their linearization formula.

Corollary 8. *The following integral formula holds:*

$$\int_0^1 J_i^a(x)\,dx = \frac{4}{i+2}\left(1-2^{-i-1}\right). \tag{109}$$

Proof. The following two formulas can be proved:

$$\int_0^1 J_{2k}^a(x)\,dx = \frac{4^{-k}a^{2k}\left(2^{2k+1}-1\right)}{k+1}, \tag{110}$$

$$\int_0^1 J_{2k+1}^a(x)\,dx = \frac{4^{-k}\,a^{2k+1}\left(4^{k+1}-1\right)}{2k+3}. \tag{111}$$

The proof of the two formulas is similar. We prove Formula (111). The proof is based on the connection formula with Bernoulli polynomials that can be deduced from (83) by setting $q=0$. Thus, integrating both sides from 0 to 1, we obtain

$$
\begin{aligned}
\int_0^1 J_{2k+1}^a(x)\,dx =& a^{2k+1}\sum_{m=0}^{k} \frac{4^{-2k+m}\left(-(2k+2)!\Gamma\left(\frac{1}{2}-k+m\right)+(-1)^{m+k}4^{k+1}\sqrt{\pi}(k+m+2)!\right)}{\sqrt{\pi}\,(2m+3)!\,(k-m)!} \times \\
& \int_0^1 B_{k-m}(x)\,dx.
\end{aligned}
$$

If we note the identity:

$$\int_0^1 B_k(x)\,dx = \begin{cases} 1, & k=0, \\ 0, & k>0, \end{cases}$$

then it is easy to reduce the above formula to

$$\int_0^1 J^a_{2k+1}(x)\,dx = \frac{4^{-k}\,a^{2k+1}\left(4^{k+1}-1\right)}{2k+3}.$$

This proves (111). Formula (110) can be similarly proved from the connection formula that can be obtained from (82) setting $q=0$. □

Corollary 9. *For all non-negative integers m and k, one has*

$$\int_0^1 x^m\, J^a_k(x)\,dx = 2^{2m} a^i \sum_{r=0}^{m} \frac{2(-1)^r\left(2-2^{-i-m-r}\right)\binom{m}{r}}{2+i+m+r}. \tag{112}$$

Proof. From the moment formula, it can be shown that

$$\int_0^1 x^m\, J^a_k(x)\,dx = 2^{2m} \sum_{r=0}^{m} (-1)^r \binom{m}{r} a^{-m-r} \int_0^1 J^a_{i+m+r}(x)\,dx. \tag{113}$$

Based on Formula (109), the last formula can be converted into

$$\int_0^1 x^m\, J^a_k(x)\,dx = 2^{2m} a^i \sum_{r=0}^{m} \frac{2(-1)^r\left(2-2^{-i-m-r}\right)\binom{m}{r}}{2+i+m+r}. \tag{114}$$

This proves Corollary 9. □

Corollary 10. *Consider any two non-negative integers r and s, the following linearization formula holds:*

$$\int_0^1 J^a_r(x)\, J^a_s(x)\,dx = \sum_{m=0}^{\lfloor \frac{r}{2} \rfloor} U_{m,r} + \sum_{m=0}^{\lfloor \frac{r}{2} \rfloor -1} \bar{U}_{m,r}, \tag{115}$$

where $U_{m,r}$ and $\bar{U}_{m,r}$ are given as follows:

$$U_{m,r} = \begin{cases} H_{m,r}, & \text{if } r \text{ is even}, \\ Z_{m,r}, & \text{if } r \text{ is odd}, \end{cases} \tag{116}$$

$$\bar{U}_{m,r} = \begin{cases} \bar{H}_{m,r}, & \text{if } r \text{ is even}, \\ \bar{Z}_{m,r}, & \text{if } r \text{ is odd}. \end{cases} \tag{117}$$

with

$$H_{m,r} = \frac{\left(4-2^{1+2m-r-s}\right)a^{r+s}\sqrt{\pi}\left(\frac{r}{2}\right)!}{(2-2m+r+s)(2m)!}\; {}_3\tilde{F}_2\left(\begin{matrix} -m,\, 1+\frac{r}{2},\, \frac{1}{2}-m \\ \frac{1}{2},\, 1-2m+\frac{r}{2} \end{matrix} \,\middle|\, 1 \right), \tag{118}$$

$$\bar{H}_{m,r} = -\frac{4\left(1-2^{2m-r-s}\right)a^{r+s}\sqrt{\pi}\left(\frac{r}{2}\right)!}{(1-2m+r+s)(2m+1)!}\; {}_3\tilde{F}_2\left(\begin{matrix} -m,\, 1+\frac{r}{2},\, -\frac{1}{2}-m \\ \frac{1}{2},\, -2m+\frac{r}{2} \end{matrix} \,\middle|\, 1 \right), \tag{119}$$

$$Z_{m,r} = \frac{2\left(1-2^{2m-r-s}\right)a^{r+s}\sqrt{\pi}\left(\frac{r+1}{2}\right)!}{(1-2m+r+s)(2m)!}\; {}_3\tilde{F}_2\left(\begin{matrix} -m,\, \frac{r+3}{2},\, \frac{1}{2}-m \\ \frac{3}{2},\, \frac{1}{2}(1-4m+r) \end{matrix} \,\middle|\, 1 \right), \tag{120}$$

$$\tilde{Z}_{m,r} = -\frac{\left(4 - 2^{3+2m-r-s}\right)a^{r+s}\sqrt{\pi}\left(\frac{r+1}{2}\right)!}{2(-2m+r+s)(2m+1)!}\,{}_3\tilde{F}_2\left(\begin{matrix} -m, \frac{r+3}{2}, -\frac{1}{2}-m \\ \frac{3}{2}, \frac{1}{2}(-1-4m+r) \end{matrix}\,\middle|\, 1\right). \tag{121}$$

Proof. Integrating both sides of the linearization formulas in (60), and (61) leads, respectively, to the following integral formulas:

$$\int_0^1 J_{2r}^a(x)\, J_s^a(x)\, dx = \sqrt{\pi}\, r!\left(\sum_{m=0}^{r} \frac{a^{2m}}{(2m)!}\,{}_3\tilde{F}_2\left(\begin{matrix} -m, 1+r, \frac{1}{2}-m \\ \frac{1}{2}, 1+r-2m \end{matrix}\,\middle|\, 1\right) G_{s+2r-2m}\right.$$
$$\left. - \sum_{m=0}^{r-1} \frac{a^{2m+1}}{(2m+1)!}\,{}_3\tilde{F}_2\left(\begin{matrix} -m, 1+r, -\frac{1}{2}-m \\ \frac{1}{2}, r-2m \end{matrix}\,\middle|\, 1\right) G_{s+2r-2m-1}\right), \tag{122}$$

$$\int_0^1 J_{2r+1}^a(x)\, J_s^a(x)\, dx = \frac{1}{2}\sqrt{\pi}\,(r+1)!\left(\sum_{m=0}^{r} \frac{a^{2m+1}}{(2m)!}\,{}_3\tilde{F}_2\left(\begin{matrix} 2+r, \frac{1}{2}-m, -m \\ \frac{3}{2}, 1+r-2m \end{matrix}\,\middle|\, 1\right) G_{s+2r-2m}\right. \tag{123}$$
$$\left. - \sum_{m=0}^{r-1} \frac{a^{2+2m}}{(2m+1)!}\,{}_3\tilde{F}_2\left(\begin{matrix} 2+r, -\frac{1}{2}-m, -m \\ \frac{3}{2}, r-2m \end{matrix}\,\middle|\, 1\right) G_{s+2r-2m-1}\right), \tag{124}$$

where

$$G_i = \int_0^1 J_i^a(x)\, dx = \frac{4}{i+2}\left(1 - 2^{-i-1}\right).$$

The above two formulas can be merged to give Formula (115). □

Remark 10. *The formula that evaluates the integrals* $\int_0^1 (J_r^a(x))^2\, dx$ *can be obtained as a special case of Formula* (115).

Corollary 11. *For the two positive integers i and j, the following integral formula holds:*

$$\begin{aligned}\int_0^1 J_{2i}^a(x)\, F_j^{A,B}(x)\, dx =& \left(-\frac{1}{4A}\right)^i a^{2i} \sum_{p=0}^{i} (-B)^p \binom{i}{p} \times \\ & {}_4F_3\left(\begin{matrix} -p, \frac{1}{2}+\frac{i}{2}, 1+\frac{i}{2}, -i+p \\ \frac{1}{4}, \frac{1}{2}, \frac{3}{4} \end{matrix}\,\middle|\, -\frac{A^2}{4B}\right) I_{i+j-2p}^{A,B}(x) \\ & + (-1)^{1+i} 2^{1-2i} a^{2i} A^{1-i} (i+1)! \sum_{p=0}^{i-1} \frac{(-B)^p}{p!(i-p-1)!} \times \\ & {}_4F_3\left(\begin{matrix} -p, 1+\frac{i}{2}, \frac{3}{2}+\frac{i}{2}, 1-i+p \\ \frac{3}{4}, \frac{5}{4}, \frac{3}{2} \end{matrix}\,\middle|\, -\frac{A^2}{4B}\right) I_{i+j-2p-1}^{A,B},\end{aligned} \tag{125}$$

$$\begin{aligned}\int_0^1 J_{2i+1}^a(x)\, F_j^{A,B}(x)\, dx =& \left(-\frac{1}{4}\right)^i a^{1+2i} A^{-i} (i+1) \sum_{p=0}^{i} (-B)^p \binom{i}{p} \times \\ & {}_4F_3\left(\begin{matrix} -p, 1+\frac{i}{2}, \frac{3}{2}+\frac{i}{2}, -i+p \\ \frac{1}{2}, \frac{3}{4}, \frac{5}{4} \end{matrix}\,\middle|\, -\frac{A^2}{4B}\right) I_{i+j-2p}^{A,B} \\ & + \frac{1}{3}(-1)^{i+1} 2^{1-2i} a^{1+2i} A^{1-i} (i+2)! \sum_{p=0}^{i-1} \frac{(-B)^p}{(i-p-1)!p!} \times \\ & {}_4F_3\left(\begin{matrix} -p, \frac{3}{2}+\frac{i}{2}, 2+\frac{i}{2}, 1-i+p \\ \frac{5}{4}, \frac{3}{2}, \frac{7}{4} \end{matrix}\,\middle|\, -\frac{A^2}{4B}\right) I_{i+j-2p-1}^{A,B},\end{aligned} \tag{126}$$

where $I_j^{A,B}$ *is given by [57]*

$$I_j^{A,B} = \int_0^1 F_j^{A,B}(x)\,dx = \begin{cases} \frac{A^j}{j+1}\, {}_2F_1\left(\begin{matrix} -\frac{1}{2} - \frac{j}{2}, -\frac{j}{2} \\ -j \end{matrix} \middle| -\frac{4B}{A^2} \right), & j \text{ even}, \\ -\frac{2B^{\frac{j+1}{2}}}{A(j+1)} + \frac{A^j}{j+1}\, {}_2F_1\left(\begin{matrix} -\frac{1}{2} - \frac{j}{2}, -\frac{j}{2} \\ -j \end{matrix} \middle| -\frac{4B}{A^2} \right), & j \text{ odd}. \end{cases} \quad (127)$$

Proof. The above two integral formulas are direct consequences of the two linearization formulas (65), and (66) along with Formula (127). □

8. Conclusions

This paper presented novel results on a certain class of the JTPs. Some new formulas concerning these polynomials were developed. Derivative expression formulas for these polynomials were established as combinations of the different polynomials. The inverse derivatives formulas were also developed. The pivotal formula was the expression of the shifted CPs of the third in terms of the generalized Jacobsthal polynomials, which led to a new inversion formula of these polynomials. Most of the formulas in this paper are new and may be employed in numerical analysis and approximation theory. In future work, we aim to investigate other generalized sequences of polynomials and utilize them to solve several differential equations.

Author Contributions: Conceptualization, W.M.A.-E.; Methodology, W.M.A.-E., O.M.A. and A.K.A.; Software, W.M.A.-E. and A.K.A.; Formal analysis, W.M.A.-E., O.M.A. and A.K.A.; Validation, W.M.A.-E., O.M.A. and A.K.A.; Writing—original draft, W.M.A.-E., O.M.A. and A.K.A.; Writing—review & editing, W.M.A.-E., O.M.A. and A.K.A.; Supervision, W.M.A.-E. All authors have read and agreed to the published version of the manuscript.

Funding: This research work was funded by Umm Al-Qura University, Saudi Arabia, Grant Code: (22UQU4331287DSR02).

Data Availability Statement: Data are contained within the article.

Acknowledgments: The authors would like to thank the Deanship of Scientific Research at Umm Al-Qura University for supporting this work by Grant Code: (22UQU4331287DSR02).

Conflicts of Interest: The authors declare no conflict of interest.

References

1. Fan, H.Y.; He, R.; Da, C.; Liang, Z.F. Optical field's quadrature excitation studied by new Hermite-polynomial operator identity. *Chin. Phys. B* **2013**, *22*, 080301. [CrossRef]
2. Fakhri, H.; Mojaveri, B. The remarkable properties of the associated Romanovski functions. *J. Phys. A Math. Theor.* **2011**, *44*, 195205. [CrossRef]
3. Nikiforov, F.; Uvarov, V.B. *Special Functions of Mathematical Physics*; Springer: Berlin/Heidelberg, Germany, 1988; Volume 205.
4. Xu, R.; Kim, T.; Kim, D.S.; Ma, Y. Probabilistic degenerate Fubini polynomials associated with random variables. *J. Nonlinear Math. Phys.* **2024**, *31*, 47. [CrossRef]
5. Kim, T.; Kim, D.S.; Kwon, J. Probabilistic degenerate Stirling polynomials of the second kind and their applications. *Math. Comput. Model. Dyn. Syst.* **2024**, *30*, 16–30. [CrossRef]
6. Aceto, L.; Malonek, H.; Tomaz, G. A unified matrix approach to the representation of Appell polynomials. *Integral Transform. Spec. Funct.* **2015**, *26*, 426–441. [CrossRef]
7. Dattoli, G. Generalized polynomials, operational identities and their applications. *J. Comput. Appl. Math.* **2000**, *118*, 111–123. [CrossRef]
8. Abd-Elhameed, W.M.; Alqubori, O.M.; Napoli, A. On convolved Fibonacci polynomials. *Mathematics* **2024**, *13*, 22. [CrossRef]
9. Pathan, M.; Khan, W.A. A new class of generalized polynomials associated with Hermite and Euler polynomials. *Mediterr. J. Math.* **2016**, *13*, 913–928. [CrossRef]

10. Isah, A. Poly-Genocchi polynomials and its applications. *AIMS Math.* **2021**, *6*, 8221–8238.
11. Costabile, F.; Gualtieri, M.; Napoli, A. Recurrence relations and determinant forms for general polynomial sequences. Application to Genocchi polynomials. *Integral Transform. Spec. Funct.* **2019**, *30*, 112–127. [CrossRef]
12. Nalli, A.; Haukkanen, P. On generalized Fibonacci and Lucas polynomials. *Chaos Solitons Fractals* **2009**, *42*, 3179–3186. [CrossRef]
13. Abd-Elhameed, W.M.; Alqubori, O.M. New results of unified Chebyshev polynomials. *AIMS Math.* **2024**, *9*, 20058–20088. [CrossRef]
14. Dehghani, A.; Mojaveri, B.; Mahdian, M. New even and odd coherent states attached to the Hermite polynomials. *Rep. Math. Phys.* **2015**, *75*, 267–277. [CrossRef]
15. Fan, H.Y.; Jiang, T.F. Two-variable Hermite polynomials as time-evolutional transition amplitude for driven harmonic oscillator. *Mod. Phys. Lett. B* **2007**, *21*, 475–480. [CrossRef]
16. Ahmed, H.M. Numerical solutions of Korteweg-de Vries and Korteweg-de Vries-Burger's equations in a Bernstein polynomial basis. *Mediterr. J. Math.* **2019**, *16*, 102. [CrossRef]
17. Haq, S.; Ali, I. Approximate solution of two-dimensional Sobolev equation using a mixed Lucas and Fibonacci polynomials. *Eng. Comput.* **2022**, *38*, 2059–2068. [CrossRef]
18. Abd-Elhameed, W.M.; Alqubori, O.M.; Atta, A.G. A collocation approach for the nonlinear fifth-order KdV equations using certain shifted Horadam polynomials. *Mathematics* **2025**, *13*, 300. [CrossRef]
19. Partohaghighi, M.; Hashemi, M.S.; Mirzazadeh, M.; El Din, S.M. Numerical method for fractional advection–dispersion equation using shifted Vieta–Lucas polynomials. *Results Phys.* **2023**, *52*, 106756. [CrossRef]
20. Kumar, S.; Kumar, R.; Osman, M.S.; Samet, B. A wavelet based numerical scheme for fractional order SEIR epidemic of measles by using Genocchi polynomials. *Numer. Methods Partial Differ. Equ.* **2021**, *37*, 1250–1268. [CrossRef]
21. Izadi, M.; Sene, N.; Adel, W.; El-Mesady, A. The Layla and Majnun mathematical model of fractional order: stability analysis and numerical study. *Results Phys.* **2023**, *51*, 106650. [CrossRef]
22. Ahmed, H.M. Numerical solutions for singular Lane-Emden equations using shifted Chebyshev polynomials of the first kind. *Contemp. Math.* **2023**, *4*, 132–149. [CrossRef]
23. Gamal, M.; Zaky, M.A.; El-Kady, M.; Abdelhakem, M. Chebyshev polynomial derivative-based spectral tau approach for solving high-order differential equations. *Comput. Appl. Math.* **2024**, *43*, 412. [CrossRef]
24. Izadi, M.; Ansari, K.J.; Srivastava, H.M. A highly accurate and efficient Genocchi-based spectral technique applied to singular fractional order boundary value problems. *Math. Methods Appl. Sci.* **2025**, *48*, 905–925. [CrossRef]
25. Adel, M.; Khader, M.M.; Algelany, S. High-dimensional chaotic Lorenz system: Numerical treatment using Changhee polynomials of the Appell type. *Fractal Fract.* **2023**, *7*, 398. [CrossRef]
26. Gasper, G. Linearization of the product of Jacobi polynomials. I. *Canad. J. Math.* **1970**, *22*, 171–175. [CrossRef]
27. Sánchez-Ruiz, J.; Dehesa, J.S. Some connection and linearization problems for polynomials in and beyond the Askey scheme. *J. Comput. Appl. Math.* **2001**, *133*, 579–591. [CrossRef]
28. Popov, B.S.; Srivastava, H.M. Linearization of a product of two polynomials of different orthogonal systems. *Facta Univ. Ser. Math. Inform.* **2003**, *18*, 1–8.
29. Srivastava, H.M.; Niukkanen, A.W. Some Clebsch-Gordan type linearization relations and associated families of Dirichlet integrals. *Math. Comput. Model.* **2003**, *37*, 245–250. [CrossRef]
30. Abd-Elhameed, W.M. New product and linearization formulae of Jacobi polynomials of certain parameters. *Integral Transform. Spec. Funct.* **2015**, *26*, 586–599. [CrossRef]
31. Ahmed, H.M. Computing expansions coefficients for Laguerre polynomials. *Integral Transforms Spec. Funct.* **2021**, *32*, 271–289. [CrossRef]
32. Abd-Elhameed, W.M. Novel expressions for the derivatives of sixth kind Chebyshev polynomials: Spectral solution of the non-linear one-dimensional Burgers' equation. *Fractal Fract.* **2021**, *5*, 53. [CrossRef]
33. Guo, D.; Chu, W. Sums of Pell/Lucas Polynomials and Fibonacci/Lucas Numbers. *Mathematics* **2022**, *10*, 2667. [CrossRef]
34. Nalli, A.; Haukkanen, P. On the generalized Fibonacci and Lucas matrix Hybrinomials. *Filomat* **2024**, *38*, 9779–9794.
35. Soykan, Y. A study on generalized Fibonacci polynomials: Sum formulas. *Int. J. Adv. Appl. Math. Mech.* **2022**, *10*, 39–118.
36. Ma, R.; Zhang, W. Several identities involving the Fibonacci numbers and Lucas numbers. *Fibonacci Q.* **2007**, *45*, 164. [CrossRef]
37. Falcon, S.; Plaza, A. On k-Fibonacci sequences and polynomials and their derivatives. *Chaos Soliton Fract.* **2009**, *39*, 1005–1019. [CrossRef]
38. Chen, L.; Wang, X. The power sums involving Fibonacci polynomials and their applications. *Symmetry* **2019**, *11*, 635. [CrossRef]
39. Özkan, E.; Altun, İ. Generalized Lucas polynomials and relationships between the Fibonacci polynomials and Lucas polynomials. *Commun. Algebra* **2019**, *47*, 4020–4030. [CrossRef]
40. Amdeberhan, T.; Chen, X.; Moll, V.H.; Sagan, B.E. Generalized Fibonacci polynomials and Fibonomial coefficients. *Ann. Comb.* **2014**, *18*, 541–562. [CrossRef]
41. Koshy, T. Infinite sums involving Jacobsthal polynomials: Generalizations. *Fibonacci Q.* **2023**, *61*, 305–311. [CrossRef]

42. Koshy, T. Products Involving Reciprocals of Jacobsthal Polynomials. *Fibonacci Q.* **2022**, *60*, 72–81. [CrossRef]
43. Koshy, T. Infinite sums involving Jacobsthal polynomial products. *Fibonacci Q.* **2021**, *59*, 338–348. [CrossRef]
44. Djordjevic, G.B. Derivative sequences of generalized Jacobsthal and Jacobsthal-Lucas polynomials. *Fibonacci Q.* **2000**, *38*, 334–338. [CrossRef]
45. Cerda-Morales, G. On third-order Jacobsthal polynomials and their properties. *Miskolc Math. Notes* **2021**, *22*, 123–132. [CrossRef]
46. Koshy, T. Infinite sums involving Jacobsthal polynomials Revisited. *Fibonacci Q.* **2022**, *60*, 229–234. [CrossRef]
47. Koshy, T.; Gao, Z. Sums involving a class of Jacobsthal polynomial Squares. *Fibonacci Q.* **2024**, *62*, 40–44. [CrossRef]
48. Saba, N.; Boussayoud, A.; Ferkioui, M.; Boughaba, S. Symmetric functions of binary products of Gaussian Jacobsthal Lucas polynomials and Chebyshev polynomials. *Palest. J. Math.* **2021**, *10*, 452.
49. Erdağ, Ö.; Peters, J.F.; Deveci, Ö. The Jacobsthal–Padovan–Fibonacci p-sequence and its application in the concise representation of vibrating systems with dual proximal groups. *J. Supercomput.* **2025**, *81*, 197. [CrossRef]
50. Saba, N.; Boussayoud, A. Gaussian (p, q)-Jacobsthal and Gaussian (p, q)-Jacobsthal Lucas numbers and their some interesting properties. *J. Math. Phys.* **2022**, *63*, 112704. [CrossRef]
51. Horadam, A.F. Extension of a synthesis for a class of polynomial sequences. *Fibonacci Q.* **1996**, *34*, 68–74. [CrossRef]
52. Djordjevic, G.B.; Milovanovic, G.M. *Special Classes of Polynomials*; University of Nis, Faculty of Technology Leskovac: Niš, Serbia, 2014.
53. Tereszkiewicz, A.; Wawreniuk, I. Generalized Jacobsthal polynomials and special points for them. *Appl. Math. Comput.* **2015**, *268*, 806–814. [CrossRef]
54. Abd-Elhameed, W.M.; Al-Harbi, M.S.; Amin, A.K.; Ahmed, H.M. Spectral treatment of high-order Emden–Fowler equations based on modified Chebyshev polynomials. *Axioms* **2023**, *12*, 99. [CrossRef]
55. Koepf, W. *Hypergeometric Summation*, 2nd ed.; Universitext Series; Springer: London, UK, 2014.
56. Bell, W.W. *Special Functions for Scientists and Engineers*; Courier Corporation: North Chelmsford, MA, USA, 2004.
57. Abd-Elhameed, W.M.; Amin, A.K. Novel identities of Bernoulli polynomials involving closed forms for some definite integrals. *Symmetry* **2022**, *14*, 2284. [CrossRef]

mathematics

MDPI

Article

On Symmetrical Sonin Kernels in Terms of Hypergeometric-Type Functions

Yuri Luchko

Department of Mathematics, Physics, and Chemistry, Berlin University of Applied Sciences and Technology, 13353 Berlin, Germany; luchko@bht-berlin.de

Abstract: In this paper, a new class of kernels of integral transforms of the Laplace convolution type that we named symmetrical Sonin kernels is introduced and investigated. For a symmetrical Sonin kernel given in terms of elementary or special functions, its associated kernel has the same form with possibly different parameter values. In the paper, several new kernels of this type are derived by means of the Sonin method in the time domain and using the Laplace integral transform in the frequency domain. Moreover, for the first time in the literature, a class of Sonin kernels in terms of the convolution series, which are a far-reaching generalization of the power series, is constructed. The new symmetrical Sonin kernels derived in the paper are represented in terms of the Wright function and the new special functions of the hypergeometric type that are extensions of the corresponding Horn functions in two variables.

Keywords: Sonin kernels; symmetrical Sonin kernels; Laplace integral transform; hypergeometric functions; Horn functions; general fractional derivative; general fractional integral

MSC: 26A33; 33C60; 33C70; 44A05; 44A10

1. Introduction

In the theory of the integral transforms of the Mellin convolution type, the functions p and q are said to form a pair of the Fourier kernels if the relations

$$F(x) = \int_0^{+\infty} p(x\xi)\, f(\xi)\, d\xi, \; x > 0, \tag{1}$$

$$f(\xi) = \int_0^{+\infty} q(\xi x)\, F(x)\, dx, \; \xi > 0 \tag{2}$$

are simultaneously valid on some functional spaces that the functions f and F belong to; see, e.g., [1] for details and particular cases. In the case $p(x) = q(x), \; x \in \mathbb{R}_+$, the kernels p and q are called symmetrical Fourier kernels.

Under the condition that the Mellin integral transforms

$$P(s) = \int_0^{+\infty} p(x)\, x^{s-1}\, dx, \;\; Q(s) = \int_0^{+\infty} q(x)\, x^{s-1}\, dx$$

of the Fourier kernels p and q exist in the domain $D = \{s \in \mathbb{C} : C_1 < \Re(s) < C_2\}$, with C_1 and C_2 being some constants from $\mathbb{R}$, the Mellin convolution theorem applied to relations (1) and (2) leads to the functional equation

$$P(s) \cdot Q(1-s) = 1, \;\; C_1 < \Re(s) < C_2 \tag{3}$$

in the frequency domain.

Because the majority of elementary and special functions are particular cases of the Meijer G- or Fox H-functions, their Mellin integral transforms can be represented in terms of quotients of products of Gamma functions. Thus, Formula (3) lets a straightforward derivation of both Fourier kernels and symmetrical Fourier kernels in terms of the Meijer G and Fox H functions [1].

In this paper, we focus on kernels of so-called general fractional integrals (GFIs),

$$F(x) = (\mathbb{I}_{(\kappa)} f)(x) := (\kappa * f)(x) = \int_0^x \kappa(x-\xi) f(\xi)\, d\xi \tag{4}$$

and general fractional derivatives (GFDs),

$$f(\xi) = (\mathbb{D}_{(k)} F)(\xi) := \frac{d}{d\xi}(\mathbb{I}_{(k)} F)(\xi) = \frac{d}{d\xi}(k * F)(\xi) = \frac{d}{d\xi}\int_0^\xi k(\xi - x) F(x)\, dx \tag{5}$$

of the Laplace convolution type with Sonin kernels κ and k ([2–6]).

In [7], Sonin extended the Abel method for solving the integral equation of type (4) with the power law kernel $\kappa(x) = x^{\alpha-1}$, $\alpha \in (0, 1)$ to the case of a general kernel, κ, that satisfies the condition

$$(\kappa * k)(x) = \int_0^x \kappa(x-\xi) k(\xi)\, d\xi = 1,\ x > 0. \tag{6}$$

Nowadays, condition (6) is referred to as the Sonin condition, and the function k is called the Sonin kernel associated with the kernel κ.

It is worth mentioning that, in the mathematical literature, the famous Russian mathematician Sonin is referred to either as Sonin (English spelling) or as Sonine (French spelling). In this paper, we employ the English spelling of his surname.

Under certain conditions, the GFD (5) with the Sonin kernel k is a left-inverse operator to the GFI (4) with its associated kernel κ; see, e.g., [2,4–6,8–10] for details and examples of Sonin kernels in terms of elementary and special functions.

If the Laplace integral transforms

$$\tilde{\kappa}(p) = \int_0^{+\infty} \kappa(x)\, e^{-px}\, dx,\ \tilde{k}(p) = \int_0^{+\infty} k(x)\, e^{-px}\, dx$$

of the Sonin kernels κ and k exist in the domain $D = \{p \in \mathbb{C} : \Re(p) > C\}$, the relation (6) is reduced to a simple formula in the Laplace domain:

$$\tilde{\kappa}(p) \cdot \tilde{k}(p) = \frac{1}{p},\ \Re(p) > C. \tag{7}$$

This formula can be used for the derivation of some particular cases of Sonin kernels using the tables of the Laplace integral transforms of elementary and special functions. However, in contrast to the case of the Fourier kernels, we cannot directly use the technique of the Mellin integral transform and provide a general description of the Sonin kernels in terms of the Meijer G and Fox H functions. In this paper, we suggest some alternative approaches for the derivation of Sonin kernels and, in particular, of so-called symmetrical Sonin kernels that will be defined in the next section.

It is worth mentioning that, recently, GFIs and GFDs with Sonin kernels became a subject of active research in both fractional calculus (FC) (see, e.g., [2–6,11–14]) and its applications (see [15–19] for the models of the general fractional dynamics, the general non-Markovian quantum dynamics, the general non-local electrodynamics, the non-local classical theory of gravity, and non-local statistical mechanics, respectively, and [20–24] for the mathematical models of anomalous diffusion and linear viscoelasticity in terms of GFIs and GFDs with Sonin kernels). Thus, the investigation of the general properties and particular cases of the Sonin kernels is an important topic both for the theory of FC and for its applications. This paper is devoted to these matters, and it aims to extend the set of known Sonin kernels in terms of the special functions of the hypergeometric type.

The rest of the paper is organized as follows. In Section 2, we provide some preliminary information regarding Sonin kernels and their examples. In particular, for the first time in the literature, we introduce a class of symmetrical Sonin kernels. Section 3 is devoted to the construction of Sonin kernels, both symmetrical and non-symmetrical, in the time domain. Following Sonin, we provide a procedure for the derivation of the Sonin kernels in the form of hypergeometric-type functions, and we present several examples of Sonin kernels, both known and new ones, obtained by means of this procedure. In particular, a new pair of symmetrical Sonin kernels in terms of the Wright function is deduced. Then, we introduce a new class of Sonin kernels in the form of the convolution series, which constitutes a far-reaching generalization of the power series, and we present some examples of this kind. In Section 4, the Laplace integral transform technique is employed for the construction of symmetrical Sonin kernels in the frequency domain. Using the inverse Laplace transform, these kernels are then represented in the time domain in terms of the hypergeometric functions in one and two variables. In particular, we present several new Sonin kernels expressed in the form of the new special functions of the hypergeometric type that are extensions of the corresponding Horn functions in two variables.

2. Definitions and Examples

For the first time, a pair of Sonin kernels appeared in the publications [25,26] by Abel devoted to the so-called tautochrone problem. The tautochrone is a curve for which the time taken for an object that slides without friction in uniform gravity to its lowest point is independent of its starting point on the curve. By the time of Abel's publications, Christiaan Huygens could already prove, through some advanced geometrical methods, that the tautochrone is a suitable part of the cycloid. In [25,26], Abel provided an analytical solution to a somewhat more general mechanical problem that is nowadays referred to as the generalized tautochrone problem, which is formulated as follows: for a given function, $F = F(x)$, find a curve for which the sliding time taken for an object sliding without friction in uniform gravity depends on the position x of its starting point on the curve as $F = F(x)$. In [25,26], Abel first derived a mathematical model of the generalized tautochrone problem in the form of the following integro-differential equation (with slightly different notations):

$$F(x) = \int_0^x \frac{f'(\xi)}{\sqrt{(x-\xi)}}\, d\xi. \tag{8}$$

Then Abel considered a more general equation:

$$F(x) = \int_0^x \frac{f'(\xi)}{(x-\xi)^{\alpha}}\, d\xi,\ 0 < \alpha < 1. \tag{9}$$

The solution to the integro-differential Equation (9) derived by Abel has the following form (according to his tautochrone model, the condition $f(0) = 0$ is valid):

$$f(x) = \frac{\sin(\alpha\,\pi)}{\pi} \int_0^x (x-\xi)^{\alpha-1}\, F(\xi)\, d\xi,\ x > 0. \tag{10}$$

It is worth mentioning that the known formula

$$\frac{\sin(\alpha\,\pi)}{\pi} = \frac{1}{\Gamma(\alpha)\Gamma(1-\alpha)}$$

immediately leads to a representation of Equations (9) and (10) in terms of the so-called Caputo fractional derivative, ${}_*D^{\alpha}_{0+}$, and the Riemann–Liouville fractional integral, I^{α}_{0+}, of the order α:

$$\frac{F(x)}{\Gamma(1-\alpha)} = ({}_*D^{\alpha}_{0+}f)(x),\ \Gamma(1-\alpha)f(x) = (I^{\alpha}_{0+}F)(x),\ x > 0,\ 0 < \alpha < 1.$$

The main ingredient of the solution method for the integro-differential Equation (9) invented by Abel was a simple formula for the kernels of the operators at the right-hand sides of Equations (9) and (10), i.e., of the kernels of the Riemann–Liouville fractional integral and the Riemann–Liouville or Caputo fractional derivatives (in modern notations):

$$(h_\alpha * h_{1-\alpha})(x) = 1,\ 0 < \alpha < 1,\ x > 0, \tag{11}$$

where the power law function h_α is defined as follows:

$$h_\alpha(x) = \frac{x^{\alpha-1}}{\Gamma(\alpha)},\ \alpha > 0. \tag{12}$$

Thus, in [25,26], Abel derived the first and a very important pair of Sonin kernels:

$$\kappa(x) = h_\alpha(x),\ k(x) = h_{1-\alpha}(x),\ 0 < \alpha < 1,\ x > 0. \tag{13}$$

In particular, the tautochrone problem (8) corresponds to kernels (13) with $\alpha = \frac{1}{2}$. In this case, the kernels κ and k have exactly the same form:

$$\kappa(x) = k(x) = h_{1/2}(x) = \frac{1}{\sqrt{\pi}}\frac{1}{\sqrt{x}},\ x > 0. \tag{14}$$

It is natural to call such kernels symmetrical Sonin kernels. However, up to a constant multiplier, this is the only pair of Sonin kernels that satisfies the relation $\kappa(x) = k(x)$, $x \in \mathbb{R}_+$ if we suppose that the Laplace integral transforms of the kernels exist. Indeed, in this case, we get the following chain of implications from the Sonin condition (7) in the frequency domain:

$$\tilde{\kappa}(p) \cdot \tilde{k}(p) = \tilde{\kappa}^2(p) = \frac{1}{p} \Rightarrow \tilde{\kappa}(p) = k(p) = \pm\frac{1}{\sqrt{p}} \Rightarrow \kappa(x) = k(x) = \pm h_{1/2}(x).$$

Even the power-law Sonin kernels (13) derived by Abel in [25,26] do not coincide unless $\alpha = 1/2$. However, they are expressed in terms of the same power law function, h_β, with different values of the parameter β, and they generate the Riemann–Liouville and Caputo fractional derivatives and the Riemann–Liouville fractional integral, which are probably the most used FC operators.

Motivated by this example, we define the symmetrical Sonin kernels as follows:

Definition 1. *A pair (κ, k) of Sonin kernels is called symmetrical if both the kernels are of the same form in terms of certain elementary or special functions with possibly different parameter values.*

According to this definition, the power-law Sonin kernels (13) can be called symmetrical. However, not all pairs of Sonin kernels are symmetrical. In particular, we mention here the following known pairs of non-symmetrical Sonin kernels (see [9,11,27]):

$$\kappa(x) = h_{\alpha,\rho}(x),\ k(x) = h_{1-\alpha,\rho}(x) + \rho\int_0^x h_{1-\alpha,\rho}(\xi)\,d\xi,\ 0 < \alpha < 1,\ \rho > 0,$$

where

$$h_{\alpha,\rho}(x) = \frac{x^{\alpha-1}}{\Gamma(\alpha)}e^{-\rho x}$$

and

$$\kappa(x) = h_{1-\beta+\alpha}(x) + h_{1-\beta}(x),\ k(x) = x^{\beta-1}E_{\alpha,\beta}(-x^\alpha),\ 0 < \alpha < \beta < 1, \tag{15}$$

where $E_{\alpha,\beta}$ stands for the two-parameter Mittag–Leffler function defined by the following convergent series:

$$E_{\alpha,\beta}(z) = \sum_{n=0}^{+\infty} \frac{z^n}{\Gamma(\alpha n + \beta)}, \ \alpha > 0, \ \beta, z \in \mathbb{C}. \tag{16}$$

For further examples of symmetrical and non-symmetrical Sonin kernels, we refer to [4,5,7–9]; see also the references therein.

It is worth mentioning that any pair, (κ, k), of the Sonin kernels generates a pair of the general FC operators: the GFI (4) with the kernel κ and the GFD (5) with the kernel k. As an example, the Sonin kernels (15) generate the GFI in the form of a sum of two Riemann–Liouville fractional integrals,

$$(\mathbb{I}_{(\kappa)} f)(x) = (I_{0+}^{1-\beta+\alpha} f)(x) + (I_{0+}^{1-\beta} f)(x), \ x > 0 \tag{17}$$

and the GFD with the Mittag–Leffler function in the kernel

$$(\mathbb{D}_{(k)} f)(x) = \frac{d}{dx} \int_0^x (x-\xi)^{\beta-1} E_{\alpha,\beta}(-(x-\xi)^\alpha) f(\xi)\, d\xi, \ 0 < \alpha < \beta < 1, \ x > 0. \tag{18}$$

In suitable spaces of functions, the GFD (18) is a left-inverse operator to the GFI (17) (see, e.g., [4,5] for details):

$$(\mathbb{D}_{(k)}\, \mathbb{I}_{(\kappa)} f)(x) = f(x).$$

As we see, in the case of non-symmetrical Sonin kernels, the formulas for the GFIs and the GFDs look very different. In the rest of this paper, we mainly deal with the symmetrical Sonin kernels and discuss the derivation of such kernels in the time and frequency domains, as well as several known and new kernels of this kind.

3. Sonin Kernels in the Time Domain

In [7], Sonin introduced an important class of Sonin kernels in the form of the products of power law functions and analytic functions:

$$\kappa(x) = x^{\beta-1} \cdot \kappa_1(x), \ \kappa_1(x) = \sum_{n=0}^{+\infty} a_n x^n, \ a_0 \neq 0, \ 0 < \beta < 1, \tag{19}$$

$$k(x) = x^{-\beta} \cdot k_1(x), \ k_1(x) = \sum_{n=0}^{+\infty} b_n x^n, \ 0 < \beta < 1. \tag{20}$$

Whereas the coefficients a_n, $n \in \mathbb{N}_0$ ($\mathbb{N}_0 = \mathbb{N} \cup \{0\}$) of the analytic function κ_1 can be arbitrarily chosen, the coefficients b_n, $n \in \mathbb{N}_0$ of the function k_1 have to satisfy the following triangular system of the linear equations:

$$\Gamma(\beta)\Gamma(1-\beta)a_0 b_0 = 1, \ \sum_{n=0}^{N} \Gamma(n+\beta)\Gamma(N-n+1-\beta) a_n b_{N-n} = 0, \ N \in \mathbb{N}. \tag{21}$$

Equations (21) are obtained via the substitution of the functions κ and k defined as in (19) and (20) into the Sonin condition (6), interchanging the order of the integration and summation operations (which is justified by the uniform convergence of the series defining the analytic functions κ_1 and k_1 at any finite interval) and by applying the formula

$$(h_\alpha * h_\beta)(x) = h_{\alpha+\beta}(x), \ \alpha, \beta > 0, \ x > 0, \tag{22}$$

that immediately follows from the well-known representation of the Euler beta function in terms of the Gamma function:

$$B(\alpha, \beta) = \int_0^1 u^{\alpha-1}(1-u)^{\beta-1}\, du = \frac{\Gamma(\alpha)\Gamma(\beta)}{\Gamma(\alpha+\beta)}, \ \alpha, \beta > 0.$$

In the following theorem, a more general construction of the Sonin kernels compared to the one suggested by Sonin in forms (19) and (20) is provided.

Theorem 1. *Let κ_1 and k_1 be analytic functions, and let the conditions*

$$0 < \beta < 1, \ \alpha > 0, \ \lambda \in \mathbb{R} \tag{23}$$

be satisfied.

The functions

$$\kappa(x) = x^{\beta-1} \cdot \kappa_1(\lambda x^{\alpha}), \ \kappa_1(x) = \sum_{n=0}^{+\infty} a_n x^n, \ a_0 \neq 0 \tag{24}$$

and

$$k(x) = x^{-\beta} \cdot k_1(\lambda x^{\alpha}), \ k_1(x) = \sum_{n=0}^{+\infty} b_n x^n \tag{25}$$

build a pair of Sonin kernels iff the coefficients a_n, $n \in \mathbb{N}_0$ and b_n, $n \in \mathbb{N}_0$ of the functions κ_1 and k_1 satisfy the following triangular system of equations:

$$\Gamma(\beta)\Gamma(1-\beta)a_0 b_0 = 1, \ \sum_{n=0}^{N} \Gamma(\alpha n + \beta)\Gamma(\alpha(N-n) + 1 - \beta) a_n b_{N-n} = 0, \ N \in \mathbb{N}. \tag{26}$$

The statement formulated in Theorem 1 is proved through the same direct calculations as the ones employed for the Sonin kernels in forms (19) and (20) (see, e.g., [9]), i.e., by substitution of the functions κ and k defined as in (24) and (25) into the Sonin condition (6), interchanging the order of the integration and summation operations, and applying the Formula (22) for the calculation of convolution integrals.

Remark 1. *It is worth mentioning that Theorem 1 also remains valid in the case of the convergence radii of the series that define the functions κ_1 and k_1 not being infinite. The essential condition for the validity of Theorem 1 is that the convergence radius of the series that defines κ_1 is greater than zero. Then, the conditions* (26) *implicate that the series for k_1 has the same convergence radius, and the functions κ and k defined by Formulas* (24) *and* (25)*, respectively, are Sonin kernels (see* [28] *for the proof of this statement in the case of $\alpha = 1$). The proof for an arbitrary $\alpha > 0$ is completely analogous to the one for $\alpha = 1$, and we omit it here.*

Now, we follow another idea suggested by Sonin in his paper [7] concerning kernels in forms (19) and (20) to derive some particular cases of Sonin kernels in forms (24) and (25), and in particular, of symmetrical Sonin kernels.

First, we mention that Equation (26) can be interpreted as just one functional equation:

$$\left(\sum_{n=0}^{+\infty} c_n x^n\right) \cdot \left(\sum_{n=0}^{+\infty} d_n x^n\right) \equiv 1, \ x > 0, \tag{27}$$

where

$$c_n := \Gamma(\alpha n + \beta) a_n \ \text{and} \ d_n := \Gamma(\alpha n + 1 - \beta) b_n, \ n \in \mathbb{N}_0. \tag{28}$$

Moreover, without any loss of generality, we can set

$$c_0 = d_0 = 1. \tag{29}$$

Remark 2. *When Equation* (27) *is employed, the Sonin kernels in the form* (24) *and* (25) *can be derived using the following simple procedure:*

Step 1: Construct an arbitrary power series with a convergence radius greater than zero:

$$\phi(x) = \sum_{n=0}^{+\infty} c_n x^n, \; c_0 = 1. \tag{30}$$

Step 2: Build the function $\frac{1}{\phi(x)}$ *and determine its Taylor series:*

$$\frac{1}{\phi(x)} = \sum_{n=0}^{+\infty} d_n x^n, \; d_0 = 1. \tag{31}$$

Step 3: The functions (24) *and* (25) *with the coefficients*

$$a_n = \frac{c_n}{\Gamma(\alpha n + \beta)} \; \text{and} \; b_n = \frac{d_n}{\Gamma(\alpha n + 1 - \beta)}, \; n \in \mathbb{N}_0, \tag{32}$$

respectively, are Sonin kernels.

Remark 3. *In the case when the functions* $\phi(x)$ *and* $\frac{1}{\phi(x)}$ *defined by the series at the right-hand sides of* (30) *and* (31)*, respectively, have the same form in terms of certain elementary or special functions with possibly different parameter values, the procedure presented in Remark 2 leads to symmetrical Sonin kernels.*

Now, we demonstrate the application of Theorem 1, Remarks 2 and 3 for the derivation of some symmetrical Sonin kernels, both already known and new ones.

Example 1. *In Formula* (30)*, we set* $\phi(x) = \exp(x)$*. Then,*

$$\phi(x) = \exp(x) = \sum_{n=0}^{+\infty} \frac{1}{n!} x^n, \; \frac{1}{\phi(x)} = \exp(-x) = \sum_{n=0}^{+\infty} \frac{(-1)^n}{n!} x^n.$$

Thus,

$$c_n = \frac{1}{n!}, \; d_n = \frac{(-1)^n}{n!}, \; n \in \mathbb{N}_0$$

and (see the relations (32)*)*

$$a_n = \frac{c_n}{\Gamma(\alpha n + \beta)} = \frac{1}{n!\Gamma(\alpha n + \beta)}, \; n \in \mathbb{N}_0, \tag{33}$$

$$b_n = \frac{d_n}{\Gamma(\alpha n + 1 - \beta)} = \frac{(-1)^n}{n!\Gamma(\alpha n + 1 - \beta)}, \; n \in \mathbb{N}_0. \tag{34}$$

The Sonin kernels (24) *and* (25) *from Theorem 1 with the coefficients as in* (33) *and* (34)*, respectively, take the form* ($\beta \in (0, 1)$, $\alpha > 0$, $\lambda \in \mathbb{R}$)

$$\kappa(x) = x^{\beta-1} \sum_{n=0}^{+\infty} \frac{(\lambda x^\alpha)^n}{n!\Gamma(\alpha n + \beta)} = x^{\beta-1} W_{\alpha,\beta}(\lambda x^\alpha) \tag{35}$$

and

$$k(x) = x^{-\beta} \sum_{n=0}^{+\infty} \frac{(-\lambda x^\alpha)^n}{n!\Gamma(\alpha n + 1 - \beta)} = x^{-\beta} W_{\alpha,1-\beta}(-\lambda x^\alpha), \tag{36}$$

where the Wright function $W_{\alpha,\beta}(z)$ *is defined by the convergent series (see* [29] *for its properties and applications):*

$$W_{\alpha,\beta}(z) := \sum_{n=0}^{+\infty} \frac{z^n}{n!\Gamma(\alpha n + \beta)}, \; z, \beta \in \mathbb{C}, \; \alpha > -1. \tag{37}$$

To the best knowledge of the author, the pair of (35) and (36) of symmetrical (in the sense of Definition 1) Sonin kernels has not yet been reported in the literature. However, in his paper [7], Sonin mentioned a particular case of the kernels (35) and (36) with $\alpha = 1$. In this case, Sonin kernels (35) and (36) can be expressed in terms of the cylinder or Bessel functions; see [7,9] for details.

Example 2. *In this example, we derive another pair of symmetrical Sonin kernels that is generated via the function $\phi(x) = (1+x)^{-\gamma}$. The Taylor series for $\phi(x)$ and its reciprocal are well known:*

$$\phi(x) = (1+x)^{-\gamma} = \sum_{n=0}^{+\infty} \frac{(-1)^n(\gamma)_n}{n!} x^n, \quad \frac{1}{\phi(x)} = (1+x)^{\gamma} = \sum_{n=0}^{+\infty} \frac{(-1)^n(-\gamma)_n}{n!} x^n,$$

where the Pochhammer symbol $(\gamma)_n$ is defined as follows:

$$(\gamma)_n := \frac{\Gamma(\gamma+n)}{\Gamma(\gamma)} = \gamma \cdot (\gamma+1) \cdot \ \ldots \ \cdot (\gamma+n-1).$$

As we see, the functions $\phi(x) = (1+x)^{-\gamma}$ and $\frac{1}{\phi(x)} = (1+x)^{\gamma}$ generate the coefficients

$$c_n = \frac{(-1)^n(\gamma)_n}{n!}, \quad d_n = \frac{(-1)^n(-\gamma)_n}{n!}, \quad n \in \mathbb{N}_0,$$

and

$$a_n = \frac{c_n}{\Gamma(\alpha n+\beta)} = \frac{(-1)^n(\gamma)_n}{n!\Gamma(\alpha n+\beta)}, \quad b_n = \frac{d_n}{\Gamma(\alpha n+1-\beta)} = \frac{(-1)^n(-\gamma)_n}{n!\Gamma(\alpha n+1-\beta)}, \quad n \in \mathbb{N}_0.$$

The Sonin kernels (24) *and* (25) *take then the form ($\beta \in (0,1)$, $\alpha > 0$, $\lambda \in \mathbb{R}$)*

$$\kappa(x) = x^{\beta-1} \sum_{n=0}^{+\infty} \frac{(-1)^n(\gamma)_n}{n!\Gamma(\alpha n+\beta)} (\lambda x^{\alpha})^n = x^{\beta-1} E^{\gamma}_{\alpha,\beta}(-\lambda x^{\alpha}) \tag{38}$$

and

$$k(x) = x^{-\beta} \sum_{n=0}^{+\infty} \frac{(-1)^n(-\gamma)_n}{n!\Gamma(\alpha n+1-\beta)} (\lambda x^{\alpha})^n = x^{-\beta} E^{-\gamma}_{\alpha,1-\beta}(-\lambda x^{\alpha}), \tag{39}$$

where the three-parameter Mittag–Leffler function or the Prabhakar function $E^{\gamma}_{\alpha,\beta}(z)$ is defined by the convergent series (see, e.g., [30,31] *for its properties and applications)*

$$E^{\gamma}_{\alpha,\beta}(z) := \sum_{n=0}^{+\infty} \frac{(\gamma)_n}{n!\Gamma(\alpha n+\beta)}, \quad z, \beta, \gamma \in \mathbb{C}, \ \alpha > 0. \tag{40}$$

Please note that the function (40) can also be interpreted as a particular case of the so-called generalized Wright or Fox–Wright function; see [29] for details.

In [7], Sonin derived a particular case of the kernels (38) and (39) with $\alpha = 1$ in the form of the power law series. As mentioned in [9], the kernels (38) and (39) with $\alpha = 1$ can be represented in terms of the confluent hypergeometric function or the Kummer function ${}_1F_1$:

$$\kappa(x) = x^{\beta-1} \sum_{n=0}^{+\infty} \frac{(-1)^n(\gamma)_n}{n!\Gamma(n+\beta)} (\lambda x)^n = \frac{x^{\beta-1}}{\Gamma(\beta)} {}_1F_1(\gamma; \beta; -\lambda x), \tag{41}$$

$$k(x) = x^{-\beta} \sum_{n=0}^{+\infty} \frac{(-1)^n(-\gamma)_n}{n!\Gamma(n+1-\beta)} (\lambda x)^n = \frac{x^{-\beta}}{\Gamma(1-\beta)} {}_1F_1(-\gamma; 1-\beta; -\lambda x), \tag{42}$$

where the Kummer function ${}_1F_1$ is defined by the convergent series

$$ {}_1F_1(\gamma;\beta;z) := \sum_{n=0}^{+\infty} \frac{(\gamma)_n}{(\beta)_n} \frac{z^n}{n!}, \ z, \beta, \gamma \in \mathbb{C}. \tag{43} $$

The integral operator in the form of (4) (which we called GFI with kernel κ) and the integro-differential operator (5) (which we called GFD with kernel k) with the Sonin kernels (41) and (42) were considered by Prabhakar in his paper [32] (see also [10], formulas (37.1) and (37.31)). In particular, in [32], the GFD (5) with the kernel (42) was shown to be a left-inverse operator to the GFI (5) with the kernel (41).

Two years after the publication of his paper [32], in [31], Prabhakar also studied the general case of the GFI (4) and the GFD (5) with the Sonin kernels (38) and (39), respectively, in terms of the three-parameter Mittag–Leffler function. For this reason, nowadays, this function is often referred to as the Prabhakar function. For a detailed presentation of the theory and applications of these operators, nowadays called the Prabhakar fractional integral and derivative, we refer the interested reader to a recent survey [30].

As mentioned in the introduction, the investigation of GFIs and GFDs with Sonin kernels is a very recent topic initialized by Kochubei in the paper [2] published in 2011. In the earlier publications by Prabhakar and other authors who investigated the operators of type (4) and (5) with kernels in terms of the Bessel function, Kummer function, three-parameter Mittag–Leffler function, etc., these operators were introduced and studied independently of the theory of GFIs and GFDs with Sonin kernels. However, recently, one started to interpret these earlier results from the viewpoint of the GFIs and the GFDs; see, e.g., [33] for a discussion of a connection between general fractional calculus (GFC) and the Prabhakar fractional integral and derivative.

Example 3. *In this example, we consider a pair of Sonin kernels generated via the function* $\phi(x) = \exp(x)(1+x)^{-\gamma}$. *The Taylor series for the function* $\phi(x)$ *and its reciprocal can be obtained through the multiplication of the Taylor series from Examples 1 and 2:*

$$ \phi(x) = \exp(x)(1+x)^{-\gamma} = \left(\sum_{n=0}^{+\infty} \frac{1}{n!} x^n\right) \cdot \left(\sum_{n=0}^{+\infty} \frac{(-1)^n (\gamma)_n}{n!} x^n\right) = \sum_{n=0}^{+\infty} c_{n,\gamma}\, x^n, $$

where

$$ c_{n,\gamma} = \sum_{m=0}^{n} \frac{(-1)^m (\gamma)_m}{m!(n-m)!}, \ n \in \mathbb{N}_0, \tag{44} $$

$$ \frac{1}{\phi(x)} = \exp(-x)(1+x)^{\gamma} = \left(\sum_{n=0}^{+\infty} \frac{(-1)^n}{n!} x^n\right) \cdot \left(\sum_{n=0}^{+\infty} \frac{(-1)^n (-\gamma)_n}{n!} x^n\right) = \sum_{n=0}^{+\infty} d_{n,\gamma}\, (-x)^n, $$

where

$$ d_{n,\gamma} = \sum_{m=0}^{n} \frac{(-\gamma)_m}{m!(n-m)!}, \ n \in \mathbb{N}_0. \tag{45} $$

Taking into account the relations (28) *and applying Theorem 1, we arrive at the following new pair of Sonin kernels* ($\beta \in (0,1)$, $\alpha > 0$, $\lambda \in \mathbb{R}$)*:*

$$ \kappa(x) = x^{\beta-1} \sum_{n=0}^{+\infty} \frac{c_{n,\gamma}}{\Gamma(\alpha n + \beta)} (\lambda x^{\alpha})^n, \ k(x) = x^{-\beta} \sum_{n=0}^{+\infty} \frac{d_{n,\gamma}}{\Gamma(\alpha n + 1 - \beta)} (-\lambda x^{\alpha})^n, \tag{46} $$

where the coefficients $c_{n,\gamma}$ *and* $d_{n,\gamma}$ *are given by Formulas* (44) *and* (45)*, respectively.*

The series in (46) *are convergent for all* $x \geq 0$ *because of the known asymptotic formulas for the Gamma function:*

$$ \Gamma(\alpha x + \beta) \sim \sqrt{2\pi} \exp(-\alpha x)(\alpha x)^{\alpha x + \beta - 1/2} \ \text{as } x \to +\infty, \ \alpha > 0, \ \beta \in \mathbb{C}, \tag{47} $$

$$\frac{\Gamma(x+a)}{\Gamma(x+b)} \sim x^{a-b} \text{ as } x \to +\infty,\ a, b \in \mathbb{C}. \tag{48}$$

Indeed, we can estimate the coefficients $c_{n,\gamma}$ as follows:

$$|c_{n,\gamma}| \le \sum_{m=0}^{n} \frac{|(\gamma)_m|}{m!(n-m)!} \le \frac{(|\gamma|)_n}{n!} \sum_{m=0}^{n} \frac{n!}{m!(n-m)!} = \frac{(|\gamma|)_n}{n!} \cdot 2^n. \tag{49}$$

Taking into account the asymptotic Formulas (47) and (48), we get the estimate

$$\left(\left|\frac{c_{n,\gamma}}{\Gamma(\alpha n+\beta)}\right|\right)^{1/n} \le C_1 \left(\frac{2^n\,(|\gamma|)_n}{n!} \exp(\alpha n)(\alpha n)^{-\alpha n-\beta+1/2}\right)^{1/n} \le C_2 n^{-\alpha} \to 0 \text{ as } n \to +\infty$$

and, thus, the first series in (46) is convergent for any $x \ge 0$. For the second series, similar estimates are evidently valid, and thus this series is also convergent for $x \ge 0$.

In the rest of this section, we discuss an important extension of Sonin kernels (19) and (20) in the form of products of the power-law functions and analytic functions to the so-called convolution series. The convolution series are a far-reaching generalization of the power-law series that was recently introduced in the framework of the general FC (see, e.g., [5,34]). First, we remind readers of their definition and properties that we need for further discussions.

Let a function, f, belong to the space $C_{-1}(0,+\infty) = \{\phi : \phi(x) = x^p\phi_1(x),\ x > 0,\ p > -1,\ \phi_1 \in C[0,+\infty)\}$ and be represented in the form

$$f(x) = x^p f_1(x),\ x > 0,\ p > 0,\ f_1 \in C[0,+\infty)$$

and let the convergence radius of the power series

$$\Sigma(x) = \sum_{n=0}^{+\infty} a_n\, x^n,\ a_n, x \in \mathbb{R}$$

be non-zero.

The convolution series generated via the function f has the form

$$\Sigma_f(x) = \sum_{n=0}^{+\infty} a_n\, f^{<n+1>}(x), \tag{50}$$

where $f^{<n>}$, $n \in \mathbb{N}$ stands for the convolution powers

$$f^{<n>}(x) := \begin{cases} f(x), & n = 1, \\ (\underbrace{f * \ldots * f}_{n \text{ times}})(x), & n = 2, 3, \ldots . \end{cases} \tag{51}$$

As was shown in [5,34], the convolution series (50) is convergent for all $x > 0$, and it defines a function from the space $C_{-1}(0,+\infty)$. Moreover, the series

$$x^{1-\alpha}\,\Sigma_f(x) = \sum_{n=0}^{+\infty} a_n\, x^{1-\alpha} f^{<n+1>}(x),\ \ \alpha = \min\{p,\, 1\} \tag{52}$$

is uniformly convergent for $x \in [0,\ X]$ for any $X > 0$.

In particular, any power series can be represented in the form of the convolution series (50) generated via the function $f(x) = h_1(x) = \frac{x^0}{\Gamma(1)} \equiv 1,\ x \ge 0$:

$$\Sigma_{h_1}(x) = \sum_{n=0}^{+\infty} a_n\, h_1^{<n+1>}(x) = \sum_{n=0}^{+\infty} a_n\, h_{n+1}(x) = \sum_{n=0}^{+\infty} a_n\, \frac{x^n}{n!}.$$

For examples and applications of the convolution series in the form (50), we refer to [5,34]. In the following theorem, we present a construction of the Sonin kernels in terms of the convolution series.

Theorem 2. *Let (κ_1, k_1) be a pair of Sonin kernels, let f be any function from the space $C_{-1}(0, +\infty)$ that is not identically equal to zero, and let the convergence radii of the power series*

$$\Sigma_a(x) = \sum_{n=0}^{+\infty} a_n\, x^n,\ a_n, x \in \mathbb{R} \text{ and } \Sigma_b(x) = \sum_{n=0}^{+\infty} b_n\, x^n,\ b_n, x \in \mathbb{R}$$

be non-zero.

Then, the functions

$$\kappa(x) = a_0 \kappa_1(x) + (\kappa_1 \,*\, \sum_{n=1}^{+\infty} a_n\, f^{<n>})(x),\ a_0 \neq 0, \tag{53}$$

$$k(x) = b_0 k_1(x) + (k_1 \,*\, \sum_{n=1}^{+\infty} b_n\, f^{<n>})(x) \tag{54}$$

build a pair of Sonin kernels iff the conditions

$$a_0 b_0 = 1,\ \sum_{m=0}^{n} a_m b_{n-m} = 0,\ n \in \mathbb{N} \tag{55}$$

hold true.

Proof. According to the Sonin condition (6) and the definition of the convolution powers, we immediately get the relations

$$(a_0\kappa_1 \,*\, b_0 k_1)(x) = a_0 b_0,\ (a_0\kappa_1 \,*\, (b_m k_1 \,*\, f^{<m>}))(x) = a_0 b_m (1 \,*\, f^{<m>})(x),$$
$$((\kappa_1 \,*\, a_i f^{<i>}) \,*\, b_0 k_1)(x) = a_i b_0 (1 \,*\, f^{<i>})(x),$$
$$((\kappa_1 \,*\, a_i f^{<i>}) \,*\, (k_1 \,*\, b_m f^{<m>}))(x) = a_i b_m (1 \,*\, f^{<i+m>})(x).$$

To calculate the convolution $(\kappa \,*\, k)(x)$ of the functions κ and k defined by (53) and (54), respectively, we interchange the orders of integration and summation (which is allowed because of the uniform convergence of the convolution series (52)) and use the relations from above. Thus, we arrive at the representation

$$(\kappa \,*\, k)(x) = a_0 b_0 + \sum_{n=1}^{+\infty} \left(\sum_{m=0}^{n} a_m b_{n-m} \right) (1 \,*\, f^{<n>})(x).$$

This formula ensures that the pair of functions κ and k given by the relations (53) and (54) are Sonin kernels iff the conditions (55) are satisfied. □

Remark 4. *The Sonin kernels* (19) *and* (20) *in the form of the products of the power law functions $x^{\beta-1}$ and $x^{-\beta}$ with $0 < \beta < 1$ and the analytic functions are a particular case of the general convolution kernels* (53) *and* (54) *with $\kappa_1(x) = h_\beta(x)$, $k_1(x) = h_{1-\beta}(x)$ and $f(x) = h_1(x) \equiv 1$. Other forms of Sonin kernels can be constructed by employing any other Sonin kernels κ_1, k_1 and any function $f \in C_{-1}(0, +\infty)$ that generates the convolution series in the Formulas* (53) *and* (54). *In particular, the Sonin kernels* (24) *and* (25) *presented in Theorem 1 correspond to the convolution kernels* (53) *and* (54) *with $\kappa_1(x) = h_\beta(x)$, $k_1(x) = h_{1-\beta}(x)$ $(0 < \beta < 1)$ and $f(x) = \lambda\, h_\alpha(x)$, $\alpha > 0$, $\lambda \in \mathbb{R}$.*

4. Sonin Kernels in the Laplace Domain

As already mentioned in the introduction, the Laplace integral transforms of any pair of Sonin kernels (if they exist) are connected to each other via the relation (7) that can be easily solved for, say, $\tilde{k}$:

$$\tilde{k}(p) = \frac{1}{p\tilde{\kappa}(p)},\ \Re(p) > C. \tag{56}$$

Using the Formula (56), several important pairs of the Sonin kernels have already been derived (see, e.g., [2,9,11,33]). In this section, we apply this formula to obtain some new symmetrical Sonin kernels in terms of the hypergeometric type functions.

Let us suppose that the Laplace integral transforms of the Sonin kernels κ and k exist. Then, the relation (56) implies that these kernels are symmetrical iff their Laplace transforms $\tilde{\kappa}(p)$ and $\tilde{k}(p) = \frac{1}{p\tilde{\kappa}(p)}$ are represented in terms of the same elementary or special function with possibly different parameter values. In this section, we consider some examples of the known and new symmetrical Sonin kernels that possess this property.

Example 4. *We start with the well-known case of the Laplace transform $\tilde{\kappa}(p)$ in the form of a power function,*

$$\tilde{\kappa}(p) = p^{-\alpha},\ \alpha > 0,\ \Re(p) > 0.$$

Then, the Laplace transform of the associated kernel, k, is given by the relation

$$\tilde{k}(p) = \frac{1}{p\tilde{\kappa}(p)} = p^{\alpha-1},\ \alpha < 1,\ \Re(p) > 0.$$

The basic formula

$$\tilde{h}_\gamma(p) = p^{-\gamma},\ \gamma > 0,\ \Re(p) > 0 \tag{57}$$

for the Laplace transform of the power function $h_\gamma(t) = t^{\gamma-1}/\Gamma(\gamma)$ leads to the well-known pair of symmetrical Sonin kernels in the time domain:

$$\kappa(t) = h_\alpha(t),\ \ k(t) = h_{1-\alpha}(t),\ 0 < \alpha < 1.$$

Example 5. *For the kernel κ with the Laplace transform*

$$\tilde{\kappa}(p) = p^{-\beta}\exp(\lambda\, p^{-\alpha}),\ \alpha > 0,\ \beta > 0,\ \lambda \in \mathbb{R},\ \Re(p) > 0, \tag{58}$$

the Laplace transform of its associated kernel k has a similar form,

$$\tilde{k}(p) = \frac{1}{p\kappa(p)} = p^{\beta-1}\exp(-\lambda\, p^{-\alpha}),\ \alpha > 0,\ \beta < 1,\ \lambda \in \mathbb{R},\ \Re(p) > 0. \tag{59}$$

We note here that the functions (58) *and* (59) *with $\lambda = 0$ have already been considered in Example 5.*

To represent the function κ in the time domain, we employ the series representation of its Laplace transform

$$\tilde{\kappa}(p) = p^{-\beta}\exp(\lambda\, p^{-\alpha}) = \sum_{n=0}^{+\infty}\frac{\lambda^n}{n!}p^{-\alpha n-\beta} \tag{60}$$

and the Formula (57), *and thus, we arrive at the expression*

$$\kappa(x) = \sum_{n=0}^{+\infty}\frac{\lambda^n}{n!}h_{\alpha n+\beta}(x) = \sum_{n=0}^{+\infty}\frac{\lambda^n}{n!}\frac{x^{\alpha n+\beta-1}}{\Gamma(\alpha n+\beta)} = x^{\beta-1}W_{\alpha,\beta}(\lambda x^\alpha),\ \alpha > 0,\ \beta > 0,\ \lambda \in \mathbb{R}, \tag{61}$$

where $W_{\alpha,\beta}$ is the Wright function (37). *Using the same method for the Laplace transform $\tilde{k}(p)$ given by* (59), *we get a representation of the associated kernel k in the time domain:*

$$k(x) = x^{-\beta}W_{\alpha,1-\beta}(-\lambda x^\alpha),\ \alpha > 0,\ \beta < 1, \tag{62}$$

where $W_{\alpha,\beta}$ is the Wright function (37).

To the best knowledge of the author, the pair of Sonin kernels in forms (61) and (62) was not yet reported in the literature. However, we already derived the same Sonin kernels in Section 3; see Example 1.

Example 6. *In this example, we set*

$$\tilde{\kappa}(p) = \frac{p^{\alpha\gamma-\beta}}{(p^\alpha+\lambda)^\gamma},\ \alpha>0,\ \beta>0,\ \lambda\in\mathbb{R},\ |\lambda p^{-\alpha}|<1. \tag{63}$$

The Laplace transform of the associated kernel k has the same form with different parameter values:

$$\tilde{k}(p) = \frac{1}{p\tilde{\kappa}(p)} = \frac{(p^\alpha+\lambda)^\gamma}{p^{\alpha\gamma-\beta+1}} = \frac{p^{-\alpha\gamma+\beta-1}}{(p^\alpha+\lambda)^{-\gamma}},\ \beta<1,\ \alpha>0,\ \lambda\in\mathbb{R},\ |\lambda p^{-\alpha}|<1. \tag{64}$$

For $\lambda=0$, (63) *and* (64) *are reduced to the functions that have been discussed in Example 4. Using the power series representation*

$$\tilde{\kappa}(p) = \frac{p^{\alpha\gamma-\beta}}{(p^\alpha+\lambda)^\gamma} = p^{-\beta}(1+\lambda p^{-\alpha})^{-\gamma} = \sum_{n=0}^{+\infty}\frac{(-1)^n(\gamma)_n\lambda^n}{n!}p^{-\alpha n-\beta} \tag{65}$$

and the Formula (57)*, we get the following result in the time domain:*

$$\kappa(x) = \sum_{n=0}^{+\infty}\frac{(-1)^n(\gamma)_n\lambda^n}{n!}h_{\alpha n+\beta}(x) = x^{\beta-1}E^{\gamma}_{\alpha,\beta}(-\lambda x^\alpha),\ \alpha>0,\ \beta>0,\ \lambda\in\mathbb{R}, \tag{66}$$

where $E^\gamma_{\alpha,\beta}$ is the three-parameter Mittag–Leffler function defined as in (40).

The same method applied to the Laplace transform (64) *easily leads to the formula*

$$k(x) = x^{-\beta}E^{-\gamma}_{\alpha,1-\beta}(-\lambda x^\alpha),\ \alpha>0,\ \beta<1,\ \lambda\in\mathbb{R}, \tag{67}$$

where $E^\gamma_{\alpha,\beta}$ is the three-parameter Mittag–Leffler function defined as in (40).

The pair of the symmetrical Sonin kernels (66) and (67) has already been discussed in Section 3; see Example 2.

Example 7. *In this example, we consider the Sonin kernel κ with the Laplace integral transform $\tilde{\kappa}$ in the form*

$$\tilde{\kappa}(p) = p^{-\beta}\frac{p^{\alpha_1\gamma}}{(p^{\alpha_1}+\lambda_1)^\gamma}\exp(\lambda_2 p^{-\alpha_2}) = p^{\alpha_1\gamma-\beta}(p^{\alpha_1}+\lambda_1)^{-\gamma}\exp(\lambda_2 p^{-\alpha_2}), \tag{68}$$

where the parameters and the Laplace variable satisfy the conditions $\alpha_1>0,\ \alpha_2>0,\ \beta>0,\ \lambda_1,\lambda_2\in\mathbb{R},\ \Re(p)>0,\ |\lambda_1 p^{-\alpha_1}|<1$.

Please note that we already considered two important particular cases of the kernels in form (68)*, namely the case of $\lambda_1=0$ in Example 5 and the case of $\lambda_2=0$ in Example 6.*

The Laplace transform of the associated kernel k has, then, a similar form:

$$\tilde{k}(p) = \frac{1}{p\tilde{\kappa}(p)} = p^{-\alpha_1\gamma+\beta-1}(p^{\alpha_1}+\lambda_1)^\gamma\exp(-\lambda_2 p^{-\alpha_2}), \tag{69}$$

where the parameters and the Laplace variable satisfy the conditions $\alpha_1>0,\ \alpha_2>0,\ \beta<1,\ \lambda_1,\lambda_2\in\mathbb{R},\ \Re(p)>0,\ |\lambda_1 p^{-\alpha_1}|<1$.

The series representations of the Functions (68) and (69) immediately follow from the Formulas (60) and (65):

$$\tilde{\kappa}(p) = \sum_{m,n=0}^{+\infty} \frac{(-\lambda_1)^m (\gamma)_m \lambda_2^n}{m!n!} p^{-\alpha_1 m - \alpha_2 n - \beta}, \tag{70}$$

$$\tilde{k}(p) = \frac{1}{p\kappa(p)} = \sum_{m,n=0}^{+\infty} \frac{(-\lambda_1)^m (-\gamma)_m (-\lambda_2)^n}{m!n!} p^{-\alpha_1 m - \alpha_2 n + \beta - 1}. \tag{71}$$

The last two formulas are valid under the conditions $\alpha_1 > 0,\ \alpha_2 > 0,\ 0 < \beta < 1$, $\lambda_1, \lambda_2 \in \mathbb{R}$, $|\lambda_1 p^{-\alpha_1}| < 1$, $\Re(p) > 0$.

Now, we apply the Formula (57) and get the following representations of Sonin kernels κ *and* k *in the time domain:*

$$\kappa(x) = \sum_{m,n=0}^{+\infty} \frac{(-\lambda_1)^m (\gamma)_m \lambda_2^n}{m!n!} h_{\alpha_1 m + \alpha_2 n + \beta}(x) = x^{\beta-1} \phi_3(\gamma; (\alpha_1, \alpha_2; \beta); -\lambda_1 x^{\alpha_1}, \lambda_2 x^{\alpha_2}), \tag{72}$$

$$k(x) = \sum_{m,n=0}^{+\infty} \frac{(-\lambda_1)^m (-\gamma)_m (-\lambda_2)^n}{m!n!} h_{\alpha_1 m + \alpha_2 n - \beta + 1}(x) =$$

$$x^{-\beta} \phi_3(-\gamma; (\alpha_1, \alpha_2; 1-\beta); -\lambda_1 x^{\alpha_1}, -\lambda_2 x^{\alpha_2}), \tag{73}$$

where $\alpha_1 > 0,\ \alpha_2 > 0,\ 0 < \beta < 1,\ \lambda_1, \lambda_2 \in \mathbb{R}$ *and* ϕ_3 *is a new special function of the hypergeometric type in two variables defined by the convergent series*

$$\phi_3(\gamma; (\alpha_1, \alpha_2; \beta); y, z) := \sum_{m,n=0}^{+\infty} \frac{(\gamma)_m}{\Gamma(\alpha_1 m + \alpha_2 n + \beta)} \frac{y^m z^n}{m!n!},\ \alpha_1 > 0,\ \alpha_2 > 0,\ \gamma, \beta, y, z \in \mathbb{C}. \tag{74}$$

The asymptotical Formulas (47) and (48) for the gamma function ensure convergence of the series in (74) for all $y, z \in \mathbb{C}$. *The proof of this fact closely follows the lines of the derivation of the convergence conditions for the Horn function* Φ_3 *([35]), and we omit it here.*

The denotation ϕ_3 is motivated by a particular case of this function for $\alpha_1 = \alpha_2 = 1$ that is reduced to the known Horn function Φ_3:

$$\phi_3(\gamma; (1,1; \beta); y, z) = \sum_{m,n=0}^{+\infty} \frac{(\gamma)_m}{\Gamma((m+n)+\beta)} \frac{y^m z^n}{m!n!} = \frac{1}{\Gamma(\beta)} \Phi_3(\gamma; \beta; y, z), \tag{75}$$

where Φ_3 is one of the Horn functions defined by the double-confluent series of the hypergeometric type (see Formula (22) in Section 5.7.1 in [35]):

$$\Phi_3(\gamma; \beta; y, z) := \sum_{m,n=0}^{+\infty} \frac{(\gamma)_m}{(\beta)_{m+n}} \frac{y^m z^n}{m!n!}. \tag{76}$$

Thus, for $\alpha_1 = \alpha_2 = 1$, the pair (72) and (73) of the symmetrical Sonin kernels is expressed in terms of the Horn function Φ_3:

$$\kappa(x) = h_\beta(x)\, \Phi_3(\gamma; \beta; -\lambda_1 x, \lambda_2 x),\ \beta > 0, \tag{77}$$

$$k(x) = h_{1-\beta}(x)\, \Phi_3(-\gamma; 1-\beta; -\lambda_1 x, -\lambda_2 x),\ \beta < 1. \tag{78}$$

The representations (77) and (78) can also be obtained by employing the Formula (2.2.3.16) from [36] that is valid under the conditions $\Re(\mu+\nu) < 0, \Re(p) > \max\{0, -\Re(b)\}$:

$$\{\mathcal{L}^{-1} p^\mu (p+b)^\nu \exp(a/p)\}(x) = h_{-\mu-\nu}(x)\, \Phi_3(-\nu; -\mu-\nu; -bx, ax), \tag{79}$$

where Φ_3 is the Horn function defined by (76), and $\{\mathcal{L}^{-1} f(p)\}(x)$ stands for the inverse Laplace transform of the function f at point $x > 0$.

To the best knowledge of the author, both functions (72) and (73) and functions (77) and (78) are new symmetrical Sonin kernels not yet mentioned in the literature.

Example 8. *In this last example, the Laplace integral transform $\tilde{\kappa}$ of the Sonin kernel κ is a product of three different power-law functions:*

$$\tilde{\kappa}(p) = p^{-\beta} \frac{p^{\alpha_1\gamma_1}}{(p^{\alpha_1}+\lambda_1)^{\gamma_1}} \frac{p^{\alpha_2\gamma_2}}{(p^{\alpha_2}+\lambda_2)^{\gamma_2}} = p^{\alpha_1\gamma_1+\alpha_2\gamma_2-\beta}(p^{\alpha_1}+\lambda_1)^{-\gamma_1}(p^{\alpha_2}+\lambda_2)^{-\gamma_2}, \quad (80)$$

where the parameters and the Laplace variable satisfy the conditions $\alpha_1 > 0,\ \alpha_2 > 0,\ \beta > 0$, $\lambda_1, \lambda_2 \in \mathbb{R},\ \Re(p) > 0,\ |\lambda_1 p^{-\alpha_1}| < 1,\ |\lambda_2 p^{-\alpha_2}| < 1$.

In the case of $\lambda_1 = 0$ or $\lambda_2 = 0$, the kernel (80) *is reduced to the kernel already considered in Example 6.*

The Laplace transform of the associated kernel k takes a similar form:

$$\tilde{k}(p) = \frac{1}{p\tilde{\kappa}(p)} = p^{-\alpha_1\gamma_1-\alpha_2\gamma_2+\beta-1}(p^{\alpha_1}+\lambda_1)^{\gamma_1}(p^{\alpha_2}+\lambda_2)^{\gamma_2}, \quad (81)$$

where the parameters and the Laplace variable satisfy the conditions $\alpha_1 > 0,\ \alpha_2 > 0,\ \beta < 1$, $\lambda_1, \lambda_2 \in \mathbb{R},\ \Re(p) > 0,\ |\lambda_1 p^{-\alpha_1}| < 1,\ |\lambda_2 p^{-\alpha_2}| < 1$.

Applying the Formula (65), *we get the following series representations of the functions as in the Formulas* (80) *and* (81) *:*

$$\tilde{\kappa}(p) = \sum_{m,n=0}^{+\infty} \frac{(-\lambda_1)^m(\gamma_1)_m(-\lambda_2)^n(\gamma_2)_n}{m!n!} p^{-\alpha_1 m-\alpha_2 n-\beta}, \quad (82)$$

$$\tilde{k}(p) = \sum_{m,n=0}^{+\infty} \frac{(-\lambda_1)^m(-\gamma_1)_m(-\lambda_2)^n(-\gamma_2)_n}{m!n!} p^{-\alpha_1 m-\alpha_2 n+\beta-1}, \quad (83)$$

that are valid under the conditions $\alpha_1 > 0,\ \alpha_2 > 0,\ 0 < \beta < 1,\ \lambda_1, \lambda_2 \in \mathbb{R},\ \Re(p) > 0$, $|\lambda_1 p^{-\alpha_1}| < 1,\ |\lambda_2 p^{-\alpha_2}| < 1$.

To transform the functions $\tilde{\kappa}$ and $\tilde{k}$ into the time domain, we again apply Formula (57) *and arrive at the following representations:*

$$\kappa(x) = \sum_{m,n=0}^{+\infty} \frac{(-\lambda_1)^m(\gamma_1)_m(-\lambda_2)^n(\gamma_2)_n}{m!n!} h_{\alpha_1 m+\alpha_2 n+\beta}(x) =$$

$$x^{\beta-1}\,\xi_2(\gamma_1;\gamma_2;(\alpha_1,\alpha_2;\beta);-\lambda_1 x^{\alpha_1},-\lambda_2 x^{\alpha_2}), \quad (84)$$

$$k(x) = \sum_{m,n=0}^{+\infty} \frac{(-\lambda_1)^m(-\gamma_1)_m(-\lambda_2)^n(-\gamma_2)_n}{m!n!} h_{\alpha_1 m+\alpha_2 n+1-\beta}(x) =$$

$$x^{-\beta}\,\xi_2(-\gamma_1;-\gamma_2;(\alpha_1,\alpha_2;1-\beta);-\lambda_1 x^{\alpha_1},-\lambda_2 x^{\alpha_2}), \quad (85)$$

where $\alpha_1 > 0,\ \alpha_2 > 0,\ 0 < \beta < 1,\ \lambda_1, \lambda_2 \in \mathbb{R}$, and ξ_2 is a new special function of the hypergeometric type in two variables defined by the convergent series

$$\xi_2(\gamma_1;\gamma_2;(\alpha_1,\alpha_2,\beta),y,z) := \sum_{m,n=0}^{+\infty} \frac{(\gamma_1)_m(\gamma_2)_n}{\Gamma(\alpha_1 m+\alpha_2 n+\beta)} \frac{y^m z^n}{m!n!}, \quad (86)$$

$$\alpha_1 > 0,\ \alpha_2 > 0,\ |y| < 1,\ \gamma_1, \gamma_2, \beta, z \in \mathbb{C}.$$

The convergence conditions for the series in (86) *follow from the asymptotical Formulas* (47) *and* (48) *for the Gamma function by applying the same arguments as in the derivation of the convergence conditions for the Horn function Ξ_2* ([35]).

Similar to the case considered in Example 7, we denoted the function defined by Equation (86) by ξ_2 because, for $\alpha_1 = \alpha_2 = 1$, it is reduced to the known Horn function Ξ_2:

$$\xi_2(\gamma_1;\gamma_2;(1,1;\beta);y,z) = \sum_{m,n=0}^{+\infty} \frac{(\gamma_1)_m(\gamma_2)_n}{\Gamma(m+n+\beta)} \frac{y^m z^n}{m!n!} = \frac{1}{\Gamma(\beta)} \Xi_2(\gamma_1;\gamma_2;\beta;y,z), \tag{87}$$

where the Horn function Ξ_2 is defined by the double-confluent series of the hypergeometric type (see Formula (26) in Section 5.7.1 in [35]):

$$\Xi_2(\gamma_1;\gamma_2;\beta;y,z) := \sum_{m,n=0}^{+\infty} \frac{(\gamma_1)_m(\gamma_2)_n}{(\beta)_{m+n}} \frac{y^m z^n}{m!n!}. \tag{88}$$

Thus, for $\alpha_1 = \alpha_2 = 1$ and under the conditions $0 < \beta < 1$, $\lambda_1, \lambda_2 \in \mathbb{R}$, the pair (84) and (85) of the symmetrical Sonin kernels is expressed in terms of the Horn function Ξ_2:

$$\kappa(x) = h_\beta(x)\, \Xi_2(\gamma_1;\gamma_2;\beta;-\lambda_1 x, -\lambda_2 x), \tag{89}$$

$$k(x) = h_{1-\beta}(x)\, \Xi_2(-\gamma_1;-\gamma_2;1-\beta;-\lambda_1 x, -\lambda_2 x). \tag{90}$$

To the best knowledge of the author, both the pair of functions (84) and (85) and its particular case in forms (89) and (90) are new symmetrical Sonin kernels not yet reported in the literature.

5. Conclusions and Some Open Problems

In this paper, we have introduced a new class of Sonin kernels referred to as symmetrical Sonin kernels, and we have discussed several methods for the derivation of Sonin kernels in terms of elementary and special functions. Even if these methods can be applied to the construction of arbitrary Sonin kernels, the focus of this paper was the case of symmetrical kernels that are expressed in terms of the same elementary or special functions with possibly different values for their parameters.

The first method discussed in this paper can be traced back to the publication [7] by Sonin, who applied this technique for the construction of several kernels, including the famous pair of kernels in terms of the Bessel and modified Bessel functions. The procedure presented in Remark 2 is a generalization of the method suggested by Sonin. By applying this technique, a new pair of symmetrical Sonin kernels in terms of the Wright function was derived in Example 1. In Example 3, we constructed another new pair of symmetrical Sonin kernels in the form of the hypergeometric-type series.

The second method for the derivation of Sonin kernels presented in this paper was not yet reported in the literature until now. In Theorem 2, we introduced a new class of Sonin kernels in the form of the convolution series that are a far-reaching generalization of the power series. The new Sonin kernels in the form of the convolution series can be constructed for any known pair of the Sonin kernels and any function from the space $C_{-1}(0,+\infty)$. In this way, we have achieved a very general representation of Sonin kernels that includes an arbitrary function from the space $C_{-1}(0,+\infty)$. In some cases, the convolution series can be represented in terms of the power series, and one obtains Sonin kernels in the conventional form; see Remark 4.

The third method discussed in this paper is based on the Laplace integral transform technique. Even if this method is known, with its help, some new and important pairs of symmetrical Sonin kernels were constructed in this paper. In Example 7, a pair of the symmetrical Sonin kernels was derived in terms of a generalization of the Horn function Φ_3, whereas, in Example 8, the symmetrical Sonin kernels were expressed by means of a generalization of the Horn function Ξ_2.

Because only very few symmetrical Sonin kernels are known in the literature (symmetrical Sonin kernels in terms of the power function, the Bessel function, the Kummer function, and the Prabhakar function), the construction of four new symmetrical Sonin kernels (Examples 1, 3, 7 and 8) can be considered an essential contribution to this subject.

In the rest of this section, we mention some open problems and directions for further research related to the topic of this paper. First of all, searching for the new Sonin kernels, and in particular for new symmetrical Sonin kernels, is a very important subject for further research. Another topic worth consideration is an investigation of the properties of Sonin kernels. In particular, Sonin kernels in terms of the power function and those in terms of the Prabhakar function are known to be completely monotonic. This property of the kernels is very essential for many applications, in particular, for applications in linear viscoelasticity. The question of whether there exist some other completely monotonic symmetrical Sonin kernels is still open.

Regarding applications of Sonin kernels, let us mention a very recent and actively developing branch of FC in form of GFIs and GFDs with Sonin kernels; see, e.g., [2–6,11–14] for their theory and [15–24] for applications in models for fractional dynamics, general non-Markovian quantum dynamics, general non-local electrodynamics, anomalous diffusion, linear viscoelasticity, and other non-local physical theories. Thus, the investigation of the general properties and particular cases of Sonin kernels is an important topic both for the theory of FC and for its applications.

It is worth mentioning that any pair of Sonin kernels, and especially any pair of symmetrical Sonin kernels, generates a kind of new FC. For instance, one can consider the GFI and the corresponding GFD with the kernels κ and k in terms of the Horn function Ξ_2, as in (89) and (90), respectively:

$$(\mathbb{I}_{(\kappa)}\, f)(x) = \int_0^x h_\beta(x-\xi)\, \Xi_2(\gamma_1; \gamma_2; \beta; -\lambda_1(x-\xi), -\lambda_2(x-\xi))\, f(\xi)\, d\xi, \tag{91}$$

$$(\mathbb{D}_{(k)}\, f)(x) = \frac{d}{dx}\int_0^x h_{1-\beta}(x-\xi)\, \Xi_2(-\gamma_1; -\gamma_2; 1-\beta; -\lambda_1(x-\xi), -\lambda_2(x-\xi))\, f(\xi)\, d\xi. \tag{92}$$

It is easy to see that all the Sonin kernels that we considered in this paper, both the known and new ones, belong to the space of functions $C_{-1}(0,+\infty)$. The GFIs and the GFDs with the Sonin kernels from this space were introduced and investigated in [4–6] and other related publications. In particular, the general theory of the GFIs and the GFDs developed in [4–6] ensures that the GFD defined by (92) is a left-inverse operator to the GFI defined by (91) on the suitable spaces of functions (see, e.g., [4] for details). However, developing a theory of these operators on other spaces of functions, the investigation of their mapping properties, the derivation of their norm estimates, etc. are among further important directions for research devoted to Sonin kernels and the FC operators with these kernels.

Funding: This research received no external funding.

Data Availability Statement: The original contributions presented in the study are included in the article; further inquiries can be directed to the corresponding author.

Conflicts of Interest: The author declares no conflicts of interest.

References

1. Fox, C. The G and H Functions as symmetrical Fourier kernels. *Trans. Am. Math. Soc.* **1961**, *98*, 395–429.
2. Kochubei, A.N. General fractional calculus, evolution equations, and renewal processes. *Integral Equ. Oper. Theory* **2011**, *71*, 583–600. [CrossRef]
3. Kochubei, A.N. General fractional calculus. In *Handbook of Fractional Calculus with Applications. Volume 1: Basic Theory*; Kochubei, A., Luchko, Y., Eds.; De Gruyter: Berlin, Germany, 2019; pp. 111–126.
4. Luchko, Y. General fractional integrals and derivatives with the Sonine kernels. *Mathematics* **2021**, *9*, 594. [CrossRef]
5. Luchko, Y. Operational calculus for the general fractional derivatives with the Sonine kernels. *Fract. Calc. Appl. Anal.* **2021**, *24*, 338–375. [CrossRef]
6. Luchko, Y. General fractional integrals and derivatives of arbitrary order. *Symmetry* **2021**, *13*, 755. [CrossRef]

7. Sonine, N. Sur la généralisation d'une formule d'Abel. *Acta Math.* **1884**, *4*, 171–176. [CrossRef]
8. Ortigueira, M.D. Searching for Sonin kernels. *Fract. Calc. Anal. Appl.* **2024**, *27*, 2219–2247. [CrossRef]
9. Samko, S.G.; Cardoso, R.P. Integral equations of the first kind of Sonine type. *Int. J. Math. Sci.* **2003**, *57*, 3609–3632. [CrossRef]
10. Samko, S.G.; Kilbas, A.A.; Marichev, O.I. *Fractional Integrals and Derivatives. Theory and Applications*; Gordon and Breach: New York, NY, USA, 1993.
11. Hanyga, A. A comment on a controversial issue: A generalized fractional derivative cannot have a regular kernel. *Fract. Calc. Anal. Appl.* **2020**, *23*, 211–223. [CrossRef]
12. Luchko, Y.; Yamamoto, M. General time-fractional diffusion equation: Some uniqueness and existence results for the initial-boundary-value problems. *Fract. Calc. Appl. Anal.* **2016**, *19*, 675–695. [CrossRef]
13. Luchko, Y.; Yamamoto, M. The general fractional derivative and related fractional differential equations. *Mathematics* **2020**, *8*, 2115. [CrossRef]
14. Tarasov, V.E. General fractional calculus: Multi-kernel approach. *Mathematics* **2021**, *9*, 1501. [CrossRef]
15. Tarasov, V.E. General fractional dynamics. *Mathematics* **2021**, *9*, 1464. [CrossRef]
16. Tarasov, V.E. General non-Markovian quantum dynamics. *Entropy* **2021**, *23*, 1006. [CrossRef] [PubMed]
17. Tarasov, V.E. General non-local electrodynamics: Equations and non-local effects. *Ann. Phys.* **2022**, *445*, 169082. [CrossRef]
18. Tarasov, V.E. Nonlocal classical theory of gravity: Massiveness of nonlocality and mass shielding by nonlocality. *Eur. Phys. J. Plus* **2022**, *137*, 1336. [CrossRef]
19. Tarasov, V.E. Nonlocal statistical mechanics: General fractional Liouville equations and their solutions. *Physica A* **2023**, *609*, 128366. [CrossRef]
20. Atanacković, T.M.; Pilipović, S. Zener model with general fractional calculus: Thermodynamical restrictions. *Fractal Fract.* **2022**, 6, 617. [CrossRef]
21. Bazhlekova, E.; Pshenichnov, S. Two integral representations for the relaxation modulus of the generalized fractional Zener model. *Fractal Fract.* **2023**, 7, 636. [CrossRef]
22. Górska, K.; Horzela, A. Subordination and memory dependent kinetics in diffusion and relaxation phenomena. *Fract. Calc. Appl. Anal.* **2023**, 26, 480–512. [CrossRef]
23. Mišković-Stanković, V.; Atanacković, T.M. On a system of equations with general fractional derivatives arising in diffusion theory. *Fractal Fract.* **2023**, 7, 518. [CrossRef]
24. Mišković-Stanković, V.; Janev, M.; Atanacković, T.M. Two compartmental fractional derivative model with general fractional derivative. *J. Pharmacokinet. Pharmacodyn.* **2023**, 50, 79–87. [PubMed]
25. Abel, N.H. Oplösning af et par opgaver ved hjelp af bestemte integraler. *Mag. Naturvidenskaberne* **1823**, *2*, 2.
26. Abel, N.H. Auflösung einer mechanischen Aufgabe. *J. Reine Angew. Math.* **1826**, *1*, 153–157.
27. Zacher, R. Boundedness of weak solutions to evolutionary partial integro-differential equations with discontinuous coefficients. *J. Math. Anal. Appl.* **2008**, *348*, 137–149. [CrossRef]
28. Wick, J. Über eine Integralgleichung vom Abelschen Typ. *Z. Angew. Math. Mech.* **1968**, *48*, T39–T41.
29. Luchko, Y. The Wright function and its applications. In *Handbook of Fractional Calculus with Applications. Volume 1: Basic Theory*; Kochubei, A., Luchko, Y., Eds.; Walter de Gruyter: Berlin, Germany; Boston, MA, USA, 2019; pp. 241–268.
30. Giusti, A.; Colombaro, I.; Garra, R.; Garrappa, R.; Polito, F.; Popolizio, M.; Mainardi, F. A practical guide to Prabhakar fractional calculus. *Fract. Calc. Anal. Appl.* **2020**, 23, 9–54. [CrossRef]
31. Prabhakar, T.R. A singular integral equation with a generalized Mittag-Leffler function in the kernel. *Yokohama Math. J.* **1971**, 19, 7–15.
32. Prabhakar, T.R. Two singular integral equations involving confluent hypergeometric functions. *Proc. Camb. Phil. Soc.* **1969**, 66, 71–89. [CrossRef]
33. Giusti, A. General fractional calculus and Prabhakar's theory. *Commun. Nonlinear Sci. Numer. Simul.* **2020**, 83, 105114. [CrossRef]
34. Luchko, Y. Convolution series and the generalized convolution Taylor formula. *Fract. Calc. Appl. Anal.* **2022**, *25*, 207–228. [CrossRef]
35. Bateman, H.; Erdelyi, A.; Magnus, W.; Oberhettinger, F.; Tricomi, F.G. *Higher Transcendental Functions*; McGraw-Hill Book Company, Inc.: New York, NY, USA, 1953; Volume I.
36. Prudnikov, A.P.; Brychkov, Y.A.; Marichev, O.I. *Integrals and Series Volume 5: Inverse Laplace Transforms*; Gordon and Breach: New York, NY, USA, 1992.

mathematics

MDPI

Article

Some Symmetry and Duality Theorems on Multiple Zeta(-Star) Values

Kwang-Wu Chen [1,*], Minking Eie [2] and Yao Lin Ong [3]

[1] Department of Mathematics, University of Taipei, Taipei 100234, Taiwan
[2] Department of Mathematics, National Chung Cheng University, Chia-Yi 62145, Taiwan; minkingeie@gmail.com
[3] Executive Master of Business Administration, Chang Jung Christian University, Tainan City 71101, Taiwan; ylong@mail.cjcu.edu.tw
* Correspondence: kwchen@utaipei.edu.tw

Abstract: In this paper, we provide a symmetric formula and a duality formula relating multiple zeta values and zeta-star values. We find that the summation $\sum_{a+b=r-1}(-1)^a\zeta^\star(a+2,\{2\}^{p-1})\zeta^\star(\{1\}^{b+1},\{2\}^q)$ equals $\zeta^\star(\{2\}^p,\{1\}^r,\{2\}^q)+(-1)^{r+1}\zeta^\star(\{2\}^q,r+2,\{2\}^{p-1})$. With the help of this equation and Zagier's $\zeta^\star(\{2\}^p,3,\{2\}^q)$ formula, we can easily determine $\zeta^\star(\{2\}^p,1,\{2\}^q)$ and several interesting expressions.

Keywords: multiple zeta value; multiple zeta-star value; duality theorem; Yamamoto's integral

MSC: 11M32; 05A15; 33B15

1. Introduction

For an r-tuple $\boldsymbol{\alpha}=(\alpha_1,\alpha_2,\dots,\alpha_r)$ of positive integers with $\alpha_r\geq 2$, a multiple zeta value $\zeta(\boldsymbol{\alpha})$ and a multiple zeta-star value $\zeta^\star(\boldsymbol{\alpha})$ are defined to be [1–3]

$$\zeta(\boldsymbol{\alpha})=\sum_{1\leq k_1<k_2<\cdots<k_r}k_1^{-\alpha_1}k_2^{-\alpha_2}\cdots k_r^{-\alpha_r},\quad\text{and}$$
$$\zeta^\star(\boldsymbol{\alpha})=\sum_{1\leq k_1\leq k_2\leq\cdots\leq k_r}k_1^{-\alpha_1}k_2^{-\alpha_2}\cdots k_r^{-\alpha_r}.$$

We denote the parameters $w(\boldsymbol{\alpha})=|\boldsymbol{\alpha}|=\alpha_1+\alpha_2+\cdots+\alpha_r$, $d(\boldsymbol{\alpha})=r$, and $h(\boldsymbol{\alpha})=\#\{i\mid\alpha_i>1,1\leq i\leq r\}$, called, respectively, the weight, the depth, and the height of $\boldsymbol{\alpha}$ (or of $\zeta(\boldsymbol{\alpha})$, or of $\zeta^\star(\boldsymbol{\alpha})$). We let $\{a\}^k$ be k repetitions of a such that $\zeta(2,\{3\}^3)=\zeta(2,3,3,3)$.

In this paper, we investigate the functions Z_U (Schur multiple zeta values of anti-hook type), Z_L (Schur multiple zeta values of hook type), and Z_B [4–6]:

$$Z_U\binom{\boldsymbol{\alpha}}{\boldsymbol{\beta}}:=\sum_{1\leq k_1<k_2<\cdots<k_r}k_1^{-\alpha_1}k_2^{-\alpha_2}\cdots k_r^{-\alpha_r}\sum_{1\leq\ell_1\leq\ell_2\leq\cdots\leq\ell_m\leq k_r}\ell_1^{-\beta_1}\ell_2^{-\beta_2}\cdots\ell_m^{-\beta_m},$$
$$Z_L\binom{\boldsymbol{\alpha}}{\boldsymbol{\beta}}:=\sum_{1\leq k_1<k_2<\cdots<k_r}k_1^{-\alpha_1}k_2^{-\alpha_2}\cdots k_r^{-\alpha_r}\sum_{k_1\leq\ell_1\leq\ell_2\leq\cdots\leq\ell_m}\ell_1^{-\beta_1}\ell_2^{-\beta_2}\cdots\ell_m^{-\beta_m},$$
$$Z_B\binom{\boldsymbol{\alpha}}{\boldsymbol{\beta}}:=\sum_{1\leq k_1<k_2<\cdots<k_r}k_1^{-\alpha_1}k_2^{-\alpha_2}\cdots k_r^{-\alpha_r}\sum_{k_1\leq\ell_1\leq\ell_2\leq\cdots\leq\ell_m\leq k_r}\ell_1^{-\beta_1}\ell_2^{-\beta_2}\cdots\ell_m^{-\beta_m}.$$

For the sake of convergence, the functions Z_U and Z_B are restricted by $\alpha_r\geq 2$, and the function Z_L is restricted by $\alpha_r\geq 2,\beta_m\geq 2$.

Yamamoto [7] introduced a combinatorial generalization of the iterated integral, the integral associated with a 2-poset. Kaneko and Yamamoto [8] conjectured that the following integral-series identity is sufficient to describe all the linear relations of multiple zeta values over $\mathbb{Q}$.

$$I\Bigg($$ 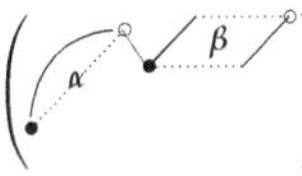 $$\Bigg) = Z_U\binom{\alpha}{\beta},$$

where the left-hand side of the above identity is an integral associated with a 2-posets introduced by Yamamoto [7] (we will introduce the associated notations in Section 2).

The use of Yamamoto's integral is prevalent among researchers studying multiple zeta values and multiple zeta-star values [8–10].

Many scholars have conducted research on the function Z_U appearing on the right-hand side of the above identity [4,5,8,11,12].

We simplify our notations with

$$\overrightarrow{\boldsymbol{\alpha}_{i,j}} = (\alpha_{i+1}, \alpha_{i+2}, \ldots, \alpha_j), \quad \overleftarrow{\boldsymbol{\alpha}_{i,j}} = (\alpha_j, \alpha_{j-1}, \ldots, \alpha_{i+1}),$$

for $i < j$. Note that if $i \geq j$, we set $\overrightarrow{\boldsymbol{\alpha}_{i,j}} = \overleftarrow{\boldsymbol{\alpha}_{i,j}} = \emptyset$. For brevity, we use the lowercase English letters and lowercase Greek letters, with or without subscripts, in summations to represent non-negative and positive integers, unless otherwise specified. To make the symbols more compact, we adopt the fact $\zeta(\emptyset) = \zeta^\star(\emptyset) = 1$.

We use Yamamoto's integral to obtain the following symmetric form between multiple zeta(-star) values in Section 3.

Theorem 1. *Let r, m, θ be nonnegative integers with $\theta \geq 2$, and the vectors $\boldsymbol{\alpha} = (\alpha_1, \alpha_2, \ldots, \alpha_r)$, $\boldsymbol{\beta} = (\beta_1, \beta_2, \ldots, \beta_m)$ with $\alpha_i \geq 2$, $\beta_m \geq 2$, for $1 \leq i \leq r$. Then*

$$\sum_{\substack{a+b=r\\c+d=m}} (-1)^{a+c} \zeta^\star(\overrightarrow{\boldsymbol{\alpha}_{0,b}}) \zeta(\overleftarrow{\boldsymbol{\beta}_{0,c}}, \theta, \overleftarrow{\boldsymbol{\alpha}_{b,r}}) \zeta^\star(\overrightarrow{\boldsymbol{\beta}_{c,m}}) = \zeta^\star(\boldsymbol{\alpha}, \theta, \boldsymbol{\beta}), \tag{1}$$

$$\sum_{\substack{a+b=r\\c+d=m}} (-1)^{a+c} \zeta(\overrightarrow{\boldsymbol{\alpha}_{0,b}}) \zeta^\star(\overleftarrow{\boldsymbol{\beta}_{0,c}}, \theta, \overleftarrow{\boldsymbol{\alpha}_{b,r}}) \zeta(\overrightarrow{\boldsymbol{\beta}_{c,m}}) = \zeta(\boldsymbol{\alpha}, \theta, \boldsymbol{\beta}). \tag{2}$$

The following symmetric formula that we have is truly exquisite.

Corollary 1. *For any nonnegative integers p, q, s, t, α with $s \geq 2, t \geq 2, \theta \geq 2$, we have*

$$\sum_{\substack{a+b=q\\c+d=p}} (-1)^{a+c} \zeta^\star(\{s\}^b) \zeta(\{s\}^a, \theta, \{t\}^c) \zeta^\star(\{t\}^d) = \zeta^\star(\{t\}^p, \theta, \{s\}^q),$$

$$\sum_{\substack{a+b=q\\c+d=p}} (-1)^{a+c} \zeta(\{s\}^b) \zeta^\star(\{s\}^a, \theta, \{t\}^c) \zeta(\{t\}^d) = \zeta(\{t\}^p, \theta, \{s\}^q).$$

We note that a version of finite sums of the above two identities can be found in [13,14].

Let $(a_1, b_1), (a_2, b_2), \ldots, (a_n, b_n)$ be n pairs of nonnegative integers. If we write

$$(\alpha_1, \alpha_2, \ldots, \alpha_r) = (\{1\}^{a_1}, b_1 + 2, \{1\}^{a_2}, b_2 + 2, \ldots, \{1\}^{a_n}, b_n + 2)$$

and set

$$(\{1\}^{b_n}, a_n + 2, \{1\}^{b_{n-1}}, a_{n-1} + 2, \ldots, \{1\}^{b_1}, a_1 + 2) = (\beta_1, \beta_2, \ldots, \beta_m),$$

then the duality theorem of multiple zeta values [15] is stated as

$$\zeta(\alpha_1, \alpha_2, \ldots, \alpha_r) = \zeta(\beta_1, \beta_2, \ldots, \beta_m).$$

We say that $\zeta(\beta_1,\ldots,\beta_m)$ is the dual of $\zeta(\alpha_1,\ldots,\alpha_r)$, and we denote it as $\zeta(\alpha_1,\ldots,\alpha_r)^\sharp = \zeta(\beta_1,\ldots,\beta_m)$.

In 2015, the first author [4] gave a formula related to Z_U:

$$Z_U\binom{\beta_1,\beta_2,\ldots,\beta_m}{\{1\}^q} = \sum_{|\boldsymbol{d}|=q} \zeta(\alpha_1+d_1,\ldots,\alpha_r+d_r)\prod_{j=1}^{r}\binom{\alpha_j+d_j-1}{d_j},$$

if $\zeta(\beta_1,\ldots,\beta_m)$ is the dual of $\zeta(\alpha_1,\ldots,\alpha_r)$.

In Section 4, we present three different methods to prove the following duality theorem between these Z_B, Z_U, and Z_L functions.

Theorem 2. *If $\zeta(\beta_1,\beta_2,\ldots,\beta_m)$ is the dual of $\zeta(\alpha_1,\alpha_2,\ldots,\alpha_r)$. Given any nonnegative integer n, we have*

$$Z_U\binom{\alpha_1,\alpha_2,\ldots,\alpha_r}{\{2\}^n} = Z_L\binom{\beta_1,\beta_2,\ldots,\beta_m}{\{2\}^n}, \quad \text{and}$$
$$Z_B\binom{\alpha_1,\alpha_2,\ldots,\alpha_r}{\{2\}^n} = Z_B\binom{\beta_1,\beta_2,\ldots,\beta_m}{\{2\}^n}.$$

Chen and Eie [5] use these three functions to give three new sum formulas for multiple zeta(-star) values with height ≤ 2 and the evaluation of $\zeta^\star(\{1\}^m,\{2\}^{n+1})$. For example, the authors use Z_B to obtain (Theorem 1.1, [5])

$$\sum_{\substack{\alpha_1+\alpha_2=n\\ \alpha_1,\alpha_2\geq 1}} \zeta^\star(\alpha_1,\{1\}^m,\alpha_2+1) = (m+n)\zeta(m+n+1).$$

We use the duality theorem on the functions Z_U and Z_L to obtain the following formula.

Theorem 3. *For any nonnegative integers p, q, and r with $p>0$, $q>0$, we have*

$$\begin{aligned}&\zeta^\star(\{2\}^p,\{1\}^r,\{2\}^q) + (-1)^{r+1}\zeta^\star(\{2\}^q,r+2,\{2\}^{p-1})\\ &= \sum_{a+b=r-1}(-1)^a\zeta^\star(a+2,\{2\}^{p-1})\zeta^\star(\{1\}^{b+1},\{2\}^q).\end{aligned} \tag{3}$$

Substituting $r=1$ into the above equation yields Equation (2) in [13]. By employing this in conjunction with Zagier's formula (ref. [16]) for computing $\zeta^\star(\{2\}^p,3,\{2\}^q)$, we can determine the values of $\zeta^\star(\{2\}^p,1,\{2\}^q)$:

$$\zeta^\star(\{2\}^p,1,\{2\}^q) = 2\sum_{k=1}^{p+q}\left[\binom{2k}{2q} - \left(1-\frac{1}{2^{2k}}\right)\binom{2k}{2p-1}\right]\zeta^\star(\{2\}^{p+q-k})\zeta(2k+1),$$

for any positive integers p and q and this result coincides with Theorem 1.6 in [13]. We will discuss Theorem 3 and its relevant applications in the final section, providing some intriguing formulas.

2. Some Preliminaries and Auxiliary Tools

In this section, we review the definitions and basic properties of 2-labeled posets (in this paper, we call them 2-posets for short) and the associated integrals first introduced by Yamamoto [7].

Definition 1 (Definition 3.1, [8])**.** *A 2-poset is a pair (X,δ_X), where $X=(X,\leq)$ is a finite partially ordered set (poset for short) and δ_X is a map from X to $\{0,1\}$. We often omit δ_X and simply say "a 2-poset X." The δ_X is called the* label map *of X.*

A 2-poset (X, δ_X) *is called admissible if* $\delta_X(x) = 0$ *for all maximal elements* $x \in X$ *and* $\delta_X(x) = 1$ *for all minimal elements* $x \in X$.

A 2-poset is depicted as a Hasse diagram in which an element x with $\delta(x) = 0$ (resp. $\delta(x) = 1$) is represented by $\circ$ (resp. $\bullet$). For example, the diagram

represents the 2-poset $X = \{x_1, x_2, x_3, x_4, x_5\}$ with order $x_1 < x_2 < x_3 > x_4 < x_5$ and label $(\delta_X(x_1), \dots, \delta_X(x_5)) = (1, 0, 0, 1, 0)$.

Definition 2 (Definition 3.2, [8]). *For an admissible 2-poset X, we define the associated integral*

$$I(X) = \int_{\Delta_X} \prod_{x \in X} \omega_{\delta_X(x)}(t_x), \tag{4}$$

where

$$\Delta_X = \{(t_x)_x \in [0,1]^X \mid t_x < t_y \text{ if } x < y\} \quad \text{and} \quad \omega_0(t) = \frac{dt}{t}, \quad \omega_1(t) = \frac{dt}{1-t}.$$

Note that the admissibility of a 2-poset corresponds to the convergence of the associated integral.

Example 1. *When an admissible 2-poset is totally ordered, the corresponding integral is exactly the iterated integral expression for a multiple zeta value. To be precise, for an index* $\boldsymbol{\alpha} = (\alpha_1, \dots, \alpha_r)$ *(admissible or not), we write the 'totally ordered' diagram:*

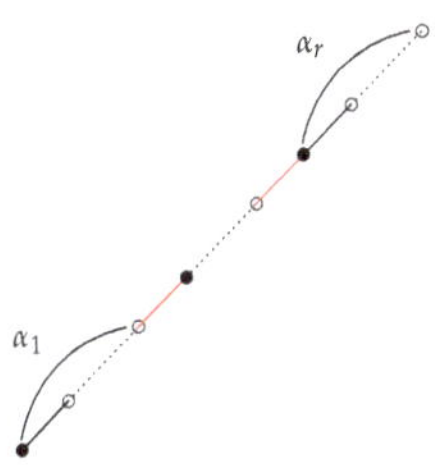

as

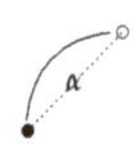

In [7], an integral expression for multiple zeta-star values is described in terms of a 2-poset. For an index $\boldsymbol{\beta} = (\beta_1, \beta_2, \dots, \beta_m)$, *we write the following diagram:*

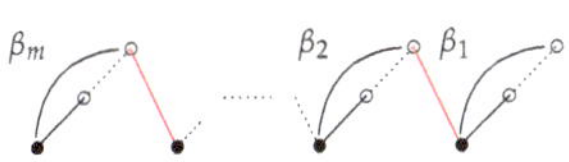

as

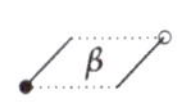

Then, if $\boldsymbol{\alpha}$ *and* $\boldsymbol{\beta}$ *are admissible, we have [10] Proposition 2.4, 2.7*

$\zeta(\boldsymbol{\alpha}) = I\Big($ 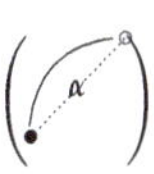 $\Big)$, *and* $\zeta^\star(\boldsymbol{\beta}) = I($ 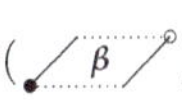 $)$. (5)

For example,

$\zeta(1,2) = I\Big($ 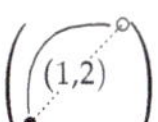 $\Big) = I\Big($  $\Big)$, $\zeta^\star(2,3) = I\Big($ 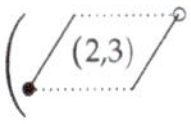 $\Big) = I\Big($ 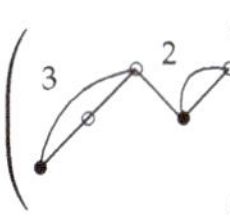 $\Big)$.

We also recall an algebraic setup for 2-posets (cf. Remark at the end of §2 of [7]). Let $\mathfrak{P}$ be the $\mathbb{Q}$-algebra generated by the isomorphism classes of 2-posets, whose multiplication is given by the disjoint union of 2-posets. Then, the integral (4) defines a $\mathbb{Q}$-algebra homomorphism $I\colon \mathfrak{P}^0 \to \mathbb{R}$ from the subalgebra $\mathfrak{P}^0$ of $\mathfrak{P}$ generated by the classes of admissible 2-posets.

Following these notations, we have

$$Z_U\begin{pmatrix}\boldsymbol{\alpha}\\ \boldsymbol{\beta}\end{pmatrix} = I\Bigg(\ \text{[diagram]}\ \Bigg), \qquad \text{and} \qquad Z_L\begin{pmatrix}\boldsymbol{\alpha}\\ \boldsymbol{\beta}\end{pmatrix} = I\Bigg(\ \text{[diagram]}\ \Bigg). \tag{6}$$

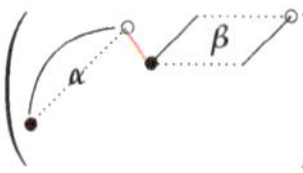

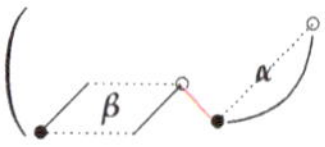

In fact, the upper left equation is the same as (Theorem 4.1, [8]). Kaneko and Yamamoto conjecture that any linear dependency of MZVs over $\mathbb{Q}$ is deduced from this equation.

We evaluate $Z_L\begin{pmatrix}1,2\\1,2\end{pmatrix}$ as an example: Let $D = \{(t_1,t_2,t_3,t_4,t_5,t_6) \in [0,1]^6 \mid t_1 < t_2 > t_3 > t_4 < t_5 < t_6\}$, we calculate

$$\begin{aligned}
I\Bigg(\ \text{[diagram]}\ \Bigg) &= \int_D \frac{dt_1}{1-t_1}\frac{dt_2}{t_2}\frac{dt_3}{1-t_3}\frac{dt_4}{1-t_4}\frac{dt_5}{1-t_5}\frac{dt_6}{t_6} \\
&= \int_{D-\{t_1\}} \left(\int_0^{t_2} \sum_{n=0}^{\infty} t_1^n\, dt_1\right) \frac{dt_2}{t_2}\frac{dt_3}{1-t_3}\frac{dt_4}{1-t_4}\frac{dt_5}{1-t_5}\frac{dt_6}{t_6} \\
&= \int_{D-\{t_1,t_2\}} \left(\int_{t_3}^{1} \sum_{\ell_2=1}^{\infty} \frac{t_2^{\ell_2-1}}{\ell_2}\, dt_2\right) \frac{dt_3}{1-t_3}\frac{dt_4}{1-t_4}\frac{dt_5}{1-t_5}\frac{dt_6}{t_6} \\
&= \sum_{\ell_2=1}^{\infty} \frac{1}{\ell_2^2} \int_{D-\{t_1,t_2,t_3\}} \left(\int_{t_4}^{1} \sum_{n=0}^{\ell_2-1} t_3^n\, dt_3\right) \frac{dt_4}{1-t_4}\frac{dt_5}{1-t_5}\frac{dt_6}{t_6} \\
&= \sum_{\ell_2=1}^{\infty} \frac{1}{\ell_2^2} \sum_{\ell_1=1}^{\ell_2} \frac{1}{\ell_1} \int_{0<t_5<t_6<1} \left(\int_0^{t_5} \sum_{n=0}^{\ell_1-1} t_4^n\, dt_4\right) \frac{dt_5}{1-t_5}\frac{dt_6}{t_6} \\
&= \sum_{\ell_2=1}^{\infty} \frac{1}{\ell_2^2} \sum_{\ell_1=1}^{\ell_2} \frac{1}{\ell_1} \sum_{k_1=1}^{\ell_1} \frac{1}{k_1} \int_0^1 \left(\int_0^{t_6} \sum_{n=0}^{\infty} t_5^{n+k_1}\, dt_5\right) \frac{dt_6}{t_6} \\
&= \sum_{\ell_2=1}^{\infty} \frac{1}{\ell_2^2} \sum_{\ell_1=1}^{\ell_2} \frac{1}{\ell_1} \sum_{k_1=1}^{\ell_1} \frac{1}{k_1} \sum_{n=1}^{\infty} \frac{1}{(n+k_1)^2} = Z_L\begin{pmatrix}1,2\\1,2\end{pmatrix}.
\end{aligned}$$

We need some properties of these three functions Z_U, Z_L and Z_B, please see [5] for details:

$$\zeta(\boldsymbol{\alpha})\zeta^\star(\boldsymbol{\beta}) = Z_L\begin{pmatrix}\alpha_1,\alpha_2,\ldots,\alpha_r\\ \beta_1,\beta_2,\ldots,\beta_m\end{pmatrix} + Z_L\begin{pmatrix}\beta_1,\alpha_1,\ldots,\alpha_r\\ \beta_2,\beta_3,\ldots,\beta_m\end{pmatrix}, \tag{7}$$

$$\zeta(\boldsymbol{\alpha})\zeta^\star(\boldsymbol{\beta}) = Z_U\begin{pmatrix}\alpha_1,\alpha_2,\ldots,\alpha_r\\ \beta_1,\beta_2,\ldots,\beta_m\end{pmatrix} + Z_U\begin{pmatrix}\alpha_1,\ldots,\alpha_r,\beta_m\\ \beta_1,\ldots,\beta_{m-1}\end{pmatrix}. \tag{8}$$

Proposition 1 (Proposition 4.1, [5]). *For an r-tuple $\boldsymbol{\alpha} = (\alpha_1,\alpha_2,\ldots,\alpha_r)$ of positive integers with $\alpha_1 \geq 2$, $\alpha_r \geq 2$, we have*

$$\sum_{k=0}^{r} (-1)^k \zeta^\star(\alpha_k,\alpha_{k-1},\ldots,\alpha_1)\zeta(\alpha_{k+1},\alpha_{k+2},\ldots,\alpha_r) = \begin{cases} 1, & \textit{if } r=0,\\ 0, & \textit{otherwise.}\end{cases} \tag{9}$$

Let $\boldsymbol{\alpha} = (s,\ldots,s) = (\{s\}^r)$ in Equation (9). We obtain the classical known result (Equation (5.8), [5])

$$\sum_{a+b=r} (-1)^a \zeta(\{s\}^a)\zeta^\star(\{s\}^b) = \begin{cases} 1, & \text{if } r=0,\\ 0, & \text{otherwise.}\end{cases} \tag{10}$$

We derive an evaluation of Z_L using Equation (7).

$$\begin{aligned} Z_L\begin{pmatrix}\alpha_1,\ldots,\alpha_r\\ \beta_1,\ldots,\beta_m\end{pmatrix} &= \zeta(\alpha_1,\ldots,\alpha_r)\zeta^\star(\beta_1,\ldots,\beta_m) - Z_L\begin{pmatrix}\beta_1,\alpha_1,\ldots,\alpha_r\\ \beta_2,\ldots,\beta_m\end{pmatrix}\\ &= \zeta(\alpha_1,\ldots,\alpha_r)\zeta^\star(\beta_1,\ldots,\beta_m) - \zeta(\beta_1,\alpha_1,\ldots,\alpha_r)\zeta^\star(\beta_2,\ldots,\beta_m)\\ &\quad + (-1)^2 Z_L\begin{pmatrix}\beta_2,\beta_1,\alpha_1,\ldots,\alpha_r\\ \beta_3,\ldots,\beta_m\end{pmatrix}. \end{aligned}$$

We use Equation (7) repeatedly until the vector in the second row is the empty set. Since

$$Z_L\begin{pmatrix}\beta_m,\beta_{m-1},\ldots,\beta_1,\alpha_1,\ldots,\alpha_r\\ \varnothing\end{pmatrix} = \zeta(\beta_m,\beta_{m-1},\ldots,\beta_1,\alpha_1,\ldots,\alpha_r),$$

we arrive a formula for the function Z_L:

$$Z_L\begin{pmatrix}\boldsymbol{\alpha}\\ \boldsymbol{\beta}\end{pmatrix} = \sum_{a+b=m}(-1)^a\zeta(\beta_a,\ldots,\beta_1,\alpha_1,\ldots,\alpha_r)\zeta^\star(\beta_{a+1},\ldots,\beta_m).$$

If we use Equation (7) in a different direction

$$Z_L\begin{pmatrix}\alpha_1,\ldots,\alpha_r\\ \beta_1,\ldots,\beta_m\end{pmatrix} = \zeta(\alpha_2,\ldots,\alpha_r)\zeta^\star(\alpha_1,\beta_1,\ldots,\beta_m) - Z_L\begin{pmatrix}\alpha_2,\ldots,\alpha_r\\ \alpha_1,\beta_1,\beta_2,\ldots,\beta_m\end{pmatrix},$$

then we obtain the following formula for Z_L.

$$Z_L\begin{pmatrix}\alpha_1,\ldots,\alpha_r\\ \beta_1,\ldots,\beta_m\end{pmatrix} = \sum_{a+b=r-1}(-1)^a\zeta(\alpha_{a+2},\ldots,\alpha_r)\zeta^\star(\alpha_{a+1},\ldots,\alpha_1,\beta_1,\ldots,\beta_m).$$

Similarly, we also use Equation (8) to obtain two formulas of the function Z_U. We conclude these four formulas in the following propositions.

Proposition 2. *For any nonnegative integers m,r, an r-tuple $\boldsymbol{\alpha} = (\alpha_1,\alpha_2,\ldots,\alpha_r)$ of positive integers, and an m-tupe $\boldsymbol{\beta} = (\beta_1,\beta_2,\ldots,\beta_m)$ of positive integers, with $\alpha_r \geq 2$, $\beta_m \geq 2$, we have*

$$\begin{aligned} Z_L\begin{pmatrix}\boldsymbol{\alpha}\\ \boldsymbol{\beta}\end{pmatrix} &= \sum_{a+b=m}(-1)^a\zeta(\beta_a,\ldots,\beta_1,\alpha_1,\ldots,\alpha_r)\zeta^\star(\beta_{a+1},\ldots,\beta_m) &(11)\\ &= \sum_{a+b=r-1}(-1)^a\zeta(\alpha_{a+2},\ldots,\alpha_r)\zeta^\star(\alpha_{a+1},\ldots,\alpha_1,\beta_1,\ldots,\beta_m). &(12) \end{aligned}$$

And

$$\begin{aligned} Z_U\begin{pmatrix}\boldsymbol{\alpha}\\ \boldsymbol{\beta}\end{pmatrix} &= \sum_{a+b=m}(-1)^a\zeta(\alpha_1,\ldots,\alpha_r,\beta_m,\ldots,\beta_{b+1})\zeta^\star(\beta_1,\ldots,\beta_b) &(13)\\ &= \sum_{a+b=r-1}(-1)^a\zeta(\alpha_1,\ldots,\alpha_b)\zeta^\star(\beta_1,\ldots,\beta_m,\alpha_r,\ldots,\alpha_{b+1}), &(14) \end{aligned}$$

where $\beta_i \geq 2$ $(1 \leq i \leq m)$ for Equation (13) and $\alpha_j \geq 2$ $(1 \leq j \leq r)$ for Equation (14).

We use a formula among the function Z_B and Z_U (Proposition 7.1, [5])

$$(-1)^m Z_B\begin{pmatrix} \alpha_{m+1},\ldots,\alpha_r \\ \alpha_m,\ldots,\alpha_1 \end{pmatrix} = \zeta(\boldsymbol{\alpha}) + \sum_{k=1}^{m}(-1)^k Z_U\begin{pmatrix} \alpha_{k+1},\ldots,\alpha_r \\ \alpha_k,\ldots,\alpha_1 \end{pmatrix}, \tag{15}$$

where $\alpha_r \geq 2$ and $1 \leq m \leq r$, and Equation (13) to obtain an explicit formula for the function Z_B:

$$Z_B\begin{pmatrix} \alpha_{m+1},\ldots,\alpha_r \\ \alpha_m,\ldots,\alpha_1 \end{pmatrix} = \sum_{0\leq j\leq d\leq m}(-1)^{m+j-d}\zeta(\alpha_{d+1},\ldots,\alpha_r,\alpha_1,\ldots,\alpha_j)\zeta^\star(\alpha_d,\ldots,\alpha_{j+1}). \tag{16}$$

3. Symmetric Formulas and Theorem 1

In order to prove Theorem 1, we apply Yamamoto's integrals to show four equalities that involve the Z_U and Z_L functions.

Proposition 3 (ref. [8]). *For any nonnegative integers m, r, θ with $\theta \geq 2$, an r-tuple $\boldsymbol{\alpha} = (\alpha_1, \alpha_2, \ldots, \alpha_r)$ of positive integers, and an m-tupe $\boldsymbol{\beta} = (\beta_1, \beta_2, \ldots, \beta_m)$ of positive integers with $\beta_m \geq 2$, we have*

$$\sum_{k=0}^{m}(-1)^k\zeta(\overrightarrow{\boldsymbol{\beta}_{k,m}})Z_U\begin{pmatrix} \boldsymbol{\alpha} \\ \overleftarrow{\boldsymbol{\beta}_{0,k}} \end{pmatrix} = \zeta(\boldsymbol{\alpha},\boldsymbol{\beta}), \quad \text{for } \alpha_r \geq 2, \tag{17}$$

$$\sum_{k=0}^{r}(-1)^{r-k}\zeta(\overrightarrow{\boldsymbol{\alpha}_{0,k}})Z_L\begin{pmatrix} \boldsymbol{\beta} \\ \overleftarrow{\boldsymbol{\alpha}_{k,r}} \end{pmatrix} = \zeta(\boldsymbol{\alpha},\boldsymbol{\beta}), \quad \text{for } \alpha_i \geq 2, 1 \leq i \leq r, \tag{18}$$

$$\sum_{k=0}^{m}(-1)^k\zeta^\star(\overrightarrow{\boldsymbol{\beta}_{k,m}})Z_U\begin{pmatrix} \overleftarrow{\boldsymbol{\beta}_{0,k}},\theta \\ \boldsymbol{\alpha} \end{pmatrix} = \zeta^\star(\boldsymbol{\alpha},\theta,\boldsymbol{\beta}), \tag{19}$$

$$\sum_{k=0}^{r}(-1)^{r-k}\zeta^\star(\overrightarrow{\boldsymbol{\alpha}_{0,k}})Z_L\begin{pmatrix} \theta,\overleftarrow{\boldsymbol{\alpha}_{k,r}} \\ \boldsymbol{\beta} \end{pmatrix} = \zeta^\star(\boldsymbol{\alpha},\theta,\boldsymbol{\beta}), \quad \text{for } \alpha_i \geq 2, 1 \leq i \leq r. \tag{20}$$

Proof. We present the process to get obtain the equation, the other equations are obtained similarly. Since $\zeta(\boldsymbol{\alpha},\boldsymbol{\beta})$ can be represented as

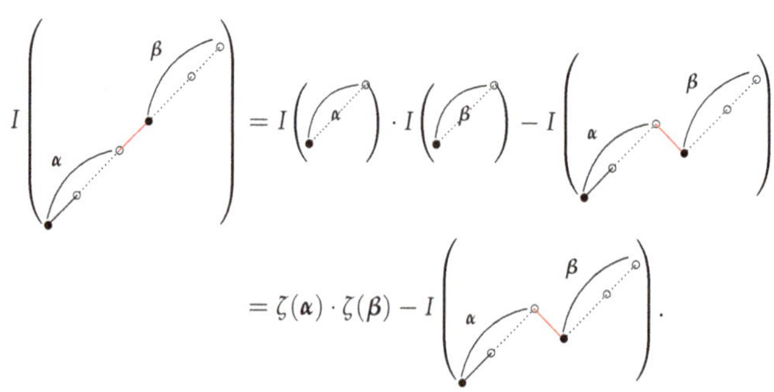

Since for an integer i with $1 \le i \le m$, we have

I 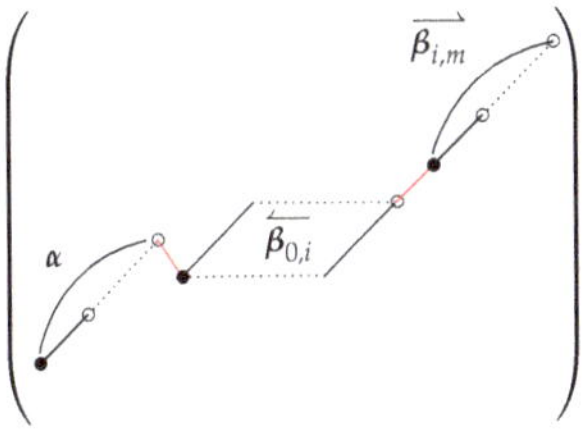

$= I$ 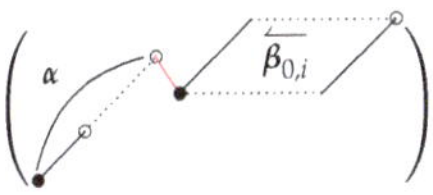 $\cdot I$ 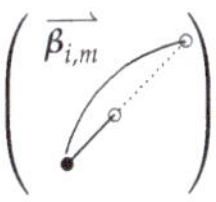 $- I$ 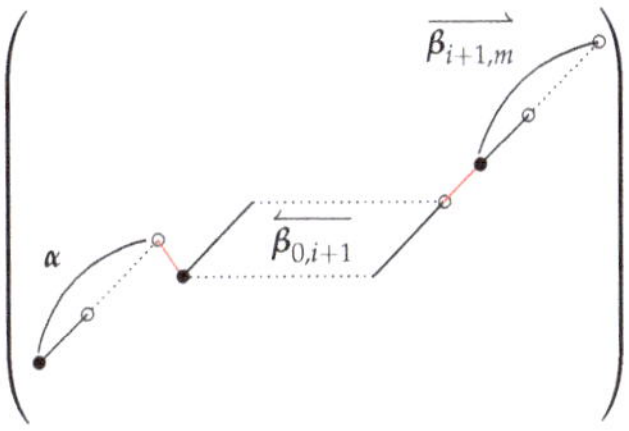

$= Z_U \begin{pmatrix} \boldsymbol{\alpha} \\ \overleftarrow{\boldsymbol{\beta}_{0,i}} \end{pmatrix} \cdot \zeta(\overrightarrow{\boldsymbol{\beta}_{i,m}}) - I$ 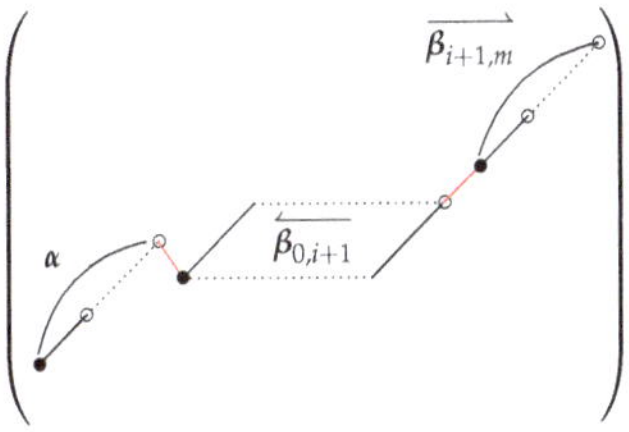 .

Continue this process we have

I 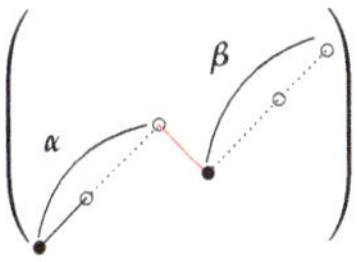 $= \sum_{k=1}^{m} (-1)^{k-1} Z_U \begin{pmatrix} \boldsymbol{\alpha} \\ \overleftarrow{\boldsymbol{\beta}_{0,k}} \end{pmatrix} \zeta(\overrightarrow{\boldsymbol{\beta}_{k,m}}).$

Substituing into the original equation, we get the conclusion. □

We can easily derive the identities in Theorem 1 using the equations from Proposition 3. First we substitute the representation Equation (13) of Z_U:

$$Z_U \begin{pmatrix} \overleftarrow{\boldsymbol{\beta}_{0,k}}, \theta \\ \boldsymbol{\alpha} \end{pmatrix} = \sum_{a+b=r} (-1)^a \zeta(\overleftarrow{\boldsymbol{\beta}_{0,k}}, \theta, \overleftarrow{\boldsymbol{\alpha}_{b,r}}) \zeta^\star(\overrightarrow{\boldsymbol{\alpha}_{0,b}})$$

into Equation (19), we have Equation (1). The other formula Equation (2) is obtained from Equation (17):

$$\sum_{c+d=m} (-1)^c \zeta(\overrightarrow{\boldsymbol{\beta}_{c,m}}) Z_U \begin{pmatrix} \boldsymbol{\alpha}, \theta \\ \overleftarrow{\boldsymbol{\beta}_{0,c}} \end{pmatrix} = \zeta(\boldsymbol{\alpha}, \theta, \boldsymbol{\beta}),$$

using the representation Equation (14) of Z_U:

$$\sum_{a+b=r} (-1)^a \zeta(\overrightarrow{\boldsymbol{\alpha}_{0,b}}) \zeta^\star(\overleftarrow{\boldsymbol{\beta}_{0,c}}, \theta, \overleftarrow{\boldsymbol{\alpha}_{b,r}}).$$

Therefore, we complete the proof of Theorem 1.

Furthermore, the beautiful equations in Corollary 1 are derived by substituting $\boldsymbol{\alpha} = \{t\}^p$ and $\boldsymbol{\beta} = \{s\}^q$ into Theorem 1.

4. Duality Theorems and Theorem 2

We will begin by proving the first equation in Theorem 2.

Theorem 4. *Let $\zeta(\boldsymbol{\beta})$ be the dual of $\zeta(\boldsymbol{\alpha})$ and n be a nonnegative integer. Then*

$$Z_U\binom{\boldsymbol{\alpha}}{\{2\}^n} = Z_L\binom{\boldsymbol{\beta}}{\{2\}^n}. \tag{21}$$

For this theorem, we provide three different methods of proof.

Method 1—The generating functions. We let $G_{\boldsymbol{\alpha}}(x)$, $g_{\boldsymbol{\alpha}}(x)$ be the generating function of $Z_U\binom{\boldsymbol{\alpha}}{\{2\}^n}$, $Z_L\binom{\boldsymbol{\alpha}}{\{2\}^n}$, respectively, that is,

$$G_{\boldsymbol{\alpha}}(x) = \sum_{n=0}^{\infty} Z_U\binom{\boldsymbol{\alpha}}{\{2\}^n} x^{2n}, \quad \text{and} \quad g_{\boldsymbol{\alpha}}(x) = \sum_{n=0}^{\infty} Z_L\binom{\boldsymbol{\alpha}}{\{2\}^n} x^{2n}.$$

We begin from the generating function $G_{\boldsymbol{\alpha}}(x)$.

$$\begin{aligned} G_{\boldsymbol{\alpha}}(x) &= \sum_{1\le k_1<k_2<\cdots<k_r} \frac{\prod_{1\le j\le k_r}\left(1-\frac{x^2}{j^2}\right)^{-1}}{k_1^{\alpha_1}k_2^{\alpha_2}\cdots k_r^{\alpha_r}} \\ &= \frac{\pi x}{\sin(\pi x)} \sum_{1\le k_1<k_2<\cdots<k_r} \frac{\prod_{j>k_r}\left(1-\frac{x^2}{j^2}\right)}{k_1^{\alpha_1}k_2^{\alpha_2}\cdots k_r^{\alpha_r}} \\ &= \frac{\pi x}{\sin(\pi x)} \sum_{n=0}^{\infty} (-1)^n \zeta(\alpha_1,\alpha_2,\ldots,\alpha_r,\{2\}^n) x^{2n}. \end{aligned}$$

Since the dual of $\zeta(\boldsymbol{\alpha})$ is $\zeta(\boldsymbol{\beta})$, we have

$$\zeta(\boldsymbol{\alpha},\{2\}^n)^\sharp = \zeta(\{2\}^n,\boldsymbol{\beta}).$$

Therefore, the generating function $G_{\boldsymbol{\alpha}}(x)$ can be rewritten as

$$\begin{aligned} &\frac{\pi x}{\sin(\pi x)} \sum_{1\le \ell_1<\ell_2<\cdots<\ell_m} \frac{\prod_{1\le j<\ell_1}\left(1-\frac{x^2}{j^2}\right)}{\ell_1^{\beta_1}\ell_2^{\beta_2}\cdots\ell_m^{\beta_m}} \\ &= \sum_{1\le \ell_1<\ell_2<\cdots<\ell_m} \frac{\prod_{\ell_1\le j}\left(1-\frac{x^2}{j^2}\right)^{-1}}{\ell_1^{\beta_1}\ell_2^{\beta_2}\cdots\ell_m^{\beta_m}} = g_{\boldsymbol{\beta}}(x). \end{aligned}$$

The coefficients of x^{2n} of both generating functions give our identity.

Method 2—Yamamoto's integral. Since the duality of the Euler sums is represented by $u_i = 1 - t_i$ in its Drinfel'd iterated integral, the corresponding 2-poset Hasse diagram appears as a vertical reflection, with ∘ and • interchanged.

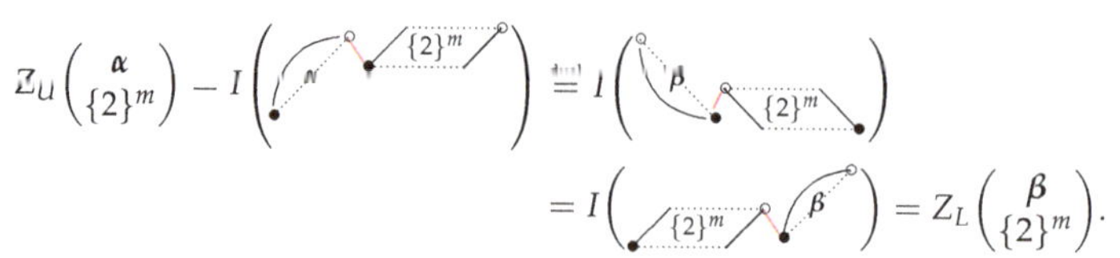

We explain it by an example with $Z_U\begin{pmatrix}3,3\\2,2\end{pmatrix}^{\#} = Z_L\begin{pmatrix}1,2,1,2\\2,2\end{pmatrix}$.

Method 3—Expressions by MZVs and MZSVs. We use Equations (13) and (11), we know that

$$Z_U\begin{pmatrix}\boldsymbol{\alpha}\\\{2\}^n\end{pmatrix} = \sum_{a+b=n}(-1)^a\zeta(\boldsymbol{\alpha},\{2\}^a)\zeta^\star(\{2\}^b),$$

$$Z_L\begin{pmatrix}\boldsymbol{\beta}\\\{2\}^n\end{pmatrix} = \sum_{a+b=n}(-1)^a\zeta(\{2\}^a,\boldsymbol{\beta})\zeta^\star(\{2\}^b).$$

Since $\zeta(\boldsymbol{\alpha})^\sharp = \zeta(\boldsymbol{\beta})$, this implies that $\zeta(\boldsymbol{\alpha},\{2\}^a)^\sharp = \zeta(\{2\}^a,\boldsymbol{\beta})$. Thus, we have

$$\begin{aligned} Z_U\begin{pmatrix}\boldsymbol{\alpha}\\\{2\}^n\end{pmatrix} &= \sum_{a+b}\zeta(\boldsymbol{\alpha},\{2\}^a)\zeta^\star(\{2\}^b)\\ &= \sum_{a+b}\zeta(\{2\}^a,\boldsymbol{\beta})\zeta^\star(\{2\}^b) = Z_L\begin{pmatrix}\boldsymbol{\beta}\\\{2\}^n\end{pmatrix}. \end{aligned}$$

Next, we proceed to prove the second equation of Theorem 2.
Using Equation (16), we know that

$$Z_B\begin{pmatrix}\boldsymbol{\alpha}\\\{2\}^m\end{pmatrix} = \sum_{a+b+c=m}(-1)^{a+b}\zeta(\{2\}^a,\boldsymbol{\alpha},\{2\}^b)\zeta^\star(\{2\}^c).$$

It is easy to see that $\zeta(\{2\}^a,\boldsymbol{\alpha},\{2\}^b)^\sharp = \zeta(\{2\}^b,\boldsymbol{\beta},\{2\}^a)$, we have

$$\begin{aligned} Z_B\begin{pmatrix}\boldsymbol{\alpha}\\\{2\}^n\end{pmatrix} &= \sum_{a+b+c=n}(-1)^{a+b}\zeta(\{2\}^a,\boldsymbol{\alpha},\{2\}^b)\zeta^\star(\{2\}^c)\\ &= \sum_{a+b+c=n}(-1)^{a+b}\zeta(\{2\}^b,\boldsymbol{\beta},\{2\}^a)\zeta^\star(\{2\}^c) = Z_B\begin{pmatrix}\boldsymbol{\beta}\\\{2\}^n\end{pmatrix}. \end{aligned}$$

Therefore, the function Z_B satisfies second equation. We complete the proof.

Nakasuji, Ohno (Theorem 4.4, [17]) use Schur multiple zeta functions to give a more general duality theorem. However, our particular duality forms are founded by the classical generating functions, or the new Yamamoto's integral.

Since $\zeta(k)^\sharp = \zeta(\{1\}^{k-2},2)$, for $k \geq 2$. Then, for any nonnegative integer n, we have

$$\begin{aligned} \zeta(2n+k) = Z_B\begin{pmatrix}k\\\{2\}^n\end{pmatrix} &= Z_B\begin{pmatrix}\{1\}^{k-2},2\\\{2\}^n\end{pmatrix}\\ &= \sum_{a+b+c=n}(-1)^{a+b}\zeta(\{2\}^a,\{1\}^{k-2},\{2\}^{b+1})\zeta^\star(\{2\}^c). \end{aligned}$$

Let $k=2$, we have the following weighted sum formula:

$$\zeta(2n+2) = \sum_{a+b=n}(-1)^b(b+1)\zeta(\{2\}^{b+1})\zeta^\star(\{2\}^a). \tag{22}$$

5. Theorem 3 and Some More Formulas

In this last section, we will start by providing the proof of Theorem 3, and then we will discuss some applications.

Proof of Theorem 3. Let

$$G(x)=\sum_{p=0}^{\infty}\zeta^{\star}(\{2\}^{p},\{1\}^{r},\{2\}^{q})x^{2p}$$

be the generating function of $\zeta^{\star}(\{2\}^{p},\{1\}^{r},\{2\}^{q})x^{2p}$. Thus,

$$\begin{aligned}G(x)&=\sum_{1\le k_1\le k_2\le\cdots\le k_{q+r}}\frac{\prod_{1\le j\le k_1}\left(1-\frac{x^2}{j^2}\right)^{-1}}{k_1k_2\cdots k_rk_{r+1}^2k_{r+2}^2\cdots k_{q+r}^2}\\&=\frac{\pi x}{\sin(\pi x)}\sum_{1\le k_1\le k_2\le\cdots\le k_{q+r}}\frac{\prod_{j>k_1}\left(1-\frac{x^2}{j^2}\right)}{k_1k_2\cdots k_rk_{r+1}^2k_{r+2}^2\cdots k_{q+r}^2}.\end{aligned}$$

We represent the above summation as

$$\zeta^{\star}(\{1\}^{r},\{2\}^{q})+\sum_{n=1}^{\infty}(-1)^{n}Z_L\binom{1,\{2\}^{n}}{\{1\}^{r-1},\{2\}^{q}}x^{2n}.$$

By convolution, we have

$$\begin{aligned}G(x)=&\sum_{n=0}^{\infty}\zeta^{\star}(\{2\}^{n})\zeta^{\star}(\{1\}^{r},\{2\}^{q})x^{2n}\\&+\sum_{p=1}^{\infty}\left(\sum_{\substack{m+n=p\\m\ge1}}(-1)^{m}\zeta^{\star}(\{2\}^{n})Z_L\binom{1,\{2\}^{m}}{\{1\}^{r-1},\{2\}^{q}}\right)x^{2p}.\end{aligned}$$

Comparing the coefficient of x^{2p}, for $p\ge1$, we have

$$\begin{aligned}\zeta^{\star}(\{2\}^{p},\{1\}^{r},\{2\}^{q})=&\,\zeta^{\star}(\{2\}^{p})\zeta^{\star}(\{1\}^{r},\{2\}^{q})\\&+\sum_{m+n=p-1}(-1)^{m+1}\zeta^{\star}(\{2\}^{n})Z_L\binom{1,\{2\}^{m+1}}{\{1\}^{r-1},\{2\}^{q}}.\end{aligned}\tag{23}$$

We use Equation (7) to the function Z_L, this gives

$$\begin{aligned}Z_L\binom{1,\{2\}^{m+1}}{\{1\}^{r-1},\{2\}^{q}}=&(-1)^{r-1}Z_L\binom{\{1\}^{r},\{2\}^{m+1}}{\{2\}^{q}}\\&+\sum_{a+b=r-2}(-1)^{a}\zeta(\{1\}^{a+1},\{2\}^{m+1})\zeta^{\star}(\{1\}^{b+1},\{2\}^{q}).\end{aligned}$$

It is clear that $\zeta(\{1\}^{a+1},\{2\}^{m+1})^{\sharp}=\zeta(\{2\}^{m},a+3)$, and we apply the dual theorem to transform

$$Z_L\binom{\{1\}^{r},\{2\}^{m+1}}{\{2\}^{q}}=Z_U\binom{\{2\}^{m},r+2}{\{2\}^{q}},$$

then we obtain

$$\begin{aligned}Z_L\binom{1,\{2\}^{m+1}}{\{1\}^{r-1},\{2\}^{q}}=&(-1)^{r-1}Z_U\binom{\{2\}^{m},r+2}{\{2\}^{q}}\\&+\sum_{a+b=r-2}(-1)^{a}\zeta(\{2\}^{m},a+3)\zeta^{\star}(\{1\}^{b+1},\{2\}^{q}).\end{aligned}$$

The summation in Equation (23) becomes

$$\sum_{m+n=p-1}(-1)^{m+r}\zeta^{\star}(\{2\}^n)Z_U\binom{\{2\}^m, r+2}{\{2\}^q}$$
$$+\sum_{m+n=p-1}\sum_{a+b=r-2}(-1)^{m+a+1}\zeta^{\star}(\{2\}^n)\zeta(\{2\}^m, a+3)\zeta^{\star}(\{1\}^{b+1},\{2\}^q).$$

The second summation of the above formula can be simplified by using Equation (9)

$$\sum_{m+n=p-1}(-1)^m\zeta^{\star}(\{2\}^n)\zeta(\{2\}^m, a+3)=\zeta^{\star}(a+3,\{2\}^{p-1}).$$

We will obtain

$$\sum_{a+b=r-2}(-1)^{a+1}\zeta^{\star}(a+3,\{2\}^{p-1})\zeta^{\star}(\{1\}^{b+1},\{2\}^q).$$

It remains to treat the summation

$$\sum_{m+n=p-1}(-1)^{m+r}\zeta^{\star}(\{2\}^n)Z_U\binom{\{2\}^m, r+2}{\{2\}^q}.$$

We apply Equation (19) with $\boldsymbol{\alpha}=(\{2\}^q)$, $\theta=r+2$, and $\boldsymbol{\beta}=(\{2\}^{p-1})$, then the above summation is equal to

$$(-1)^r\zeta^{\star}(\{2\}^q, r+2,\{2\}^{p-1}).$$

Therefore, Equation (23) becomes

$$\begin{aligned}\zeta^{\star}(\{2\}^p,\{1\}^r,\{2\}^q)&=\zeta^{\star}(\{2\}^p)\zeta^{\star}(\{1\}^r,\{2\}^q)+(-1)^r\zeta(\{2\}^q, r+2,\{2\}^{p-1})\\&\quad+\sum_{a+b=r-2}(-1)^{a+1}\zeta^{\star}(a+3,\{2\}^{p-1})\zeta^{\star}(\{1\}^{b+1},\{2\}^q)\\&=(-1)^r\zeta^{\star}(\{2\}^q, r+2,\{2\}^{p-1})\\&\quad+\sum_{a+b=r-1}(-1)^a\zeta^{\star}(a+2,\{2\}^{p-1})\zeta^{\star}(\{1\}^{b+1},\{2\}^q).\end{aligned}$$

This finishes our work. □

It is well-known that (ref. [18]) $\zeta^{\star}(1,\{2\}^q)=2\zeta(2q+1)$, and we leverage Zagier's formula (ref. [16]) to compute $\zeta^{\star}(\{2\}^q,3,\{2\}^{p-1})$:

$$\zeta^{\star}(\{2\}^q,3,\{2\}^{p-1})=-2\sum_{k=1}^{p+q}\left[\binom{2k}{2q}-\delta_{k,q}-\left(1-\frac{1}{2^{2k}}\right)\binom{2k}{2p-1}\right]\zeta^{\star}(\{2\}^{p+q-k})\zeta(2k+1).$$

By substituting $r=1$ in Equation (3), we obtain an evaluation of $\zeta^{\star}(\{2\}^p,1,\{2\}^q)$, for any positive integers p and q (Theorem 1.6, [13]):

$$\zeta^{\star}(\{2\}^p,1,\{2\}^q)=2\sum_{k=1}^{p+q}\left[\binom{2k}{2q}-\left(1-\frac{1}{2^{2k}}\right)\binom{2k}{2p-1}\right]\zeta^{\star}(\{2\}^{p+q-k})\zeta(2k+1).$$

On the other hand, if we apply $p=q=1$ in Equation (3), then

$$\sum_{a+b=r}(-1)^a(b+1)\zeta(a+2)\zeta(b+2)=\zeta^{\star}(2,\{1\}^r,2)+(-1)^r\zeta(r+2,2),$$

for any nonnegative integer r, by using the fact (ref. [5]) $\zeta^{\star}(\{1\}^{b+1},2)=(b+2)\zeta(b+3)$.

Author Contributions: Conceptualization, K.-W.C. and M.E.; methodology, K.-W.C. and M.E.; validation, K.-W.C.; data curation, Y.L.O.; writing—original draft preparation, K.-W.C. and M.E.; writing—review and editing, K.-W.C.; funding acquisition, K.-W.C. All authors have read and agreed to the published version of the manuscript.

Funding: The first author was funded by the Ministry of Science and Technology, Taiwan, R.O.C., under grant number MOST 111-2115-M-845-001, and also by the National Science and Technology Council, Taiwan, R.O.C., under grant NSTC 113-2115-M-845-001.

Data Availability Statement: Data are contained within the article.

Conflicts of Interest: The authors declare no conflicts of interest.

References

1. Hoffman, M.E. Multiple harmonic series. *Pac. J. Math.* **1992**, *152*, 275–290. [CrossRef]
2. Ohno, Y. Sum relations for multiple zeta values. *In Zeta Functions, Topology and Quantum Physics, Developments in Mathematics;* Aoki, T., Kanemitsu, S., Nakahara, M., Ohno, Y., Eds.; Springer: Boston, MA, USA, 2005; Volume 14, pp. 131–144.
3. Zagier, D. Values of zeta functions and their applications. In *First European Congress of Mathematics Paris;* Birkhäuser: Baesl, Switzerland, 1994; Volume II, pp. 497–512.
4. Chen, K.-W. Generalized harmonic numbers and Euler sums. *Int. J. Number Theory* **2017**, *13*, 513–528. [CrossRef]
5. Chen, K.-W.; Eie, M. On three general forms of multiple zeta(-star) values. *Expo. Math.* **2023**, *41*, 299–315. [CrossRef]
6. Chen, K.-W.; Chung, C.-L.; Eie, M. Sum formulas and duality theorems of multiple zeta values. *J. Number Theory* **2016**, *158*, 33–53. [CrossRef]
7. Yamamoto, S. Multiple zeta-star values and multiple integrals. *RIMS Kôkyr̂oku Bessatsu* **2017**, *B68*, 3–14.
8. Kaneko, M.; Yamamoto, S. A new integral-series identity of multiple zeta values and regularizations. *Sel. Math. New Ser.* **2018**, *24*, 2499–2521. [CrossRef]
9. Hirose, M.; Murahara, H.; Ono, M. On variants of symmetric multiple zeta-star values and the cyclic sum formula. *Ramanujan J.* **2021**, *56*, 467–489. [CrossRef]
10. Yamamoto, S. Integrals associated with 2-posets and applications to multiple zeta values. *RIMS Kôkyr̂oku Bessatsu* **2020**, *B83*, 27–46.
11. Nakasuji, M.; Phuksuwan, O.; Yamasaki, Y. On Schur multiple zeta functions: A combinatoric generalization of multiple zeta functions. *Adv. Math.* **2018**, *333*, 570–619. [CrossRef]
12. Nakasuji, M.; Takeda, W. Shuffle product formula of the Schur multiple zeta values of hook type. *arXiv* **2022**, arXiv:2202.01402v2.
13. Tasaka, K.; Yamamoto, S. On some multiple zeta-star values of one-two-three indices. *Inter. J. Number Theory* **2013**, *9*, 1171–1184. [CrossRef]
14. Xu, C. Evaluations of nonlinear Euler sums of weight ten. *Appl. Math. Comput.* **2019**, *346*, 594–611. [CrossRef]
15. Ohno, Y. A generalization of the duality and sum formulas on the multiple zeta values. *J. Number Theory* **1999**, *74*, 39–43. [CrossRef]
16. Zagier, D. Evaluation of the multiple zeta value $\zeta(2,\ldots,2,3,2,\ldots,2)$. *Ann. Math.* **2012**, *175*, 977–1000. [CrossRef]
17. Nakasuji, M.; Ohno, Y. Duality formula and its generalization for Schur multiple zeta functions. *arXiv* **2019**, arXiv:2109.14362v1.
18. Zlobin, S.A. Generating functions for the values of a multiple zeta function. *Vestnik Moskov. Univ. Ser. 1 Mat. Mekh.* **2005**, *2*, 55–59.

mathematics

MDPI

Article

On the Containment of the Unit Disc Image by Analytical Functions in the Lemniscate and Nephroid Domains

Saiful R. Mondal

Department of Mathematics and Statistics, College of Science, King Faisal University, P.O. Box 400, Al-Ahsa 31982, Saudi Arabia; smondal@kfu.edu.sa

Abstract: Suppose that $\mathcal{A}_1$ is a class of analytic functions $f : \mathfrak{D} = \{z \in \mathbb{C} : |z| < 1\} \to \mathbb{C}$ with normalization $f(0) = 1$. Consider two functions $\mathcal{P}_l(z) = \sqrt{1+z}$ and $\Phi_{N_e}(z) = 1 + z - z^3/3$, which map the boundary of $\mathfrak{D}$ to a cusp of lemniscate and to a twi-cusped kidney-shaped nephroid curve in the right half plane, respectively. In this article, we aim to construct functions $f \in \mathcal{A}_0$ for which (i) $f(\mathfrak{D}) \subset \mathcal{P}_l(\mathfrak{D}) \cap \Phi_{N_e}(\mathfrak{D})$ (ii) $f(\mathfrak{D}) \subset \mathcal{P}_l(\mathfrak{D})$, but $f(\mathfrak{D}) \not\subset \Phi_{N_e}(\mathfrak{D})$ (iii) $f(\mathfrak{D}) \subset \Phi_{N_e}(\mathfrak{D})$, but $f(\mathfrak{D}) \not\subset \mathcal{P}_l(\mathfrak{D})$. We validate the results graphically and analytically. To prove the results analytically, we use the concept of subordination. In this process, we establish the connection lemniscate (and nephroid) domain and functions, including $g_\alpha(z) := \sqrt{1+\alpha z^2}$, $|\alpha| \leq 1$, the polynomial $g_{\alpha,\beta}(z) := 1 + \alpha z + \beta z^3$, $\alpha, \beta \in \mathbb{R}$, as well as Lerch's transcendent function, Incomplete gamma function, Bessel and Modified Bessel functions, and confluent and generalized hypergeometric functions.

Keywords: subordination; lemniscate; nephroid curve; incomplete gamma function; Lerch transcendent; Bessel function

MSC: 33C10; 33C15; 33B20; 30C45

1. Introduction

Recently, research into the theory of geometric functions related to nephroid and leminscate domains has gained prominence [1–6]. Here, the leminscate domain refers to the image of $\mathfrak{D} = \{z : |z| < 1\}$ through the function $\mathcal{P}_l(z) = \sqrt{1+z}$, while the image of $\mathfrak{D}$ through the function $\Phi_{N_e}(z) = 1 + z - z^3/3$ is known as the nephroid domain. The mapping of boundary of unit disc $\mathfrak{D}$ by $\mathcal{P}_l$ and Φ_{N_e} is given in Figure 1.

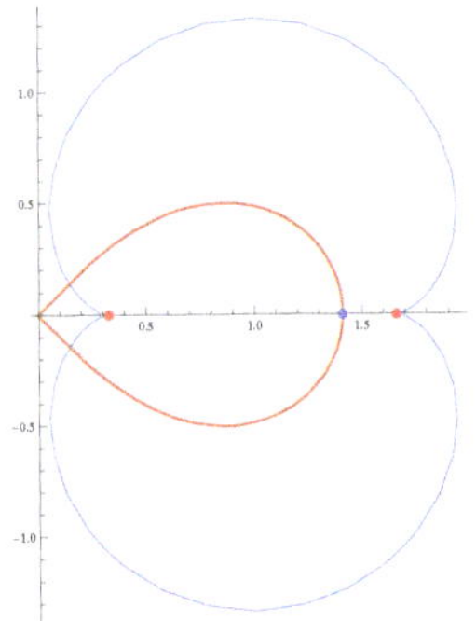

Figure 1. Mapping of the boundary of the unit disc using the lemniscate and nephroid curve.

Now, we recall a few basic concepts of the geometric function theory. The class of functions f defined on the open unit disk $\mathfrak{D} = \{z : |z| < 1\}$, and normalized by the conditions $f(0) = 0 = f'(0) - 1$, is denoted by $\mathcal{A}$. We say $f \in \mathcal{A}_1$ if $f(0) = 1$ is the normalized condition. Generally, $f \in \mathcal{A}$ possess power series

$$f(z) = z + \sum_{n=2}^{\infty} a_n z^n,$$

while $f \in \mathcal{A}_1$ has the power series

$$f(z) = 1 + \sum_{n=1}^{\infty} b_n z^n.$$

Definition 1 (Subordination). *For two functions f and g, which are analytic in $\mathfrak{D}$, we say that f is subordinate to g, and write $f \prec g$ in $\mathfrak{D}$, if there exists a Schwartz function $w(z)$, which is analytic in $\mathfrak{D}$ with $w(0) = 0$ and $|w(z)| < 1$ $(z \in \mathfrak{D})$, such that $f(z) = g(w(z))$.*

Subordination [7] is one of the important concepts of geometric function theory that is useful in studying the geometric properties of analytic functions. There are several important sub-classes of $\mathcal{A}$, namely the class of starlike and convex functions denoted by $\mathcal{S}^*$ and $\mathcal{C}$, respectively. The Cárath}eodory class $\mathcal{P}$ includes analytic functions p that satisfy $p(0) = 1$ and $\operatorname{Re} p(z) > 0$ in $\mathfrak{D}$. These sub-classes are related to each other. In analytical terms, $f \in \mathcal{S}^*$ if $zf'(z)/f(z) \in \mathcal{P}$, and $f \in \mathcal{C}$ if $1 + zf''(z)/f'(z) \in \mathcal{P}$.

If $1 + (zf''(z)/f'(z))$ is within the region bounded by the right half of the lemniscate of Bernoulli, denoted by $\{w : |w^2 - 1| = 1\}$, then the function $f \in \mathcal{A}$ is known as the lemniscate convex. This is equivalent to subordination $1 + (zf''(z)/f'(z)) \prec \sqrt{1+z}$. In an analogous way, if $zf'(z)/f(z) \prec \sqrt{1+z}$, then the function f is lemniscate starlike. Moreover, if $f'(z) \prec \sqrt{1+z}$, then the function $f \in \mathcal{A}$ is lemniscate Carathéodory. It is evident that the lemniscate Carathéodory function is univalent as it is a Carathéodory function. More details about the geometric properties associated with lemniscate can be seen in [5,8,9].

In this article, we are going to study the following functions or a combination of them. Details about the nature of the functions are provided in the associated section or subsection. The listed functions are as follows:

1. Section 2: The function $g_\alpha(z) := \sqrt{1 + \alpha z^2}, \quad |\alpha| \le 1$,
2. Section 3: The polynomial $g_{\alpha,\beta}(z) := 1 + \alpha z + \beta z^3$, $\alpha, \beta \in \mathbb{R}$,
3. Section 5: Lerch's transcendent function,
4. Section 6: Incomplete gamma function,
5. Section 7: Bessel and Modified Bessel functions.

Our aim is to derive the condition for which an analytic function or a polynomial, let us denote it as f, maps the unit disc to a domain such that following implication holds: (i) $f(\mathfrak{D}) \subset \mathcal{P}_l(\mathfrak{D}) \cap \Phi_{N_e}(\mathfrak{D})$ (ii) $f(\mathfrak{D}) \subset \mathcal{P}_l(\mathfrak{D})$, but $f(\mathfrak{D}) \not\subset \Phi_{N_e}(\mathfrak{D})$ (iii) $f(\mathfrak{D}) \subset \Phi_{N_e}(\mathfrak{D})$, but $f(\mathfrak{D}) \not\subset \mathcal{P}_l(\mathfrak{D})$.

2. Results Involving $g_\alpha(z) := \sqrt{1 + \alpha z^2}$

In this section, we consider the function $g_\alpha(z) := \sqrt{1 + \alpha z^2}$, $|\alpha| \le 1$. Using the definition of subordination, we derived conditions on the parameter α for which $g_\alpha(z) \prec \sqrt{1+z}$ and $g_\alpha(z) \prec \Phi_{N_e}(z)$. We also validate the result through graphical representation. Using g_α, we also construct a function that is lemniscate and nephroid starlike under the same condition as α.

Theorem 1. *The containment $g_\alpha(\mathfrak{D}) \subset \mathcal{P}_l(\mathfrak{D})$ holds for $|\alpha| \le 1$, while the containment $g_\alpha(\mathfrak{D}) \subset \Phi_{N_e}(\mathfrak{D})$ is true for $|\alpha| \le 8/9$.*

Proof. Consider the function $\omega(z) = \alpha z^2$. Then, $\omega(0) = 0$ and $|\omega(z)| < |\alpha| \leq 1$. Thus, by the definition of subordination,

$$\sqrt{1+\alpha z^2} = \sqrt{1+w(z)} \implies \sqrt{1+\alpha z^2} \prec \sqrt{1+z}. \tag{1}$$

Hence, $g_\alpha(\mathfrak{D}) \subset \mathcal{P}_l(\mathfrak{D})$ holds for $|\alpha| \leq 1$.

For the second part, first we note that Φ_{N_e} intercepts the x-axis, at $\Phi_{N_e}(-1) = 1/3$ and $\Phi_{N_e}(1) = 5/3$. Furthermore, g_α intercepts the x-axis, at $g_\alpha(\pm i) = \sqrt{1-\alpha}$ and at $g_\alpha(\pm 1) = \sqrt{1+\alpha}$. From Figure 1, it is evident that $g_\alpha(\mathfrak{D}) \subset \mathcal{P}_l(\mathfrak{D})$ implies $g_\alpha(\mathfrak{D}) \subset \Phi_{N_e}(\mathfrak{D})$, provided the left side intercept of g_α with the x-axis is above $1/3$.

In this aspect, $g_\alpha(z) \prec \Phi_{N_e}(z)$ implies the validity of the following inequalities:

$$\frac{1}{3} < g_1(\pm i) < 1 < g_1(\pm 1) < \frac{5}{3}, \quad \text{when} \quad 0 \leq \alpha \leq 1. \tag{2}$$

$$\frac{1}{3} < g_1(\pm 1) < 1 < g_1(\pm i) < \frac{5}{3}, \quad \text{when} \quad -1 \leq \alpha < 0. \tag{3}$$

In (2), the left side inequality holds if $\sqrt{1-\alpha} > 1/3$, which is equivalent to $0 < \alpha < 8/9$. On the other hand, the right hand side inequality holds if $\sqrt{1+\alpha} < 5/3$ is equivalent to $0 < \alpha < 16/9$. Thus, both inequalities hold when $0 < \alpha < 8/9$. Similarly, in (3), the left side inequality holds if $\sqrt{1+\alpha} > 1/3$, which is equivalent to $\alpha > -8/9$, and the right hand side inequality holds if $\sqrt{1-\alpha} < 5/3$ is equivalent to $\alpha > -16/9$. Thus, both inequalities hold when $0 > \alpha > -8/9$. Finally, we conclude that $\sqrt{1+\alpha z^2} \prec \Phi_{N_e}(z)$, equivalently $g_\alpha(\mathfrak{D}) \subset \Phi_{N_e}(\mathfrak{D})$ holds only when $|\alpha| < 8/9$. □

We can interpret the result in Theorem 1 from the following visualization (Figure 2) by considering different α, namely $\alpha = -35/36, -1/2, 1/2, 8/9, 35/36$.

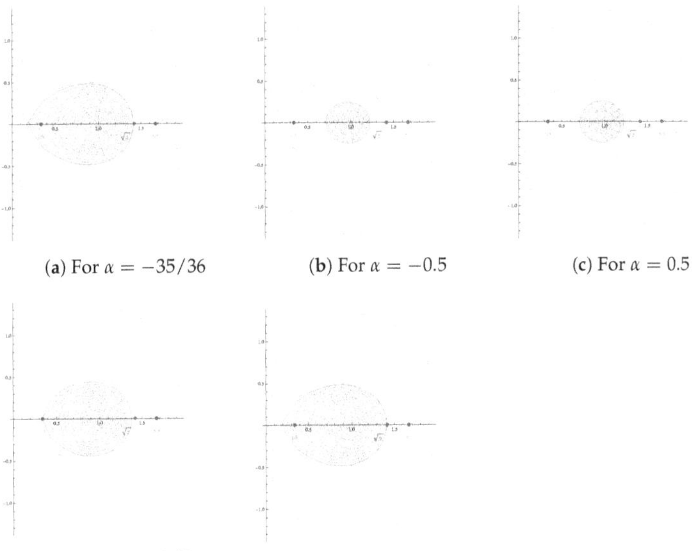

(**a**) For $\alpha = -35/36$ (**b**) For $\alpha = -0.5$ (**c**) For $\alpha = 0.5$ (**d**) For $\alpha = 8/9$ (**e**) For $\alpha = 35/36$

Figure 2. Graphical interpretation of Theorem 1 for different α.

Theorem 2. *For $\alpha, \beta \in \mathbb{R}$ and $z \in \mathfrak{D}$, the function*

$$\mathtt{F}_\alpha(z) := \frac{2}{e} \frac{z\, exp\left(\sqrt{1+\alpha z^2}\right)}{1+\sqrt{1+\alpha z^2}}, \tag{4}$$

is lemniscate starlike for $|\alpha| \leq 1$ and nephriod starlike when $|\alpha| < 8/9$.

Proof. To show lemniscate or nephroid starlikeness, our aim is to prove, respectively,

$$\frac{z\mathtt{F}'_\alpha(z)}{\mathtt{F}_\alpha(z)} \prec \sqrt{1+z} \quad \text{and} \quad \frac{z\mathtt{F}'_\alpha(z)}{\mathtt{F}_\alpha(z)} \prec 1+z-\tfrac{z^3}{3}.$$

It is clear that $\mathtt{F}_\alpha(0) = 0$, and a logarithmic differentiation of both sides in (4) yields

$$\begin{aligned} \frac{\mathtt{F}'_\alpha(z)}{\mathtt{F}_\alpha(z)} &= \frac{\alpha z}{\sqrt{\alpha z^2+1}} - \frac{\alpha z}{\sqrt{\alpha z^2+1}\left(\sqrt{\alpha z^2+1}+1\right)} + \frac{1}{z} \\ &= \frac{\alpha z}{\sqrt{\alpha z^2+1}+1} + \frac{1}{z} \\ &= \frac{\alpha z^2 + \sqrt{\alpha z^2+1}+1}{z\left(\sqrt{\alpha z^2+1}+1\right)} \\ &= \frac{\sqrt{\alpha z^2+1}}{z}. \end{aligned} \tag{5}$$

Further simplification of (5) leads

$$\mathtt{F}'_\alpha(z) = \frac{\sqrt{\alpha z^2+1}}{z}\mathtt{F}_\alpha(z) = \frac{2}{e}\frac{\exp\left(\sqrt{1+\alpha z^2}\right)\sqrt{\alpha z^2+1}}{1+\sqrt{1+\alpha z^2}}. \tag{6}$$

Thus, $\mathtt{F}'_\alpha(0) = 1$. It is also follows from (5) that

$$\frac{z\mathtt{F}'_\alpha(z)}{\mathtt{F}_\alpha(z)} = \sqrt{1+\alpha z^2} = \mathtt{g}_\alpha(z). \tag{7}$$

As Theorem 1 provides us $\mathtt{g}_\alpha(z) \prec \mathcal{P}_l(z)$ for $|\alpha| \leq 1$ and $\mathtt{g}_\alpha(z) \prec \Phi_{N_e}(z)$ for $|\alpha| \leq 8/9$, we have the conclusion from (7). □

3. Result Related to $g_{\alpha,\beta}(z) = 1 + \alpha z + 3\beta z^3$

For $\alpha, \beta \in \mathbb{R}$, define the function

$$\mathtt{G}_{\alpha,\beta}(z) = z e^{\alpha z + \beta z^3}. \tag{8}$$

Clearly, $\mathtt{G}_{\alpha,\beta}(0) = 0$ and $\mathtt{G}'_{\alpha,\beta}(0) = 1$. In our next result, we will find conditions for α and β for which the function $\mathtt{G}_{\alpha,\beta}(z)$ is lemniscate and nephroid starlike. First, we need the following result.

Theorem 3. *For $\alpha, \beta \in \mathbb{R}$, the function $g_{\alpha,\beta}(z) = 1 + \alpha z + 3\beta z^3 \prec \sqrt{1+z}$ for $|\alpha| + 3|\beta| \leq \sqrt{2}-1$ and $g_{\alpha,\beta}(z) \prec 1 + z - z^3/3$ when $|\alpha| \leq 1$ and $\beta = -\alpha^3/9$.*

Proof. Consider the function $w_1(z) = 2(\alpha z + 3\beta z^3) + (\alpha z + 3\beta z^3)^2$. Clearly, $w_1(0) = 0$ and

$$\sqrt{1+w_1(z)} = \sqrt{1+2(\alpha z+3\beta z^3)+(\alpha z+3\beta z^3)^2} = 1+\alpha z+3\beta z^3.$$

Now, for $|z| < 1$ and $|\alpha| + 3|\beta| \leq \sqrt{2} - 1$, it follows

$$|w_1(z)| < 2(|\alpha| + 3|\beta|) + (|\alpha| + 3|\beta|)^2 = (1 + |\alpha| + 3|\beta|)^2 - 1 \leq 1.$$

From the definition of subordination, we can conclude that $1 + \alpha z + 3\beta z^3 \prec \sqrt{1+z}$.

In similar way, the second part of the result follows if we consider $w_2(z) = \alpha z$. Clearly, $w_2(0) = 0$ and $|w_2(z)| < |\alpha| \leq 1$. Now, by taking $\beta = -\alpha^3/9$, we have

$$1 + w_2(z) - \frac{w_2^3(z)}{3} = 1 + \alpha z - \frac{\alpha^3}{3} z^3 = 1 + \alpha z + \beta z^3.$$

This provides the required subordination. □

A logarithmic differentiation of (8) yields

$$\frac{z\mathtt{G}'_{\alpha,\beta}(z)}{\mathtt{G}_{\alpha,\beta}(z)} = g_{\alpha,\beta}(z).$$

Therefore, Theorem 3 immediately leads to the following conclusion.

Theorem 4. *For $\alpha, \beta \in \mathbb{R}$, and $z \in \mathfrak{D}$, the function $\mathtt{G}_{\alpha,\beta}(z)$ is lemniscate starlike for $|\alpha| + 3|\beta| \leq \sqrt{2} - 1$ and nephroid starlike when $|\alpha| \leq 1$ and $\beta = -\alpha^3/9$.*

4. Results Related to Taylor Series of an Analytic Functions and It's Partial Sum

Consider a function $\mathfrak{A} : \mathbb{N} \times [1/2, \infty)$, such that

$$\sum_{k=1}^{\infty} (k\beta + 1)|\mathfrak{A}(k, \beta)|$$

is convergent for $\beta \geq 1/2$, and also the function

$$f_\beta(z) = 1 + \sum_{k=1}^{\infty} \mathfrak{A}(k, \beta) z^k \in \mathcal{A}_1. \tag{9}$$

We denote the n-th partial sum of the series f_β as $S_n(f_\beta, z)$.

For our next result, we need following

Lemma 1 ([6], Theorem 3.2). *Suppose that the function $p(z) \in \mathcal{A}_1$ satisfies the subordination $p(z) + \beta z p'(z) \prec 1 + z$ for $\beta > 0$. Then, $p(z) \prec \Phi_{N_e}(z)$ whenever $\beta \geq 1/2$, and this estimate on β is sharp.*

Theorem 5. *For $\beta \geq 1/2$ and $z \in \mathfrak{D}$, the partial sum $S_n(f_\beta, z) \prec 1 + z - z^3/3$ provided*

$$\sum_{k=1}^{n} (k\beta + 1)|\mathfrak{A}(k, \beta)| \leq 1. \tag{10}$$

In general, the function $f_\beta(z) = \lim_{n \to \infty} S_n(f_\beta, z) \prec 1 + z - z^3/3$ provided

$$\sum_{k=1}^{\infty} (k\beta + 1)|\mathfrak{A}(k, \beta)| \leq 1. \tag{11}$$

Proof. Denote $p_1(z) = S_n(f_\beta, z)$. Then, a calculation yields

$$p_1(z) + \beta z p_1'(z) = 1 + \sum_{k=1}^{n} (k\beta + 1) \mathfrak{A}(k, \beta) z^k.$$

Now, consider the Schwarz function

$$w(z) = \sum_{k=1}^{n} (k\beta + 1)\mathfrak{A}(k, \beta) z^k.$$

Clearly, $w(0) = 0$. As $|z| < 1$, the hypothesis (10) implies

$$|w(z)| \leq \sum_{k=1}^{n} (k\beta + 1)|\mathfrak{A}(k, \beta)||z|^k < \sum_{k=1}^{n} (k\beta + 1)|\mathfrak{A}(k, \beta)| \leq 1.$$

Finally, $p_1(z) + \beta z p_1'(z) = 1 + w(z)$ yields $p_1(z) + \beta z p_1'(z) \prec 1 + z$. The final conclusion follows from Lemma 1.

Similarly, the general part holds by considering the Schwarz function as

$$w(z) = \sum_{k=1}^{\infty} (k\beta + 1)\mathfrak{A}(k, \beta) z^k.$$

We omit the details proof for this part. □

Remark 1. *Instead of the partial sum $S_n(f_\beta, z)$, the result is still holds if we consider the n th degree polynomial defined by $P_n(z) := 1 + \sum_{k=1}^{n} \mathfrak{A}(k, \beta) z^k$.*

Now, judicious choice of $\mathfrak{A}(k, \beta)$ in Theorem 5 leads to several interesting examples. Because of the independent significance of each example, we present them as a theorem.

Theorem 6. *For $\beta \geq 1/2$ and $z \in \mathfrak{D}$, the polynomials $\mathfrak{F}_\beta(z) = 1 \pm z/(1 + \beta) \prec \Phi_{N_e}(z)$.*

Proof. In virtue of Theorem 5 and Remark 1, we have $\mathfrak{A}(k, \beta) = \pm\frac{1}{k\beta+1}$, $n = 1$ and, hence, $k = 1$. Thus, $P_1(z) = \mathfrak{F}_\beta(z)$. Clearly, $(k\beta + 1)|\mathfrak{A}(k, \beta)| = 1$. Thus, the result follows from Theorem 5. □

Remark 2. *The function $\mathfrak{F}_{1/2}(z)$ is one of the best fitting subordinated functions of $\Phi_{N_e}(z)$, as is evident from the Figure 3.*

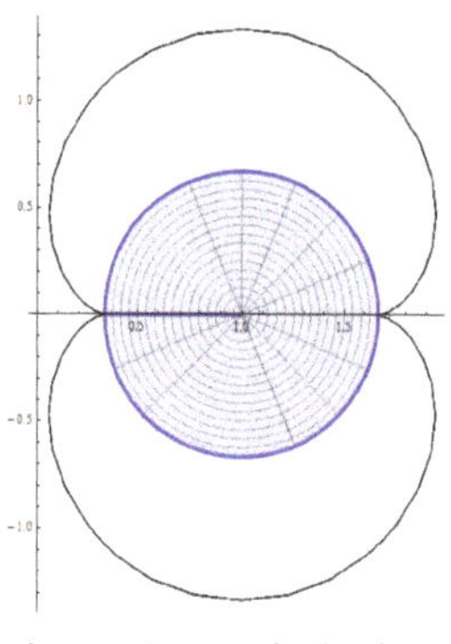

Figure 3. Image of $\mathfrak{D}$ by the polynomial $\mathfrak{F}_{1/2}(z)$.

5. Results Related to Lerch's Transcendent Functions

Next, we consider the function

$$\varpi_n(z, r, a) := \sum_{k=0}^{n} \frac{a^r z^k}{(k + a)^r}, \quad n \in \mathbb{N} \quad \text{and} \quad r \in \mathbb{R}. \tag{12}$$

Here, $a \neq 0, -1, -2, -3, \ldots, -n$ when $r > 0$ and a is any real number when $r \leq 0$.

For $n \to \infty$, the function $\lim_{n\to\infty} \varpi_n(z,r,a) = a^r\Phi(z,r,a)$ which is well known Lerch's transcendent. The Lerch's transcendent $\Phi(z,r,a)$ is given by its power series as

$$\Phi(z,r,a) = \sum_{k=0}^{\infty} \frac{z^k}{(k+a)^r}, \tag{13}$$

which is convergent for $a \notin -\mathbb{N}$ when $z \in \mathfrak{D}$. For this study, we consider $r > -1$ and $a > -1$. Our aim is to find the answer to the following problem.

Problem 1. *Find the triplet (r,a,n), such that $\varpi_n(z,r,a)$ and $\Phi(z,r,a)$ are subordinate by $\mathcal{P}_l(z)$ and $\Phi_{N_e}(z)$.*

To answer Problem 1, we need to further discuss $\Phi(z,r,a)$. The Lerch's transcendent generalized various special functions, namely

1. The Hurwitz Zeta function: The function is defined when $z = 1$ and is represented as

$$\zeta(r,a) = \Phi(1,r,a) = \sum_{k=0}^{\infty} \frac{1}{(k+a)^s}. \tag{14}$$

2. Poly-logarithm function: The function is defined as

$$Li_r(z) = z\Phi(z,r,1) = \sum_{k=1}^{\infty} \frac{z^k}{k^s}. \tag{15}$$

For more details about this function, see [10].

Theorem 7. *For $r > -1$, $a > -1$, and $z \in \mathfrak{D}$, the function $\varpi_n(z,r,a) \prec \sqrt{1+z}$ provides*

$$a^r\left(\zeta(r,1+a) - \zeta(r,1+a+n)\right) < \sqrt{2} - 1. \tag{16}$$

Proof. Define

$$W_n(z) := 2\sum_{k=1}^{n} \frac{a^r z^k}{(k+a)^r} + \left(\sum_{k=1}^{n} \frac{a^r z^k}{(k+a)^r}\right)^2. \tag{17}$$

Clearly, $W_n(0) = 0$. Now, to find the condition for which $|W_n(z)| < 1$, we rearrange the terms $\zeta(r,a)$, and it follows from (14) that

$$\begin{aligned}
\sum_{k=1}^{n} \frac{a^r}{(k+a)^r} &= \sum_{k=0}^{\infty} \frac{a^r}{(k+1+a)^r} - \sum_{k=n+1}^{\infty} \frac{a^r}{(k+a)^r} \\
&= a^r\zeta(r,1+a) - a^r \sum_{k=0}^{\infty} \frac{1}{(k+n+1+a)^r} \\
&= a^r\left(\zeta(r,1+a) - \zeta(r,1+a+n)\right).
\end{aligned}$$

Now, for $|z| < 1$, the hypothesis in (16) yields

$$\begin{aligned}
|W_n(z)| &< 2\sum_{k=1}^{n} \frac{a^r}{(k+a)^r} + \left(\sum_{k=1}^{n} \frac{a^r}{(k+a)^r}\right)^2, \\
&= 2a^r\left(\zeta(r,1+a) - \zeta(r,1+a+n)\right) + a^{2r}\left(\zeta(r,1+a) - \zeta(r,1+a+n)\right)^2 \\
&= \left(1 + a^r\zeta(r,1+a) - a^r\zeta(r,1+a+n)\right)^2 - 1 < 1.
\end{aligned}$$

The result follows from the definition of subordination. □

A natural question arises about the existence of triplet (r, a, n), for which the hypothesis (16) of Theorem 7 is true. We investigate numerically two possible cases to explain that such triplets exist.

- **Fixed r and n**: In the following table, we present a_0, such that the inequality (16) holds for fixed n, r. Here, a_0 is the solution to the equation

$$a^r(\zeta(r, 1+a) - \zeta(r, 1+a+n)) = \sqrt{2} - 1.$$

Denote, $\mathrm{H}(a) := a^r(\zeta(r, 1+a) - \zeta(r, 1+a+n)) - \sqrt{2} + 1$. Then,

$$\begin{aligned} H'(a) &= -ra^r\zeta(r+1, 1+a) + ra^r\zeta(r+1, 1+a+n) \\ &= -ra^r \sum_{k=0}^{\infty} \frac{1}{(k+1+a)^{r+1}} + ra^r \sum_{k=0}^{\infty} \frac{1}{(k+1+a+n)^{r+1}} \\ &= ra^r \sum_{k=0}^{\infty} \frac{(k+1+a)^{r+1} - (k+1+a+n)^{r+1}}{(k+1+a+n)^{r+1}(k+1+a)^{r+1}} < 0. \end{aligned}$$

Thus, $\mathrm{H}(a)$ is a decreasing function of a, and hence the inequality (16) holds for $a \geq a_0$. Table 1 lists a few values for a_0 with fixed r and n.

Table 1. The values for a_0 with fixed r and n.

	1/2	**3/2**	**2**	**5/2**	**3**
1	0.207107	1.25057	1.80579	2.3658	2.92823
2	0.0617472	0.733443	1.13638	1.55064	1.97081
3	0.033622	0.607962	0.980932	1.36935	1.76586
4	0.0224263	0.549594	0.911624	1.29195	1.68176
5	0.0165764	0.515237	0.872399	1.24991	1.63784
6	0.0130345	0.492324	0.847168	1.2239	1.61168
7	0.0106812	0.475811	0.82958	1.20642	1.5947
8	0.00901404	0.463262	0.816619	1.19397	1.58302
9	0.00777637	0.453352	0.806673	1.18471	1.5746
10	0.00682406	0.445295	0.798799	1.1776	1.56834

- **Fixed r and a**: In this part, we fix r and a and test the validity of inequality (16) by finding the numerical values of $a^r(\zeta(r, 1+a) - \zeta(r, 1+a+n))$ for $n = 1, 2, 3, 4, 5$. If the values is less than $\sqrt{2} - 1 = 0.414214$, we have the triplet (r, a, n).
  The standout values are bigger than $\sqrt{2} - 1 = 0.414214$ and the combination of (r, a, n) is not of interest to us. The trend for higher n and a can be easily observed from the data in Table 2.

From Table 2, one can observe that the number of standout values reduces when r increases. Now, we test the inequality (16) when $r = 3$, $a = 1, 2, 3, 4, 5$, and n is large, for example, $n = 100, 500, 1000, 2000, 5000, 10000, 100000$, and the outcome is presented in Table 3. It is clear from Table 3 that, for a large n, the value of $a^r(\zeta(r, 1+a) - \zeta(r, 1+a+n))$ may converge to a specific real number. This observation is conducted for each row individually. This raises questions regarding how the exact values should be formulated when $n \to \infty$. The answer can be found in the following result.

Table 2. Validation of inequality (16) for fixed $r = 0.5, 2, 2.5, 3$.

a/n	1	2	3	4	5
r = 0.5					
0.1	0.301511	~~0.519729~~	~~0.699335~~	~~0.855508~~	~~0.995536~~
0.2	0.408248	~~0.70976~~	~~0.95976~~	~~1.17798~~	~~1.37409~~
0.33	~~0.5~~	~~0.877964~~	~~1.19419~~	~~1.47154~~	~~1.72154~~
r = 2					
0.1	0.00826446	0.010532	0.0115726	0.0121675	0.012552
0.2	0.0277778	0.0360422	0.0399485	0.0422161	0.0436954
0.33	0.0615637	0.081623	0.0914436	0.097252	0.101085
0.5	0.111111	0.151111	0.171519	0.183865	0.192129
0.75	0.183673	0.258054	0.298054	0.322984	0.339998
1	0.25	0.361111	~~0.423611~~	~~0.463611~~	~~0.491389~~
r = 2.5					
0.1	0.00249183	0.00298665	0.00317355	0.00326645	0.00332029
0.2	0.0113402	0.0138321	0.0148086	0.0153034	0.0155936
0.33	0.0306659	0.038215	0.0413065	0.04291	0.0438638
0.5	0.06415	0.0820386	0.0897521	0.0938674	0.0963592
0.75	0.120243	0.159086	0.176975	0.186881	0.193026
1	0.176777	0.240927	0.272177	0.290065	0.301405
1.25	0.230048	0.32179	0.368704	0.396365	~~0.414254~~
1.5	0.278855	0.399097	~~0.463247~~	~~0.502091~~	~~0.527674~~
1.75	0.323045	~~0.471816~~	~~0.554203~~	~~0.605304~~	~~0.639528~~
r = 3					
0.1	0.000751315	0.000859295	0.000892862	0.000907371	0.00091491
0.2	0.00462963	0.00538094	0.00562509	0.00573306	0.00578996
0.33	0.0152752	0.0181162	0.0190894	0.0195321	0.0197694
0.5	0.037037	0.045037	0.0479525	0.0493242	0.0500755
0.75	0.0787172	0.0990027	0.107003	0.110939	0.113158
1	0.125	0.162037	0.177662	0.185662	0.190292
1.25	0.171468	0.228364	0.253806	0.267304	0.275304
1.5	0.216	0.294717	0.331754	0.35204	0.364329
1.75	0.257701	0.359331	0.409338	~~0.437529~~	~~0.454955~~
2	0.296296	~~0.421296~~	~~0.485296~~	~~0.522333~~	~~0.545657~~

Table 3. Validation of inequality (16) for fixed $r = 3$ and higher values of n.

a/n	100	500	1000	10,000	15,000	20,000
0.1	0.000930679	0.000930727	0.000930728	0.00093073	0.00093073	0.00093073
0.2	0.00591175	0.00591213	0.00591214	0.0059121	0.0059121	0.0059121
0.33	0.0202925	0.0202942	0.0202943	0.0202943	0.0202943	0.0202943
0.5	0.0517937	0.0517995	0.0517997	0.0517998	0.0517998	0.0517998
0.75	0.118504	0.118523	0.118524	0.118524	0.118524	0.118524
1	0.202008	0.202055	0.202056	0.202057	0.202057	0.202057
1.5	0.398432	0.398588	0.398593	0.398594	0.398594	0.398594
1.52	0.406829	0.40699	0.406996	0.406997	0.406997	0.406997
1.53	0.411039	0.411204	0.411209	0.411211	0.411211	0.411211

Theorem 8. *The Lerch's transcendent* $a^r\Phi(z,r,a) \prec \sqrt{1+z}$ *when* $a^r\zeta(r,1+a) < \sqrt{2}-1$.

Theorem 8 can be obtained by considering

$$W(z) = 2\sum_{k=1}^{\infty} \frac{a^r z^k}{(k+a)^r} + \left(\sum_{k=1}^{\infty} \frac{a^r z^k}{(k+a)^r}\right)^2.$$

Next, we will find the pair (r,a), such that the inequality $a^r\zeta(r,1+a) < \sqrt{2}-1$ holds well. We discuss this part numerically with a fixed a and find a range of r. It is to be noted here that $\zeta(r,1+a)$ is not defined for $r=1$. So, we will consider the case for $r \in (1,\infty)$.

- For $r > 1$, the inequality holds for $r > r_{0.5}$, where $r_{0.5} = 1.7085$ is the root of $(0.5)^r\zeta(r,1.5) = \sqrt{2}-1$ in $(1,\infty)$. The range of r with fixed $a = 0.5$ is presented in Figure 4.
- Finally, for any $a > 0$, there exists r_a, the root of $a^r\zeta(r,1+a) = \sqrt{2}-1$ in $(1,\infty)$ such that $a^r\zeta(r,1+a) < \sqrt{2}-1$ for $r > r_a$. We consider a few arbitrary values of a and determine r_a. The outcome is presented in Table 4. It can be observed that r_a is increasing along with a.

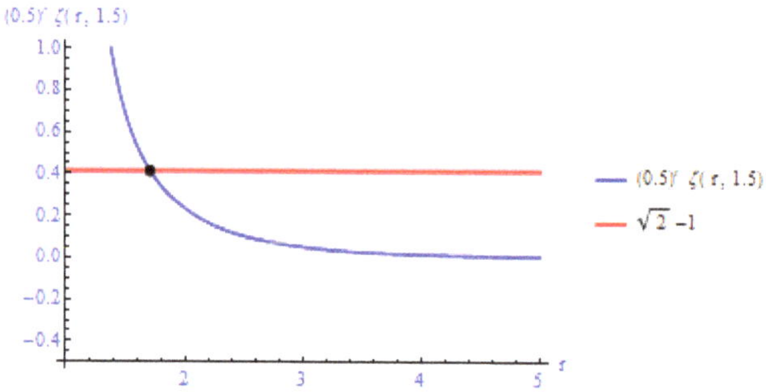

Figure 4. Range of r with fixed $a = 0.5$.

Table 4. Range of r for arbitrary a.

a	r_a	a	r_a
0.001	1.00024	0.01	1.02208
0.05	1.09511	0.09	1.15867
0.1	1.17379	0.2	1.31624
0.33	1.48966	0.5	1.7085
0.75	2.0236	1	2.33521
1.25	2.64515	1.5	2.95417
1.75	3.26265	2	3.57076
5	7.25935	15	19.5408
20	25.6808	30	37.9605
40	50.2401	50	62.5197
100	123.917	500	615.096

Theorem 9. *Suppose that* $\beta \geq 1/2$. *Then, the polynomial* $\beta^r\varpi_n(z,r,\beta) \prec \Phi_{N_e}(z)$ *provided*

$$\beta^{1-r}\left(\zeta\left(r-1,\frac{\beta+1}{\beta}\right) - \zeta\left(r-1,n+\frac{\beta+1}{\beta}\right)\right) < 1. \tag{18}$$

In general, $\beta^r\Phi(z,r,\beta) \prec \Phi_{N_e}(z)$ *when*

$$\beta^{1-r}\zeta\left(r-1,\frac{\beta+1}{\beta}\right) < 1. \tag{19}$$

Next, we need to find out the existence of (β, r, n) and (β, r) for which the inequalities (18) and (19) hold well. We answer this problem numerically.

- **Case I:** $(1/2, 2, n)$: Taking $\beta = 1/2$ and $r = 2$, we will try to find the range of n for which the inequality (18) holds. The numerical values for different n are tabulated in Table 5.
  It is clear that for $n \geq 762$, the inequality (18) failed.
- **Case II:** $(1/2, 3)$: In this case, we consider $\beta = 1/2$ and $r = 3$ to validate the inequality (18). The numerical values for different n are tabulated in Table 6.
  It is clear from Table 6 that the value is increasing with n, but if we take $n \to \infty$, we have

$$\sum_{k=1}^{\infty} \frac{a^r(k\beta + 1)}{(k+a)^r} = \frac{1}{8}\sum_{k=1}^{\infty} \frac{(k\frac{1}{2} + 1)}{(k + \frac{1}{2})^3} = \frac{1}{32}\Big(21\zeta(3) + \pi^2 - 32\Big) = 0.097275. \tag{20}$$

Thus, in this case, inequality (18) holds for all n and inequality (19) is also true. This case implies

$$\frac{1}{8}\,\Phi\Big(z, 3, \tfrac{1}{2}\Big) \prec \Phi_{N_e}(z).$$

Table 5. Validity of inequality (18) for $\beta = 1/2 = a$ and $r = 2$.

1	0.166667	2	0.246667	3	0.297687	4	0.334724
5	0.36365	6	0.387318	10	0.45346	20	0.542364
40	0.630341	100	0.745748	761	0.999961	762	1.00013

Table 6. Validity of inequality (19) for $\beta = 1/2 = a$ and $r = 3$.

1	0.0555556	2	0.0715556	3	0.0788442	4	0.0829594
5	0.085589	6	0.0874097	7	0.088743	8	0.0897607
9	0.0905626	10	0.0912105	11	0.0912105	12	0.0921927
13	0.0925737	14	0.0929018	15	0.0931871	16	0.0934375
17	0.0936591	18	0.0938565	19	0.0940335	20	0.0941931

6. Results Involving Incomplete Gamma Function

Our next example involves incomplete gamma function. The Euler's integral form of gamma function is defined as

$$\Gamma(a) = \int_0^\infty e^{-t}t^{a-1}dt. \tag{21}$$

The incomplete gamma function arises by decomposing the integration (21) into two parts as

$$\gamma(a,z) = \int_0^z e^{-t}t^{a-1}dt \tag{22}$$

$$\Gamma(a,z) = \int_z^\infty e^{-t}t^{a-1}dt. \tag{23}$$

The function $\gamma(a,z)$ is well-known as a lower incomplete gamma function and $\Gamma(a,z)$ is an upper incomplete function. Next, define the function $\Gamma(a, z_1, z_2) = \Gamma(a, z_1) - \Gamma(a, z_2)$. Then,

$$\Gamma(a, z_1, z_2) = \int_{z_1}^{z_2} e^{-t}t^{a-1}dt. \tag{24}$$

Theorem 10. *For $\beta \geq 1/2$, the function*

$$\frac{1}{2} + \frac{z^{-1/\beta}}{2\beta}\Gamma\left(\frac{1}{\beta}, 0, z\right) \prec \Phi_{N_e}(z). \tag{25}$$

Proof. From (24), it follows

$$\begin{aligned}
\frac{z^{-1/\beta}}{2\beta}\Gamma\left(\frac{1}{\beta}, 0, z\right) &= \frac{z^{-1/\beta}}{2\beta}\int_0^z e^{-t}t^{\frac{1}{\beta}-1}dt \\
&= \frac{z^{-1/\beta}}{2\beta}\sum_{k=0}^{\infty}\frac{(-1)^k}{k!}\int_0^z t^{k+\frac{1}{\beta}-1}dt \\
&= \frac{z^{-1/\beta}}{2\beta}\sum_{k=0}^{\infty}\frac{(-1)^k}{k!}\frac{z^{k+\frac{1}{\beta}}}{k+\frac{1}{\beta}} \\
&= \frac{1}{2}\sum_{k=0}^{\infty}\frac{(-1)^k}{k!}\frac{z^k}{k\beta+1}.
\end{aligned}$$

Thus,

$$\frac{1}{2} + \frac{z^{-1/\beta}}{2\beta}\Gamma\left(\frac{1}{\beta}, 0, z\right) = 1 + \frac{1}{2}\sum_{k=1}^{\infty}\frac{(-1)^k}{k!}\frac{z^k}{k\beta+1}.$$

Now,

$$\frac{1}{2} + \sum_{k=1}^{\infty}\frac{k\beta+1}{k!}\frac{1}{k\beta+1} = \frac{1}{2}\sum_{k=1}^{\infty}\frac{1}{k!} = \frac{e-1}{2} = 0.859141 < 1.$$

Finally, the result follows from Theorem 5. □

The result stated in Theorem 10 is visible in Figure 5 for $\beta = 1/2$ and $\beta = 1$.

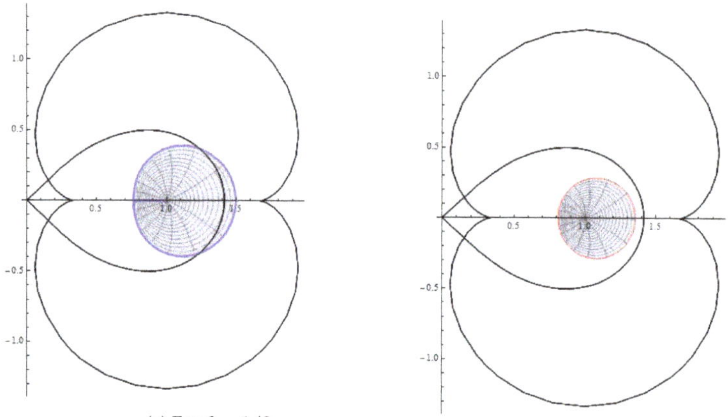

(**a**) For $\beta = 1/2$

(**b**) For $\beta = 1$

Figure 5. Graphical interpretation of Theorem 10 for different $\beta = 1/2$ and $\beta = 1$.

7. Results Involving Bessel and Modified-Bessel Function

Next, we consider a function involving well-known Bessel and modified-Bessel functions, which have series form

$$J_v(z) = \frac{z^v}{2^v}\sum_{n=0}^{\infty}\frac{(-1)^n z^{2n}}{4^n n!\Gamma(n+v+1)} \tag{26}$$

$$I_v(z) = \frac{z^v}{2^v}\sum_{n=0}^{\infty}\frac{z^{2n}}{4^n n!\Gamma(n+v+1)}. \tag{27}$$

For further use, we recall here the notation $(x)_n$, the well known Pochhammer symbol, defined as

$$(x)_n = x(x+1)\dots(x+n-1) = \frac{\Gamma(x+n)}{\Gamma(x)}.$$

Theorem 11. *Suppose that $\beta \geq 1/2$ and $\alpha > 0$. Then, the functions*

$$\mathcal{I}_{\alpha,\beta}(z) = \frac{1}{2} + \frac{1}{2}\Gamma(\alpha+\beta)z^{\frac{1-\alpha-\beta}{2}} I_{\alpha+\beta-1}(2\sqrt{z}) \prec \Phi_{N_e}(z), \tag{28}$$

$$\mathcal{J}_{\alpha,\beta}(z) = \frac{1}{2} + \frac{1}{2}\Gamma(\alpha+\beta)z^{\frac{1-\alpha-\beta}{2}} J_{\alpha+\beta-1}(2\sqrt{z}) \prec \Phi_{N_e}(z), \tag{29}$$

when

$$\beta\Gamma(\alpha+\beta)I_{\alpha+\beta}(2) + {}_0F_1(\alpha+\beta;1) < 3. \tag{30}$$

In particular, for $\beta = 1/2$, the result holds for $\alpha > \alpha_0(1/2)$. Here, $\alpha_0(1/2) = 0.532446$ is the solution of

$$\Gamma(\alpha+\tfrac{1}{2})I_{\alpha+\frac{1}{2}}(2) + 2{}_0F_1\left(\alpha+\tfrac{1}{2},1\right) = 6. \tag{31}$$

Proof. From the series (27), it follows that

$$\begin{aligned}
\mathcal{I}_{\alpha,\beta}(z) &= \frac{1}{2} + \frac{1}{2}\Gamma(\alpha+\beta)z^{\frac{1-\alpha-\beta}{2}} I_{\alpha+\beta-1}(2\sqrt{z}) \\
&= \frac{1}{2} + \frac{1}{2}\Gamma(\alpha+\beta)\sum_{n=0}^{\infty}\frac{z^n}{n!\Gamma(n+\alpha+\beta)} \\
&= 1 + \sum_{n=1}^{\infty}\frac{z^n}{2n!(\alpha+\beta)_n}.
\end{aligned}$$

Similarly, from the series (26), we have

$$\mathcal{J}_{\alpha,\beta}(z) = 1 + \frac{1}{2}\sum_{n=1}^{\infty}\frac{(-1)^n z^n}{n!(\alpha+\beta)_n}.$$

Now, define

$$\mathfrak{h}(\alpha,\beta) := \frac{1}{2}\sum_{n=1}^{\infty}\frac{\beta n+1}{n!(\alpha+\beta)_n}.$$

It is easy to verify that for any fixed $\beta \geq 1/2$, the function $\mathfrak{h}(\alpha,\beta)$ is a decreasing function of α. Our aim is to find the range of α for which $\mathfrak{h}(\alpha,\beta) < 1$ for all $\beta \geq 1/2$.

A careful re-arrangement of terms of $\mathfrak{h}(\alpha,\beta)$ along with (27) leads to

$$\begin{aligned}\mathfrak{h}(\alpha,\beta) &= \frac{\beta}{2}\sum_{n=1}^{\infty}\frac{n}{n!(\alpha+\beta)_n}+\frac{1}{2}\sum_{n=1}^{\infty}\frac{1}{n!(\alpha+\beta)_n}\\ &= \frac{\beta}{2}\sum_{n=1}^{\infty}\frac{\Gamma(\alpha+\beta)}{(n-1)!\Gamma(n+\alpha+\beta)}+\frac{1}{2}\sum_{n=1}^{\infty}\frac{1}{n!(\alpha+\beta)_n}\\ &= \frac{\beta\Gamma(\alpha+\beta)}{2}\sum_{n=0}^{\infty}\frac{1}{n!\Gamma(n+1+\alpha+\beta)}+\frac{1}{2}\Big({}_0F_1(\alpha+\beta;1)-1\Big)\\ &= \frac{1}{2}\Big(\beta\Gamma(\alpha+\beta)I_{\alpha+\beta}(2)+{}_0F_1(\alpha+\beta;1)-1\Big).\end{aligned}$$

Thus, $\mathfrak{h}(\alpha,\beta)<1$ is equivalent to

$$\beta\Gamma(\alpha+\beta)I_{\alpha+\beta}(2)+{}_0F_1(\alpha+\beta;1)<3. \tag{32}$$

For a fixed β, the inequality (32) holds for $\alpha\geq\alpha_0(\beta)$, where $\alpha_0(\beta)$ is the root of the equation

$$\beta\Gamma(\alpha+\beta)I_{\alpha+\beta}(2)+{}_0F_1(\alpha+\beta;1)=3.$$

The root $\alpha_0(\beta)$ depends on β and decreases for increasing β. Thus, the result holds for all $\beta\geq 1/2$ and $\alpha\geq\alpha_0(1/2)$. This is equivalent to $\alpha\geq\alpha_0(1/2)=0.532446$, where $\alpha_0(1/2)$ is the root of

$$\Gamma(\alpha+\tfrac{1}{2})I_{\alpha+\frac{1}{2}}(2)+2\,{}_0F_1(\alpha+\tfrac{1}{2};1)=6.$$

The inequality (32) reduces to

$$\Gamma(\alpha+\tfrac{1}{2})I_{\alpha+\frac{1}{2}}(2)+2\,{}_0F_1(\alpha+\tfrac{1}{2};1)<6. \tag{33}$$

This completes the proof. □

One of the most important functions in the literature is the generalized and normalized Bessel functions of the form

$$\mathtt{U}_{p,b,c}(z)=\sum_{n=0}^{\infty}\frac{(-1)^n c^n}{4^n(p+\frac{b+1}{2})_n}\frac{z^n}{n!}, \tag{34}$$

where $b\in\mathbb{R}$, such that $p+(b+1)/2\neq 0,-2,-4,-6,\ldots$.

The function $\mathtt{U}_{p,b,c}$ yields the Spherical Bessel function for $b=2$, $c=1$ and reduces to the normalized classical Bessel (modified Bessel) functions of order p when $b=c=1$ ($b=-c=1$). There is a large amount research related to the inclusion of $\mathtt{U}_p$ in different subclasses of univalent functions theory [11–16] and some references therein. In [11], the lemniscate convexity and additional properties of $\mathtt{U}_p$ are examined in detail. The lemniscate starlikeness of $z\mathtt{U}_p$ is discussed in [1].

For this study, we introduce the function $\mathfrak{V}_{p,b,c,\beta}$ defined as

$$\mathfrak{V}_{p,b,c,\beta}(z):=\sum_{n=0}^{\infty}\frac{(-1)^n c^n}{4^n(p+\frac{b}{2}+\beta)_n}\frac{z^n}{n!}. \tag{35}$$

We note here that $\mathfrak{V}_{p,b,c,1/2}(z)=\mathtt{U}_{p,b,c}(z)$. Now, we state and prove the following result involving $\mathfrak{V}_{p,b,c,\beta}$.

Theorem 12. *For $\beta \geq 1/2$, the function $\mathfrak{V}_{p,b,c,\beta}(z) \prec \Phi_{N_e}(z)$ if*

$$\beta|c|\mathfrak{V}_{p+1,b,|c|,\beta}(-1) + 4\left(p + \tfrac{b}{2} + \beta\right)\mathfrak{V}_{p,b,|c|,\beta}(-1) < 16\left(p + \tfrac{b}{2} + \beta\right). \tag{36}$$

In particular, $\mathtt{U}_{p,b,c}(z) \prec \Phi_{N_e}(z)$ if

$$|c|\mathtt{U}_{p+1,b,|c|}(-1) + 8\left(p + \tfrac{b+1}{2}\right)\mathtt{U}_{p,b,|c|}(-1) < 16\left(p + \tfrac{b+1}{2}\right). \tag{37}$$

Proof. The proof is based on Theorem 5. Let us denote

$$\mathfrak{U}(n,\beta) = \frac{(-1)^n c^n}{4^n (p + \frac{b}{2} + \beta)_n n!}.$$

Then,

$$\begin{aligned}
\sum_{n=1}^{\infty}(n\beta+1)|\mathfrak{U}(n,\beta)| &= \sum_{n=1}^{\infty} \frac{(n\beta+1)|c|^n}{4^n (p+\frac{b}{2}+\beta)_n} \frac{1}{n!} \\
&= \beta \sum_{n=1}^{\infty} \frac{|c|^n}{4^n (p+\frac{b}{2}+\beta)_n (n-1)!} + \sum_{n=1}^{\infty} \frac{|c|^n}{4^n (p+\frac{b}{2}+\beta)_n n!} \\
&= \frac{\beta|c|}{4\left(p+\frac{b}{2}+\beta\right)} \sum_{n=1}^{\infty} \frac{|c|^{n-1}}{4^{n-1}(p+1+\frac{b}{2}+\beta)_{n-1}(n-1)!} + \sum_{n=1}^{\infty} \frac{|c|^n}{4^n (p+\frac{b}{2}+\beta)_n n!} \\
&= \frac{\beta|c|}{4\left(p+\frac{b}{2}+\beta\right)} \mathfrak{V}_{p+1,b,|c|,\beta}(-1) + \mathfrak{V}_{p,b,|c|,\beta}(-1) - 1
\end{aligned}$$

Now, inequality (11) holds if

$$\frac{\beta|c|}{4\left(p+\frac{b}{2}+\beta\right)} \mathfrak{V}_{p+1,b,|c|,\beta}(-1) + \mathfrak{V}_{p,b,|c|,\beta}(-1) - 1 < 1$$

After a routine simplification, we have

$$\beta|c|\mathfrak{V}_{p+1,b,|c|,\beta}(-1) + 4\left(p + \tfrac{b}{2} + \beta\right)\mathfrak{V}_{p,b,|c|,\beta}(-1) < 8\left(p + \tfrac{b}{2} + \beta\right). \tag{38}$$

As stated before, if $\beta = 1/2$, then $\mathfrak{V}_{p+1,b,c,1/2}(z) = \mathtt{U}_{p,b,c}(z)$. Thus, taking $\beta = 1/2$ in (38), we have $\mathtt{U}_{p,b,c}(z) \prec \Phi_{N_e}(z)$ if

$$|c|\mathtt{U}_{p+1,b,|c|}(-1) + 8\left(p + \tfrac{b+1}{2}\right)\mathtt{U}_{p,b,|c|}(-1) < 16\left(p + \tfrac{b+1}{2}\right). \tag{39}$$

This completes the proof. □

The normalized form of the classical Bessel and Modified Bessel functions as defined in (26) and (27) are given as

$$\mathtt{J}_v(z) = \frac{z^{-v}}{2^{-v}}\Gamma(v+1)J_v(\sqrt{z}) = \sum_{n=0}^{\infty} \frac{(-1)^n z^n}{4^n n!(v+1)_n} \tag{40}$$

$$\mathtt{I}_v(z) = \frac{z^{-v}}{2^{-v}}\Gamma(v+1)I_v(\sqrt{z}) = \sum_{n=0}^{\infty} \frac{z^n}{4^n n!(v+1)_n} \tag{41}$$

Notice that $\mathtt{J}_v(-1) = \mathtt{I}_v(1)$. Now, by taking $b = c = 1$ and $b = -c = 1$ in (39), we have the following result from Theorem 12.

Corollary 1. *For $\nu \geq \nu_0$, the subordination $\mathtt{J}_\nu(z) \prec \Phi_{N_e}(z)$ and $\mathtt{I}_\nu(z) \prec \Phi_{N_e}(z)$. Here, $\nu_0 \approx -0.5791$ is the root of the equation*

$$\delta(\mu) : \mathtt{I}_{\nu+1}(1) + 8(\nu+1)\mathtt{I}_\nu(1) - 16(\nu+1) = 0. \tag{42}$$

We calculate the value of ν_0 using *Mathematica Software* and the validity of inequality can be observed from Figure 6.

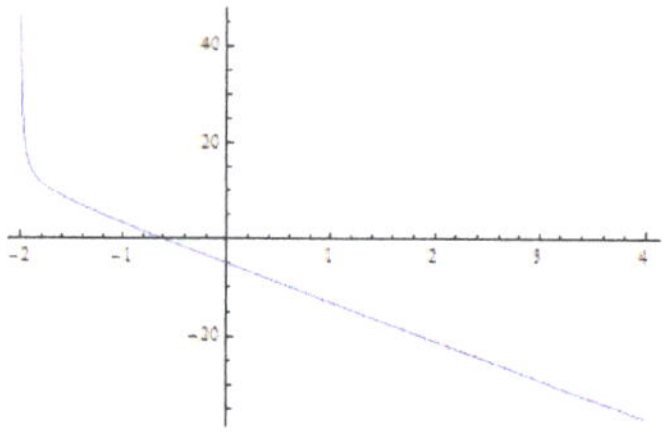

Figure 6. The graph of $\delta(\mu)$.

We visualize the subordination $\mathtt{J}_\nu(z) \prec \Phi_{N_e}(z)$ and $\mathtt{I}_\nu(z) \prec \Phi_{N_e}(z)$ for $\nu = \nu_0, -0.5, 0.5$, and present it in Figure 7 and Figure 8, respectively. We further note that

$$\mathtt{J}_{-0.5}(z) = \cos(\sqrt{z}) \qquad \mathtt{J}_{0.5}(z) = \frac{\sin(\sqrt{z})}{\sqrt{z}}$$

$$\mathtt{I}_{-0.5}(z) = \cosh(\sqrt{z}) \qquad \mathtt{I}_{0.5}(z) = \frac{\sinh(\sqrt{z})}{\sqrt{z}}.$$

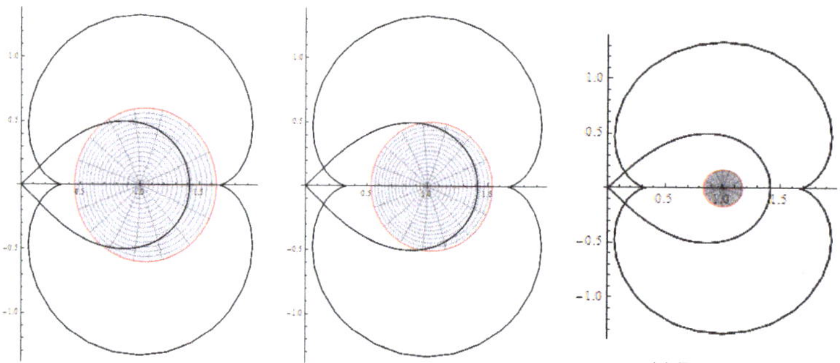

(**a**) For $\nu = \nu_0$ (**b**) For $\nu = -0.5$ (**c**) For $\nu = 0.5$

Figure 7. Image of $\mathtt{J}_\nu(\mathbb{D})$ for $\nu = \nu_0, -0.5, 0.5$.

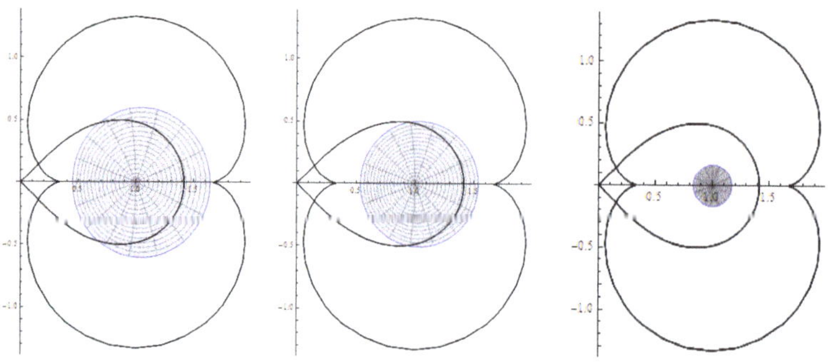

(**a**) For $\nu = \nu_0$ (**b**) For $\nu = 0.5$ (**c**) For $\nu = 0.5$

Figure 8. Image of $\mathtt{I}_\nu(\mathbb{D})$ for $\nu = \nu_0, -0.5, 0.5$.

8. Results Involving Confluent and Generalized Hypergeometric Function

The well-known confluent hypergeometric function ${}_1F_1(\alpha, \beta, z)$ is represented by series

$$ {}_1F_1(\alpha_1, \alpha_2, z) = \sum_{n=0}^{\infty} \frac{(\alpha_1)_n z^n}{(\alpha_2)_n n!}. \tag{43} $$

Here, $\alpha_2 \neq -1, -2, \ldots$ In the context of geometric functions theory, the confluent hypergeometric functions has a high significance. Miller and Mocanu [17] proved that $\operatorname{Re} {}_1F_1(\alpha_1, \alpha_2, z) > 0$ in $\mathfrak{D}$ for real α_1 and α_2, satisfying either $\alpha_1 > 0$ and $\alpha_2 \geq \alpha_1$, or $\alpha_1 \leq 0$ and $\alpha_2 \geq 1 + \sqrt{1 + \alpha_1^2}$. Conditions for which $\operatorname{Re} {}_1F_1(\alpha_1, \alpha_2, z) > \delta$, $0 \leq \delta \leq 1/2$ are obtained by Ponnusamy and Vuorinen ([18] Theorem 1.9, p. 77). In addition, they established that $(\alpha_2/\alpha_1)({}_1F_1(\alpha_1, \alpha_2, z) - 1)$ is close-to-convex of the positive order with respect to the identity function. A connection between the confluent and lemniscate is established in [19,20] and the references therein.

Now, we state and prove a result involving ${}_1F_1$.

Theorem 13. *For $\beta \geq 1/2$, the confluent hypergeometric function ${}_1F_1(1/2; \beta + 1; z) \prec \Phi_{N_e}(z)$, provided*

$$ \beta\, {}_1F_1\left(\frac{3}{2}; \beta + 2; 1\right) + 2(\beta + 1)\, {}_1F_1\left(\frac{1}{2}; \beta + 1; 1\right) \leq 4(\beta + 1). \tag{44} $$

Proof. By following the notion of Theorem 5 and series (43), we have

$$ \sum_{n=1}^{\infty} \frac{(\beta n + 1)\left(\frac{1}{2}\right)_n}{(1 + \beta)_n n!} = \frac{\beta\, {}_1F_1(\frac{3}{2}; \beta + 2; 1)}{2(\beta + 1)} + {}_1F_1\left(\frac{1}{2}; \beta + 1; 1\right) - 1 < 1 \tag{45} $$

when the hypothesis (44) holds. The conclusion follows from Theorem 5. □

Remark 3. *Let us denote*

$$ \mathfrak{P}(\beta) = \beta\, {}_1F_1\left(\frac{3}{2}; \beta + 2; 1\right) + 2(\beta + 1)\, {}_1F_1\left(\frac{1}{2}; \beta + 1; 1\right) - 4(\beta + 1). $$

Numerical calculation provides $\mathfrak{P}(1/2) = -0.252904$ and from Figure 9, it is clear that $\mathfrak{P}(\beta)$ is a decreasing function of β when $\beta \geq 1/2$.

Thus, the inequality (44) holds for all $\beta \geq 1/2$, and hence the condition (44) can be relaxed from Theorem 13. However, as we are not able to prove this inequality analytically, we keep the condition (44).

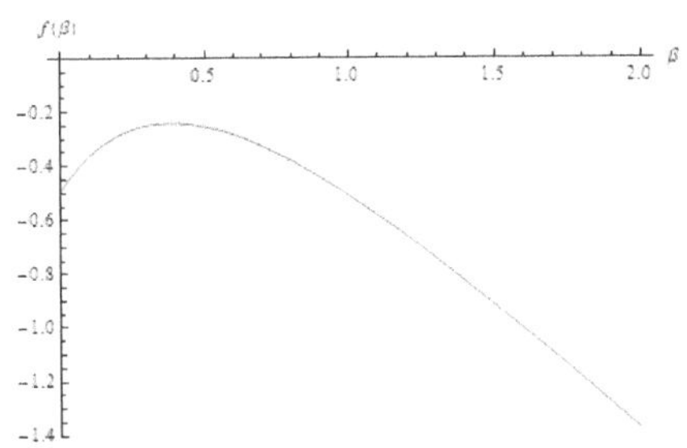

Figure 9. Graph of $\mathfrak{P}(\beta)$.

Our last example is on generalized hypergeometric functions.

Consider

$$\mathfrak{A}(n,\beta) = \frac{(\beta-1)_n}{n!(\beta)_n(\beta+1)_n};$$

substituting in (11), we have

$$\sum_{n=1}^{\infty}(n\beta+1)|\mathfrak{A}(n,\beta)| = \frac{(\beta-1)\,{}_1F_2(\beta;\beta+1,\beta+2;1)}{\beta+1} + {}_1F_2(\beta-1;\beta,\beta+1;1). \tag{46}$$

Here, ${}_1F_2$ is known as generalized hypergeometric functions. The generalized hypergeometric functions denoted by

$${}_mF_n(a_1,a_2,\ldots,a_m;b_1,b_2,\ldots,b_n;z)$$

with series representation

$${}_mF_n(a_1,a_2,\ldots,a_m;b_1,b_2,\ldots,b_n;z) = \sum_{r=0}^{\infty}\frac{(a_1)_r(a_2)_r\ldots(a_m)_r}{(b_1)_r(b_2)_r\ldots(b_n)_r}\frac{z^n}{n!} \tag{47}$$

where $b_i, 1 \leq i \leq n$ are positive. The series (47) converges if

(i) Any of $a_j, 1 \leq j \leq m$ are non-positive.

(ii) $m < n+1$, the series converges for any finite value of z and, hence, is entire.

Now, for $\beta \geq 1/2$, the graphical representation of the right side of (46) is given in Figure 10. As the graph is asymptotic about the parallel line $y = 1$, we have that

$$\sum_{n=1}^{\infty}(n\beta+1)|\mathfrak{A}(n,\beta)| = \frac{(\beta-1)\,{}_1F_2(\beta;\beta+1,\beta+2;1)}{\beta+1} + {}_1F_2(\beta-1;\beta,\beta+1;1) < 1.$$

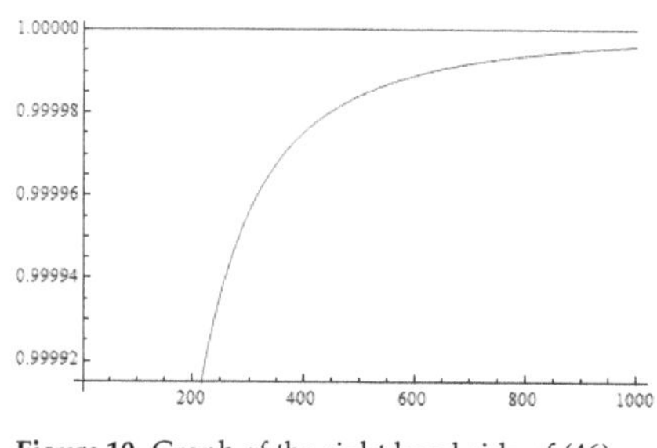

Figure 10. Graph of the right hand side of (46).

Based on this observation, we have the following result:

Theorem 14. *For $\beta \geq 1/2$, the generalized hypergeometric function ${}_1F_2(\beta-1;\beta,\beta+1;1) \prec \Phi_{N_e}(z)$.*

9. Conclusions

The article presents several analytic functions that map the unit disk to domain that are subordinated by lemniscate and nephroid curves. Analogous problems involving subordination implications have been examined previously [2,3,5,6,11,20–23]. The current article adopts the concept of subordination as its primary approach. In the context of subordination by Φ_{N_e}, we have established an extremal function. As far as the author is aware, there is no known result in geometric functions theory involving incomplete gamma functions. Likewise, there is no evidence linking Lerch transcendent to the lemniscate and nephrooid domains. Both relations are established in this work. The relation of the Bessel function and modified Bessel function with nephroid domains is also presented.

The results also establish following:

1. $f(\mathfrak{D}) \subset \mathcal{P}_l(\mathfrak{D}) \cap \Phi_{N_e}(\mathfrak{D})$: This is the easiest example because of the large intersecting parts between $\mathcal{P}_l(\mathfrak{D})$ and $\Phi_{N_e}(\mathfrak{D})$ and the existence of such a function is evident in Figures 2b–d and 5b (Involving incomplete gamma function), Figure 7c ($\cos(\sqrt{z})$), and Figure 8c ($\cosh(\sqrt{z})$).
2. $f(\mathfrak{D}) \subset \mathcal{P}_l(\mathfrak{D})$, but $f(\mathfrak{D}) \not\subset \Phi_{N_e}(\mathfrak{D})$: This is the toughest part to establish as an example, as a very small section of $\mathcal{P}_l(\mathfrak{D})$ is out of $\Phi_{N_e}(\mathfrak{D})$, but we have been able to construct an example in Figure 2a,e.
3. $f(\mathfrak{D}) \subset \Phi_{N_e}(\mathfrak{D})$, but $f(\mathfrak{D}) \not\subset \mathcal{P}_l(\mathfrak{D})$: Figure 5a ((Involving incomplete gamma function), Figure 7b ($\cos(\sqrt{z})$), Figure 8b ($\cosh(\sqrt{z})$), Figures 7a and 8a.

Finally, we remark that we were restricted by using only a few examples. Using Theorem 5 and series representation of functions, we can include many other functions such as Struve functions, Gaussian hypergeometric functions, and Bessel–Struve functions.

Funding: This research received no external funding

Data Availability Statement: Data are contained within the article.

Conflicts of Interest: The author declares no conflicts of interest.

References

1. Mondal, S.R. On Lemniscate Starlikeness of the Solution of General Differential Equations. *Mathematics* **2022**, *10*, 3254. [CrossRef]
2. Mondal, S.R. Mapping Properties of Associate Laguerre Polynomials in Leminiscate, Exponential and Nephroid Domain. *Symmetry* **2022**, *14*, 2303. [CrossRef]
3. Mondal, S.R. Subordination Involving Regular Coulomb Wave Functions. *Symmetry* **2022**, *14*, 1007. [CrossRef]
4. Alarifi, N.M.; Mondal, S.R. On Geometric Properties of Bessel-Struve Kernel Functions in Unit Disc. *Mathematics* **2022**, *10*, 2516. [CrossRef]
5. Madaan, V.; Kumar, A.; Ravichandran, V. Starlikeness associated with lemniscate of Bernoulli. *Filomat* **2019**, *33*, 1937–1955. [CrossRef]
6. Swaminathan, A.; Wani, L.A. Sufficiency for nephroid starlikeness using hypergeometric functions. *Math. Methods Appl. Sci.* **2022**, *45*, 5388–5401. [CrossRef]
7. Duren, P.L. *Univalent Functions; Grundlehren der Mathematischen Wissenschaften [Fundamental Principles of Mathematical Sciences]*; Springer: New York, NY, USA, 1983; Volume 259, p. xiv+382.
8. Ali, R.M.; Cho, N.E.; Ravichandran, V.; Sivaprasad Kumar, S. Differential subordination for functions associated with the lemniscate of Bernoulli. *Taiwanese J. Math.* **2012**, *16*, 1017–1026. [CrossRef]
9. Kumar, S.S.; Kumar, V.; Ravichandran, V.; Cho, N.E. Sufficient conditions for starlike functions associated with the lemniscate of Bernoulli. *J. Inequal. Appl.* **2013**, 176. [CrossRef]
10. Abramowitz, M.; Stegun, I.A. *Handbook of Mathematical Functions with Formulas, Graphs, and Mathematical Tables;* US Government Printing Office: Washington, DC, USA, 1968; Volume 55.
11. Madaan, V.; Kumar, A.; Ravichandran, V. Lemniscate convexity of generalized Bessel functions. *Studia Sci. Math. Hungar.* **2019**, *56*, 404–419. [CrossRef]
12. Baricz, A. *Generalized Bessel Functions of the First Kind;* Lecture Notes in Mathematics; Springer: Berlin, Germany, 2010; Volume 1994, p. xiv+206. [CrossRef]
13. Baricz, A.; Ponnusamy, S. Starlikeness and convexity of generalized Bessel functions. *Integral Transform Spec. Funct.* **2010**, *21*, 641–653. [CrossRef]
14. Baricz, A.; Szász, R. The radius of convexity of normalized Bessel functions of the first kind. *Anal. Appl. (Singap.)* **2014**, *12*, 485–509. [CrossRef]
15. Baricz, A. Geometric properties of generalized Bessel functions. *Publ. Math. Debrecen* **2008**, *73*, 155–178. [CrossRef]
16. Baricz, A. Geometric properties of generalized Bessel functions of complex order. *Mathematica* **2006**, *48*, 13–18.
17. Miller, S.S.; Mocanu, P.T. Differential subordinations and inequalities in the complex plane. *J. Differ. Equ.* **1987**, *67*, 199–211. [CrossRef]
18. Ponnusamy, S.; Vuorinen, M. Univalence and convexity properties for confluent hypergeometric functions. *Complex Var. Theory Appl.* **1998**, *36*, 73–97. [CrossRef]
19. Alzahrani, R.; Mondal, S.R. Geometric Nature of Special Functions on Domain Enclosed by Nephroid and Leminscate Curve. *Symmetry* **2023**, *16*, 19. [CrossRef]
20. Bohra, N.; Ravichandran, V. On confluent hypergeometric functions and generalized Bessel functions. *Anal. Math.* **2017**, *43*, 533–545. [CrossRef]
21. Naz, A.; Nagpal, S.; Ravichandran, V. Exponential starlikeness and convexity of confluent hypergeometric, Lommel, and Struve functions. *Mediterr. J. Math.* **2020**, *17*, 204. [CrossRef]

22. Wani, L.A.; Swaminathan, A. Starlike and convex functions associated with a nephroid domain. *Bull. Malays. Math. Sci. Soc.* **2021**, *44*, 79–104. [CrossRef]
23. Aktaş, I. Lemniscate and exponential starlikeness of regular Coulomb wave functions. *Studia Sci. Math. Hungar.* **2020**, *57*, 372–384. [CrossRef]

mathematics

MDPI

Article

Absolute Monotonicity of Normalized Tail of Power Series Expansion of Exponential Function †

Feng Qi [1,2,3]

[1] School of Mathematics and Informatics, Henan Polytechnic University, Jiaozuo 454010, China; qifeng618@gmail.com
[2] School of Mathematics and Physics, Hulunbuir University, Hulunbuir 021008, China
[3] Independent Researcher, University Village, Dallas, TX 75252-8024, USA

† This paper is dedicated to my father Shu-Gong Qi for his 82nd birthday.

Abstract: In this work, the author reviews the origination of normalized tails of the Maclaurin power series expansions of infinitely differentiable functions, presents that the ratio between two normalized tails of the Maclaurin power series expansion of the exponential function is decreasing on the positive axis, and proves that the normalized tail of the Maclaurin power series expansion of the exponential function is absolutely monotonic on the whole real axis.

Keywords: absolutely monotonic function; ratio; normalized tail; Maclaurin power series expansion; exponential function; monotonicity rule

MSC: 41A58; 26A48; 33B10

1. A Short Review of Normalized Tails

In April 2023, Qi and several mathematicians considered the decreasing property of the ratio $\frac{F(u)}{G(u)}$ on $\left(0, \frac{\pi}{2}\right)$, where

$$F(u) = \begin{cases} \ln \dfrac{3(\tan u - u)}{u^3}, & 0 < |u| < \dfrac{\pi}{2} \\ 0, & u = 0 \end{cases} \tag{1}$$

and

$$G(u) = \begin{cases} \ln \dfrac{\tan u}{u}, & 0 < |u| < \dfrac{\pi}{2} \\ 0, & u = 0 \end{cases} \tag{2}$$

are both even functions on $\left(-\frac{\pi}{2}, \frac{\pi}{2}\right)$. The reason why we investigated the ratio $\frac{F(u)}{G(u)}$ and its monotonicity on $\left(-\frac{\pi}{2}, \frac{\pi}{2}\right)$ was stated in [1] (Remark 10).

By the study of the ratio $\frac{F(u)}{G(u)}$ in [1], the authors observed that the functions

$$\frac{\tan u}{u} \quad \text{and} \quad \frac{3(\tan u - u)}{u^3} = \frac{\tan u - u}{u^3/3} \tag{3}$$

are closely related to the first two terms in the Maclaurin power series expansion

$$\tan u = \sum_{j=1}^{\infty} \frac{2^{2j}\left(2^{2j}-1\right)}{(2j)!}|B_{2j}|u^{2j-1} = u + \frac{u^3}{3} + \frac{2u^5}{15} + \frac{17u^7}{315} + \cdots, \quad |u| < \frac{\pi}{2}, \tag{4}$$

where the Bernoulli numbers B_j are generated by

$$\frac{u}{e^u - 1} = \sum_{j=0}^{\infty} B_j \frac{u^j}{j!} = 1 - \frac{u}{2} + \sum_{j=1}^{\infty} B_{2j} \frac{u^{2j}}{(2j)!}, \quad 0 < |u| < 2\pi. \tag{5}$$

Motivated by the above observation, basing on the first two terms in the Maclaurin power series expansions

$$\cos u = \sum_{j=0}^{\infty} (-1)^j \frac{u^{2j}}{(2j)!} = 1 - \frac{u^2}{2} + \frac{u^4}{24} - \frac{u^6}{720} + \frac{u^8}{40320} - \cdots, \quad u \in \mathbb{R} \tag{6}$$

and

$$\sin u = \sum_{j=0}^{\infty} (-1)^j \frac{u^{2j+1}}{(2j+1)!} = u - \frac{u^3}{6} + \frac{u^5}{120} - \frac{u^7}{5040} + \frac{u^9}{362880} - \cdots, \quad u \in \mathbb{R}, \tag{7}$$

Qi and his coauthors further constructed the even functions

$$\begin{cases} \ln \dfrac{2(1-\cos u)}{u^2}, & 0 < |u| < 2\pi; \\ 0, & u = 0, \end{cases} \tag{8}$$

$$\begin{cases} \dfrac{\ln \frac{2(1-\cos u)}{u^2}}{\ln \cos u}, & 0 < |u| < \dfrac{\pi}{2}; \\ \dfrac{1}{6}, & u = 0; \\ 0, & u = \pm \dfrac{\pi}{2}, \end{cases} \tag{9}$$

$$\begin{cases} \ln \dfrac{6(u-\sin u)}{u^3}, & 0 < |u| < \infty; \\ 0, & u = 0, \end{cases} \tag{10}$$

and

$$\begin{cases} \dfrac{\ln \frac{6(u-\sin u)}{u^3}}{\ln \frac{\sin u}{u}}, & |u| \in (0, \pi); \\ \dfrac{3}{10}, & u = 0; \\ 0, & u = \pm\pi \end{cases} \tag{11}$$

in the papers [2,3], respectively.

For generalizing the above observations, in the papers [4–7] and [8] (Remark 7), Qi and his coauthors introduced the concept of the normalized tails (also known as the normalized remainders) of the Maclaurin power series expansions (6) and (7) by

$$\operatorname{CosR}_n(u) = \begin{cases} (-1)^n \dfrac{(2n)!}{u^{2n}} \left[\cos u - \displaystyle\sum_{j=0}^{n-1} (-1)^j \frac{u^{2j}}{(2j)!} \right], & u \neq 0 \\ 1, & u = 0 \end{cases}$$

and

$$\operatorname{SinR}_n(u) = \begin{cases} (-1)^n \dfrac{(2n+1)!}{u^{2n+1}} \left[\sin u - \displaystyle\sum_{j=0}^{n-1} (-1)^j \frac{u^{2j+1}}{(2j+1)!} \right], & u \neq 0 \\ 1, & u = 0 \end{cases}$$

for $n \in \mathbb{N}$ and $u \in \mathbb{R}$. These two normalized tails are generalizations of the functions

$$\cos u = \frac{\cos u}{1}, \quad \frac{2(1-\cos u)}{u^2} = \frac{\cos u - 1}{-u^2/2}, \quad \frac{\sin u}{u}, \quad \frac{6(u-\sin u)}{u^3} = \frac{\sin u - u}{-u^3/6}$$

which appeared in (8), (9), (10), and (11), respectively.

In [9], basing on the Maclaurin power series expansion (5), Qi and his joint authors invented the normalized tail:

$$\begin{cases} \dfrac{1}{B_{2n+2}} \dfrac{(2n+2)!}{u^{2n+2}} \left[\dfrac{u}{\mathrm{e}^u - 1} - 1 + \dfrac{u}{2} - \displaystyle\sum_{j=1}^{n} B_{2j} \frac{u^{2j}}{(2j)!} \right], & u \neq 0; \\ 1, & u = 0. \end{cases}$$

Through studying this normalized tail, some new knowledge about the Bernoulli polynomials was obtained in [9] (Proposition 1) and the arXiv preprint at https://doi.org/10.48550/arxiv.2405.05280.

On the basis of the Maclaurin power series expansion (4) and utilizing the idea and thought mentioned above, Qi and his coauthors introduced the following normalized tail

$$\begin{cases} \dfrac{(2n)!}{2^{2n}(2^{2n}-1)} \dfrac{1}{|B_{2n}| u^{2n-1}} \left[\tan u - \displaystyle\sum_{j=1}^{n-1} \frac{2^{2j}(2^{2j}-1)}{(2j)!} |B_{2j}| u^{2j-1} \right], & 0 < |u| < \dfrac{\pi}{2}; \\ 1, & u = 0. \end{cases}$$

This normalized tail is a generalization of the functions in (3), which appeared in (1) and (2). Qi and his coauthors have investigated this normalized tail in a forthcoming paper.

In the paper [10] (p. 798) and the handbook [11] (pp. 42 and 55), we can find the Maclaurin power series expansion

$$\tan^2 u = \sum_{j=1}^{\infty} \frac{2^{2j+2}(2^{2j+2}-1)(2j+1)}{(2j+2)!} |B_{2j+2}| u^{2j} \tag{12}$$

for $|u| < \frac{\pi}{2}$. Basing on the series expansion (12), imitating the above observations, and employing the above initiating idea and thought to define the normalized tails, Zhang and Qi built the normalized tail

$$h_n(u) = \begin{cases} \dfrac{(2n+2)! \left[\tan^2 u - \displaystyle\sum_{\ell=1}^{n-1} \frac{2^{2\ell+2}(2^{2\ell+2}-1)(2\ell+1)}{(2\ell+2)!} |B_{2\ell+2}| u^{2\ell} \right]}{2^{2n+2}(2^{2n+2}-1)(2n+1)|B_{2n+2}| u^{2n}}, & u \neq 0 \\ 1, & u = 0 \end{cases}$$

for $n \in \mathbb{N}$ and $|u| < \frac{\pi}{2}$ in the paper [12].

Considering the relation $\sec^2 u = 1 + \tan^2 u$, we reformulate the normalized tail $h_n(u)$ as

$$h_n(u) = \begin{cases} \dfrac{(2n+2)! \left[\sec^2 u - \displaystyle\sum_{\ell=0}^{n-1} \frac{2^{2\ell+2}(2^{2\ell+2}-1)(2\ell+1)}{(2\ell+2)!} |B_{2\ell+2}| u^{2\ell} \right]}{2^{2n+2}(2^{2n+2}-1)(2n+1)|B_{2n+2}| u^{2n}}, & u \neq 0 \\ 1, & u = 0 \end{cases}$$

for $n \in \mathbb{N}$ and $|u| < \frac{\pi}{2}$. Hence, the quantity $h_n(u)$ is also the normalized tail of the Maclaurin power series expansion of the square $\sec^2 u$ about $u = 0$.

In [13] (Section 5), the authors summed up the above ideas and thoughts to design normalized tails as follows:

Lemma 4 ([26] (p. 22, Problem 94)). *Let a_n and $b_n > 0$ for $n \in \mathbb{N}_0$ be two sequences such that the infinite series $\sum_{n=0}^{\infty} b_n t^n$ converges for $t \in \mathbb{R}$ and $\lim_{n\to\infty} \frac{a_n}{b_n} = s$. Then, the infinite series $\sum_{n=0}^{\infty} a_n t^n$ converges too for $t \in \mathbb{R}$; in addition,*

$$\lim_{t\to\infty} \frac{\sum_{n=0}^{\infty} a_n t^n}{\sum_{n=0}^{\infty} b_n t^n} = s.$$

Remark 1. *In the paper [27], motivated by [28], Yang and Chu employed Lemma 4 to bind the modified Bessel function of the first kind $\sum_{n=0}^{\infty} \frac{1}{(n!)^2} \left(\frac{t}{2}\right)^{2n}$ and the Toader–Qi mean*

$$\frac{2}{\pi} \int_0^{\pi/2} a^{\cos^2\theta} b^{\sin^2\theta} \, \mathrm{d}\theta.$$

4. Decreasing Property on Positive Half-Axis

In this section, we verify that the ratio $\frac{f_{n+1}(u)}{f_n(u)}$ is decreasing in $u \in (0, \infty)$.

Theorem 1. *For $n \in \mathbb{N}$, the ratio $\frac{f_{n+1}(u)}{f_n(u)}$ is decreasing in $u \in (0, \infty)$.*

Proof. Making use of the Maclaurin power series expansion (14), we can write the normalized tail $f_n(u)$ as defined by (15) for $n \in \mathbb{N}$ as

$$f_n(u) = \sum_{j=0}^{\infty} \frac{1}{\binom{j+n}{n}} \frac{u^j}{j!}, \quad u \in \mathbb{R}. \tag{18}$$

Then, for $u \in \mathbb{R}$ and $n \in \mathbb{N}$, we have

$$\frac{f_{n+1}(u)}{f_n(u)} = \frac{\sum_{j=0}^{\infty} \frac{1}{\binom{j+n+1}{n+1}} \frac{u^j}{j!}}{\sum_{j=0}^{\infty} \frac{1}{\binom{j+n}{n}} \frac{u^j}{j!}}. \tag{19}$$

The ratio between coefficients of u^j of two series in the above fraction is

$$\frac{\frac{1}{\binom{j+n+1}{n+1}} \frac{1}{j!}}{\frac{1}{\binom{j+n}{n}} \frac{1}{j!}} = \frac{\binom{j+n}{n}}{\binom{j+n+1}{n+1}} = \frac{(j+n)!}{n!j!} \frac{(n+1)!j!}{(j+n+1)!} = \frac{n+1}{j+n+1}$$

and it is decreasing in $j \in \mathbb{N}_0$ for given $n \in \mathbb{N}$. Considering Lemma 1, we conclude that the ratio $\frac{f_{n+1}(u)}{f_n(u)}$ is decreasing in $u \in (0, \infty)$ for a given $n \in \mathbb{N}$. The proof of Theorem 1 is complete. □

5. Absolute Monotonicity

In this section, we discover the absolute monotonicity of the normalized tail $f_n(u)$ in $u \in \mathbb{R}$ for $n \in \mathbb{N}$.

Theorem 2. *For $n \in \mathbb{N}$, the normalized tail $f_n(u)$ is an absolutely monotonic function in $u \in \mathbb{R}$.*

Proof. When $u > 0$, from the Maclaurin power series expansion (18), it follows immediately that the normalized tail $f_n(u)$ for $n \in \mathbb{N}$ is an absolutely monotonic function in $u > 0$.

Utilizing Lemma 2, we arrive at

$$f_n(u) = 1 + u \int_0^1 v^n \, \mathrm{e}^{u(1-v)} \, \mathrm{d}v, \quad u \in \mathbb{R} \tag{20}$$

and $f_n(0) = 1$ for $n \in \mathbb{N}$. For $m \in \mathbb{N}$, a direct differentiation gives

$$\begin{aligned} f_n^{(m)}(u) &= \mathrm{e}^u \left[u \int_0^1 v^n (1-v)^m \mathrm{e}^{-uv} \,\mathrm{d}v + m \int_0^1 v^n (1-v)^{m-1} \mathrm{e}^{-uv} \,\mathrm{d}v \right] \\ &\to m \int_0^1 v^n (1-v)^{m-1} \,\mathrm{d}v, \quad u \to 0 \\ &= \frac{m!n!}{(m+n)!} \\ &> 0, \quad m,n \in \mathbb{N}. \end{aligned}$$

Accordingly, in order to prove the absolute monotonicity of $f_n(u)$ in $u < 0$ for $n \in \mathbb{N}$, we need to show

$$\frac{u \int_0^1 v^n (1-v)^m \mathrm{e}^{-uv} \,\mathrm{d}v}{\int_0^1 v^n (1-v)^{m-1} \mathrm{e}^{-uv} \,\mathrm{d}v} \ge -m \tag{21}$$

for $m, n \in \mathbb{N}$ and $u < 0$.

It is easy to see that, via integration in part,

$$u \int_0^1 v^n (1-v)^m \mathrm{e}^{-uv} \,\mathrm{d}v = -\int_0^1 v^n (1-v)^m \frac{\mathrm{d}\,\mathrm{e}^{-uv}}{\mathrm{d}v} \,\mathrm{d}v = \int_0^1 [v^n (1-v)^m]' \mathrm{e}^{-uv} \,\mathrm{d}v$$

for $m, n \in \mathbb{N}$ and $u < 0$. Applying Lemma 3 to

$$W(u,v) = \mathrm{e}^{-uv} > 0, \quad U(v) = [v^n (1-v)^m]', \quad V(v) = v^n (1-v)^{m-1} > 0$$

for $v \in (0,1)$ and $m, n \in \mathbb{N}$, which satisfy that both

$$\frac{\partial [\ln W(v,u)]}{\partial u} = \frac{\partial W(v,u)/\partial u}{W(v,u)} = -v$$

and

$$\frac{U(v)}{V(v)} = \frac{[v^n (1-v)^m]'}{v^n (1-v)^{m-1}} = \frac{n}{v} - m - n$$

are decreasing in $v \in (0,1)$, reveals that the ratio

$$\frac{u \int_0^1 v^n (1-v)^m \mathrm{e}^{-uv} \,\mathrm{d}v}{\int_0^1 v^n (1-v)^{m-1} \mathrm{e}^{-uv} \,\mathrm{d}v} = \frac{\int_0^1 [v^n (1-v)^m]' \mathrm{e}^{-uv} \,\mathrm{d}v}{\int_0^1 v^n (1-v)^{m-1} \mathrm{e}^{-uv} \,\mathrm{d}v} \tag{22}$$

is increasing in $u < 0$ for $m, n \in \mathbb{N}$.

In light of Equation (22), we acquire

$$\begin{aligned} \frac{u \int_0^1 v^n (1-v)^m \mathrm{e}^{-uv} \,\mathrm{d}v}{\int_0^1 v^n (1-v)^{m-1} \mathrm{e}^{-uv} \,\mathrm{d}v} &= \frac{\int_0^1 [n v^{n-1} (1-v)^m - m v^n (1-v)^{m-1}] \mathrm{e}^{-uv} \,\mathrm{d}v}{\int_0^1 v^n (1-v)^{m-1} \mathrm{e}^{-uv} \,\mathrm{d}v} \\ &= n \frac{\int_0^1 v^{n-1} (1-v)^m \mathrm{e}^{-uv} \,\mathrm{d}v}{\int_0^1 v^n (1-v)^{m-1} \mathrm{e}^{-uv} \,\mathrm{d}v} - m \end{aligned}$$

for $m, n \in \mathbb{N}$ and $u \in \mathbb{R}$. When $u \to -\infty$, making use of Lemma 4, we obtain

$$\begin{aligned} \lim_{u \to -\infty} \frac{\int_0^1 v^{n-1} (1-v)^m \mathrm{e}^{-uv} \,\mathrm{d}v}{\int_0^1 v^n (1-v)^{m-1} \mathrm{e}^{-uv} \,\mathrm{d}v} &= \lim_{u \to -\infty} \frac{\sum_{k=0}^{\infty} (-1)^k \frac{u^k}{k!} \int_0^1 v^{n+k-1} (1-v)^m \,\mathrm{d}v}{\sum_{k=0}^{\infty} (-1)^k \frac{u^k}{k!} \int_0^1 v^{n+k} (1-v)^{m-1} \,\mathrm{d}v} \\ &= \lim_{u \to \infty} \frac{\sum_{k=0}^{\infty} \frac{u^k}{k!} \frac{m!(n+k-1)!}{(m+n+k)!}}{\sum_{k=0}^{\infty} \frac{u^k}{k!} \frac{(n+k)!(m-1)!}{(m+n+k)!}} \end{aligned}$$

$$
\begin{aligned}
&= \lim_{k\to\infty} \frac{\frac{1}{k!}\frac{m!(n+k-1)!}{(m+n+k)!}}{\frac{1}{k!}\frac{(n+k)!(m-1)!}{(m+n+k)!}} \\
&= \lim_{k\to\infty} \frac{m}{n+k} \\
&= 0
\end{aligned}
$$

for $m, n \in \mathbb{N}$. Consequently, the inequality (21) is sound. The proof of Theorem 2 is complete. □

6. More Remarks

In this section, we give some remarks about our main results.

Remark 2. *By the definition* (15)*, we acquire*

$$
\frac{f_{n+1}(u)}{f_n(u)} = \frac{\frac{(n+1)!}{u^{n+1}}\left(e^u - \sum_{j=0}^{n}\frac{u^j}{j!}\right)}{\frac{n!}{u^n}\left(e^u - \sum_{j=0}^{n-1}\frac{u^j}{j!}\right)} = (n+1)\frac{e^u - \sum_{j=0}^{n}\frac{u^j}{j!}}{u\left(e^u - \sum_{j=0}^{n-1}\frac{u^j}{j!}\right)} \to \begin{cases} 0, & u\to\infty \\ 1, & u\to 0 \\ \dfrac{n+1}{n}, & u\to-\infty \end{cases}
$$

for $n \in \mathbb{N}$. Accordingly, Theorem 1 implies the inequality $f_{n+1}(u) < f_n(u)$ for $u \in (0,\infty)$ and $n \in \mathbb{N}$. In particular, when $n = 1$, we acquire

$$
\frac{2(e^u - 1 - u)}{u^2} < \frac{e^u - 1}{u}, \quad u \in (0,\infty),
$$

which can be further reformulated as

$$
e^u < \frac{2+u}{2-u}, \quad u \in (0,2).
$$

Generally, utilizing Theorem 1, for $n \in \mathbb{N}$, we have

$$
e^u < \sum_{k=0}^{n-1}\frac{u^k}{k!} + \frac{n+1}{n+1-u}\frac{u^n}{n!}, \quad u \in (0, n+1). \tag{23}
$$

This inequality extends and refines an inequality

$$
e^u < \sum_{k=0}^{n-1}\frac{u^k}{k!} + \frac{n}{n-u}\frac{u^n}{n!}, \quad u \in (0, n) \tag{24}
$$

collected in [29] (p. 269, Entry 3.6.6). This demonstrates that Theorem 1 and the notion of the normalized tail $f_n(u)$ of the Maclaurin power series expansion (14) *of the exponential function e^u are significant in mathematics.*

In the paper [14], Qi constructed many inequalities similar to (23) *and* (24)*.*

Remark 3. *Taking $n = 1, 2, 3$ in Theorem 2 gives that the functions*

$$
f_1(u) = \frac{e^u - 1}{u}, \quad f_2(u) = \frac{2(e^u - 1 - u)}{u^2}, \quad f_3(u) = \frac{6\left(e^u - 1 - u - \frac{u^2}{2}\right)}{u^3}
$$

are absolutely monotonic on $\mathbb{R}$. These special cases are not trivial for $u < 0$.

Remark 4. *In [15] (p. 369), it was stated that if f is a completely monotonic function such that $f^{(k)}(t) \neq 0$ for $k \in \mathbb{N}_0$, then*

$$
a_i = \ln\left[(-1)^{i-1} f^{(i-1)}(t)\right], \quad i \in \mathbb{N}
$$

is a convex sequence. By virtue of this conclusion or [16] (p. 167, Corollary 16), we see that the absolute monotonicity of $f_n(u)$ in $u \in \mathbb{R}$ for $n \in \mathbb{N}$ in Theorem 2 is stronger than the logarithmic convexity of $f_n(u)$ in $u \in \mathbb{R}$ for $n \in \mathbb{N}$ in [13] (Corollary 1).

Remark 5. *We guess that the ratio $\frac{f_{n+1}(u)}{f_n(u)}$ is decreasing for $n \in \mathbb{N}$ in $u \in (-\infty, 0)$.*

A direct differentiation on both sides of (19) yields

$$\frac{\mathrm{d}}{\mathrm{d}u}\left[\frac{f_{n+1}(u)}{f_n(u)}\right] = \frac{\left[\sum_{j=1}^{\infty}\frac{1}{\binom{j+n+1}{n+1}}\frac{u^{j-1}}{(j-1)!}\right]\left[\sum_{j=0}^{\infty}\frac{1}{\binom{j+n}{n}}\frac{u^j}{j!}\right] - \left[\sum_{j=0}^{\infty}\frac{1}{\binom{j+n+1}{n+1}}\frac{u^j}{j!}\right]\left[\sum_{j=1}^{\infty}\frac{1}{\binom{j+n}{n}}\frac{u^{j-1}}{(j-1)!}\right]}{\left[\sum_{j=0}^{\infty}\frac{1}{\binom{j+n}{n}}\frac{u^j}{j!}\right]^2}$$
$$= \frac{\left[\sum_{j=0}^{\infty}\frac{1}{\binom{j+n+2}{n+1}}\frac{u^j}{j!}\right]\left[\sum_{j=0}^{\infty}\frac{1}{\binom{j+n}{n}}\frac{u^j}{j!}\right] - \left[\sum_{j=0}^{\infty}\frac{1}{\binom{j+n+1}{n+1}}\frac{u^j}{j!}\right]\left[\sum_{j=0}^{\infty}\frac{1}{\binom{j+n+1}{n}}\frac{u^j}{j!}\right]}{\left[\sum_{j=0}^{\infty}\frac{1}{\binom{j+n}{n}}\frac{u^j}{j!}\right]^2} \tag{25}$$

for $u \in \mathbb{R}$ and $n \in \mathbb{N}$. Accordingly, in order to prove the decreasing property of the ratio $\frac{f_{n+1}(u)}{f_n(u)}$ for $n \in \mathbb{N}$ in $u \in (-\infty, 0)$, it suffices to show that the inequality

$$\left[\sum_{j=0}^{\infty}\frac{1}{\binom{j+n+2}{n+1}}\frac{u^j}{j!}\right]\left[\sum_{j=0}^{\infty}\frac{1}{\binom{j+n}{n}}\frac{u^j}{j!}\right] \le \left[\sum_{j=0}^{\infty}\frac{1}{\binom{j+n+1}{n+1}}\frac{u^j}{j!}\right]\sum_{j=0}^{\infty}\frac{1}{\binom{j+n+1}{n}}\frac{u^j}{j!}\Bigg] \tag{26}$$

is sound for $u \in \mathbb{R}$ and $n \in \mathbb{N}$. See the first problem at the website https://math.stackexchange.com/q/4956563 (accessed on 11 August 2024).

The case $u > 0$ of the inequality (26) can be easily deduced from the combination of Theorem 1 with the derivative in (25).

The inequality (26) can be rearranged as

$$\frac{\sum_{j=0}^{\infty}\frac{1}{\binom{j+n+2}{n+1}}\frac{u^j}{j!}}{\sum_{j=0}^{\infty}\frac{1}{\binom{j+n+1}{n+1}}\frac{u^j}{j!}} \le \frac{\sum_{j=0}^{\infty}\frac{1}{\binom{j+n+1}{n}}\frac{u^j}{j!}}{\sum_{j=0}^{\infty}\frac{1}{\binom{j+n}{n}}\frac{u^j}{j!}}$$

for $u \in \mathbb{R}$ and $n \in \mathbb{N}$. See the third problem at the website https://math.stackexchange.com/q/4956563 (accessed on 11 August 2024). Accordingly, in order to prove the inequality (26), it is sufficient to show that the sequence

$$\frac{\sum_{j=0}^{\infty}\frac{1}{\binom{j+n+1}{n}}\frac{u^j}{j!}}{\sum_{j=0}^{\infty}\frac{1}{\binom{j+n}{n}}\frac{u^j}{j!}} = \frac{\sum_{j=0}^{\infty}\frac{(j+1)u^j}{(j+n+1)!}}{\sum_{j=0}^{\infty}\frac{u^j}{(j+n)!}}$$

is decreasing in $n \in \mathbb{N}$ for $u < 0$.

Remark 6. *If the guess in Remark 5 is true, making use of the limits in Remark 2, we conclude the inequality $\frac{f_{n+1}(u)}{f_n(u)} < \frac{n+1}{n}$ for $n \in \mathbb{N}$ and $u \in \mathbb{R}$. Equivalently, the inequality*

$$\frac{R_{n+1}(u)}{u^{n+1}} < \frac{1}{n}\frac{R_n(u)}{u^n}$$

is sound for $n \in \mathbb{N}$ and $u \in \mathbb{R}$. Therefore, for $n \in \mathbb{N}$, the inequality

$$(n-u)\frac{R_n(u)}{u^n} < \frac{1}{(n-1)!}$$

is valid in $u > 0$ and reverses in $u < 0$.

Remark 7. *For $n \in \mathbb{N}$ and $u \in \mathbb{R}$, let*

$$G_n(u) = \left[\sum_{j=0}^{\infty} \frac{1}{\binom{j+n+1}{n+1}} \frac{u^j}{j!}\right]\left[\sum_{j=0}^{\infty} \frac{1}{\binom{j+n+1}{n}} \frac{u^j}{j!}\right] - \left[\sum_{j=0}^{\infty} \frac{1}{\binom{j+n+2}{n+1}} \frac{u^j}{j!}\right]\left[\sum_{j=0}^{\infty} \frac{1}{\binom{j+n}{n}} \frac{u^j}{j!}\right]$$

and

$$H_n(u) = \left[\sum_{j=0}^{\infty} \frac{1}{\binom{j+n+2}{n}} \frac{u^j}{j!}\right]\left[\sum_{j=0}^{\infty} \frac{1}{\binom{j+n}{n}} \frac{u^j}{j!}\right] - \left[\sum_{j=0}^{\infty} \frac{1}{\binom{j+n+1}{n}} \frac{u^j}{j!}\right]^2.$$

We guess that the functions $G_n(u)$ and $H_n(u)$ for $n \in \mathbb{N}$ are absolutely monotonic in $u \in \mathbb{R}$. This guess is stronger than the inequalities (16) *and* (26).

7. Conclusions

In this paper, we reviewed the origination of the notion of normalized tails of infinitely differentiable functions' Maclaurin power series expansions, presenting that the ratio $\frac{f_{n+1}(u)}{f_n(u)}$ between the normalized tails $f_{n+1}(u)$ and $f_n(u)$ for $n \in \mathbb{N}$ is decreasing in $u \in (0, \infty)$, as well as proving that the normalized tail $f_n(u)$ for $n \in \mathbb{N}$ is absolutely monotonic in $u \in \mathbb{R}$.

Moreover, the guesses posed in Remarks 5 and 7 are interesting in mathematics.

Funding: This research received no external funding.

Data Availability Statement: No new data were created or analyzed in this study.

Acknowledgments: The author is thankful to anonymous reviewers for their careful corrections, helpful suggestions, and valuable comments on the original version of this article.

Conflicts of Interest: The author declares no conflicts of interest.

References

1. Li, Y.-W.; Qi, F.; Du, W.-S. Two forms for Maclaurin power series expansion of logarithmic expression involving tangent function. *Symmetry* **2023**, *15*, 1686. [CrossRef]
2. Li, Y.-F.; Qi, F. A series expansion of a logarithmic expression and a decreasing property of the ratio of two logarithmic expressions containing cosine. *Open Math.* **2023**, *21*, 20230159. [CrossRef]
3. Liu, X.-L.; Long, H.-X.; Qi, F. A series expansion of a logarithmic expression and a decreasing property of the ratio of two logarithmic expressions containing sine. *Mathematics* **2023**, *11*, 3107. [CrossRef]
4. Niu, D.-W.; Qi, F. Monotonicity results of ratios between normalized tails of Maclaurin power series expansions of sine and cosine. *Mathematics* **2024**, *12*, 1781. [CrossRef]
5. Wan, A.; Qi, F. Power series expansion, decreasing property, and concavity related to logarithm of normalized tail of power series expansion of cosine. *Electron. Res. Arch.* **2024**, *32*, 3130–3144. [CrossRef]
6. Wang, F.; Qi, F. Power series expansion and decreasing property related to normalized remainders of power series expansion of sine. *Filomat* 2024. Available online: https://www.researchgate.net/publication/382386328 (accessed on 17 July 2024).
7. Zhang, T.; Yang, Z.-H.; Qi, F.; Du, W.-S. Some properties of normalized tails of Maclaurin power series expansions of sine and cosine. *Fractal Fract.* **2024**, *8*, 257. [CrossRef]
8. Li, Y.-W.; Qi, F. A new closed-form formula of the Gauss hypergeometric function at specific arguments. *Axioms* **2024**, *13*, 317. [CrossRef]
9. Zhang, G.-Z.; Yang, Z.-H.; Qi, F. On normalized tails of series expansion of generating function of Bernoulli numbers. *Proc. Am. Math. Soc.* **2024**. [CrossRef]
10. Brychkov, Y.A. Power expansions of powers of trigonometric functions and series containing Bernoulli and Euler polynomials. *Integral Transform. Spec. Funct.* **2009**, *20*, 797–804. [CrossRef]

11. Gradshteyn, I.S.; Ryzhik, I.M. *Table of Integrals, Series, and Products;* Translated from the Russian, Translation edited and with a preface by Daniel Zwillinger and Victor Moll, Eighth edition, Revised from the seventh edition; Elsevier: Amsterdam, The Netherlands; Academic Press: Cambridge, MA, USA, 2015. [CrossRef]
12. Zhang, G.-Z.; Qi, F. On convexity and power series expansion for logarithm of normalized tail of power series expansion for square of tangent. *J. Math. Inequal.* 2025, *in press*. Available online: https://www.researchgate.net/publication/383273005 (accessed on 21 August 2024).
13. Bao, Z.-H.; Agarwal, R.P.; Qi, F.; Du, W.-S. Some properties on normalized tails of Maclaurin power series expansion of exponential function. *Symmetry* **2024**, *16*, 989. [CrossRef]
14. Qi, F. A method of constructing inequalities about e^x. *Univ. Beograd. Publ. Elektrotehn. Fak. Ser. Mat.* **1997**, *8*, 16–23.
15. Mitrinović, D.S.; Pečarić, J.E.; Fink, A.M. *Classical and New Inequalities in Analysis;* Kluwer Academic Publishers: Dordrecht, The Netherlands; Boston, MA, USA; London, UK, 1993. [CrossRef]
16. Widder, D.V. *The Laplace Transform;* Princeton Mathematical Series 6; Princeton University Press: Princeton, NJ, USA, 1946.
17. Schilling, R.L.; Song, R.; Vondraček, Z. *Bernstein Functions*, 2nd ed.; de Gruyter Studies in Mathematics 37; Walter de Gruyter: Berlin, Germany, 2012. [CrossRef]
18. Berg, C. Integral representation of some functions related to the gamma function. *Mediterr. J. Math.* **2004**, *1*, 433–439. [CrossRef]
19. Guo, B.-N.; Qi, F. A property of logarithmically absolutely monotonic functions and the logarithmically complete monotonicity of a power-exponential function. *Politehn. Univ. Bucharest Sci. Bull. Ser. A Appl. Math. Phys.* **2010**, *72*, 21–30.
20. Qi, F.; Chen, C.-P. A complete monotonicity property of the gamma function. *J. Math. Anal. Appl.* **2004**, *296*, 603–607. [CrossRef]
21. Biernacki, M.; Krzyż, J. On the monotonity of certain functionals in the theory of analytic functions. *Ann. Univ. Mariae Curie-Skłodowska Sect. A* **1955**, *9*, 135–147.
22. Heikkala, V.; Vamanamurthy, M.K.; Vuorinen, M. Generalized elliptic integrals. *Comput. Methods Funct. Theory* **2009**, *9*, 75–109. [CrossRef]
23. Ponnusamy, S.; Vuorinen, M. Asymptotic expansions and inequalities for hypergeometric functions. *Mathematika* **1997**, *44*, 278–301. [CrossRef]
24. Alzer, H.; Brenner, J.L.; Ruehr, O.G. Inequalities for the tails of some elementary series. *J. Math. Anal. Appl.* **1993**, *179*, 500–506. [CrossRef]
25. Qi, F. Decreasing properties of two ratios defined by three and four polygamma functions. *Comptes Rendus Math.* **2022**, *360*, 89–101. [CrossRef]
26. Pólya, G.; Szegö, G. *Problems and Theorems in Analysis, Volume I, Series, Integral Calculus, Theory of Functions;* Translated from the German by D. Aeppli. Corrected printing of the revised translation of the fourth German edition. Grundlehren der Mathematischen Wissenschaften, 193; Springer: Berlin/Heidelberg, Germany; New York, NY, USA, 1978.
27. Yang, Z.-H.; Chu, Y.-M. On approximating the modified Bessel function of the first kind and Toader-Qi mean. *J. Inequal. Appl.* **2016**, *2016*, 40. [CrossRef]
28. Qi, F.; Shi, X.-T.; Liu, F.-F.; Yang, Z.-H. A double inequality for an integral mean in terms of the exponential and logarithmic means. *Period. Math. Hung.* **2017**, *75*, 180–189. [CrossRef]
29. Mitrinović, D.S. *Analytic Inequalities;* Springer: Berlin/Heidelberg, Germany, 1970.

Σ mathematics

MDPI

Article

On Polar Jacobi Polynomials

Roberto S. Costas-Santos

Department of Quantitative Methods, Universidad Loyola Andalucía, 41704 Seville, Spain; rscosa@gmail.com

Abstract: In the present work, we investigate certain algebraic and differential properties of the orthogonal polynomials with respect to a discrete–continuous Sobolev-type inner product defined in terms of the Jacobi measure.

Keywords: orthogonal polynomials; Jacobi polynomials; recurrence relations; polar polynomials; location of zeros; asymptotic behavior

MSC: 42C05; 33C45; 12D10; 34D05

1. Introduction

Let us consider a measure μ supported on the subset of the complex plane γ.

In the vector space of polynomials with complex coefficients $\mathbb{P}$, let us introduce the following inner product:

$$\langle f, g \rangle_\xi := M f(\xi) g(\xi) + \int_\gamma f'(z) g'(z) d\mu(z), \quad M, \xi \in \mathbb{C}, \tag{1}$$

assuming that the integral exists. The inner product Equation (1) is called discrete–continuous Sobolev-type, which is a particular case of the Sobolev-type inner products. Algebraic and analytical properties and the limiting behavior of the families of orthogonal polynomials with respect to Sobolev-type inner products have been thoroughly used for the last 25 years. For an overview of this subject, see [1], or the introduction of [2] as well as [3].

Discrete–continuous Sobolev inner products were introduced in [4] to study the behavior of the optimal polynomial approximation of absolutely continuous functions in the norm generated by a Sobolev inner product as Equation (1). Later, in [5], R. Koekoek considered the Laguerre case with $d\mu = x^\alpha e^{-x} dx$, $\alpha > -1$, $\gamma = [0, +\infty)$ and $\xi = 0$. The Gegenbauer case was studied by Bavinck and Meijer in [6,7], with $d\mu = (1 - x^2)^{\lambda - 1/2} dx$, $\lambda > -1/2$, $\gamma = [-1, 1]$ and $\xi_1 = -1$ and $\xi_2 = 1$.

The families of orthogonal polynomials with respect to Equation (1) have been studied as an extension of the Bochner–Krall theory (i.e., polynomial sequences which are simultaneously eigenfunctions of a differential operator and orthogonal with respect to an inner product), see for the discrete–continuous case [8–10].

The starting point of our work is the orthogonality with respect to the Jacobi case. Let (Q_n) be the monic orthogonal polynomial sequence with respect to the Sobolev inner product

$$\langle f, g \rangle := f(\xi) g(\xi) + \int_\gamma f'(z) g'(z) (1 - z)^\alpha (1 + z)^\beta dz, \tag{2}$$

where $\alpha, \beta \in \mathbb{C}$, γ is a path encircling the points $+1$ and -1 first in a positive sense and then in a negative sense, as shown in Figure 2.1 in [11], $M = 1$ and $\xi \in \mathbb{C}$.

Let us consider $\left(P_n^{(\alpha,\beta)}(z)\right)$ as the monic Jacobi polynomials, i.e., the monic orthogonal polynomial sequence with respect to the measure $d\mu(z) = (1-z)^{\alpha}(1+z)^{\beta}dz$. Therefore, for each $n \in \mathbb{N}$, $P_n^{(\alpha,\beta)}(z)$ satisfies

$$\int_{\gamma} P_n^{(\alpha,\beta)}(z) z^k (1-z)^{\alpha}(1+z)^{\beta} dz = 0, \quad k = 0,1,\ldots,n-1, \tag{3}$$

and let $\Pi_{n+1,\xi}$ be the polynomial primitive of $(n+1)P_n^{(\alpha,\beta)}$ that has a zero at ξ, i.e., for all $n \geq 1$, we have

$$\Pi_{n+1,\xi}(\xi) = 0, \qquad \frac{d}{dz}\Pi_{n+1,\xi}(z) = (n+1)P_n^{(\alpha,\beta)}(z). \tag{4}$$

Then, by definition of Q_n, it is clear that $\Pi_{n+1,\xi}(z) = Q_{n+1}(z)$ for all $n = 0,1,2,\ldots$. It is straightforward to prove that the polynomial of degree n which is orthogonal with respect to Equation (2) can be written as follows (one must consider $Q_0(z) = 1$):

$$Q_n(z) = (z-\xi)P_{n-1}(z),$$

where P_n is called the `polar polynomial associated with` μ (see [12]) and ξ from now on will be called the `pole`. Let us define the differential operator $L_{\xi} : \mathcal{H}^1(\gamma) \to L^2(\gamma)$ as

$$L_{\xi}[f(z)] = f(z) + (z-\xi)\frac{d}{dz}f(z), \tag{5}$$

where $\mathcal{H}^1(\gamma) := \{f \in L^2(\gamma) : f'(z) \in L^2(\gamma)\}$ is the Sobolev space of index 1. Taking into account that Q_n is orthogonal with respect to the inner product Equation (2), we have

$$\int_{\gamma} L_{\xi}[P_n(z)] z^k (1-z)^{\alpha}(1+z)^{\beta} dz = \int_{\gamma} (P_n(z) + (z-\xi)P_n'(z)) z^k (1-z)^{\alpha}(1+z)^{\beta} dz = 0,$$

for $k = 0,1,\ldots,n-1$. Therefore, P_n is the monic orthogonal polynomial of degree n with respect to the differential operator L_{ξ}, and the measure $d\mu$ (see [12–17]). In such a case, for $n \in \mathbb{N}_0$, we have

$$P_n(z) + (z-\xi)P_n'(z) = (n+1)P_n^{(\alpha,\beta)}(z). \tag{6}$$

The main aim of this work is to study algebraic (zero localization) and differential properties of the polynomial sequences that are orthogonal with respect to the inner product Equation (2) for the Jacobi weight case, which is a natural extension of the Legendre case [12].

In Section 2, we obtain several algebraic relations between the polar Jacobi polynomials and the Jacobi polynomials and some differential and different identities related to the polar Jacobi polynomials. Finally, in Section 3 we study the location of the zeros for the polynomials P_n.

2. Algebraic Properties of the Polar Jacobi Polynomials

Let us start by summarizing some basic properties of the Jacobi orthogonal polynomials to be used in the sequel to Chapter 18 in [18]

Proposition 1. *Let $\left(P_n^{(\alpha,\beta)}(z)\right)$ be the classical monic Jacobi orthogonal polynomial sequence. The following statements hold:*

1. *Three-term recurrence relation.*

$$P_{n+1}^{(\alpha,\beta)}(z) = (z-\beta_n)P_n^{(\alpha,\beta)}(z) - \gamma_n P_{n-1}^{(\alpha,\beta)}(z), \quad n = 0,1,\ldots, \tag{7}$$

with initial condition $P_0^{(\alpha,\beta)}(z) = 1$, and recurrence coefficients

$$\beta_n = \frac{\beta^2 - \alpha^2}{(\alpha+\beta+2n)(\alpha+\beta+2n+2)}, \quad \gamma_n = \frac{4n(\alpha+n)(\beta+n)(\alpha+\beta+n)}{(\alpha+\beta+2n-1)(\alpha+\beta+2n)^2(\alpha+\beta+2n+1)}.$$

2. *First structure relation.*

$$(1-z^2)\frac{d}{dz}P_n^{(\alpha,\beta)}(z) = -nP_{n+1}^{(\alpha,\beta)}(z) + \widehat{\beta}_n P_n^{(\alpha,\beta)}(z) + \widehat{\gamma}_n P_{n-1}^{(\alpha,\beta)}(z), \quad n = 0,1,\ldots, \tag{8}$$

with coefficients

$$\widehat{\beta}_n = \frac{2n(\alpha-\beta)(\alpha+\beta+n+1)}{(\alpha+\beta+2n)(\alpha+\beta+2n+2)}, \quad \widehat{\gamma}_n = \frac{4n(\alpha+n)(\beta+n)(\alpha+\beta+n)(\alpha+\beta+n+1)}{(\alpha+\beta+2n-1)(\alpha+\beta+2n)^2(\alpha+\beta+2n+1)}.$$

3. *Second structure relation.*

$$P_{n+1}^{(\alpha-1,\beta-1)}(z) = P_{n+1}^{(\alpha,\beta)}(z) + \widetilde{\beta}_n P_n^{(\alpha,\beta)}(z) + \widetilde{\gamma}_n P_{n-1}^{(\alpha,\beta)}(z), \quad n = 0,1,\ldots, \tag{9}$$

$$\widetilde{\beta}_n = \frac{(2n+2)(\alpha-\beta)}{(\alpha+\beta+2n)(\alpha+\beta+2n+2)}, \quad \widetilde{\gamma}_n = -\frac{4n(n+1)(\alpha+n)(\beta+n)}{(\alpha+\beta+2n-1)(\alpha+\beta+2n)^2(\alpha+\beta+2n+1)}.$$

4. *Squared Norm. For every $n \geq 0$,*

$$\left\|P_n^{(\alpha,\beta)}(z)\right\|^2 = \int_\gamma \left(P_n^{(\alpha,\beta)}(z)\right)^2 \omega(z;\alpha,\beta)\,dz = \frac{2^{2n+\alpha+\beta+1} n!\Gamma(\alpha+n+1)\Gamma(\beta+n+1)\Gamma(\alpha+\beta+n+1)}{\Gamma(\alpha+\beta+2n+1)\Gamma(\alpha+\beta+2n+2)}. \tag{10}$$

5. *Second-order difference equation. For every $n \geq 0$,*

$$(1-z^2)\frac{d^2}{dz^2}P_n^{(\alpha,\beta)}(z) + (\beta-\alpha-z(\alpha+\beta+2))\frac{d}{dz}P_n^{(\alpha,\beta)}(z) = -n(\alpha+\beta+n+1)P_n^{(\alpha,\beta)}(z). \tag{11}$$

6. *Forward shift operator.*

$$\frac{d}{dz}P_n^{(\alpha,\beta)}(z) = nP_{n-1}^{(\alpha+1,\beta+1)}(z), \quad n = 0,1,\ldots, \tag{12}$$

7. *Asymptotic formula. Let $z \in \mathbb{C} \setminus [-1,1]$. Put $\varphi(z) = z + \sqrt{z^2-1}$ where the branch of the square root is chosen so that $|z + \sqrt{z^2-1}| > 1$ for $z \in \mathbb{C} \setminus [-1,1]$. Then,*

$$P_n^{(\alpha,\beta)}(z) = \frac{\varphi^n(z)}{\sqrt{n}}\left(c(\alpha,\beta,z) + \mathcal{O}(n^{-1})\right), \tag{13}$$

where $c(\alpha,\beta,z)$ is a function of α and β and x independent of n. The relation holds uniformly on compact sets of $\mathbb{C} \setminus [-1,1]$.

Let us obtain the algebraic relations between the Jacobi polynomials and the polar Jacobi polynomials.

Lemma 1. *For any $\alpha, \beta, \xi \in \mathbb{C}$. The polar Jacobi polynomials can be written in terms of the Jacobi polynomials as follows:*

$$\begin{aligned} P_n(z) &= \frac{P_{n+1}^{(\alpha-1,\beta-1)}(z) - P_{n+1}^{(\alpha-1,\beta-1)}(\xi)}{z-\xi} \\ &= \frac{1}{\alpha+\beta+n}\left[(z+\xi)\frac{d}{dz}P_n^{(\alpha,\beta)}(z) + \frac{\xi^2-1}{z-\xi}\left(\frac{d}{dz}P_n^{(\alpha,\beta)}(z) - \frac{d}{dz}P_n^{(\alpha,\beta)}(\xi)\right)\right. \end{aligned} \tag{14}$$

$$+(\alpha+\beta)P_n^{(\alpha,\beta)}(z)+\frac{\alpha-\beta+\xi(\alpha+\beta)}{z-\xi}\left(P_n^{(\alpha,\beta)}(z)-P_n^{(\alpha,\beta)}(\xi)\right)\Bigg]. \tag{15}$$

Therefore,

$$(z-\xi)P_n(z)=P_{n+1}^{(\alpha,\beta)}(z)+\widetilde{\beta}_nP_n^{(\alpha,\beta)}(z)+\widetilde{\gamma}_nP_{n-1}^{(\alpha,\beta)}(z)-P_{n+1}^{(\alpha-1,\beta-1)}(\xi). \tag{16}$$

Proof. From Equation (6), we have

$$(n+1)P_n^{(\alpha,\beta)}(z)=\frac{d}{dz}((z-\xi)P_n(z)).$$

Therefore, by using the forward shift operator Equation (12), we have

$$(z-\xi)P_n(z)=(n+1)\int_\xi^z P_n^{(\alpha,\beta)}(z)\,dz=\int_\xi^z\frac{d}{dz}\left(P_{n+1}^{(\alpha-1,\beta-1)}(z)\right)dz. \tag{17}$$

From Equation (17), the identity (14) follows. Using Equation (14) and the second structure relation (9) the expression (16) follows.

Let us now to prove Equation (15): by using the second-order differential Equation (11) with n,α,β being shifted to $n+1,\alpha-1,\beta-1$, respectively, and the forward shift operator of the Jacobi polynomials, we obtain

$$(1-z^2)\frac{d}{dz}P_n^{(\alpha,\beta)}(z)+(\beta-\alpha-z(\alpha+\beta))P_n^{(\alpha,\beta)}(z)=-(\alpha+\beta+n)P_{n+1}^{(\alpha-1,\beta-1)}(z). \tag{18}$$

By using the differential Equation (18) and the identity

$$\frac{f(z)g(z)-f(\xi)g(\xi)}{z-\xi}=\frac{f(z)-f(\xi)}{z-\xi}g(z)+f(\xi)\frac{g(z)-g(\xi)}{z-\xi},$$

then Equation (15) follows and hence the result holds. □

The following additional property of orthogonality holds.

Theorem 1. *The polar Jacobi polynomial P_n with pole $\xi\in\mathbb{C}$ fulfills the following property of orthogonality:*

$$\int_\gamma\left(P_n(z)+(z-\xi)\frac{d}{dz}P_n(z)\right)P_m^{(\alpha,\beta)}(z)\omega(z;\alpha,\beta)dz=\begin{cases}0, & m\neq n,\\ (n+1)\left\|P_n^{(\alpha,\beta)}(z)\right\|^2, & m=n.\end{cases} \tag{19}$$

Furthermore, if $n>1$, then

$$\int_\gamma(z-\xi)P_n(z)P_m^{(\alpha,\beta)}(z)\omega(z;\alpha,\beta)dz=\begin{cases}-\dfrac{2^{\alpha+\beta+1}\Gamma(\alpha+1)\Gamma(\beta+1)}{\Gamma(\alpha+\beta+2)}P_{n+1}^{(\alpha-1,\beta-1)}(\xi), & m=0,\\ 0, & 0<m<n-1,\\ \widetilde{\gamma}_n\left\|P_{n-1}^{(\alpha,\beta)}(z)\right\|^2, & n-1=m,\\ \widetilde{\beta}_n\left\|P_n^{(\alpha,\beta)}(z)\right\|^2, & n=m,\\ \left\|P_{n+1}^{(\alpha,\beta)}(z)\right\|^2, & n+1=m,\\ 0, & n+1<m.\end{cases} \tag{20}$$

Proof. Taking into account Equation (6), we have

$$\int_{\gamma}\left(P_n(z)+(z-\xi)\frac{d}{dz}P_n(z)\right)P_m^{(\alpha,\beta)}(z)\omega(z;\alpha,\beta)\,dz=(n+1)\int_{\gamma}P_n^{(\alpha,\beta)}(z)P_m^{(\alpha,\beta)}(z)\omega(z;\alpha,\beta)\,dz.$$

So, the first property of orthogonality follows. By using the relation (16) and considering the property of orthogonality of the Jacobi polynomials, the second property of orthogonality follows. Hence, the result holds. □

Theorem 2. *The sequence of polar Jacobi polynomials (P_n) with pole $\xi\in\mathbb{C}$ satisfies the following recurrence relation:*

$$P_{n+1}(z)=zP_n(z)+a_nP_n(z)+b_nP_{n-1}(z)+P_{n+1}^{(\alpha-1,\beta-1)}(\xi),\quad n=0,1,\dots,\tag{21}$$

with initial conditions $P_{-1}(z)=0$ and $P_0(z)=1$, and coefficients

$$a_n=\frac{(\alpha+\beta-2)(\alpha-\beta)}{(\alpha+\beta+2n)(\alpha+\beta+2n+2)},\quad b_n=-\frac{4(n+1)(\alpha+n)(\beta+n)(\alpha+\beta+n-1)}{(\alpha+\beta+2n-1)(\alpha+\beta+2n)^2(\alpha+\beta+2n+1)}.$$

Proof. Let the sequence $(\nu_{n,k})$ be such that

$$(z-\xi)P_n(z)=\sum_{k=0}^{n+1}\nu_{n,k}P_k(z),$$

where $\nu_{n,n+1}=1$.

Then, by using Equation (6), we obtain

$$\begin{aligned}(z-\xi)\left(P_n(z)+(n+1)P_n^{(\alpha,\beta)}(z)\right)&=(z-\xi)\left(P_n(z)+((z-\xi)P_n(z))'\right)\\&=\sum_{k=0}^{n+1}\nu_{n,k}\left(P_k(z)+(z-\xi)\frac{d}{dz}P_k(z)\right).\end{aligned}\tag{22}$$

By the property of orthogonality Equation (19), we have

$$\sum_{k=0}^{n+1}\nu_{n,k}\int_{\gamma}\left(P_k(z)+(z-\xi)\frac{d}{dz}P_k(z)\right)P_m^{(\alpha,\beta)}(z)\omega(z;\alpha,\beta)\,dz=\nu_{n,k}(m+1)\left\|P_m^{(\alpha,\beta)}(z)\right\|^2,\tag{23}$$

for $m=0,1,\dots,n$.

On the other hand, let us denote

$$I_{n,m}=\int_{\gamma}(z-\xi)P_m^{(\alpha,\beta)}(z)\left(P_n(z)+(n+1)P_n^{(\alpha,\beta)}(z)\right)\omega(z;\alpha,\beta)\,dz.$$

From the orthogonality of the Jacobi polynomials and the property of orthogonality (20), we obtain

$$I_{n,m}=\begin{cases}-2^{\alpha+\beta+1}P_{n+1}^{(\alpha-1,\beta-1)}(\xi)\dfrac{\Gamma(\alpha+1)\Gamma(\beta+1)}{\Gamma(\alpha+\beta+2)}, & m=0,\\ 0, & 0<m<n-1,\\ -\widetilde{\gamma}_n(\alpha+\beta+n-1)\left\|P_{n-1}^{(\alpha,\beta)}(z)\right\|^2, & n-1=m\\ \left(\dfrac{2-\alpha-\beta}{2}\widetilde{\beta}_n-\xi(n+1)\right)\left\|P_n^{(\alpha,\beta)}(z)\right\|^2, & n=m.\end{cases}\tag{24}$$

Thus, multiplying Equation (22) by $P_m^{(\alpha,\beta)}(z)$, integrating over γ, and using Equations (23) and (24), we obtain

$$\nu_{n,m} = \frac{I_{n,m}}{(m+1)\left\|P_m^{(\alpha,\beta)}(z)\right\|^2} = \begin{cases} -P_{n+1}^{(\alpha-1,\beta-1)}(\xi), & m = 0, \\ 0, & 0 < m < n-1, \\ -b_n, & m = n-1, \\ \frac{2-\alpha-\beta}{2(n+1)}\widetilde{\beta}_n - \xi, & m = n. \end{cases}$$

The expression (21) is obtained after a straightforward calculation. □

A direct consequence of this result is the following.

Corollary 1 (The polar ultraspherical case). *The sequence of symmetric polar Jacobi polynomials with pole $\xi \in \mathbb{C}$, i.e., the sequence of polar ultraspherical polynomial with pole $\xi \in \mathbb{C}$, satisfies, namely P_n, the following recurrence relation:*

$$\mathsf{P}_{n+1}(z) = z\mathsf{P}_n(z) - \frac{(n+1)(2\alpha+n-1)}{(2\alpha+2n-1)(2\alpha+2n+1)}\mathsf{P}_{n-1}(z) + \mathsf{P}_{n+1}^{(\alpha-1,\alpha-1)}(\xi), \quad n = 0,1,\ldots, \tag{25}$$

with initial conditions $\mathsf{P}_{-1}(z) = 0$ and $\mathsf{P}_0(z) = 1$.

Another direct consequence is the fact that when one, or both, of the parameters is a negative integer, we can factorize the Jacobi polynomial. In fact (see (1.2) in [11]),

$$P_n^{(-k,\beta)}(z) = (z-1)^k P_{n-k}^{(k,\beta)}, \tag{26}$$

$$P_n^{(\alpha,-k)}(z) = (z+1)^k P_{n-k}^{(\alpha,k)}. \tag{27}$$

Remark 1. *Since in some results we will consider the polar Jacobi polynomials with different parameters and poles, to avoid such possible confusion, we will denote by $P_n(z;\alpha,\beta;\xi)$ the polar Jacobi polynomial of degree n with parameters α and β, and pole at ξ.*

Corollary 2 (The factorization). *For any positive integer k, the following identities hold:*

$$P_{n+k}(z;-k,\beta;1) = (z-1)^k P_n^{k+1,\beta-1}(z) \tag{28}$$

$$= (z-1)^k\Big((z-1)P_{n-1}(z;k+2,\beta;1) + P_n^{k+1,\beta-1}(1)\Big), \tag{29}$$

$$P_{n+k}(z;\alpha,-k;-1) = (z+1)^k P_n^{\alpha-1,k+1}(z) \tag{30}$$

$$= (z+1)^k\Big((z+1)P_{n-1}(z;\alpha,k+2;-1) + P_n^{\alpha-1,k+1}(-1)\Big). \tag{31}$$

Moreover, the recurrence coefficients satisfy the following relations:

$$a_{n+k}(-k,\beta;1) = a_{n-1}(k+2,\beta;1), \quad b_{n+k}(-k,\beta;1) = b_{n-1}(k+2,\beta;1),$$

and

$$a_{n+k}(\alpha,-k;-1) = a_{n-1}(\alpha,k+2;-1), \quad b_{n+k}(\alpha,-k;-1) = b_{n-1}(\alpha,k+2;-1).$$

Proof. The identities (28)–(31) follow by using the factorization of the Jacobi polynomials Equations (26) and (27). In order to obtain the relation between the recurrence coefficients defined in Theorem 2, we must use the former factorization(s), and after a straightforward calculation the identities follow. □

The last result of this section is due the parity relation of the Jacobi polynomials, i.e.,

$$P_n^{(\alpha,\beta)}(z) = (-1)^n P_n^{(\beta,\alpha)}(-z). \tag{32}$$

Lemma 2. *For any $\xi \in \mathbb{C}$, the following identity holds:*

$$P_n(z;\alpha,\beta;\xi) = (-1)^n P_n(-z;\beta,\alpha;-\xi). \tag{33}$$

Proof. Starting from Equation (14) and using Equation (32), we have

$$\begin{aligned} P_n(z;\alpha,\beta;\xi) =& \frac{P_{n+1}^{\alpha-1,\beta-1}(z) - P_{n+1}^{\alpha-1,\beta-1}(\xi)}{z-\xi} = (-1)^{n+1}\frac{P_{n+1}^{\beta-1,\alpha-1}(-z) - P_{n+1}^{\beta-1,\alpha-1}(-\xi)}{z-\xi} \\ =&(-1)^n\frac{P_{n+1}^{\beta-1,\alpha-1}(-z) - P_{n+1}^{\beta-1,\alpha-1}(-\xi)}{-z-(-\xi)} = (-1)^n P_n(-z;\beta,\alpha;-\xi). \end{aligned}$$

□

3. Zero Location

Finding the roots of polynomials is a problem of interest in both mathematics and in areas of application such as physical systems, which can be reduced to solving certain equations. There are very interesting geometric relationships between the roots of a polynomial $f_n(z)$ and those of $f_n'(z)$. The most important result is the following.

Theorem 3 (The Gauß–Lucas theorem [19]). *Let $f_n(z) \in \mathbb{C}[z]$ be a polynomial of degree of at least one. All zeros of $f_n'(z)$ lie in the convex hull of the zeros of the zeros of $f_n(z)$.*

In this section, we are going to study the zero distribution for the polar Jacobi polynomials. The next result, which was obtained by G. Szegő, is useful to estimate where such zeros are located.

Theorem 4 (Szegő's theorem [20,21]). *Let $a(z)$ and $b(z)$ be polynomials of the form*

$$a(z) = \sum_{\ell=0}^{n} a_\ell \binom{n}{\ell} z^\ell, \quad b(z) = \sum_{\ell=0}^{n} b_\ell \binom{n}{\ell} z^\ell.$$

If the zeros of $a(z)$ lie in a closed disk $\overline{\mathrm{D}}$ and $\lambda_1, \ldots, \lambda_n$ are the zeros of $b(z)$, then the zeros of the "composition" of the two

$$c(z) = \sum_{\ell=0}^{n} a_\ell b_\ell \binom{n}{\ell} z^\ell,$$

have the form $\lambda_\ell \gamma_\ell$, where $\gamma_\ell \in \overline{\mathrm{D}}$.

By using this result, we are going to locate the disk within which all the zeros of the polar Jacobi are located.

Theorem 5. *For any $\Re\alpha, \Re\beta > -1$ and $\xi \in \mathbb{C}$, the zeros of $P_n(z;\alpha,\beta;\xi)$ lie inside the closed disk $\overline{D}(0, 2+|\xi|)$.*

Proof. Starting from Equation (6) and assuming that

$$a(z) = P_n^{(\alpha,\beta)}(w) = \sum_{k=0}^{n} \mu_k w^k, \quad c(z) = P_n(z;\alpha,\beta;w) = \sum_{k=0}^{n} \eta_k w^k,$$

where $w := z - \xi$, then $\eta_k = (n+1)/(k+1)\mu_k$. In order to apply Szegő's theorem, we consider

$$b(z) = \sum_{k=0}^{n} \binom{n}{k} \frac{n+1}{k+1} w^k = \sum_{k=0}^{n} \binom{n+1}{k+1} w^k = \frac{(w+1)^{n+1} - 1}{w}.$$

If $b(w_1) = 0$, then $|w_1 + 1| = 1$, so $|z_1| \leq 2 + |\xi|$. Moreover, if $a(z_2) = 0$, i.e., z_2 is a zero of $a(z)$, then $|z_2| \leq 1$. Therefore, combining these inequalities and applying Szegő's theorem one obtains that if $c(z_3) = 0$, i.e., z_3 is a zero of $c(z)$, then $|z_3| \leq 2 + |\xi|$ and hence the result follows. □

In Figure 1, we illustrate on the one hand how accurate Theorem 5 is, and on the other hand, we show the behavior of the zeros of the same polar Jacobi polynomial when the pole travels along a specific circle (observe $I = \sqrt{-1}$).

In Figure 2, we illustrate an example of Jacobi polar polynomials where the parameters $\Re\alpha \leq -1$ or $\Re\beta \leq -1$; therefore, the zeros of the Jacobi polynomial can move away from the interval $[-1, 1]$ in a somewhat uncontrolled way. Therefore, Theorem 5 cannot be applied in such a case. However, observe that in the considered example $-2 < \Re(\alpha + \beta) = -1.95 < -1$.

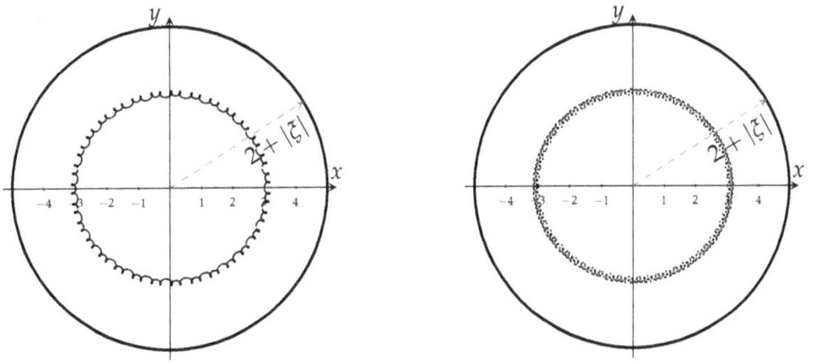

Figure 1. Left: Zeros of the polar Jacobi polynomial $P_{30}(z; 1/2, 2; 3\exp(2\pi kI/30))$ for $k = 0, 1, \ldots, 29$. Right: Zeros of the polar Jacobi polynomial $P_{30}(z; \sqrt{3}, \pi; 3\exp(2\pi kI/23))$ for $k = 0, 1, \ldots, 22$.

The next theorem gives the location of the zeros of the polar Jacobi polynomial of degree n and its multiplicity, or equivalently the location of source points and their corresponding strength.

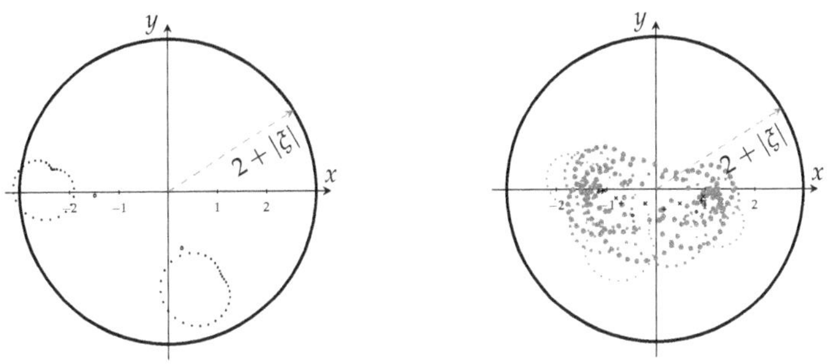

Figure 2. Left: Zeros of the polar Jacobi polynomial $P_2(z; -1/2 + I, -1.45 - I/2; \exp(2\pi kI/30))$ for $k = 0, 1, \ldots, 29$ (dots) and zeros of the Jacobi polynomials $P_2^{(-1/2+I, -1.45-I/2)}(z)$ (circles). Right: Zeros of the polar Jacobi polynomial $P_n(z; -1/2 + I, -1.45 - I/2; \exp(2\pi kI/30))$ for $k = 0, 1, \ldots, 29$ (gray dots) and zeros of the Jacobi polynomials $P_n^{(-1/2+I, -1.45-I/2)}(z)$ (+, ×, and circles) for $k = 0, 1, \ldots, 29$, $n = 3, 4, 5$.

Theorem 6. *For any $\Re\alpha, \Re\beta > -1$ and $\xi \in \mathbb{C}$. The following statements hold:*

1. *If $\zeta \in \mathbb{C}^*$ is a zero of $P_n(z;\alpha,\beta;\xi)$, then $z = -\zeta$ is a zero of $P_n(z;\beta,\alpha;-\xi)$.*
2. *If $\zeta \in \mathbb{C}^*$ is a zero of $P_n^{(\alpha,\beta)}(z)$, then ζ is a zero of $P_n(z)$.*
3. *The zeros of $P_n(z)$ have multiplicity of at most 2 and their multiple zeros are located on $[-1,1]$.*
4. *All the zeros of $P_n(z)$ are located on the curve*

$$\mathscr{L}_n(\xi) = \left\{ z \in \mathbb{C} \,:\, P_{n+1}^{(\alpha-1,\beta-1)}(z) = P_{n+1}^{(\alpha-1,\beta-1)}(\xi) \right\} \setminus \{\xi\}. \tag{34}$$

Proof. The first statement holds true due to Equation (34), the second statement holds true due to Equation (6), and the fourth statement holds true due to Equation (14).

Suppose that ω is a zero P_n of multiplicity greater than two; then, by (6), ω is a zero of $P_n^{(\alpha,\beta)}$ and also a zero of $\left(P_n^{(\alpha,\beta)}\right)'$. Thus, ω is a zero of multiplicity 2 of $P_n^{(\alpha,\beta)}$. This is a contradiction since the zeros of the Jacobi polynomials are all simple. Therefore, statement 3 holds true. □

Remark 2.

- *Observe that the zeros of P_n do not have to be simple. Let $\xi_+ = (1+2\sqrt{6})/5$ or $\xi_- = (1-2\sqrt{6})/5$; then, the polar polynomial of degree two $P_2(z;0,1,\xi_+) = \left(z - \frac{1-\sqrt{6}}{5}\right)^2$, or $P_2(z;0,1,\xi_-) = \left(z - \frac{1+\sqrt{6}}{5}\right)^2$.*
- *When the parameters are not standard, i.e., $\Re\alpha < -1$ or $\Re\beta < -1$ then, by Corollary 2, statement 3 of Theorem 6 is no longer true. For example, if $\alpha = -4$, $\beta = 1 > 0$, and $n = 5$, then $P_5(z;-4,1,1) = (z-1)^4(z-5/7)$.*

We can establish the following result concerning the boundedness of the zeros of the polar polynomials.

Lemma 3. *Given $\xi \in \mathbb{C}$, let us define the two numbers $\Delta_\xi := \sup\{|\xi - z| : z \in [-1,1]\}$ and $\delta_\xi := \inf\{|\xi - z| : z \in [-1,1]\}$. Then, the following can be stated:*

1. *All zeros of the polar Jacobi polynomials with pole ξ are contained in $|z| \le \Delta_\xi + 1$.*
2. *If $\delta_\xi > 1$, the zeros of the polar Jacobi polynomials with pole ξ are simple and contained in the exterior of the ellipse $|z+1| + |z-1| = 2\alpha$, where $1 < \alpha < \delta_\xi$.*

Proof. By Equation (14), the zeros of $P_n(z)$ are located in $\mathscr{L}_n(\xi)$. Since $\left|P_{n+1}^{(\alpha-1,\beta-1)}(\xi)\right| < \Delta_\xi^{n+1}$, they are contained in the interior of the set $\left|P_{n+1}^{(\alpha-1,\beta-1)}(z)\right| = \Delta_\xi^{n+1}$. It is known that the zeros of $P_{n+1}^{(\alpha-1,\beta-1)}(z)$, namely $x_{n+1,k}$, satisfy $|x_{n+1,k}| \le 1$. Therefore, for any $t \in \mathbb{C}$, such that $|t| > 1 + \Delta_\xi$, we have

$$\left|P_{n+1}^{(\alpha-1,\beta-1)}(z)\right| = \prod_{k=0}^{n} |z - x_{n+1,k}| \ge \prod_{k=0}^{n} \big||z| - |x_{n+1,k}|\big| > \Delta_\xi^{n+1}.$$

Hence, the first statement holds.

Concerning the second statement, let z be such that $|z+1| + |z-1| = 2\alpha$. From the well-known arithmetic–geometric mean inequality, we have

$$\left|P_{n+1}^{(\alpha-1,\beta-1)}(z)\right| \le \left(\frac{1}{n+1}\sum_{k=0}^{n} |z - x_{n+1,k}|\right)^{n+1} < \alpha^{n+1}.$$

If ω is a zero of P_n, we obtain, in view of Equation (34),

$$\left|P_{n+1}^{(\alpha-1,\beta-1)}(\omega)\right| = \left|P_{n+1}^{(\alpha-1,\beta-1)}(\xi)\right| = \prod_{k=0}^{n} |\xi - x_{n+1,k}| > \delta_{\xi}^{n+1} > \alpha^{n+1}.$$

Therefore, the result holds. □

The last result is about the asymptotic behavior of the zeros of the polar Jacobi polynomials.

Theorem 7 (Theorem 22 in [16]). *The accumulation points of zeros of* (P_n) *are located on the set* $\mathscr{E}(\xi) \cup [-1,1]$, *where* $\mathscr{E}(\xi)$ *is the ellipse*

$$\mathscr{E}(\xi) = \{z \in \mathbb{C} : z = \cosh(\log|\varphi(\xi)| + i\theta),\ 0 \le \theta < 2\pi\} = \left\{z \in \mathbb{C} : \left|z + \sqrt{z^2-1}\right| = |\varphi(\xi)|\right\},$$

where $\varphi(z) = z + \sqrt{z^2-1}$.

Funding: This research received no external funding.

Data Availability Statement: The original contributions presented in the study are included in the article, further inquiries can be directed to the corresponding author.

Conflicts of Interest: The author declares no conflicts of interest.

References

1. Martínez-Finkelshtein, A. Analytic aspects of Sobolev orthogonal polynomials revisited. *J. Comput. Appl. Math.* **2001**, *127*, 255–266. [CrossRef]
2. Lagomasino, G.L.; Español, F.M.; Cabrera, H. Logarithmic asymptotics of contracted Sobolev extremal polynomials on the real line. *J. Approx. Theory* **2006**, *143*, 62–73. [CrossRef]
3. Marcellán, F.; Xu, Y. On Sobolev orthogonal polynomials. *Expo. Math.* **2015**, *33*, 308–352. [CrossRef]
4. Cohen, E.A., Jr. Theoretical properties of best polynomial approximation in $W^{1,2}[-1,1]$. *SIAM J. Math. Anal.* **1971**, *2*, 187–192. [CrossRef]
5. Koekoek, R. Generalizations of Laguerre polynomials. *J. Math. Anal. Appl.* **1990**, *153*, 576–590. [CrossRef]
6. Bavinck, H.; Meijer, H.G. Orthogonal polynomials with respect to a symmetric inner product involving derivatives. *Appl. Anal.* **1989**, *33*, 103–117. [CrossRef]
7. Bavinck, H.; Meijer, H.G. On orthogonal polynomials with respect to an inner product involving derivatives: Zeros and recurrence relations. *Indag. Math. New Ser.* **1990**, *1*, 7–14. [CrossRef]
8. Alfaro, M.; Pérez, T.E.; Piñar, M.A.; Rezola, M.L. Sobolev orthogonal polynomials: The discrete-continuous case. *Methods Appl. Anal.* **1999**, *6*, 593–616. [CrossRef]
9. Jung, I.H.; Kwon, K.H.; Lee, J.K. Sobolev orthogonal polynomials relative to $\lambda p(c)q(c) + \langle\tau, p'(x)q'(x)\rangle$. *Commun. Korean Math. Soc.* **1997**, *12*, 603–617.
10. Kwon, K.H.; Littlejohn, L.L. Sobolev orthogonal polynomials and second-order differential equations. *Rocky Mt. J. Math.* **1998**, *28*, 547–594. [CrossRef]
11. Kuijlaars, A.B.J.; Martinez-Finkelshtein, A.; Orive, R. Orthogonality of Jacobi polynomials with general parameters. *arXiv* **2003**, arXiv:math/0301037.
12. Pijeira Cabrera, H.; Bello Cruz, J.Y.; Urbina Romero, W. On polar Legendre polynomials. *Rocky Mt. J. Math.* **2010**, *40*, 2025–2036. [CrossRef]
13. Aptekarev, A.I.; López Lagomasino, G.T.; Marcellán, F. Orthogonal polynomials with respect to a differential operator. Existence and uniqueness. *Rocky Mt. J. Math.* **2002**, *32*, 467–481. [CrossRef]
14. Borrego-Morell, J.; Pijeira-Cabrera, H. Orthogonality with respect to a Jacobi differential operator and applications. *J. Math. Anal. Appl.* **2013**, *404*, 491–500. [CrossRef]
15. Borrego-Morell, J.; Pijeira-Cabrera, H. Differential orthogonality: Laguerre and Hermite cases with applications. *J. Approx. Theory* **2015**, *196*, 111–130. [CrossRef]
16. Borrego Morell, J.A. On orthogonal polynomials with respect to a class of differential operators. *Appl. Math. Comput.* **2013**, *219*, 7853–7871. [CrossRef]
17. Pijeira-Cabrera, H.; Rivero-Castillo, D. Iterated integrals of Jacobi polynomials. *Bull. Malays. Math. Sci. Soc.* **2020**, *43*, 2745–2756. [CrossRef]
18. Olver, F.W.J.; Olde Daalhuis, A.B.; Lozier, D.W.; Schneider, B.I.; Boisvert, R.F.; Clark, C.W.; Miller, B.R.; Saunders, B.V.; Cohl, H.S.; McClain, M.A. (Eds.) *NIST Digital Library of Mathematical Functions, Release 1.2.1 of 2024-06-15*; National Institute of Standards and Technology: Gaithersburg, MD, USA, 2024.

19. Lucas, F. Theorems on algebraic equations. *C. R. Acad. Sci.* **1874**, *78*, 431–433.
20. Borwein, P.; Erdélyi, T. *Polynomials and Polynomial Inequalities*; Graduate Texts in Mathematics; Springer: New York, NY, USA, 1995; Volume 161, pp. x+480. [CrossRef]
21. Szegő, G. Bemerkungen zu einem Satz von J. H. Grace über die Wurzeln algebraischer Gleichungen. *Math. Z.* **1922**, *13*, 28–55. [CrossRef]

mathematics MDPI

Article

Generating Functions for Binomial Series Involving Harmonic-like Numbers

Chunli Li [1] **and Wenchang Chu** [2,*]

[1] School of Mathematics and Statistics, Zhoukou Normal University, Zhoukou 466001, China; lichunlizk@zknu.edu.cn or lichunlizk@outlook.com
[2] Department of Mathematics and Physics, University of Salento, 73100 Lecce, Italy
* Correspondence: wenchang.chu@unisalento.it or hypergeometricx@outlook.com

Abstract: By employing the coefficient extraction method, a class of binomial series involving harmonic numbers will be reviewed through three hypergeometric ${}_2F_1(y^2)$-series. Numerous closed-form generating functions for infinite series containing binomial coefficients and harmonic numbers will be established, including several conjectured ones.

Keywords: harmonic numbers; central binomial coefficient; hypergeometric series

MSC: 11B65; 33C20; 65B10

1. Introduction and Motivation

Harmonic numbers and their variants have been examined since Euler's era for more than three centuries and involved in many mathematical fields (cf. [1–6]), such as the analysis of algorithms (cf. [7]) in computer science, various topics of number theory (cf. [8–11]), and combinatorial analysis (cf. [12–14]). In this paper, we are going to review a particular class of binomial series (cf. [15–18]) with a free variable "y" and harmonic-like numbers. In order to proceed smoothly, it is necessary to go over some basic facts about harmonic numbers, the "coefficient extraction" method (cf. [19–21]), and classical hypergeometric series.

For the sake of brevity, we shall make use of the following notations throughout the paper for Catalan's constant and the Riemann zeta function (cf. [22]):

$$G=\sum_{k=1}^{\infty}\frac{(-1)^{k-1}}{(2k-1)^2}\quad\text{and}\quad\zeta(m)=\sum_{k=1}^{\infty}\frac{1}{k^m}\quad\text{for}\quad m>1.$$

1.1. Harmonic Numbers

For $\lambda\in\mathbb{R}$ and $m,n\in\mathbb{N}_0$, the harmonic-like numbers are defined by

$$\mathbf{H}_n^{\langle m\rangle}(\lambda)=\sum_{k=0}^{n-1}\frac{1}{(\lambda+k)^m},\quad \mathbf{O}_n^{\langle m\rangle}=\sum_{k=0}^{n-1}\frac{1}{(1+2k)^m};$$
$$\bar{\mathbf{H}}_n^{\langle m\rangle}(\lambda)=\sum_{k=0}^{n-1}\frac{(-1)^k}{(\lambda+k)^m},\quad \bar{\mathbf{O}}_n^{\langle m\rangle}=\sum_{k=0}^{n-1}\frac{(-1)^k}{(1+2k)^m}.$$

When $m=1$ and/or $\lambda=1$, they will be omitted from these notations. We also record the following simple but useful relations:

$$\mathbf{H}_n^{\langle m\rangle}(\tfrac{1}{2})=2^m\mathbf{O}_n^{\langle m\rangle},\qquad \mathbf{H}_{2n}^{\langle m\rangle}=\mathbf{O}_n^{\langle m\rangle}+2^{-m}\mathbf{H}_n^{\langle m\rangle};$$
$$\bar{\mathbf{H}}_n^{\langle m\rangle}(\tfrac{1}{2})=2^m\bar{\mathbf{O}}_n^{\langle m\rangle},\qquad \bar{\mathbf{H}}_{2n}^{\langle m\rangle}=\mathbf{O}_n^{\langle m\rangle}-2^{-m}\mathbf{H}_n^{\langle m\rangle}.$$

1.2. Coefficient Extraction

For $n \in \mathbb{N}_0$ and an indeterminate x, the shifted factorials are usually defined (cf. Bailey [23] §1.1) by

$$(x)_0 = 1 \quad \text{and} \quad (x)_n = x(x+1)\cdots(x+n-1) \quad \text{for} \quad n \in \mathbb{N}.$$

Let $[x^m]\phi(x)$ stand for the coefficient of x^m in the formal power series $\phi(x)$. Then, the harmonic-like numbers can be expressed as coefficients extracted from factorial quotients:

$$\begin{aligned}
&[x]\frac{(1+x)_n}{n!} = \mathbf{H}_n, && [x^2]\frac{(1+x)_n}{n!} = \frac{\mathbf{H}_n^2 - \mathbf{H}_n^{\langle 2\rangle}}{2},\\
&[x]\frac{n!}{(1-x)_n} = \mathbf{H}_n, && [x^2]\frac{n!}{(1-x)_n} = \frac{\mathbf{H}_n^2 + \mathbf{H}_n^{\langle 2\rangle}}{2},\\
&[x]\frac{(\frac12+x)_n}{(\frac12)_n} = 2\mathbf{O}_n, && [x^2]\frac{(\frac12+x)_n}{(\frac12)_n} = 2(\mathbf{O}_n^2 - \mathbf{O}_n^{\langle 2\rangle}),\\
&[x]\frac{(\frac12)_n}{(\frac12-x)_n} = 2\mathbf{O}_n, && [x^2]\frac{(\frac12)_n}{(\frac12-x)_n} = 2(\mathbf{O}_n^2 + \mathbf{O}_n^{\langle 2\rangle}).
\end{aligned}$$

For a real number $\lambda \notin \mathbb{Z}\backslash\mathbb{N}$, it is not difficult to verify that

$$\mathbf{H}_n(\lambda) = [x]\frac{(\lambda+x)_n}{(\lambda)_n} = [x]\frac{(\lambda)_n}{(\lambda-x)_n}.$$

In general, the following formulae hold (cf. Chu [5,21]):

$$[x^m]\frac{(\lambda-x)_n}{(\lambda)_n} = \Omega_m\Big\{-\mathbf{H}_n^{\langle k\rangle}(\lambda)\Big\} \quad \text{and} \quad [x^m]\frac{(\lambda)_n}{(\lambda-x)_n} = \Omega_m\Big\{\mathbf{H}_n^{\langle k\rangle}(\lambda)\Big\}, \tag{1}$$

where the Bell polynomials (cf. [24] §3.3) are expressed by the multiple sum

$$\Omega_m\Big\{\pm\mathbf{H}_n^{\langle k\rangle}(\lambda)\Big\} = \sum_{\omega(m)}\prod_{k=1}^{m}\frac{\{\pm\mathbf{H}_n^{\langle k\rangle}(\lambda)\}^{i_k}}{i_k!\,k^{i_k}}, \tag{2}$$

with $\omega(m)$ standing for the set of m-partitions represented by $(i_1, i_2, \cdots, i_m) \in \mathbb{N}_0^m$ subject to the linear condition $\sum\limits_{k=1}^{m} k i_k = m$.

1.3. Three ${}_2F_1(y^2)$-Series

By making use of the "coefficient extraction" method, we shall examine three closed formulae for ${}_2F_1$-series (cf. Chu [25]) convergent with $|y| < 1$ and establish several infinite series identities.

$$\boxed{A(x,y)} \qquad {}_2F_1\left[\begin{matrix}x, -x\\ \frac12\end{matrix}\,\middle|\,y^2\right] = \sum_{n=0}^{\infty}\frac{(x)_n(-x)_n}{n!(\frac12)_n}y^{2n} = \cos(2x\arcsin y),$$

$$\boxed{B(x,y)} \qquad {}_2F_1\left[\begin{matrix}x, 1-x\\ \frac12\end{matrix}\,\middle|\,y^2\right] = \sum_{n=0}^{\infty}\frac{(x)_n(1-x)_n}{n!(\frac12)_n}y^{2n} = \frac{\cos((2x-1)\arcsin y)}{\sqrt{1-y^2}},$$

$$\boxed{C(x,y)} \qquad {}_2F_1\left[\begin{matrix}x, 1-x\\ \frac32\end{matrix}\,\middle|\,y^2\right] = \sum_{n=0}^{\infty}\frac{(x)_n(1-x)_n}{n!(\frac32)_n}y^{2n} = \frac{\sin((2x-1)\arcsin y)}{(2x-1)y}.$$

The above three equalities are analytic in the neighborhood of $x = 0$ and can be expanded into Maclaurin series. For a real number λ, $m \in \mathbb{N}_0$, and $W \in \{A, B, C\}$, we denote by $W_m(\lambda+x, y) = [x^m]W(\lambda+x, y)$ the resulting equality from the coefficients of x^m extracted across the equality $W(\lambda+x, y)$. Then, numerous infinite series identities can be established using the "coefficient extraction method". The aim of this paper is to utilize the above three series to review the summation formulae involving both the binomial coefficient and harmonic-like numbers.

The rest of the paper will be divided into five sections in accordance with the binomial/multinomial structures. Each section consists of several algebraic formulae for infinite series involving harmonic-like numbers, which can be considered generating functions (cf. Wilf [26]) for binomial sequences, together with the harmonic-like numbers. A number of known results will be recorded for comparison, including several series conjectured by Sun [27–29]. In order to assure accuracy, all the displayed equalities are verified numerically through appropriately devised Mathematica commands.

2. Series with the Central Binomial Coefficient $\binom{2n}{n}$ in the Denominator

This section is devoted to harmonic series with the central binomial coefficient in the denominator.

2.1. Series from $\boxed{A(x,y)}$

Since $A(x,y)$ can be expanded into a power series of x, the initial coefficients give rise to the following three infinite series identities, where $\boxed{A_4(x,y)}$ can be found in Sun [29] (Equation 1.4).

$$\boxed{A_2(x,y)} \qquad \sum_{n=1}^{\infty} \frac{(2y)^{2n}}{n^2\binom{2n}{n}} = 2\arcsin^2 y,$$

$$\boxed{A_4(x,y)} \qquad \sum_{n=1}^{\infty} \frac{(2y)^{2n}}{n^2\binom{2n}{n}} \mathbf{H}_{n-1}^{\langle 2\rangle} = \frac{2\arcsin^4 y}{3},$$

$$\boxed{A_6(x,y)} \qquad \sum_{n=1}^{\infty} \frac{(2y)^{2n}}{n^2\binom{2n}{n}} \Big\{ \big(\mathbf{H}_{n-1}^{\langle 2\rangle}\big)^2 - \mathbf{H}_{n-1}^{\langle 4\rangle} \Big\} = \frac{8\arcsin^6 y}{45}.$$

We remark that these series are examples of the formula discovered by Borwein and Chamberland [30]. Some interesting numerical series are recorded as follows.

- Two numerical series from $A_2(x,y)$: $\boxed{\varphi = \frac{1+\sqrt{5}}{2},\ \bar{\varphi} = \frac{1-\sqrt{5}}{2}}$.

$$\boxed{A_2(x,\tfrac{\varphi}{2})} \qquad \sum_{n=1}^{\infty} \frac{\varphi^{2n}}{n^2\binom{2n}{n}} = 2\arcsin^2\Big(\frac{\varphi}{2}\Big),$$

$$\boxed{A_2(x,\tfrac{\bar{\varphi}}{2})} \qquad \sum_{n=1}^{\infty} \frac{\bar{\varphi}^{2n}}{n^2\binom{2n}{n}} = 2\arcsin^2\Big(\frac{\bar{\varphi}}{2}\Big).$$

Their linear combination leads to the following identity conjectured by Sun [27] (Page 7):

$$\sum_{n=1}^{\infty} \frac{L_{2n}}{n^2\binom{2n}{n}} = \frac{\pi^2}{5},$$

where the Lucas numbers are given by

$$L_{n+1} = L_n + L_{n-1} \quad \text{with} \quad L_0 = 2 \quad \text{and} \quad L_1 = 1$$

and can be expressed by Binet's formula

$$L_n = \varphi^n + \bar{\varphi}^n.$$

- Two further numerical series from $A_2(x,y)$:

$$\boxed{A_2(x,\tfrac{\sqrt{5}\varphi}{2})} \qquad \sum_{n=1}^{\infty}\frac{5^n\varphi^{2n}}{n^2\binom{2n}{n}} = 2\arcsin^2\Big(\frac{\sqrt{5}\varphi}{2}\Big),$$
$$\boxed{A_2(x,\tfrac{\sqrt{5}\bar{\varphi}}{2})} \qquad \sum_{n=1}^{\infty}\frac{5^n\bar{\varphi}^{2n}}{n^2\binom{2n}{n}} = 2\arcsin^2\Big(\frac{\sqrt{5}\bar{\varphi}}{2}\Big).$$

These are refined identities of the following identity conjectured by Sun [27] (Page 7):

$$\sum_{n=1}^{\infty}\frac{V_n}{n^2\binom{2n}{n}} = \frac{2\pi^2}{5},$$

where the V-sequence is defined by

$$V_{n+1} = 5(V_n - V_{n-1}) \quad \text{with} \quad V_0 = 2 \quad \text{and} \quad V_1 = 5$$

and can be expressed by Binet's formula

$$V_n = (\sqrt{5})^n\{\varphi^n + (-\bar{\varphi})^n\}.$$

- Analogous evaluations detected by Sun [28] (Conjectures 10.62 and 10.63):

$$\sum_{n=1}^{\infty}\frac{L_{2n}}{n^2\binom{2n}{n}}\Big\{\mathbf{H}_{2n} - \mathbf{H}_{n-1}\Big\} = \frac{41\zeta(3) + 4\pi^2\ln\varphi}{25},$$
$$\sum_{n=1}^{\infty}\frac{V_n}{n^2\binom{2n}{n}}\Big\{\mathbf{H}_{2n} - \mathbf{H}_{n-1}\Big\} = \frac{124\zeta(3) + \pi^2\ln(5^5\varphi^6)}{50}.$$

- Numerical series from $A_4(x,y)$:

$$\boxed{A_4(x,\tfrac{\sqrt{2}}{2})} \qquad \sum_{n=1}^{\infty}\frac{2^n\mathbf{H}^{\langle 2\rangle}_{n-1}}{n^2\binom{2n}{n}} = \frac{\pi^4}{384},$$
$$\boxed{A_4(x,\frac{\sqrt{3}}{2})} \qquad \sum_{n=1}^{\infty}\frac{3^n\mathbf{H}^{\langle 2\rangle}_{n-1}}{n^2\binom{2n}{n}} = \frac{2\pi^4}{243},$$
$$\boxed{A_4(x,\frac{\varphi}{2})} \qquad \sum_{n=1}^{\infty}\frac{\varphi^{2n}\mathbf{H}^{\langle 2\rangle}_{n-1}}{n^2\binom{2n}{n}} = \frac{27\pi^4}{5000},$$
$$\boxed{A_4(x,\frac{\bar{\varphi}}{2})} \qquad \sum_{n=1}^{\infty}\frac{\bar{\varphi}^{2n}\mathbf{H}^{\langle 2\rangle}_{n-1}}{n^2\binom{2n}{n}} = \frac{\pi^4}{15000}.$$

- Numerical series from $A_6(x,y)$:

$$\boxed{A_6(x,\tfrac{\sqrt{2}}{2})} \qquad \sum_{n=1}^{\infty}\frac{2^n\{(\mathbf{H}^{\langle 2\rangle}_{n-1})^2 - \mathbf{H}^{\langle 4\rangle}_{n-1}\}}{n^2\binom{2n}{n}} = \frac{21\zeta(6)}{512},$$
$$\boxed{A_6(x,\tfrac{\sqrt{3}}{2})} \qquad \sum_{n=1}^{\infty}\frac{3^n\{(\mathbf{H}^{\langle 2\rangle}_{n-1})^2 - \mathbf{H}^{\langle 4\rangle}_{n-1}\}}{n^2\binom{2n}{n}} = \frac{56\zeta(6)}{243},$$
$$\boxed{A_6(x,\tfrac{\varphi}{2})} \qquad \sum_{n=1}^{\infty}\frac{\varphi^{2n}\{(\mathbf{H}^{\langle 2\rangle}_{n-1})^2 - \mathbf{H}^{\langle 4\rangle}_{n-1}\}}{n^2\binom{2n}{n}} = \frac{15309\zeta(6)}{125000},$$
$$\boxed{A_6(x,\frac{\bar{\varphi}}{2})} \qquad \sum_{n=1}^{\infty}\frac{\bar{\varphi}^{2n}\{(\mathbf{H}^{\langle 2\rangle}_{n-1})^2 - \mathbf{H}^{\langle 4\rangle}_{n-1}\}}{n^2\binom{2n}{n}} = \frac{21\zeta(6)}{125000}.$$

- Particularly for $y = \frac{1}{2}$, we deduce two numerical series

$$\boxed{A_4(x,\tfrac{1}{2})} \qquad \sum_{n=1}^{\infty} \frac{\mathbf{H}_{n-1}^{\langle 2\rangle}}{n^2\binom{2n}{n}} = \frac{\pi^4}{1944},$$

$$\boxed{A_6(x,\tfrac{1}{2})} \qquad \sum_{n=1}^{\infty} \frac{\big(\mathbf{H}_{n-1}^{\langle 2\rangle}\big)^2 - \mathbf{H}_{n-1}^{\langle 4\rangle}}{n^2\binom{2n}{n}} = \frac{\pi^6}{262440}.$$

The former is a combination of the following two formulae (cf. Comtet [24] (Page 89) and Chu [20] (Example 3.8)):

$$\sum_{n=1}^{\infty} \frac{1}{n^4\binom{2n}{n}} = \frac{17\pi^4}{3240} \quad \text{and} \quad \sum_{n=1}^{\infty} \frac{\mathbf{H}_{n}^{\langle 2\rangle}}{n^2\binom{2n}{n}} = \frac{7\pi^4}{1215};$$

while for the latter, three refined formulae exist (cf. Chu [20])

$$\sum_{n=1}^{\infty} \frac{7 - 3n^4\big(\mathbf{H}_{n}^{\langle 2\rangle}\big)^2}{n^6\binom{2n}{n}} = \frac{65\pi^6}{34992},$$

$$\sum_{n=1}^{\infty} \frac{2 - n^2\mathbf{H}_{n}^{\langle 2\rangle}}{n^6\binom{2n}{n}} = \frac{313\pi^6}{612360},$$

$$\sum_{n=1}^{\infty} \frac{3n^4\mathbf{H}_{n}^{\langle 4\rangle} - 1}{n^6\binom{2n}{n}} = \frac{163\pi^6}{136080}.$$

It should be pointed out that the last two identities were first found by Bailey et al. [31], and amusingly, conjectured by Sun [32] (Equations 4.6 and 4.7) subsequently.

2.2. *Series from* $\boxed{B(x,y)}$

Considering that $B(x,y)$ is a power series of x, the initial coefficients yield the identities below.

$$\boxed{B_1(x,y)} \qquad \sum_{n=1}^{\infty} \frac{(2y)^{2n}}{n\binom{2n}{n}} = \frac{2y\arcsin y}{\sqrt{1-y^2}},$$

$$\boxed{B_3(x,y)} \qquad \sum_{n=1}^{\infty} \frac{(2y)^{2n}}{n\binom{2n}{n}}\mathbf{H}_{n-1}^{\langle 2\rangle} = \frac{4y\arcsin^3 y}{3\sqrt{1-y^2}},$$

$$\boxed{B_5(x,y)} \qquad \sum_{n=1}^{\infty} \frac{(2y)^{2n}}{n\binom{2n}{n}}\Big\{\big(\mathbf{H}_{n-1}^{\langle 2\rangle}\big)^2 - \mathbf{H}_{n-1}^{\langle 4\rangle}\Big\} = \frac{8y\arcsin^5 y}{15\sqrt{1-y^2}}.$$

For comparison, we record five sample series conjectured experimentally by Sun [27], where the fourth and fifth series were evaluated by Chu [20].

$$\sum_{k=1}^{\infty} \frac{2^k\mathbf{H}_k}{k^2\binom{2k}{k}} = \frac{7\zeta(3)}{16} + \frac{\pi^2}{8}\ln 2,$$

$$\sum_{k=1}^{\infty} \frac{2^k\mathbf{O}_k}{k^2\binom{2k}{k}} = \frac{7\zeta(3)}{2} - \pi G,$$

$$\sum_{k=1}^{\infty} \frac{3^k(1+2k\mathbf{H}_k)}{k^3\binom{2k}{k}} = \frac{2\pi^2}{3}\ln 3,$$

$$\sum_{k=1}^{\infty} \frac{\mathbf{H}_{2k} + 2\mathbf{H}_k}{k^2\binom{2k}{k}} = \frac{5\zeta(3)}{3},$$

$$\sum_{k=1}^{\infty} \frac{\mathbf{H}_{k}^{\langle 3\rangle}}{k^2\binom{2k}{k}} = \frac{\zeta(5) + 2\zeta(2)\zeta(3)}{9}.$$

2.3. *Series from* $\boxed{C(x,y)}$

By expanding $C(x,y)$ into a power series of x, we record the following infinite series identities from the initial coefficients.

$$\boxed{C_1(x,y)}\ \sum_{n=1}^{\infty}\frac{(2y)^{2n}}{n\binom{2n}{n}(2n+1)}=2-\frac{2\sqrt{1-y^2}\arcsin y}{y},$$

$$\boxed{C_2(x,y)}\ \sum_{n=1}^{\infty}\frac{(2y)^{2n}}{n^2\binom{2n}{n}(2n+1)}=2\arcsin^2 y-4+\frac{4\sqrt{1-y^2}\arcsin y}{y},$$

$$\boxed{C_3(x,y)}\ \sum_{n=1}^{\infty}\frac{(2y)^{2n}\mathbf{H}^{\langle 2\rangle}_{n-1}}{n\binom{2n}{n}(2n+1)}=4\arcsin^2 y-8-\frac{4\sqrt{1-y^2}}{3y}\Big\{\arcsin^3 y-6\arcsin y\Big\},$$

$$\boxed{C_4(x,y)}\ \sum_{n=1}^{\infty}\frac{(2y)^{2n}\mathbf{H}^{\langle 2\rangle}_{n-1}}{n^2\binom{2n}{n}(2n+1)}=16-8\arcsin^2 y+\tfrac{2}{3}\arcsin^4 y+\tfrac{8\sqrt{1-y^2}}{3y}\Big\{\arcsin^3 y-6\arcsin y\Big\},$$

$$\boxed{C_5(x,y)}\ \sum_{n=1}^{\infty}\frac{(2y)^{2n}}{n\binom{2n}{n}}\frac{\big(\mathbf{H}^{\langle 2\rangle}_{n-1}\big)^2-\mathbf{H}^{\langle 4\rangle}_{n-1}}{(2n+1)}=\left\{\begin{matrix}\frac{8}{3}\arcsin^4 y-32\arcsin^2 y+64\\ -\frac{8\sqrt{1-y^2}}{15y}\Big[120\arcsin y-20\arcsin^3 y+\arcsin^5 y\Big]\end{matrix}\right\},$$

$$\boxed{C_6(x,y)}\ \sum_{n=1}^{\infty}\frac{(2y)^{2n}}{n^2\binom{2n}{n}}\frac{\big(\mathbf{H}^{\langle 2\rangle}_{n-1}\big)^2-\mathbf{H}^{\langle 4\rangle}_{n-1}}{(2n+1)}=\left\{\begin{matrix}\frac{8}{45}\arcsin^6 y-\frac{16}{3}\arcsin^4 y+64\arcsin^2 y-128\\ +\frac{16\sqrt{1-y^2}}{15y}\Big[120\arcsin y-20\arcsin^3 y+\arcsin^5 y\Big]\end{matrix}\right\}.$$

3. Series with the Central Binomial Coefficient $\binom{2n}{n}$ in the Numerator

This section is devoted to harmonic series with the central binomial coefficient in the numerator.

3.1. *Series from* $\boxed{A\Big(\frac{1}{2}+x,y\Big)}$

Since $A(\frac{1}{2}+x,y)$ can be expanded into a power series of x, the initial coefficients give rise to the following six infinite series identities.

$$\boxed{A_0(\tfrac{1}{2}+x,y)}\ \sum_{n=0}^{\infty}\Big(\frac{y}{2}\Big)^{2n}\binom{2n}{n}\frac{1}{2n-1}=-\sqrt{1-y^2},$$

$$\boxed{A_1(\tfrac{1}{2}+x,y)}\ \sum_{n=0}^{\infty}\Big(\frac{y}{2}\Big)^{2n}\binom{2n}{n}\frac{2n}{(2n-1)^2}=y\arcsin y,$$

$$\boxed{A_2(\tfrac{1}{2}+x,y)}\ \sum_{n=1}^{\infty}\Big(\frac{y}{2}\Big)^{2n}\binom{2n}{n}\bigg\{\frac{\mathbf{O}^{\langle 2\rangle}_{n-1}}{2n-1}-\frac{1}{(2n-1)^2}\bigg\}=\frac{\sqrt{1-y^2}\arcsin^2 y}{-2},$$

$$\boxed{A_3(\tfrac{1}{2}+x,y)}\ \sum_{n=1}^{\infty}\Big(\frac{y}{2}\Big)^{2n}\binom{2n}{n}\frac{n\mathbf{O}^{\langle 2\rangle}_{n-1}}{(2n-1)^2}=\frac{y\arcsin^3 y}{12},$$

$$\boxed{A_4(\tfrac{1}{2}+x,y)}\ \sum_{n=1}^{\infty}\Big(\frac{y}{2}\Big)^{2n}\binom{2n}{n}\bigg\{\frac{(\mathbf{O}^{\langle 2\rangle}_{n-1})^2-\mathbf{O}^{\langle 4\rangle}_{n-1}}{2n-1}-\frac{2\mathbf{O}^{\langle 2\rangle}_{n-1}}{(2n-1)^2}\bigg\}=\frac{\sqrt{1-y^2}\arcsin^4 y}{-12},$$

$$\boxed{A_5(\tfrac{1}{2}+x,y)}\ \sum_{n=1}^{\infty}\Big(\frac{y}{2}\Big)^{2n}\binom{2n}{n}\frac{n\{(\mathbf{O}^{\langle 2\rangle}_{n-1})^2-\mathbf{O}^{\langle 4\rangle}_{n-1}\}}{(2n-1)^2}=\frac{y\arcsin^5 y}{120}.$$

3.2. *Series from* $\boxed{B\Big(\frac{1}{2}+x,y\Big)}$

Considering that $B(\frac{1}{2}+x,y)$ is a power series of x, the initial coefficients yield the identities below, where $\boxed{B_2(\frac{1}{2}+x,y)}$ is equivalent to the formula by Sun [29] (Equation 1.5).

$$\boxed{B_0(\tfrac{1}{2}+x,y)}\quad \sum_{n=0}^{\infty}\Big(\frac{y}{2}\Big)^{2n}\binom{2n}{n}=\frac{1}{\sqrt{1-y^2}},$$

$$\boxed{B_2(\tfrac{1}{2}+x,y)}\quad \sum_{n=1}^{\infty}\Big(\frac{y}{2}\Big)^{2n}\binom{2n}{n}\mathbf{O}_n^{\langle 2\rangle}=\frac{\arcsin^2 y}{2\sqrt{1-y^2}},$$

$$\boxed{B_4(\tfrac{1}{2}+x,y)}\quad \sum_{n=1}^{\infty}\Big(\frac{y}{2}\Big)^{2n}\binom{2n}{n}\Big\{(\mathbf{O}_n^{\langle 2\rangle})^2-\mathbf{O}_n^{\langle 4\rangle}\Big\}=\frac{\arcsin^4 y}{12\sqrt{1-y^2}},$$

$$\boxed{B_6(\tfrac{1}{2}+x,y)}\quad \sum_{n=1}^{\infty}\Big(\frac{y}{2}\Big)^{2n}\binom{2n}{n}\Big\{(\mathbf{O}_n^{\langle 2\rangle})^3-3\mathbf{O}_n^{\langle 2\rangle}\mathbf{O}_n^{\langle 4\rangle}+2\mathbf{O}_n^{\langle 6\rangle}\Big\}=\frac{\arcsin^6 y}{120\sqrt{1-y^2}}.$$

Unlike these series, there are two similar identities conjectured by Sun [29] (Equations 2.4 and 2.5):

$$\sum_{k=0}^{\infty}\frac{\binom{2k}{k}}{8^k}\mathbf{O}_k^{\langle 3\rangle}=\frac{35\sqrt{2}}{64}\zeta(3)-\frac{\sqrt{2}}{8}\pi G\quad\text{and}\quad\sum_{k=0}^{\infty}\frac{\binom{2k}{k}}{16^k}\mathbf{O}_k^{\langle 3\rangle}=\frac{2\zeta(3)}{3\sqrt{3}}-\frac{\pi K}{8}.$$

The former was confirmed by the authors [33] (Theorem 19), while the latter remains unproven.

3.3. Series from $\boxed{C\Big(\frac{1}{2}+x,y\Big)}$

By expanding $C(\frac{1}{2}+x,y)$ into a power series of x, we record the following infinite series identities from the initial coefficients, which are particular cases of a more general formula appearing in [30].

$$\boxed{C_0(\tfrac{1}{2}+x,y)}\quad \sum_{n=0}^{\infty}\Big(\frac{y}{2}\Big)^{2n}\binom{2n}{n}\frac{1}{2n+1}=\frac{\arcsin y}{y},$$

$$\boxed{C_2(\tfrac{1}{2}+x,y)}\quad \sum_{n=1}^{\infty}\Big(\frac{y}{2}\Big)^{2n}\binom{2n}{n}\frac{\mathbf{O}_n^{\langle 2\rangle}}{2n+1}=\frac{\arcsin^3 y}{6y},$$

$$\boxed{C_4(\tfrac{1}{2}+x,y)}\quad \sum_{n=1}^{\infty}\Big(\frac{y}{2}\Big)^{2n}\binom{2n}{n}\frac{(\mathbf{O}_n^{\langle 2\rangle})^2-\mathbf{O}_n^{\langle 4\rangle}}{2n+1}=\frac{\arcsin^5 y}{60y},$$

$$\boxed{C_6(\tfrac{1}{2}+x,y)}\quad \sum_{n=1}^{\infty}\Big(\frac{y}{2}\Big)^{2n}\binom{2n}{n}\frac{(\mathbf{O}_n^{\langle 2\rangle})^3-3\mathbf{O}_n^{\langle 2\rangle}\mathbf{O}_n^{\langle 4\rangle}+2\mathbf{O}_n^{\langle 6\rangle}}{2n+1}=\frac{\arcsin^7 y}{840y}.$$

For these identities, many numerical series related to them exist in the literature.

- Numerical series from $C_2(\frac{1}{2}+x,y)$:

$$\boxed{C_2(\tfrac{1}{2}+x,\tfrac{1}{2})}\quad \sum_{n=1}^{\infty}\Big(\frac{1}{16}\Big)^{n}\frac{\binom{2n}{n}\mathbf{O}_n^{\langle 2\rangle}}{2n+1}=\frac{\pi^3}{648},$$

$$\boxed{C_2(\tfrac{1}{2}+x,\tfrac{\sqrt{2}}{2})}\quad \sum_{n=1}^{\infty}\Big(\frac{1}{8}\Big)^{n}\frac{\binom{2n}{n}\mathbf{O}_n^{\langle 2\rangle}}{2n+1}=\frac{\pi^3}{192\sqrt{2}},$$

$$\boxed{C_2(\tfrac{1}{2}+x,\tfrac{\sqrt{3}}{2})}\quad \sum_{n=1}^{\infty}\Big(\frac{3}{16}\Big)^{n}\frac{\binom{2n}{n}\mathbf{O}_n^{\langle 2\rangle}}{2n+1}=\frac{\pi^3}{81\sqrt{3}},$$

$$\boxed{C_2(\tfrac{1}{2}+x,\tfrac{\varphi}{2})}\quad \sum_{n=1}^{\infty}\Big(\frac{\varphi}{4}\Big)^{2n}\frac{\binom{2n}{n}\mathbf{O}_n^{\langle 2\rangle}}{2n+1}=\frac{9\pi^3}{1000\varphi},$$

$$\boxed{C_2(\tfrac{1}{2}+x,\tfrac{\bar{\varphi}}{2})}\quad \sum_{n=1}^{\infty}\Big(\frac{\bar{\varphi}}{4}\Big)^{2n}\frac{\binom{2n}{n}\mathbf{O}_n^{\langle 2\rangle}}{2n+1}=\frac{\pi^3\varphi}{3000}.$$

- Numerical series from $C_4(\frac{1}{2}+x, y)$:

$$\boxed{C_4(\tfrac{1}{2}+x,\tfrac{1}{2})} \quad \sum_{n=1}^{\infty}\Big(\frac{1}{16}\Big)^n \frac{\binom{2n}{n}}{2n+1}\Big\{(\mathbf{O}_n^{\langle 2\rangle})^2-\mathbf{O}_n^{\langle 4\rangle}\Big\} = \frac{\pi^5}{233280},$$

$$\boxed{C_4(\tfrac{1}{2}+x,\tfrac{i}{2})} \quad \sum_{n=1}^{\infty}\Big(\frac{-1}{16}\Big)^n \frac{\binom{2n}{n}}{2n+1}\Big\{(\mathbf{O}_n^{\langle 2\rangle})^2-\mathbf{O}_n^{\langle 4\rangle}\Big\} = \frac{\ln^5(\frac{1+\sqrt{5}}{2})}{30},$$

$$\boxed{C_4(\tfrac{1}{2}+x,\tfrac{\sqrt{2}}{2})} \quad \sum_{n=1}^{\infty}\Big(\frac{1}{8}\Big)^n \frac{\binom{2n}{n}}{2n+1}\Big\{(\mathbf{O}_n^{\langle 2\rangle})^2-\mathbf{O}_n^{\langle 4\rangle}\Big\} = \frac{\pi^5}{30720\sqrt{2}},$$

$$\boxed{C_4(\tfrac{1}{2}+x,\tfrac{\sqrt{3}}{2})} \quad \sum_{n=1}^{\infty}\Big(\frac{3}{16}\Big)^n \frac{\binom{2n}{n}}{2n+1}\Big\{(\mathbf{O}_n^{\langle 2\rangle})^2-\mathbf{O}_n^{\langle 4\rangle}\Big\} = \frac{\pi^5}{7290\sqrt{3}},$$

$$\boxed{C_4(\tfrac{1}{2}+x,\tfrac{\varphi}{2})} \quad \sum_{n=1}^{\infty}\Big(\frac{\varphi}{4}\Big)^{2n} \frac{\binom{2n}{n}}{2n+1}\Big\{(\mathbf{O}_n^{\langle 2\rangle})^2-\mathbf{O}_n^{\langle 4\rangle}\Big\} = \frac{81\pi^5}{10^6\varphi},$$

$$\boxed{C_4(\tfrac{1}{2}+x,\tfrac{\bar{\varphi}}{2})} \quad \sum_{n=1}^{\infty}\Big(\frac{\bar{\varphi}}{4}\Big)^{2n} \frac{\binom{2n}{n}}{2n+1}\Big\{(\mathbf{O}_n^{\langle 2\rangle})^2-\mathbf{O}_n^{\langle 4\rangle}\Big\} = \frac{\pi^5\varphi}{3\times 10^6}.$$

- The identity corresponding to $\boxed{C_4(\frac{1}{2}+x,\frac{1}{2})}$ was refined by the following ones due to Li and Chu [21] (Equations 30 and 32):

$$\sum_{n=0}^{\infty}\Big(\frac{1}{16}\Big)^n \frac{\binom{2n}{n}}{2n+1}\Big\{3\mathbf{O}_n^{\langle 4\rangle}+\frac{2}{(2n+1)^4}\Big\} = \frac{121\pi^5}{17280},$$

$$\sum_{n=0}^{\infty}\Big(\frac{1}{16}\Big)^n \frac{\binom{2n}{n}}{2n+1}\Big\{3(\mathbf{O}_n^{\langle 2\rangle})^2+\frac{2}{(2n+1)^4}\Big\} = \frac{1091\pi^5}{155520};$$

where the former was experimentally detected by Sun [27] (Equation 1.50).

- We remark that for the formula corresponding to $C_4(\frac{1}{2}+x,\frac{i}{2})$, the following counterpart exists:

$$\sum_{n=0}^{\infty}\frac{\binom{2n}{n}}{(2n+1)^2(-16)^k}\Big\{5\mathbf{O}_n^{\langle 4\rangle}+\frac{1}{(2n+1)^4}\Big\} = \frac{7\pi^6}{7200},$$

which was conjectured by Sun [28] (Conjecture 10.74) and confirmed in [5] (Equation 7).

- For comparison, we record below variant series involving skew harmonic numbers in odd order, conjectured by Sun [27,28] and evaluated by Li and Chu [5,21]:
  - ⋆ Sun [27] (Equation 1.43) and Li–Chu [21] (Equation 25):

$$\sum_{n=0}^{\infty}\frac{\binom{2n}{n}\mathbf{O}_{n+1}^{\langle 3\rangle}}{(2n+1)16^k} = \frac{5\pi}{18}\zeta(3).$$

  - ⋆ Sun [28] (Conjecture 10.71) and Li–Chu [5] (Equation 6):

$$\sum_{n=0}^{\infty}\frac{\binom{2n}{n}}{(2n+1)^2(-16)^k}\Big\{5\mathbf{O}_{n+1}^{\langle 3\rangle}+\frac{1}{(2n+1)^3}\Big\} = \frac{\pi^2}{2}\zeta(3).$$

  - ⋆ Sun [27] (Equation 1.50) and Li–Chu [21] (Equation 35):

$$\sum_{n=0}^{\infty}\frac{\binom{2n}{n}}{(2n+1)16^k}\Big\{33\mathbf{O}_{n+1}^{\langle 5\rangle}+\frac{4}{(2n+1)^5}\Big\} = \frac{35\pi^3}{288}\zeta(3)+\frac{1003\pi}{96}\zeta(5).$$

- ⋆ Sun [27] (Equation 1.56) and Li–Chu [21] (Equation 34):

$$\sum_{n=0}^{\infty} \frac{\binom{2n}{n}}{(2n+1)^3 16^k} \left\{ 33\mathbf{O}_{n+1}^{\langle 3 \rangle} + \frac{8}{(2n+1)^3} \right\} = \frac{245\pi^3}{216}\zeta(3) - \frac{49\pi}{144}\zeta(5).$$

4. Series Containing the Binomial Coefficient $\binom{3n}{n}$

This section is devoted to harmonic series with the binomial coefficient $\binom{3n}{n}$. By integrating Lambert's series and manipulating the cubic transformations for the ${}_3F_2$-series, the authors evaluated several similar series in a recent paper [34]. Adegoke–Frontczak–Goy [35] evaluated different series without harmonic numbers.

4.1. *Series from* $\boxed{A\left(\frac{1}{3}+x,y\right)}$

Since $A(\frac{1}{3}+x,y)$ can be expanded into a power series of x, the initial coefficients give rise to the following three infinite series identities.

$$\boxed{A_0(\tfrac{1}{3}+x,y)} \quad \sum_{n=0}^{\infty} \left(\frac{4y^2}{27}\right)^n \binom{3n}{n} \frac{1}{3n-1} = -\cos\left(\tfrac{2\arcsin y}{3}\right),$$

$$\boxed{A_1(\tfrac{1}{3}+x,y)} \quad \sum_{n=0}^{\infty} \left(\frac{4y^2}{27}\right)^n \binom{3n}{n} \left\{ \frac{\mathbf{H}_n(\frac{1}{3})-\mathbf{H}_n(\frac{2}{3})}{3n-1} + \frac{9n}{(3n-1)^2} \right\} = 2\arcsin y \sin\left(\tfrac{2\arcsin y}{3}\right),$$

$$\boxed{A_2(\tfrac{1}{3}+x,y)} \quad \sum_{n=0}^{\infty} \left(\frac{4y^2}{27}\right)^n \binom{3n}{n} \left\{ \begin{array}{c} \frac{\mathbf{H}_n^{\langle 2 \rangle}(\frac{1}{3})+\mathbf{H}_n^{\langle 2 \rangle}(\frac{2}{3})-\left[\mathbf{H}_n(\frac{1}{3})-\mathbf{H}_n(\frac{2}{3})\right]^2}{2(3n-1)} \\ -\frac{9n\left[\mathbf{H}_n(\frac{1}{3})-\mathbf{H}_n(\frac{2}{3})\right]}{(3n-1)^2} - \frac{27n}{(3n-1)^3} \end{array} \right\} = -2\arcsin^2 y \cos\left(\tfrac{2\arcsin y}{3}\right).$$

4.2. *Series from* $\boxed{B\left(\frac{1}{3}+x,y\right)}$

Considering that $B(\frac{1}{3}+x,y)$ is a power series of x, the initial coefficients yield the identities below.

$$\boxed{B_0(\tfrac{1}{3}+x,y)} \quad \sum_{n=0}^{\infty} \left(\frac{4y^2}{27}\right)^n \binom{3n}{n} = \frac{\cos(\frac{\arcsin y}{3})}{\sqrt{1-y^2}},$$

$$\boxed{B_1(\tfrac{1}{3}+x,y)} \quad \sum_{n=0}^{\infty} \left(\frac{4y^2}{27}\right)^n \binom{3n}{n} \left\{ \mathbf{H}_n(\tfrac{1}{3}) - \mathbf{H}_n(\tfrac{2}{3}) \right\} = \frac{2\arcsin y \sin(\frac{\arcsin y}{3})}{\sqrt{1-y^2}},$$

$$\boxed{B_2(\tfrac{1}{3}+x,y)} \quad \sum_{n=0}^{\infty} \left(\frac{4y^2}{27}\right)^n \binom{3n}{n} \left\{ \begin{array}{c} \mathbf{H}_n^{\langle 2 \rangle}(\frac{1}{3}) + \mathbf{H}_n^{\langle 2 \rangle}(\frac{2}{3}) \\ -\left[\mathbf{H}_n(\frac{1}{3}) - \mathbf{H}_n(\frac{2}{3})\right]^2 \end{array} \right\} = \frac{4\arcsin^2 y \cos(\frac{\arcsin y}{3})}{\sqrt{1-y^2}}.$$

4.3. *Series from* $\boxed{C\left(\frac{1}{3}+x,y\right)}$

By expanding $C(\frac{1}{3}+x,y)$ into a power series of x, we record the following infinite series identities from the initial coefficients.

$$\boxed{C_0(\tfrac{1}{3}+x,y)}\ \sum_{n=0}^{\infty}\Big(\frac{4y^2}{27}\Big)^n\binom{3n}{n}\frac{1}{2n+1}=\frac{3\sin(\frac{\arcsin y}{3})}{y},$$

$$\boxed{C_1(\tfrac{1}{3}+x,y)}\ \sum_{n=0}^{\infty}\Big(\frac{4y^2}{27}\Big)^n\binom{3n}{n}\frac{\mathbf{H}_n(\frac{1}{3})-\mathbf{H}_n(\frac{2}{3})}{2n+1}$$
$$=\frac{18}{y}\sin\big(\tfrac{\arcsin y}{3}\big)-\frac{6}{y}\arcsin y\cos\big(\tfrac{\arcsin y}{3}\big),$$

$$\boxed{C_2(\tfrac{1}{3}+x,y)}\ \sum_{n=0}^{\infty}\Big(\frac{4y^2}{27}\Big)^n\binom{3n}{n}\frac{\mathbf{H}^{\langle 2\rangle}_n(\frac{1}{3})+\mathbf{H}^{\langle 2\rangle}_n(\frac{2}{3})-\big[\mathbf{H}_n(\frac{1}{3})-\mathbf{H}_n(\frac{2}{3})\big]^2}{2n+1}$$
$$=\frac{12}{y}(\arcsin^2 y-18)\sin\big(\tfrac{\arcsin y}{3}\big)+\frac{72}{y}\arcsin y\cos\big(\tfrac{\arcsin y}{3}\big).$$

5. Series Containing the Central Binomial Coefficient $\binom{4n}{2n}$

This section is devoted to harmonic series with the central binomial coefficient $\binom{4n}{2n}$.

5.1. *Series from* $\boxed{A\big(\frac{1}{4}+x,y\big)}$

Since $A(\frac{1}{4}+x,y)$ can be expanded into a power series of x, the initial coefficients give rise to the following three infinite series identities.

$$\boxed{A_0(\tfrac{1}{4}+x,y)}\ \sum_{n=0}^{\infty}\Big(\frac{y^2}{16}\Big)^n\binom{4n}{2n}\frac{1}{4n-1}=\frac{\sqrt{1+\sqrt{1-y^2}}}{-\sqrt{2}},$$

$$\boxed{A_1(\tfrac{1}{4}+x,y)}\ \sum_{n=1}^{\infty}\Big(\frac{y^2}{16}\Big)^n\binom{4n}{2n}\Big\{\frac{\bar{\mathbf{O}}_{2n-1}}{4n-1}+\frac{1}{4n-1}\Big\}=\frac{y\arcsin y}{2\sqrt{2}\sqrt{1+\sqrt{1-y^2}}},$$

$$\boxed{A_2(\tfrac{1}{4}+x,y)}\ \sum_{n=1}^{\infty}\Big(\frac{y^2}{16}\Big)^n\binom{4n}{2n}\Big\{\frac{\mathbf{O}^{\langle 2\rangle}_{2n-1}-\bar{\mathbf{O}}^2_{2n-1}}{4n-1}-\frac{2\bar{\mathbf{O}}_{2n-1}}{4n-1}\Big\}=\frac{\arcsin^2 y\sqrt{1+\sqrt{1-y^2}}}{-4\sqrt{2}}.$$

5.2. *Series from* $\boxed{B\big(\frac{1}{4}+x,y\big)}$

Considering that $B(\frac{1}{4}+x,y)$ is a power series of x, the initial coefficients yield the identities below.

$$\boxed{B_0(\tfrac{1}{4}+x,y)}\qquad \sum_{n=0}^{\infty}\Big(\frac{y^2}{16}\Big)^n\binom{4n}{2n}=\frac{\sqrt{1+\sqrt{1-y^2}}}{\sqrt{2}\sqrt{1-y^2}},$$

$$\boxed{B_1(\tfrac{1}{4}+x,y)}\qquad \sum_{n=0}^{\infty}\Big(\frac{y^2}{16}\Big)^n\binom{4n}{2n}\bar{\mathbf{O}}_{2n}=\frac{y\arcsin y}{2\sqrt{2}\sqrt{1-y^2}\sqrt{1+\sqrt{1-y^2}}},$$

$$\boxed{B_2(\tfrac{1}{4}+x,y)}\qquad \sum_{n=0}^{\infty}\Big(\frac{y^2}{16}\Big)^n\binom{4n}{2n}\Big\{\mathbf{O}^{\langle 2\rangle}_{2n}-\bar{\mathbf{O}}^2_{2n}\Big\}=\frac{\arcsin^2 y\sqrt{1+\sqrt{1-y^2}}}{4\sqrt{2}\sqrt{1-y^2}}.$$

Among these identities, Sun [29] (Remark 2.8) recorded an equivalent formula for $\boxed{B_0(\frac{1}{4}+x,y)}$ and conjectured the following counterpart for $\boxed{B_1(\frac{1}{4}+x,y)}$ (see [29] Equation 2.16):

$$\sum_{k=0}^{\infty}\Big(\frac{x(1-x)}{4}\Big)^k\binom{4k}{2k}\Big\{\mathbf{O}_{2k}-\mathbf{O}_k\Big\}=\frac{\sqrt{1-x}}{2(2x-1)}\ln(1-x).$$

5.3. *Series from* $\boxed{C\left(\frac{1}{4}+x,y\right)}$

By expanding $C(\frac{1}{4}+x,y)$ into a power series of x, we record the following infinite series identities from the initial coefficients.

$$\boxed{C_0(\tfrac{1}{4}+x,y)}\ \sum_{n=0}^{\infty}\left(\frac{y^2}{16}\right)^n\binom{4n}{2n}\frac{1}{2n+1}=\frac{\sqrt{2}}{\sqrt{1+\sqrt{1-y^2}}},$$

$$\boxed{C_1(\tfrac{1}{4}+x,y)}\ \sum_{n=0}^{\infty}\left(\frac{y^2}{16}\right)^n\binom{4n}{2n}\frac{\bar{\mathbf{O}}_{2n}}{2n+1}=\frac{2y-(1+\sqrt{1-y^2})\arcsin y}{y\sqrt{2}\sqrt{1+\sqrt{1-y^2}}},$$

$$\boxed{C_2(\tfrac{1}{4}+x,y)}\ \sum_{n=0}^{\infty}\left(\frac{y^2}{16}\right)^n\binom{4n}{2n}\frac{\mathbf{O}_{2n}^{\langle 2\rangle}-\bar{\mathbf{O}}_{2n}^2}{2n+1}=\frac{8y-4\left(1+\sqrt{1-y^2}\right)\arcsin y-y\arcsin^2 y}{-2y\sqrt{2}\sqrt{1+\sqrt{1-y^2}}}.$$

6. Series Involving Trinomial/Binomial Quotient $\binom{6n}{n,2n,3n}\Big/\binom{2n}{n}$

This section is devoted to harmonic series with a trinomial/binomial quotient.

6.1. *Series from* $\boxed{A\left(\frac{1}{6}+x,y\right)}$

Since $A(\frac{1}{6}+x,y)$ can be expanded into a power series of x, the initial coefficients give rise to the following three infinite series identities.

$$\boxed{A_0(\tfrac{1}{6}+x,y)}\ \sum_{n=0}^{\infty}\left(\frac{y^2}{108}\right)^n\frac{\binom{6n}{n,2n,3n}}{\binom{2n}{n}}\frac{1}{6n-1}=-\cos\left(\tfrac{\arcsin y}{3}\right),$$

$$\boxed{A_1(\tfrac{1}{6}+x,y)}\ \sum_{n=0}^{\infty}\left(\frac{y^2}{108}\right)^n\frac{\binom{6n}{n,2n,3n}}{\binom{2n}{n}}\left\{\frac{\mathbf{H}_n\left(\frac{1}{6}\right)-\mathbf{H}_n\left(\frac{5}{6}\right)}{6n-1}+\frac{36n}{(6n-1)^2}\right\}=2\arcsin y\sin\left(\tfrac{\arcsin y}{3}\right),$$

$$\boxed{A_2(\tfrac{1}{6}+x,y)}\ \sum_{n=0}^{\infty}\left(\frac{y^2}{108}\right)^n\frac{\binom{6n}{n,2n,3n}}{\binom{2n}{n}}\left\{\begin{array}{c}\frac{\mathbf{H}_n^{\langle 2\rangle}\left(\frac{1}{6}\right)+\mathbf{H}_n^{\langle 2\rangle}\left(\frac{5}{6}\right)-\left[\mathbf{H}_n\left(\frac{1}{6}\right)-\mathbf{H}_n\left(\frac{5}{6}\right)\right]^2}{2(6n-1)}\\ -\frac{36n\left[\mathbf{H}_n\left(\frac{1}{6}\right)-\mathbf{H}_n\left(\frac{5}{6}\right)\right]}{(6n-1)^2}-\frac{216n}{(6n-1)^3}\end{array}\right\}$$
$$=-2\arcsin^2 y\cos\left(\tfrac{\arcsin y}{3}\right).$$

6.2. *Series from* $\boxed{B\left(\frac{1}{6}+x,y\right)}$

Considering that $B(\frac{1}{6}+x,y)$ is a power series of x, the initial coefficients yield the identities below.

$$\boxed{B_0(\tfrac{1}{6}+x,y)}\ \sum_{n=0}^{\infty}\left(\frac{y^2}{108}\right)^n\frac{\binom{6n}{n,2n,3n}}{\binom{2n}{n}}=\frac{\cos\left(\frac{2\arcsin y}{3}\right)}{\sqrt{1-y^2}},$$

$$\boxed{B_1(\tfrac{1}{6}+x,y)}\ \sum_{n=0}^{\infty}\left(\frac{y^2}{108}\right)^n\frac{\binom{6n}{n,2n,3n}}{\binom{2n}{n}}\left\{\mathbf{H}_n\left(\tfrac{1}{6}\right)-\mathbf{H}_n\left(\tfrac{5}{6}\right)\right\}=\frac{2\arcsin y\sin\left(\frac{2\arcsin y}{3}\right)}{\sqrt{1-y^2}},$$

$$\boxed{B_2(\tfrac{1}{6}+x,y)}\ \sum_{n=0}^{\infty}\left(\frac{y^2}{108}\right)^n\frac{\binom{6n}{n,2n,3n}}{\binom{2n}{n}}\left\{\begin{array}{c}\mathbf{H}_n^{\langle 2\rangle}\left(\frac{1}{6}\right)+\mathbf{H}_n^{\langle 2\rangle}\left(\frac{5}{6}\right)\\ -\left[\mathbf{H}_n\left(\frac{1}{6}\right)-\mathbf{H}_n\left(\frac{5}{6}\right)\right]^2\end{array}\right\}=\frac{4\arcsin^2 y\cos\left(\frac{2\arcsin y}{3}\right)}{\sqrt{1-y^2}}.$$

6.3. *Series from* $\boxed{C\left(\frac{1}{6}+x,y\right)}$

By expanding $C(\frac{1}{6}+x,y)$ into a power series of x, we record the following infinite series identities from the initial coefficients.

$$\boxed{C_0(\tfrac{1}{6}+x,y)}\ \sum_{n=0}^{\infty}\Big(\frac{y^2}{108}\Big)^n\frac{\binom{6n}{n,2n,3n}}{\binom{2n}{n}}\frac{1}{2n+1}=\frac{3\sin(\frac{2\arcsin y}{3})}{2y},$$

$$\boxed{C_1(\tfrac{1}{6}+x,y)}\ \sum_{n=0}^{\infty}\Big(\frac{y^2}{108}\Big)^n\frac{\binom{6n}{n,2n,3n}}{\binom{2n}{n}}\frac{\mathbf{H}_n(\frac{1}{6})-\mathbf{H}_n(\frac{5}{6})}{2n+1}$$
$$=\frac{9}{2y}\sin\Big(\frac{2\arcsin y}{3}\Big)-\frac{3}{y}\arcsin y\cos\Big(\frac{2\arcsin y}{3}\Big),$$

$$\boxed{C_2(\tfrac{1}{6}+x,y)}\ \sum_{n=0}^{\infty}\Big(\frac{y^2}{108}\Big)^n\frac{\binom{6n}{n,2n,3n}}{\binom{2n}{n}}\frac{\mathbf{H}^{\langle 2\rangle}_n(\frac{1}{6})+\mathbf{H}^{\langle 2\rangle}_n(\frac{5}{6})-\big[\mathbf{H}_n(\frac{1}{6})-\mathbf{H}_n(\frac{5}{6})\big]^2}{2n+1}$$
$$=\frac{18\arcsin y\cos\big(\frac{2\arcsin y}{3}\big)+6\arcsin^2 y\sin\big(\frac{2\arcsin y}{3}\big)-27\sin\big(\frac{2\arcsin y}{3}\big)}{y}.$$

7. Concluding Remarks

By means of the "coefficient extraction" method, we succeeded in deriving several algebraic formulae for harmonic series containing a free variable y. This fact is remarkable since almost all of the binomial series conjectured by Sun [27–29] are numerical series without variables.

7.1. General Forms of Power Series Expansions

For simplicity, throughout the paper, we examined Maclaurin polynomials only up to x^6 for three functions $A(x,y), B(x,y)$, and $C(x,y)$. In fact, it is possible to expand these functions to higher degrees. Here, we record three examples as representatives. The remaining ones can be determined similarly.

- Coefficient of x^{2m+2} in $A(x,y)$ (general form of Section 2.1):

$$\sum_{n=1}^{\infty}\frac{(2y)^{2n}}{\binom{2n}{n}n^2}\Omega_m\big(-\mathbf{H}^{\langle 2k\rangle}_{n-1}\big)=(-1)^m\frac{(2\arcsin y)^{2m+2}}{(2m+2)!}.$$

- Coefficient of x^{2m} in $B(\frac{1}{2}+x,y)$ (general form of Section 3.2):

$$\sum_{n=0}^{\infty}\binom{2n}{n}\Big(\frac{y}{2}\Big)^{2n}\Omega_m\Big(-\mathbf{H}^{\langle 2k\rangle}_n(\tfrac{1}{2})\Big)=(-1)^m\frac{(2\arcsin y)^{2m}}{(2m)!\sqrt{1-y^2}}.$$

- Coefficient of x^m in $C(\frac{1}{3}+x,y)$ (general form of Section 4.3):

$$\sum_{n=0}^{\infty}\frac{\binom{3n}{n}}{2n+1}\Big(\frac{4y^2}{27}\Big)^n\sum_{\ell=0}^{m}(-1)^{\ell}\Omega_{\ell}\Big(-\mathbf{H}^{\langle k\rangle}_n(\tfrac{1}{3})\Big)\Omega_{m-\ell}\Big(-\mathbf{H}^{\langle k\rangle}_n(\tfrac{2}{3})\Big)$$
$$=\frac{3}{y}\sin\Big(\frac{\arcsin y}{3}\Big)\sum_{k=0}^{\lfloor\frac{m}{2}\rfloor}\frac{(-1)^k}{(2k)!}(2\arcsin y)^{2k}6^{m-2k}$$
$$+\frac{18}{y}\cos\Big(\frac{\arcsin y}{3}\Big)\sum_{k=1}^{\lceil\frac{m}{2}\rceil}\frac{(-1)^k}{(2k-1)!}(2\arcsin y)^{2k-1}6^{m-2k}.$$

7.2. Linearly Combined Series

Some of our series can be combined further to produce closed formulae for simpler series.

- $\boxed{A_2(\tfrac{1}{2}+x,y)+A_1(\tfrac{1}{2}+x,y)-A_0(\tfrac{1}{2}+x,y)}$

$$\sum_{n=1}^{\infty}\Big(\frac{y}{2}\Big)^{2n}\binom{2n}{n}\frac{\mathbf{O}^{\langle 2\rangle}_{n-1}}{2n-1}=y\arcsin y-1+\frac{\sqrt{1-y^2}}{2}\Big\{2-\arcsin^2 y\Big\}.$$

- $\boxed{A_1(\tfrac{1}{4}+x,y)-A_0(\tfrac{1}{4}+x,y)}$

$$\sum_{n=1}^{\infty}\Big(\frac{y^2}{16}\Big)^n\binom{4n}{2n}\frac{\bar{\mathbf{O}}_{2n-1}}{4n-1}=\frac{\sqrt{1+\sqrt{1-y^2}}}{\sqrt{2}}-1+\frac{y\arcsin y}{\sqrt{8}\sqrt{1+\sqrt{1-y^2}}}.$$

- $\boxed{2A_3(\tfrac{1}{2}+x,y)-A_2(\tfrac{1}{2}+x,y)-A_1(\tfrac{1}{2}+x,y)+A_0(\tfrac{1}{2}+x,y)}$

$$\sum_{n=1}^{\infty}\Big(\frac{y}{2}\Big)^{2n}\binom{2n}{n}\frac{\mathbf{O}_{n-1}^{\langle 2\rangle}}{(2n-1)^2}=1-y\arcsin y+\frac{y\arcsin^3 y}{6}-\frac{\sqrt{1-y^2}}{2}\Big\{2-\arcsin^2 y\Big\}.$$

- $\boxed{A_2(\tfrac{1}{4}+x,y)+2A_1(\tfrac{1}{4}+x,y)-2A_0(\tfrac{1}{4}+x,y)}$

$$\begin{aligned}\sum_{n=1}^{\infty}\Big(\frac{y^2}{16}\Big)^n\binom{4n}{2n}\frac{\mathbf{O}_{2n-1}^{\langle 2\rangle}-\bar{\mathbf{O}}_{2n-1}^{2}}{4n-1}&=\sqrt{2}\sqrt{1+\sqrt{1-y^2}}+\frac{y\arcsin y}{\sqrt{2}\sqrt{1+\sqrt{1-y^2}}}\\&-2-\frac{\arcsin^2 y\sqrt{1+\sqrt{1-y^2}}}{4\sqrt{2}}.\end{aligned}$$

- $\boxed{A_4(\tfrac{1}{2}+x,y)+4A_3(\tfrac{1}{2}+x,y)-2A_2(\tfrac{1}{2}+x,y)-2A_1(\tfrac{1}{2}+x,y)+2A_0(\tfrac{1}{2}+x,y)}$

$$\begin{aligned}\sum_{n=1}^{\infty}\Big(\frac{y}{2}\Big)^{2n}\binom{2n}{n}\frac{(\mathbf{O}_{n-1}^{\langle 2\rangle})^2-\mathbf{O}_{n-1}^{\langle 4\rangle}}{2n-1}&=2-2y\arcsin y+\frac{y\arcsin^3 y}{3}\\&-\frac{\sqrt{1-y^2}}{12}\Big\{24-12\arcsin^2 y+\arcsin^4 y\Big\}.\end{aligned}$$

- $\boxed{\begin{array}{c}2A_5(\tfrac{1}{2}+x,y)-A_4(\tfrac{1}{2}+x,y)-4A_3(\tfrac{1}{2}+x,y)\\+2A_2(\tfrac{1}{2}+x,y)+2A_1(\tfrac{1}{2}+x,y)-2A_0(\tfrac{1}{2}+x,y)\end{array}}$

$$\begin{aligned}\sum_{n=1}^{\infty}\Big(\frac{y}{2}\Big)^{2n}\binom{2n}{n}\frac{(\mathbf{O}_{n-1}^{\langle 2\rangle})^2-\mathbf{O}_{n-1}^{\langle 4\rangle}}{(2n-1)^2}&=2y\arcsin y-\frac{y\arcsin^3 y}{3}+\frac{y\arcsin^5 y}{60}\\&+\frac{\sqrt{1-y^2}}{12}\Big\{24-12\arcsin^2 y+\arcsin^4 y\Big\}.\end{aligned}$$

7.3. Further Contiguous Series

Besides the three series $A(x,y)$, $B(x,y)$ and $C(x,y)$ examined in this paper, several contiguous series were evaluated by Chu [25]. For instance, the formula displayed in [25] (Corollary 15) can be reproduced as

$$\begin{aligned}\Lambda(x,y)={}_2F_1\left[\begin{matrix}1+x,\,1-x\\ \frac{5}{2}\end{matrix}\Big|\,y^2\right]&=\sum_{n=0}^{\infty}\frac{(1+x)_n(1-x)_n}{n!(\frac{5}{2})_n}y^{2n}\\&=\frac{3\cos(2x\arcsin y)}{y^2(1-4x^2)}-\frac{3\sqrt{1-y^2}\sin(2x\arcsin y)}{2xy^3(1-4x^2)}.\end{aligned}$$

Three initial coefficients of the Maclaurin series in x are recorded as follows:

$$\boxed{\Lambda_0(x,y)}\quad \sum_{n=0}^{\infty}\frac{(2y)^{2n}}{\binom{2n}{n}(2n+1)(2n+3)}=\frac{1}{y^2}-\frac{\sqrt{1-y^2}}{y^3}\arcsin y,$$

$$\boxed{\Lambda_2(x,y)}\quad \sum_{n=0}^{\infty}\frac{(2y)^{2n}\mathbf{H}_n^{\langle 2\rangle}}{\binom{2n}{n}(2n+1)(2n+3)}=\frac{2}{y^2}\Big\{\arcsin^2 y-2\Big\}+\tfrac{2\sqrt{1-y^2}}{3y^3}\Big\{6\arcsin y-\arcsin^3 y\Big\},$$

$$\boxed{\Lambda_4(x,y)}\quad \sum_{n=0}^{\infty}\frac{(2y)^{2n}\{(\mathbf{H}_n^{\langle 2\rangle})^2-\mathbf{H}_n^{\langle 4\rangle}\}}{\binom{2n}{n}(2n+1)(2n+3)}=\frac{4(24-12\arcsin^2 y+\arcsin^4 y)}{3y^2}$$
$$-\frac{4\sqrt{1-y^2}}{15y^3}\Big\{120\arcsin y-20\arcsin^3 y+\arcsin^5 y\Big\}.$$

More identities of a similar nature can be derived. Interested readers may make further explorations.

Author Contributions: Investigation, writing and editing, C.L.; writing—review and editing, supervision, W.C. All authors have read and agreed to the published version of the manuscript.

Funding: This research received no external funding.

Data Availability Statement: The original contributions presented in the study are included in the article, further inquiries can be directed to the corresponding author.

Conflicts of Interest: The authors declare no conflicts of interest.

References

1. Choi, J. Certain summation formulas involving harmonic numbers and generalized harmonic numbers. *Appl. Math. Comput.* **2011**, *218*, 734–740. [CrossRef]
2. Frontczak, R. Binomial Sums with Skew-Harmonic Numbers. *Palest. J. Math.* **2021**, *10*, 756–763.
3. Furdui, O. Series involving products of two harmonic numbers. *Math. Mag.* **2011**, *84*, 371–377. [CrossRef]
4. Jung, M.Y.; Cho, J.; Choi, J. Euler sums evaluable from integrals. *Commun. Korean Math. Soc.* **2004**, *19*, 545–555. [CrossRef]
5. Li, C.L.; Chu, W. Series of Convergence Rate -1/4 Containing Harmonic Numbers. *Axioms* **2023**, *12*, 513. [CrossRef]
6. Vălean, C.I.; Furdui, O. Reviving the quadratic series of Au-Yeung. *J. Class. Anal.* **2015**, *6*, 113–118. [CrossRef]
7. Greene, D.H.; Knuth, D.E. *Mathematics for the Analysis of Algorithms*, 2nd ed.; Birkhäuser: Boston, MA, USA; Basel, Switzerland; Stuttgart, Germany, 1982.
8. Chen, K.W. Generalized harmonic numbers and Euler sums. *Int. J. Number Theory* **2017**, *13*, 513–528. [CrossRef]
9. Genčev, M. Binomial sums involving harmonic numbers. *Math. Slovaca* **2011**, *61*, 21–226. [CrossRef]
10. Lehmer, D.H. Interesting series involving the central binomial coefficient. *Amer. Math. Mon.* **1985**, *92*, 449–457. [CrossRef]
11. Zucker, I.J. On the series $\sum_{k=1}^{\infty}\binom{2k}{k}^{-1}k^{-n}$. *J. Number Theory* **1985**, *20*, 92–102. [CrossRef]
12. Adegoke, K.; Frontczak, R.; Goy, T. Combinatorial sums, series and integrals involving odd harmonic numbers. *arXiv* **2024**, arXiv:2401.02470v1.
13. Chen, K.W.; Chen, Y.H. Infinite series containing generalized harmonic functions. *Notes Number Theory Discret. Math.* **2020**, *26*, 85–104. [CrossRef]
14. Choi, J. Summation formulas involving binomial coefficients, harmonic numbers, and generalized harmonic numbers. *Abstr. Appl. Anal.* **2014**, *2014*, 501906. [CrossRef]
15. Boyadzhiev, K.N. Series with central binomial coefficients, Catalan numbers, and harmonic numbers. *J. Integer. Seq.* **2012**, *15*, 12.1.7.
16. Chen, H. Interesting series associated with central binomial coefficients, Catalan numbers and harmonic numbers. *J. Integer. Seq.* **2016**, *19*, 16.1.5.
17. Choi, J. Finite summation formulas involving binomial coefficients, harmonic numbers and generalized harmonic numbers. *J. Inequal. Appl.* **2013**, *2013*, 49. [CrossRef]
18. Elsner, C. On sums with binomial coefficient. *Fibonacci Quart.* **2005**, *43*, 31–45.
19. Chu, W. Hypergeometric series and the Riemann Zeta function. *Acta Arith.* **1997**, *82*, 103–118. [CrossRef]
20. Chu, W. Further Apéry–like series for Riemann zeta function. *Math. Notes* **2021**, *109*, 136–146. [CrossRef]
21. Li, C.L.; Chu, W. Infinite Series about Harmonic Numbers Inspired by Ramanujan–Like Formulae. *Electron. Res. Arch.* **2023**, *31*, 4611–4636. [CrossRef]
22. Apostol, T.M. Hurwitz zeta function. In *NIST Handbook of Mathematical Functions*; Olver, F.W.J., Boisvert, R.F., Eds.; Cambridge University Press: Cambridge, UK, 2010.

23. Bailey, W.N. *Generalized Hypergeometric Series;* Cambridge University Press: Cambridge, UK, 1935.
24. Comtet, L. *Advanced Combinatorics;* Holland: Dordrecht, The Netherlands, 1974.
25. Chu, W. Trigonometric expressions for Gaussian ${}_2F_1$-series. *Turk. J. Math.* **2019**, *43*, 1823–1836. [CrossRef]
26. Wilf, H.S. *Generatingfunctionology*, 2nd ed.; Academic Press Inc.: London, UK, 1994.
27. Sun, Z.-W. List of conjectural series for powers of π and other constants. *arXiv* **2014**, arXiv:1102.5649v47.
28. Sun, Z.-W. *New Conjectures in Number Theory and Combinatorics;* Harbin Institute of Technology: Harbin, China, 2021. (In Chinese)
29. Sun, Z.-W. Series with summands involving harmonic numbers. *arXiv* **2023**, arXiv:2210.07238v8.
30. Borwein, J.M.; Chamberland, M. Integer Powers of Arcsin. *Int. J. Math. Math. Sci.* **2007**, *2007*, 19381. [CrossRef]
31. Bailey, D.H.; Borwein, J.M.; Bradley, D.M. Experimental determination of Ap'ery-like identities for $\zeta(2n+2)$. *Exp. Math.* **2006**, *15*, 281–289. [CrossRef]
32. Sun, Z.-W. New series for some special values of L-functions. *Nanjing Univ. J. Math. Biquarterly* **2015**, *32*, 189–218.
33. Li, C.L.; Chu, W. Binomial Series Involving Harmonic-like Numbers. *Axioms* **2024**, *13*, 162. [CrossRef]
34. Li, C.L.; Chu, W. Remarkable series concerning $\binom{3n}{n}$ and harmonic numbers in numerators. *AIMS Math.* **2024**, *9*, 17234–17258. [CrossRef]
35. Adegoke, K.; Frontczak, R.; Goy, T. On some series involving the binomial coefficients $\binom{3n}{n}$. *Notes Number Theory Discret. Math.* **2024**, *30*, 319–334. [CrossRef]

MDPI AG
Grosspeteranlage 5
4052 Basel
Switzerland
Tel.: +41 61 683 77 34

Mathematics Editorial Office
E-mail: mathematics@mdpi.com
www.mdpi.com/journal/mathematics

www.ingramcontent.com/pod-product-compliance
Lightning Source LLC
Chambersburg PA
CBHW061458210926
51850CB00008B/1749